Library of
Davidson College

Economic Growth in Developing Countries— Material and Human Resources

edited by
Yohanan Ramati

Published in cooperation with the
Continuation Committee of the
Rehovot Conference

The Praeger Special Studies program—utilizing the most modern and efficient book production techniques and a selective worldwide distribution network—makes available to the academic, government, and business communities significant, timely research in U.S. and international economic, social, and political development.

Economic Growth in Developing Countries— Material and Human Resources

Proceedings of the Seventh Rehovot Conference

PRAEGER SPECIAL STUDIES IN INTERNATIONAL ECONOMICS AND DEVELOPMENT

Praeger Publishers New York Washington London

Library of Congress Cataloging in Publication Data

Main entry under title:

Economic growth in developing countries—material and
  human resources.

  (Praeger special studies in international economics
and development)
  1. Underdeveloped areas—Economic policy—Congresses.   2. Economic development—Congresses.
I. Ramati, Yohanan, ed.
HC59.7.E29   338.91'172'4   74-4387
ISBN 0-275-09300-X

338.91
E191m

75-5206

PRAEGER PUBLISHERS
111 Fourth Avenue, New York, N.Y. 10003, U.S.A.
5, Cromwell Place, London SW7 2JL, England

Published in the United States of America in 1975
by Praeger Publishers, Inc.

All rights reserved

© 1975 by Praeger Publishers, Inc.

Printed in the United States of America

FOREWORD
Yohanan Ramati

In these days, when oil-producing Arab states attempt—not always without success—to alter the policies of the Western world, and economic power is shifting temporarily to the oil-rich, the once clear-cut definitions of "developed" and "developing" states are becoming blurred. A tremendous shift in the world's wealth is taking place before our eyes, with vast financial resources flowing from the developed countries into the coffers of Middle Eastern and other oil producers.

If, as late as 1972, it could fairly be claimed that the developed world was the sole source of capital essential to assure the economic progress of the less developed countries, this is no longer true in 1974 and will be even less true in 1976, though it is not yet certain that the surplus financial resources accumulated by oil-producing states will be used for foreign aid on·a really significant scale.

Yet if the shift in financial wealth is obvious, there has been no parallel shift in the distribution of technological know-how. Less developed countries, whether oil-rich or not, must still rely on the know-how of the developed. Without it they cannot exploit their potential wealth.

In this sphere the shift has been much slower. And since every country has its own special problems that have to be taken into consideration when technologies are chosen or adapted to local conditions, there is a particularly wide scope for the interchange of ideas.

Problems of planning, and especially the degree to which various planning targets—such as growth of national product and more equitable income distribution—are mutually exclusive, are yet another sphere where contact between experts and policy makers is of the greatest importance.

The Seventh Rehovot Conference attempted to deal with problems of this nature. On the eve of a war that provided the catalyst for well-nigh revolutionary economic developments, it brought together a formidable array of experts with policy makers for developing states in Africa, Latin America and Southeast Asia. It reflects credit on the participants that the subjects discussed and the conclusions drawn have remained virtually unaffected by the tremors that have shaken the economic structure of the world since the conference dispersed last September. Perhaps the states of the European Economic Community may now find it more difficult to undertake or sponsor investments in developing countries, but the basic issues of association patterns remain. Trade and aid between the EEC and the developing world still have to be regulated, and in this respect the Rehovot papers and discussions are even more pertinent than before. The same applies to the other subjects raised.

Mr. Abba Eban, Minister of Foreign Affairs of Israel, has been the moving spirit behind the seven Rehovot Conferences that have already taken place. Among others who helped to make the Seventh Conference a success, the chairman of the scientific preparatory committee, Mr. David Horowitz; its deputy chairman, Mr. David Kochav; and the secretary-general of the Conference, Dr. Amos Manor, are deserving of special mention.

The Seventh Conference opened on the fifth of September 1973, just a month before the outbreak of the Middle Eastern war. The opening session laid down the general framework within which the broad subject of natural and human resources as factors in development, as well as the problems of planning and the quality of life were to be discussed.

Then the Conference broke up into three study groups, the first dealing with resources, technology and income distribution, the second with external constraints on development and trade, and the third with planning. There followed a short closing session on September 11.

Papers read at the Conference have been shortened here with the participants' permission. The discussions have been reported to the extent that the scope of the book permits. In cases where the discussion was held on two papers simultaneously, it follows the second paper.

The war that broke out in October 1973 has delayed the publication of this book for unavoidable technical reasons. However, it has made the subject matter of the Rehovot Conference of greater immediate importance. The entire framework of relations between developed and developing states has been shaken out of established routines and is undergoing fairly rapid changes. In this context, the practical significance of views exchanged and contacts established at the Conference is likely to be much more far-reaching.

CONTENTS

	Page
FOREWORD Yohanan Ramati	v
LIST OF TABLES	xiii

Section

PART I: SOME GENERAL ASPECTS

INTRODUCTORY REMARKS
    Abba Eban and Golda Meir   3
    Mohamed Diawara   4

NATURAL AND HUMAN RESOURCES AS AGENTS
OF ECONOMIC GROWTH
    David Horowitz   5

ISRAEL'S DEVELOPMENT FORMULA
    Moshe Sanbar   11

POSTWAR GROWTH OF LESS DEVELOPED
COUNTRIES
    Simon Kuznets   15

ALTERNATIVE STRATEGIES FOR DEVELOPMENT
    Hollis B. Chenery   22

DEVELOPMENT PLANNING: SOME LESSONS
FROM EXPERIENCE
    John P. Lewis   36

HUMAN RESOURCES IN THE DEVELOPING
WORLD—A FORWARD LOOK
    Victor L. Urquidi   44

Section	Page
ECONOMIC GROWTH AND THE QUALITY OF LIFE 　　Richard Hoggart	53
THE FINANCIAL ASPECTS OF ECONOMIC GROWTH 　　Felipe Herrera	61

PART II: RESOURCES, TECHNOLOGY, AND INCOME DISTRIBUTION

Section	Page
DISTRIBUTION OF INCOME, WEALTH, AND POWER 　　Gustav F. Papanek	75
INCOME DISTRIBUTION AND REFORM OF RURAL INSTITUTIONS 　　Thomas Carroll	97
ECONOMIC AND SOCIAL COSTS OF MODERNIZATION AND DEVELOPMENT 　　Tarlok Singh	103
ECONOMIC AND SOCIAL COSTS OF MODERNIZATION AND DEVELOPMENT 　　Wilfred Beckerman	112
FINANCIAL INCENTIVES TO REDUCE FERTILITY 　　Stephen Enke	126
POPULATION POLICIES 　　Nusret H. Fisek	138
THE EVALUATION OF POPULATION POLICY—SOME MISSING LINKS 　　Elihu Bergman	149
EMPLOYMENT AND LABOR ABSORPTION IN DEVELOPMENT 　　Gustav Ranis	156

Section	Page
LABOR ABSORPTION IN DEVELOPING COUNTRIES Jorge Mendez	172
AGRICULTURAL STRATEGY AND INDUSTRIAL GROWTH Bruce F. Johnston	181
THE ROLES OF INDUSTRY AND AGRICULTURE IN THE DEVELOPMENT OF DEVELOPING COUNTRIES William Brian Reddaway	193
LATIN AMERICAN AGRARIAN REFORM IN ACTION Solon Barraclough	202
RAPPORTEUR'S REPORT—GROUP A John Adler	216

PART III: EXTERNAL CONSTRAINTS ON DEVELOPMENT

THE USE AND ABUSE OF CAPITAL IN DEVELOPING COUNTRIES I. M. D. Little	221
PROS AND CONS OF PROTECTION AND IMPORT SUBSTITUTION Helen Hughes	230
PROS AND CONS OF PROTECTION AND IMPORT SUBSTITUTION In Sang Song	237
TURNING FROM IMPORT SUBSTITUTION TO EXPORT PROMOTION IN COLOMBIA Carlos F. Diaz-Alejandro	244
OBSTACLES TO EXPANSION OF MANUFACTURED EXPORTS IN LDCS Juergen Donges	257

Section	Page
PRICE AND SCALE OBSTACLES TO EXPORT EXPANSION IN LESS DEVELOPED COUNTRIES Daniel Schydlowsky	269
THE ENLARGED COMMUNITY AND DEVELOPING COUNTRIES Hans Broder Krohn	285
EFFECTS OF THE EXPANDING EUROPEAN COMMON MARKET ON DEVELOPING COUNTRIES Pius Okigbo	296
THE TRANSFER OF MANAGERIAL AND TECHNICAL KNOWLEDGE Harvey Leibenstein	307
A POLICY FOR THE PURCHASE OF TECHNOLOGY BY LATIN AMERICAN COUNTRIES Jose Maria Dagnino Pastore	322
RAPPORTEUR'S REPORT—GROUP B Meir Heth	335
PART IV: PLANNING AND IMPLEMENTATION	
DEVELOPMENT PLANNING—TOOL OR TOY? John Adler	341
PLANNING AND PERFORMANCE Koichi Mera	358
PLANNING AND THE MARKET IN ECONOMIC DEVELOPMENT Peter Bauer	365
POLITICAL, SOCIAL, AND ADMINISTRATIVE CONSTRAINTS ON PLANNING Ephraim Kleiman	377

Section	Page
POLITICAL, SOCIAL, AND ADMINISTRATIVE CONSTRAINTS ON PLANNING Leopoldo Solis M.	385
THE USE AND ABUSE OF MODELS IN DEVELOPMENT PLANNING Paul Streeten	395
USEFULNESS OF PLANNING MODELS Bernard Ullmo	407
A MICROECONOMIC PLANNING MODEL OF KOREA Irma Adelman and Sherman Robinson	417
TRANSLATING PLANNING INTO RESULTS— THE CASE OF THE IVORY COAST Mohamed Diawara	425
PLANASA: A DYNAMIC PLAN FOR A DYNAMIC PROBLEM—PARTIAL INDICATIVE PLANNING IN THE BRAZILIAN EXPERIENCE Rubens Vas da Costa	438
DETERMINANTS AND CONSEQUENCES OF GROWTH OF ISRAEL AGRICULTURE Yair Mundlak	446
REALISM IN EDUCATIONAL PLANNING IN LDCS Eli Ginzberg	458
THE OVEREXPANSION OF HIGHER EDUCATION IN LESS DEVELOPED COUNTRIES AND ITS REMEDY Mark Blaug	467
RAPPORTEUR'S REPORT— GROUP C David Kochav	484

Section	Page
PART V: CLOSING ADDRESSES	
CLOSING ADDRESS Simon Kuznets	489
CLOSING ADDRESS Abba Eban	490
Appendix A Organization of the Seventh Rehovot Conference	492
Appendix B List of Participants	494
ABOUT THE EDITOR	503

LIST OF TABLES

Table		Page
1	Growth in Private and Public Enterprise Countries	77
2	Growth and Investment in India and Pakistan	78
3	Education and Income Distribution	81
4	Income Distribution in Israel—1957	82
5	Income Distribution in India and Pakistan	86
6	Real Wages in India and Pakistan	87
7	Average Income of Poorest Groups at Different Levels of Development	88
8	Changes in Adjustments to Net National Product to Derive Measure of Economic Welfare—United States, 1929-65	118
9	Distribution of Land, Labor, and Production—Chile, 1972	208
10	Export of Selected Korean Products	241
11	Nominal and Effective Tariff Rates for Industries of Selected Nations	242
12	Exports to LAFTA as Percentage of Total Exports	246
13	Growth Rates and Commodity Structure of LDCs' Exports	258

Table		Page
14	Manufactured Exports of Selected LDCs	259
15	Manufactured Exports and Economic Policy Indicators in Selected LDCs	260
16	Rates of Effective Protection and Degree of Antiexport Bias in Manufacturing Industry in Brazil and the Philippines	263
17	Sources of Manufactured Export Growth in Developing Regions, 1960-70	265
18	The Inefficiency Illusion in Argentina	272
19	The Six and The Ten	298
20	Trade Flow from Developing Africa	305
21	Data on Development Plans and Public Sector Management	342
22	Major Development Policy Objectives	346
23	Output and Inputs—Quantity Indexes, 1952-71	447
24	Output and Inputs—Average Rates of Growth	449
25	Rates of Change of Per Capita Consumption and Relative Prices	450
26	The Relative Importance of Agriculture in the Economy	451
27	Distribution of Farm Labor Force—The 1971 Census	452

Table		Page
28	Ratio of Total Costs by Educational Level Per Student Year	468
29	Ratio of Average Annual Earnings Before Tax of Labor by Educational Level	468
30	Social Rates of Return on Investment in Levels of Education	469

APPENDIX TABLE 1

    DEVELOPMENT PLANNING AND PLANNING OBJECTIVES   351

PART

I

SOME
GENERAL ASPECTS

INTRODUCTORY REMARKS
Abba Eban,
Golda Meir,
and Mohamed Diawara

ABBA EBAN (MINISTER OF FOREIGN AFFAIRS,
ISRAEL)

After welcoming delegates from over 50 countries attending the Conference, Mr. Eban continued:
"Over 90 percent of the human race now lives under their own sovereign flags. But freedom has not been accompanied by a parallel growth of economic and social welfare. After many years of neglect by colonial regimes, the new states lack education, managerial manpower and an indigenous scientific tradition. An insufficient proportion of the world's capital resources is at their disposal.

Hence, the inequalities between advanced and developing countries are growing wider. At the beginning of the 1970s, average per capita annual income in developing states was $200, as against $5,000 in North America and $4,000 in the advanced states of Western Europe. In developing states, real income has barely kept pace with population growth.

The leaders of the new nations are now looking to scientific research and technology to provide an answer to their problems. Here, Israel can play a special role. A small nation, with few resources, we have achieved a rapid rate of development. We have an indigenous scientific community and believe small states are capable of training their own natural and social scientists. We offer our experience as a guide.

MRS. GOLDA MEIR (PRIME MINISTER OF ISRAEL)

We now realize that world peace depends largely on the erasing of glaring differences between developed countries and nations that recently won their freedom but remained poor. Israel has always held that nations enjoying the benefits of science and technology should assist those seeking to raise living standards and develop their resources. We see this as a great opportunity to help those wronged by history. Within Israel's modest means, we shall play our role in the worldwide effort, and are proud that the former Governor of the Bank of Israel produced a plan to transfer capital from developed to developing countries which has been endorsed by the United States Congress as a means of economic aid.

MOHAMED DIAWARA (MINISTER OF PLANNING, IVORY COAST)

Economic growth is of special importance to us. Every statesman, every government says it is the main objective. People now want concrete results, not vague ideas, and there have been disappointments and sometimes—bitterness.

Plans are worth nothing if they are not accompanied by tenacity and the political will to implement them. This political will, the persistence of populations to realize clearly formulated and precise objectives, are perhaps the factors most lacking in developing countries. This is not something professors, scientists or theoreticians can teach us.

Israel can serve us as an example. Here, it has been proved that deserts can be made fertile, that a people without a tradition of manual labor can develop modern industrial production and not only satisfy its agricultural requirements but even export. After exchanging our experiences with you, we shall be able to leave Israel with a little more hope.

NATURAL AND HUMAN RESOURCES AS AGENTS OF ECONOMIC GROWTH
David Horowitz

Our era is characterized by the shift of importance from natural to human resources in economic growth.

Higher productivity per man-day of labor would be the direct consequence of more intensive use of productive resources. In all periods, population density has been determined in part by historical and economic factors; natural conditions have never completely explained the difference between areas. The freeing of population potentialities from too close dependence on natural resources is a trend accentuated by the development of modern technology. The idea that economic growth is tightly linked to available space and natural resources, does not square with present circumstances. With agriculture no longer the central branch in progressive communities, the importance of natural resources has decreased. Many new physical and economic factors bear on economic growth, and the possibility of consciously shaping conditions through economic policy must now be taken into account.

How seriously can a dearth of natural resources constrain economic growth? The answer boils down to the interchangeability of natural wealth with human resources of capital, skill, know-how, and technology.

Sismondi says: "The true problem is to find the ratio of population to wealth which will assure most happiness to the human race on a given area." The complexity of the modern economy makes this task exceedingly difficult. Mutation of economic conditions, technical discovery and invention, development of potential resources, and shifts in consumption and markets must all be considered. Such elements as capital and scientific and technical knowledge are subject to almost endless change. Cultural and technical levels, economic and social systems, structure and quality of population and occupational distribution, and the dynamic interaction of all these factors are infinite in their variety.

Experience in Japan, Hong Kong, and Israel indicates that physical conditions and material resources are decreasing in importance and in their impact on economic growth, while economic and social conditions play an immensely important role in conditioning economic expansion. The interaction of population and physical background cannot therefore be disregarded.

Some of the factors influencing the distribution and density of population are, in part at least, susceptible to control by organized human effort. The capacity of a country to sustain its population is today an undefined concept, probably not measurable in fixed, arithmetic terms. It is the function of many variables that depend on the particular experience of each country. The level of cultural and technical development in the country is one obvious influence. The economic and social system, the structure and quality of the population, and the occupational distribution are other influences. In most instances, several of these factors are at work and their dynamic interaction is itself important.

An analysis of economic history shows that population density differs radically from country to country as a result of human acitivity rather than natural conditions. The location of centers of production is not fixed. Changes in productivity are frequently an effect of artificial conditions created by economic, political, or other national policies.

The level of agricultural productivity and of industrialization, as well as occupational distribution, largely determine not only the economic condition of a country but also its population density. Political, social, constitutional, and ethnic considerations also play their part in determining which areas shall be densely and which sparsely inhabited. Geography alone has never provided a satisfactory explanation of the difference in population density between one area and another. Today, the forces of history (the importance of which is increasing) and the forces of nature (the importance of which is decreasing) are the factors that determine, within certain physical limits, a country's capacity to sustain its population and to raise its standard of living. The tendency towards the emancipation of population potentialities from close dependence on natural resources has been reinforced by the development of the machine age. Modern economic development inevitably influences the capacity of a country to support its population.

Since agriculture has ceased to be the major occupation in progressive communities, the importance of such natural resources in estimating the economic potential of a country has diminished. Many new factors, physical and economic, have a direct bearing on this potential. There can no longer be any rigid limit on economic possibilities. It is important, therefore, that the relative weight and interaction of the new factors be assessed.

When agriculture was the predominant occupation, it was less difficult to assess the prospects of economic growth for a growing population: of necessity, the starting point was the land area and fertility, both more in the nature of constants than of variables. But as agriculture advanced even this foundation underwent changes.

Such modern farming methods as rotation of crops, irrigation, fertilization, development of new strains congenial to soil long considered uncultivable, and recently the "Green Revolution", heralding new strains of wheat, rice, and sorghum, have transformed many accepted standards.

In 1925, a comparison was made of population density in Japan and other countries. The figures seemed to signify overpopulation in Japan. But already in the 1920s there was a spectacular rise in standards of life in that country, and production far outpaced the growth of population. After nearly half a century, Japan today is the third industrial power in the world, with a high level of economic development despite scarcity of natural resources.

An extreme case is Hong Kong, which is virtually devoid of natural resources and must rely on imports for its vital needs, including part of the water supply, and which crowds a population of four million in an area less than 5 percent that of Israel. For all that, Hong Kong enjoys full employment, an economic boom, and, after Japan, the largest per capita income in East Asia. Admittedly, this is a freak case because of the proximity of the Chinese giant interested in the entrepot trade. However, Hong Kong offers additional evidence that human and natural resources are more and more interchangeable in economic growth.

On the other extreme, the countries of the Middle East contain the bulk of the oil reserves of the world, that is, the most valuable sources of energy. They enjoy the benefit of high and growing royalties, determined by shortage of energy in other parts of the world and rapid industrial expansion, particularly in Western Europe and North America. Despite these most favorable conditions, the constraints on industrialization and the backwardness of agriculture in the Middle East are evident.

The economic potential of a country is a relative concept, affected by the relative importance of the human factor as against natural resources. For example, the limits within which a given supply of agricultural land can support and absorb an increase in population have been greatly extended, mainly because modern methods have increased productivity per acre, thus emancipating agriculture from its close dependence on land area as a determinant of production.

Both interspatial and intertemporal comparisons show that the range between minimum and maximum yields per unit of land and differences in productivity per unit and per worker are so great as to defeat any attempt at estimating the technical and natural capacity of a country to produce an increasing volume of foodstuffs. However, where values are quoted in intertemporal comparisons, certain increases may represent a shift in the value of crops.

Thus a factor extending the limits within which production values may increase is the shift from less valuable to more valuable crops. The tendency to accelerate this shift is the result of two distinct but parallel processes: the increase in national income of the more developed countries, both aggregate and per capita; and the progress of nutritional science. Both these processes tend to promote the substitution of the more valuable, high-protein foodstuffs for the cheaper energy-producing foods, if only by altering the relative weight of these two ingredients in the national diet.

The interaction of all these factors—the increased productivity of the soil per unit of land and per earner; the accumulation of knowledge as well as of capital; interchangeability of space, capital, and knowledge; the shift away from energy producing to protective foodstuffs and the introduction of new crops—has had a far-reaching influence on agriculture.

The tendency of industry towards decentralization and the far-reaching effects of its ceasing to depend on local raw material and other indigenous factors reflect the trend of world industrial development. In the past, industry tended to concentrate in certain specially favored areas, where a large market, transport, banking, skilled labor, and auxiliary industries were available.

Technical progress, however, has reduced the importance of these considerations. New, simplified industrial processes can easily be imitated in new countries, and shifts in consumer centers have given the impetus to the establishment of new industries in new areas. Thus industry is concentrating increasingly in areas not endowed with plentiful natural resources. In industry, natural resources are becoming interchangeable with capital, skill, and knowledge, and with a deliberate national policy of industrialization. Marketing facilities also are becoming a decisive factor in determining industry location.

Expanding markets reduce costs and increase the productivity of industry by facilitating the full utilization of productive capacity. At the same time, a growing population with a rising standard of living diversifies the production of an increasing number of industrial goods.

The development of secondary and tertiary stages of production has little to do with population density. Natural resources do not indicate the capacity of a country to support an expanding population. The static concept of a constant base of natural resources is, in the light of experience, an obvious fallacy. The dynamic aspect of resources is more important than the static and what count are not only the actual but the potential resources.

Essentially, the subjective qualities of its human material determine a country's capacity for economic growth. The ferment of ideas can never be reckoned with in any static conception of economic growth. Thus the quality of the population, and more particularly the ratio the skilled and trained population bears to the whole, is becoming more important.

Moreover, economic capacity and growth are plainly affected by the equilibrium of the components of an economy in dynamic interaction, in their technical, cultural, and social interlocking, such as distribution of wealth and income.

An increment of output per man-day of labor flows straight from fuller use of productive resources. Wherever a certain degree of development has been reached and a growing population permits natural resources to be more thoroughly utilized, individual productivity goes up as the population rises. This is particularly true in countries where the effects of the law of diminishing returns compelled a switch to lines of production in which larger investment of capital and labor yields a higher income and larger populations often increase the yield of capital. This may explain the high productivity of Denmark and the Netherlands and the low productivity of some sparsely populated areas. The most striking evidence of high productivity correlated with high density of population is provided by Japan. Last but not least, the flexibility of conditions conducive to economic growth is demonstrated in the case of Israel, a country with a pronounced scarcity of natural resources and an outstanding record of rapid economic development.

The shift in the relative importance of the factors determining economic growth is basic to present-day economic development. Changes in occupational distribution, resulting from the division of labor and the transition to new forms of production, influence the capacity of a country to support its population and raise its living standard. New population strata, created by the shift in occupational distribution and accretion of capital, cannot be accounted for by any estimate of cultivable land. They are the outcome of structural and socioeconomic changes that react on the whole nation, transforming it from a subsistence to an exchange economy. The idea of self-sufficiency in food is being abandoned and trade has replaced some of the factors that used to determine the productive capacity of a given area.

Diversified demand, consequent upon higher income, has increased the share of secondary and tertiary stages of production. When productivity is increasing, there should be fewer producers in the primary stage of production; otherwise, no market will be found for their products. Thus, the alternatives are either many producers with low productivity, as in the backward countries, or high productivity with fewer primary producers, as in the more developed nations.

Within the limits of controlled population growth, the capacity of a country to support its population and to raise its standard of living is largely a function of three factors: natural resources; skill and know-how of the population; and the capital available for the development of resources. These factors are, to a very great extent, interchangeable; a country can do with fewer natural resources if it has highly skilled labor force and ample capital equipment, and vice versa. This has a bearing on the whole problem of development and growth in countries with a low standard of living and limited resources.

The utilization of available resources is at least as important as their availability. Higher productivity per man per work day is the direct result of a more intensive utilization of productive resource Wherever industrial techniques and the economy attained a certain degree of development, wherever the population has reached a period of cooperation and interaction, wherever a population increase makes for more efficient use of natural resources, the productivity of the individual worker increased.

The evaluation of the importance of the human material and of its training, knowledge, and skill must be made in the broader context of the technical civilization and the institutional organization of knowledge and research. Large fixed investments are represented in the special skills of the expert. Finally, there is knowledge and industrial techniques based upon it. This human resource is concentrated in libraries, in laboratories, in universities and public school systems, in the traditions of science and the scientific spirit.

Israel's experience corroborates these general conclusions. The wide disparity between the scarcity of natural resources and limitations of space and water on the one hand and the rapid growth of the economy and population on the other hand is clearly reflected by all of the country's economic indicators. Subsequent developments contradicted and disproved virtually all forecasts of the economic future of Palestine under the Mandate, and of Israel, based on evaluations of its potential resources, some of them by unbiased experts.

The rate of economic growth achieved by Israel and the degree of economic integration of the immigrant populations, despite the country's natural handicaps, together with the contradiction between its predicted potentialities and the present realities, provides a test of the interchangeability of human and material resources.

The forces of history increasingly make and modify economic growth, with the forces of nature of progressively diminishing importance. In this gradual release of population potential from too irksome a dependence on natural resources, the developments of the machine age count a great deal, contributing as they do to shifts and changes in the significance of the factors that condition economic growth and the capacity for it. It is now not natural but human resources that count decisively.

ISRAEL'S DEVELOPMENT FORMULA
Moshe Sanbar

During the last two decades, development assistance policy was characterized by almost exclusive concentration on projects aimed to increase the GNP, "progress" being evaluated in terms of GNP per capita. This line of thinking is only now being slowly reviewed.

Economic expansion per se is an important goal, and as such a valid yardstick of development. It should not, however, be the sole aim but rather part of an overall policy in which social goals play an equal role.

Developing countries share many similar problems, but no single all-purpose development formula can be applied to all of them. The solutions to their problems must meet the specific conditions of each country, for each is unique, differing from the others in some of its physical, economic, social, demographic, and political characteristics. Yet lessons can be learned from the failures and successes of others, which serve as general guidelines.

Hence, a few words about Israel's development formula, which can be summed up as "rapid economic expansion combined with social effort." Its goal is a society marked by social justice and equality, within the framework of national revival and survival. Centuries-old traditions of charity and concern for the underprivileged have been grafted on to newer, though not less important, socialist and humanitarian ideals.

In the 25 years since Israel achieved independence, phenomenal progress was made. The average annual increase in total GNP was 10 percent and in GNP per capita - 5.5 percent. Exports grew from a negligible $30 million in 1949 to almost $600 million in 1962 and over $2,100 million in 1972. Other aspects of Israel's development, such as high morale and the spirit of national unity, cannot be expressed in figures, but may, in fact, be of far greater importance.

The economy's sound agricultural base, dating back to the preindependence Zionist pioneering period, aided development. Here too, social aspects were reflected by two unique types of community—the cooperative Moshav and the collective Kibbutz. These social experiments proved economically successful, but the pioneers were always striving to achieve "the good life" in spiritual rather than material terms.

Starting from a modest base, we built a modern industrial economy, with products ranging from simple manufactures to sophisticated electronic equipment, ships, and aircraft. The share of agriculture gradually declined.

Steady and relatively rapid economic growth has been essential to our society, not merely to raise our living standards but to ensure our survival. Our difficulties included hostile neighbors, the consequent heavy burden of defense expenditure, a dearth of natural resources, and the four fold growth of our population since 1948.

To fulfill its role as a National Homeland for Jews, Israel must keep its portals open and absorb immigrants rapidly into the social, economic, and political fabric of its society. Since immigrants came from tens of different countries and a wide variety of socioeconomic and political backgrounds, this was no easy task, particularly considering that immigration arrived in intermittent, unplanned waves.

Full employment was always one of our aims. During the 1948- period, over 15 percent of the labor force was unemployed, following huge waves of immigration. But since the late 1950s, except for a brief recession in the mid-sixties, we succeeded in maintaining relatively full employment, though often at the price of strong inflationary pressures.

It is not enough to provide everyone with work. Each individual must be made to feel that he has a fair share of the benefits being reaped. Here again the dominant factor of social justice is evident in Israel's development. The government and the trade union movement (which here includes almost 90 percent of all employees) have consistently striven for a more equitable distribution of income and wealth, in order to ensure equality of opportunity for the coming generations. They tried to keep income differentials small, often in the face of serious opposition from the highly skilled. When direct wage payments and progressive income tax policies were inadequate or inappropriate to achieve this aim, income was redistributed more equitably by providing such benefits as education and health services, children's allowances, welfare and old age benefits, subsidized housing and transportation.

The policy was, on the one hand, to reward skill, industriousness, and initiative, so as not to impede the will to work and invest, but, on the other hand, to aid the weak and underprivileged, so as to avoid an internally destructive socioeconomic polarization. Great emphasis was placed on raising the educational level of all parts of the population, this being one of the best means of improving living standards and distributing income more equitably in future. With some exceptions most adult male immigrants from Asian and African countries had received little education in their countries of birth. One-third were illiterate, and the median number of their years at school is less than 6, as compared with almost 11 among adult male immigrants from Europe or America. There is a sizeable gap between the income levels of these two groups of immigrants, a gap largely due to their widely differing educational backgrounds, which we are trying to narrow through adult education and job training. But the area for major educational activity must be among the younger generation and generations to come.

About 15 percent of the current government budget and some 7.5 percent of the GNP are devoted to education. Particular emphasis is being placed on raising the educational level of young children from disadvantaged backgrounds. The methods used include the provision of preschool nurseries for these children from the age of 3, a school day lengthened by 2 to 4 hours, smaller classes, and intensified supervision.

It is commonly held that rapid economic expansion in developing states must increase the inequality of income distribution. Israel's experience in the last two decades shows that this need not necessarily happen. Although initially some trade-off between economic expansion and social equality may occur, it is possible to achieve and sustain rapid economic growth and a better life for all. I would go even further: It is a misguided approach to place rapid economic expansion above all other considerations, because real progress can never be attained when poverty and ignorance are the portion of major segments of the population.

Israel's achievements in the field of income distribution are intimately linked with its development policy. We believe in a pluralistic economy where the public, the trade union, and the private sectors can function efficiently side by side, often cooperating with each other. The government of Israel has fostered private initiative in industry, services, and tourism by its allocation of investment resources. However, there are many areas, geographic and economic, where managers of private capital fear to tread because of the scope of the investment, a high risk element, or a lack of assured, high, and rapid return. The government has therefore invested directly in many spheres, occasionally in cooperation with the trade union or the private sector, but often on its own. The government sector is relatively large. However, government enterprises are often sold when they reach economic viability, the proceeds being invested in further development.

We have made mistakes and are likely to make more—I will confine myself to one example. Full employment was and is a vital part of our development policy. However, during periods of serious unemployment we made the error of practising "full employment at any price." Labor-intensive enterprises not requiring a big initial capital investment were created, many of which were later overprotected by tariff barriers and subsidies long after they had proved unprofitable. While in the short run this policy reduced unemployment and increased the GNP, it tied up resources that at a later stage should have been allocated in a more rational manner, eventually becoming an impediment to development and rapid growth. We have paid a high price to correct this.

In some ways Israel was fortunate. Large inflows of capital and technical know-how accelerated our development, because they were reinforced by a strong sense of national unity. The former, without the latter, would have achieved little. And the sense of national unity could not have been attained if our people did not believe that they are sharing equitably in both the burdens and the benefits of development.

Tremendous tasks still lie ahead. We ardently desire peace. With peace the future holds immense promise, since more of our resources and energy could be devoted not only to the development of our own human and economic potential but also to the building of a better future for all the peoples of the Middle East, together with our neighbours.

While waiting for peace, we have not been idle. In the past 25 years, we raised the standards of living, education, and health of the Arab citizens of Israel to a level among the highest in the Middle East. Since the 1967 war a good deal was done for the population of the territories administered by Israel. Perhaps for the first time in their history there is full employment in these areas. Living conditions have been greatly improved and the mortality rate has dropped sharply.

Experience has shown that coexistence between Jews and Arabs is not only possible, but is of benefit to both sides. The achievements attained in the administered territories within such a short period of time, and our profound desire for finding an understanding with our neighbours, strengthen our belief that when our conflict is finally resolved we can cooperate in making the Middle East a region of peace and prosperity.

POSTWAR GROWTH OF LESS DEVELOPED COUNTRIES
Simon Kuznets

This paper discusses the economic growth of less developed market economies during the 1950s and the 1960s. Communist less developed countries are excluded, as measures of their growth fully comparable with those of the market economies are not easily secured.

Less developed countries (LDCs) have a relatively low per capita income, which indicates a major deficiency in exploiting the productive potential of modern technology. The low average income suggests, under the usual type of income distribution, low welfare yields to the majority of the people. The failure to exploit the potentials of modern productive technology suggests a relative lack of a modern economic and social structure.

Our group of LDCs comprises three large regions: East and Southeast Asia, excluding Japan (referred to below as Asia), which covers all of non-Communist Asia except the few countries west of Afghanistan, Pakistan, and India; Africa, excluding South Africa, Southern Rhodesia, and Libya (hereafter referred to as Africa); and Latin America. This group accounted for over 90 percent of the population included by the UN Statistical Office under its definition of "developing market economies." (In 1970 the population in these economies was 1.68 billion, in "developed market economies" 0.70 billion, and in the rest of the world 1.25 billion. The total world population was 3.63 billion.)

For these three major regions combined, per capita gross domestic product increased by 48 percent over the twenty-year period from 1950 to 1970, implying an annual growth rate of 2.0 percent. Over the same period, population grew more than 60 percent, or at an annual rate of close to 2.5 percent. This meant that total output, gross domestic policy (GDP), rose by almost 140 percent, at an annual rate of almost 4.5 percent.

These calculations do not refer to all developing countries, due to the irrelevance of including most of the Middle East, Western Asia, and countries like Libya where oil dominates an otherwise backward economy and society, producing astronomical rates of growth due largely to external forces and factors.

The growth rates differ somewhat among the three regions, which also differ substantially in per capita product. In the 1950s, Latin America had a per capita GDP three times as high as that of Asia and Africa (273 dollars at 1965 prices, compared with about $90 for the other two regions). Its per capita product rose about 57 percent (or 2.3 percent per year), compared with 42 percent for Asia and 23 percent for Africa over the two decades. The population of Latin America also grew somewhat faster (about 2.9 percent per year) than that of Asia-Africa (2.4 percent). Thus the higher income region among the LDCs grew most rapidly in population and per capita product, while the lower income regions grew less.

In the conventional calculation of average growth in per capita product, the incomes and populations of all LDCs are pooled—a procedure implying the unrealistic assumption that the growth of income and population of one LDC (or region) has positive significance for all other LDCs. Thus a unit percentage increase of the per capita product of Latin America is weighted three times the weight of a unit percentage increase of the per capita product of Asia or Africa; and the greater growth of population in Latin America, which raises the overall average, is assumed to have positive significance for all LDCs. The alternative calculation treats each country as a separate unit; and the growth rate of its per capita product is important only as measured by the size of its population, and no greater if its per capita product is greater. It is these population-weighted aggregates that will be referred to in the discussion henceforth. On this basis the average annual growth rate for LDCs was not 2 percent but only 1.6 percent.

Even 1.6 percent per year may exceed the true growth rate in GDP per capita for the LDCs over the last two decades. The available estimates may not fully reflect the actual growth of countries affected by civil war or other major conflicts, because such disturbances usually mean failure in collection of relevant data. To cite conspicuous examples, the political upheavals in Indonesia, the division of Pakistan, and the civil wars in the Congo and Nigeria, are not fully reflected in the data. The available growth rates in the production sectors of the LDCs raise further questions. Thus, for Asia the growth rate of the services sector (commerce and other services) is much higher than that for agriculture and industry combined, the latter including construction, transportation, and communications. As a result, on a per capita basis the growth rate for A+I sectors over the period is about a sixth lower than for the total product. In Latin America the growth rate for industry is very high, but its weight may reflect the internal price structure in which, due largely to policy measures, the prices of manufactured products relative to those of other sectors are much higher than in the international markets. A reasonable rough approximation of these additional corrections would reduce the growth rate of GDP per capita to between 1 and 1.4 percent per year, or between 22 and 32 percent over the two decades.

While long-term records of growth for the LDCs are extremely scanty, it is fairly clear that for Asia and Africa the rates summarized above for the last two decades are far higher than those of the long-term past. Even a rate of 1 percent per year means a multiplication factor for per capita product of 2.7 over a century. Since per capita product around 1950 for these two regions was estimated at about $90, at 1965 purchasing power, and since one may assume a lower limit of about 50 such dollars, a growth rate of even 1 percent per year was unlikely over long periods in the past. In fact, we know that the growth rate of the per capita product in India, where some development began toward the end of the nineteenth century, was a fraction of a percent per year. In Latin America the growth rate suggested for the last two decades, of about 2 percent per year in per capita product after adjustment, may have been experienced in the past. But we know that in Brazil, Mexico, and some other countries high growth rates have been attained only in recent decades. Since the acceleration in population growth, in all three less developed regions but particularly Asia and Africa, is also recent, the rates of growth of total product in the 1950s and the 1960s must have far exceeded those in the long-term past of most LDCs, particularly the populous ones in Asia. This notable acceleration in the growth of per capita product, population, and total product must be borne in mind in any evaluation of the recent experience of the LDCs.

While the long-term growth rates of the developed states displayed some interesting and significant differences, the typical growth rate of the per capita product over the long period before World War II can reasonably be set at about 2 percent per year. This, combined with a growth rate of population of somewhat over 1 percent, means a growth rate of total product of somewhat over 3 percent per year. By this standard, the growth parameters suggested for the LDCs in the last two decades measure up not unfavorably in comparison with those of the DCs in their long pre-World War II past.

The average growth rates for all LDCs, and even for the three regions, conceal substantial diversity in space and variability over time. Per capita product in many countries showed little or no growth over the 20 years, and many more states failed to grow over shorter periods within this span. On the other hand, the average per capita income and product of developed states when they entered into the period of modern economic growth and industrialization was much higher than that of most countries in Asia and Africa in the early 1950s. For a country with a higher per capita product a showdown in growth is far less painful than for a country with a low average per capita product. (The latter implies that a large proportion of the population is living close to the subsistence level.) And there have been few parallels to the large numbers of less-developed countries that showed decline or no growth in per capita product, or to the marked annual variations in the growth rates associated with crop or weather failures, or internal disturbances.

The developed states during the long decades of their growth, were more advanced than the rest of the world. The overseas offshoots of Europe, such as the United States, Canada, Australia, and New Zealand, and up to a point, Argentina, enjoyed high income per capita well before they became industrialized. Today the LDCs must live and grow in a concert of nations including many much further advanced in economic capacity and power. The LDCs may therefore be subject to greater strains and pressures than the current DCs felt when they were entering the process of modern economic growth in a world in which they themselves were the leaders.

The backlog of technological and other potentials that permit a high growth rate has increased at a tremendous rate. This means that the LDCs today can take advantage of a stock of useful knowledge, both technological and social, that is much larger than that available to the DCs when they entered their period of modern economic growth. The advance in material and social technology that has occurred in the world since the 1880s when Japan finally managed to initiate its modern growth, or even the late 1920s when the second industrialization and growth spurt began in Russia, has been striking and impressive. One would thus expect that the LDCs could attain a much higher growth rate than that of the DCs before World War II. This argument is reinforced by the achievements of the DCs during the same period.

The UN Statistical Office includes in its group of developed market economies all non-Communist Europe, North America, Oceania, Japan, South Africa, and Israel. Its population in 1970 was about 0.70 billion people, compared with 1.68 billion for the LDCs. For our purposes it seemed best to limit the group to Europe and North America, with somewhat over 570 million people in 1970. North America, with a 1950 per capita product about three times higher than that of Europe, shows a distinctly lower growth rate, 2.2 percent per year compared with 3.9 percent for Europe. The correlation for the DCs between per capita product and the growth rate is negative. Consequently, when we reweight the growth rates of per capita product for them by constant population, the average rises to 3.34 percent per year, in contrast with the reduction to 1.58 percent, calculated similarly for the LDCs. If we assume a growth of per capita product by 1.4 percent per year for the LDCs, and by 3.3 percent for the DCs, total growth over the twenty year period would be 32 percent and 91 percent respectively.

The preceding comment implies a widening relative disparity in the per capita products of the LDCs and DCs. For the three LDC regions and the two DC regions, the widening of DC/LDC differentials in per capita product between 1950 and 1970 would depend on the choice of calculation bases. In the conventional aggregation, the change would be from a ratio of 13 to 1 in 1950 to 16 to 1 in 1970. In an aggregation consistent with weighting growth rates of per capita product by constant population, the change would be from a ratio of 12.5 to 1 in 1950 to 17 to 1 in 1970.

The rate of growth of per capita product of the LDCs over the last two decades was probably less than half that of the DCs. The relative gap, already wide in the 1950s, was even wider by 1970. The important implication is that the aspirations of the LDCs may be more related to the performance of the DCs than to some absolute fixed target. The demonstration effect of the higher growth rate of the DCs sets up a situation in which the LDCs realize that they are slipping behind, relative to some desirable goal. And perception of the widening gap becomes sharper, the closer the contact between the two groups of countries.

The diversity of per capita growth rates among LDCs was clearly much wider than among DCs in the last two decades. A large proportion of LDC population was in countries in which there was little, if any, growth in per capita product (and even less in per capita consumption). During the period 1960-68, the lower quartile of LDC population is in countries for which average growth of per capita product was less than 0.1 percent per year, that is, almost no growth at all, while the average for the top quartile was 3.45 percent per year. For the DCs, the average for the lowest quartile was 2.74 percent per year, for the upper 4.40 percent per year. Thus, for a quarter of LDC population there was no growth of per capita product, even though the population weighted average for the period for all LDCs was over 1.4 percent per year.

The income distribution in the LDCs became more unequal, partly because of the lower growth rate of agriculture than of other sectors, partly because of widening inequality within the urban sector of the population. These trends are extremely important, but because our information is scanty they are still conjectural. Cross-section studies indicate a more unequal income distribution in LDCs than in DCs; and, since distribution of income in the DCs has tended to move towards equality, the contrast is striking. A combination of initially low average income, low rate of growth in income per capita, and widening inequality in income distribution may mean that the possibility of raising the incomes of the lower income groups is distressingly limited.

The lower growth rate of per capita product and consumption in the LDCs was associated, during the 1950-70 period, with a high population growth rate. The latter is often assumed to be the cause of the former. But the simple argument overlooks major factors in the situation. First, the high growth rate of population in the LDCs was accompanied by a growth rate of 1.8 percent per year in the labor force, which was over twice as high as the 0.8 percent rate for the labor force of the DCs. The LDCs could hardly attain so high a growth rate of total product if their labor force had grown much more slowly. Second, and more important, slower population growth would require changes in the economic and social structure favoring a lower birth rate—through a reduction in the death rates at the youngest ages—and greater investment in training and other human capital in the next generation in expectation of adequate individual and social returns. Such changes would modify conditions affecting economic growth in favor of more rapid transformation and a higher growth rate. But the institutional and other conditions that account for the high growth rate of population in the LDCs are the very ones that keep the growth rate of per capita product moderate. Technological obstacles to birth control or survival of traditional views are minor elements in the LDCs compared to effects of social and economic institutions that make low birth rates inconsistent with the family's economic and social interests.

Two approaches to the exploration of factors behind the growth record of the LDCs in the last two decades can be suggested: Using the first, we would be dealing with production sectors and their inputs and outputs, the interconnections between production, consumption, savings, and investments, domestic flows of resources and product, and the flows from and to abroad, and so on through the long list of national accounts components, supplemented by data of population, labor, and wealth.

The second approach views the recent growth experience of the LDCs largely as an attempt to change the social and economic institutions as a precondition for better exploitation of the potential of modern technology. This might reveal that, while the backlog of technology available for exploitation by the LDCs is huge, and much greater than that available to the DCs in the past, its effective use imposes requirements, in the way of adequate social institutions and practices, that are difficult for the LDCs to meet. These requirements are not so much for some minimum amount of capital, or even for some minimum supply of labor of minimum skills, both of which may be relatively easy to attain. They are far more for an organization of society that provides viable stability, within which socially desirable economic interests can be consistently pursued. Two prerequisites seem of primary importance: a system of social institutions that provides adequate compensation for socially valuable labor with a fair distribution of the product, and a social organization that combines stability with the capacity to resolve flexibly and peacefully the internal conflicts of interest that are continually generated by economic growth.

The proper social channeling of modern economic growth has been a difficult task even for developed countries. History shows that the formation of a stable, politically and socially unified body to administer a country's economic growth was a slow and difficult process. Equally impressive is the frequency in the recent history of the LDCs of breakdowns in national and social unity essential for sustained economic growth. These breakdowns—in the Congo, in several North African states, in Nigeria, Ghana, Indonesia, and Pakistan—and the frequent, erratic changes of power in many Latin American republics make for relatively low rates of growth. High growth rates are impossible when overt internal conflicts rage; and rapid growth itself may be dangerously disruptive if internal tensions are exacerbated by further inequalities such growth may generate, in absence of a social and institutional structure capable of making the needed adjustments.

**ALTERNATIVE STRATEGIES
FOR DEVELOPMENT**
Hollis B. Chenery

Many experts assume that different types of economies require different development models, depending upon the level of income, the role of international trade, and the extent of surplus labor. The present paper proposes an alternative approach, classifying countries according to basic differences in their development strategies. A strategy is affected by the structural characteristics of the economy, by social objectives, and by the government's choice of policies. An analysis comparing countries trying to carry out similar policies rather than countries having only a similar starting point will, therefore, enable us to ask if a government has chosen a strategy suited to the country's resources and social objectives.

It has been observed that there are uniform patterns of change in the structure of production, demand, trade, and labor use as income levels rise. These conclusions are derived from data covering virtually all developing states. The patterns have been analysed, permitting the description of a particular country's experience in relative terms.

Patterns of trade and resource allocation provide the primary basis for distinguishing between strategies. I classified some 50 countries according to these criteria, outlining the sequence of observable structural changes. A state's performance should be assessed in relation to its strategy, rather than to average standards for all states. Since each strategy requires a different sequence of structural change, different policies may be appropriate at different stages. The major strategies should be reexamined for differences in social aims, such as income distribution and employment.

COMMON ELEMENTS OF DEVELOPMENT STRATEGIES

There are common structural elements affecting all states, such as similar demand patterns, access to similar technologies, and participation in the same international economy. Moreover, most less developed countries agree that increasing the gross national product should be the initial policy objective and use similar methods to accomplish this. Indeed, development patterns have been more uniform than the differences in resources, social objectives, and economic starting points of the newly-independent states warrant.

By 1960 development was under way in most states. These early efforts were largely unplanned, and the main focus of development strategies soon shifted to the avoidance of bottlenecks, mainly through action in the spheres of international trade and the sectoral allocation of investments.

Assuming similar aims and methods, differences in resource allocation should reflect the country's initial fund of natural resources, capital, and skills, the size of its domestic market, and its access to external capital. Development strategy is an attempt to increase consumption and investment by adjusting the production and trade patterns to fit the state's factor endowments and external environment. Variations in capital inflow, investment rates, and other constraints on policy can be allowed for.

The shift of emphasis from accumulation to resource allocation has important corollaries. A successful strategy must secure supplies of the goods needed for continued growth from local production or imports. Failure to achieve consistency in the balance of payments has in the past decade been a more important cause of poor results than failure to mobilize adequate savings.

In a rapidly growing economy, good allocation of resources requires continuous change in the production and investment patterns and in foreign currency sources. Excluding petroleum products, average earnings from primary exports during the past decade rose by about 3 percent per year. Since without import substitution import requirements grow about 50 percent faster than GNP, states must devise feasible combinations of import substitution, expansion of new exports, and external borrowing to sustain rapid growth.

NORMAL ALLOCATION PATTERNS

Average patterns of production and exports* at selected income levels were analysed for some 90 states over the 1950-70 period. The major problem of resource allocation during transition from primary specialization to a modern industrial structure is to balance production with relatively inflexible levels of primary exports and

---

*Since there is much less variation in the composition of imports, exports are the major determinant of the trade pattern.

domestic demand. In a state with 10 million inhabitants and average resources, per capita earnings from primary exports rise fairly rapidly up to an income level of $300, and more slowly thereafter. Exports of manufactured goods and services rise steadily, exceeding primary exports above income levels of $350. Thus the share of exports in GNP grows at higher income levels.

Changes in production and investment are the composite result of changes in domestic demand and exports. In the average production pattern, about half the increase in the share of industry is caused by changes in the composition of domestic demand, the other half being due to changes in the composition of exports and to import substitution. Large countries, having a more favorable domestic market, tend to industrialize earlier and to have lower proportions of primary exports (and hence of total exports).

The supply of natural resources has a dominant effect on trade patterns at lower income levels. Natural resources are more important for resource allocation in small countries than in large, since trade affects a larger proportion of the total commodity supply. The 64 small states in the sample have been classified according to their export patterns as relatively "primary-oriented" or "industry and service-oriented". Industrialization occurs much later in the primary-oriented group.

For primary-oriented small states per capita primary exports normally exceed $50 during the transition and in states of extreme specialization (Venezuela, Zambia, Malaysia) they exceed $100. When plentiful natural resources are combined with favorable export markets, further investment in primary production for export is more productive than import substitution, and industrialization is delayed.

Industry (or service) orientation in trade arises from a lack of a favorable natural resources base for exports. In such countries as Hong Kong, Taiwan, Israel, Greece, Lebanon, Tunisia, and Portugal primary exports did not reach $20 per capita. This shortage of foreign exchange may be offset by a capital inflow in the short run, but over time nonprimary exports must be developed. At middle income levels the small industry-oriented country lags somewhat behind the typical large state in industrialization, but at high income levels its specialization in manufactured exports leads to a higher degree in industrialization than in large countries, which tend to more balanced economies.

Four indices are useful in classifying the patterns of resource allocation followed by individual countries:

- The relative export level: the ratio of actual to normal level of exports for a given size and income level.
- The trade orientation: the difference between the actual export bias and the normal bias for a given income level and size.

- The production orientation: the difference between the actual production bias and the normal production bias.
- The capital inflow: measured as the deviation from normal. Capital inflow has a marked effect on trade and production patterns. There is also a significant relation between capital inflow and a state's size and income level.

The proposed classification is logical chiefly in respect of states where development is already underway. The basic sample therefore includes all states:
- which had reached an income level of $80 per capita,* and were not yet fully developed;
- for which the required statistical measures can be estimated;
- whose economies were not too disrupted by wars and disturbances;
- which are large enough to be representative.

The first two criteria yield 63 states in the transitional range of $100 to $1,000 for at least part of the decade 1960-70. From this group, 6 politically disturbed countries with low growth (South Vietnam, Cambodia, Dominican Republic, Haiti, Nigeria, and Indonesia) and 6 small, unrepresentative countries (Honduras, Paraguay, Jordan, Libya, Papua, and Panama) have been deleted, leaving 51.

Only 7 transitional countries with populations exceeding 5 million—Cameroon, Mozambique, Malagasy Republic, South Vietnam, Cambodia, Nigeria, and Indonesia—have been excluded.

Four patterns can be identified:

1. Primary Specialization, characterized by
    a) primary-oriented exports
    b) primary-oriented production
    c) export level above normal

This group corresponds to the concept of an export-led growth pattern based on favorable primary resources. In the 1960s it included 14 of the sample states with a total population of 130 million (plus Nigeria, temporarily disrupted by civil war).

2. Balanced Production and Trade, characterized by
    a) normal export orientation
    b) normal production orientation

This group of 11 states can be subdivided into 7 having normal levels of capital inflow and exports, and 4 with high capital inflow. Its total population is 160 million.

---

*All values in this paper are in 1964 U.S. dollars.

3. Import Substitution, characterized by
   a) primary export orientation
   b) low total exports
   c) production not primary-oriented

   This group includes 9 states with a total population of 220 million plus India (a special case).

4. Industrial Specialization, characterized by
   a) industrial export orientation
   b) industrial production orientation

   The total population for the whole group was 240 million in 1965, but, as of now, Bangladesh would be separated from Pakistan and this would reduce the total to 180 million.

On the basis of 1965 data, all but 6 of the 51 states could be assigned to one of these four major allocation patterns without difficulty. Each of these patterns of resource allocation applied in 1970 to 200 million to 300 million people in transitional states, India being treated as a separate category because of its size.

Let us compare each country's intentions, as represented by its development program, with the results accomplished. Two of the main features observed reflect policy failures rather than intended results: Almost all states with import substitution patterns (group 3) had planned to expand manufactured exports during the past decade and in some cases had taken extensive measures to do so. Had these measures produced average levels of industrial exports, both the country's total export level and its trade bias would have become normal and it would be classed in group 2. Therefore, the type 3 pattern is a transitory phase that occurs frequently, but is not consistent with sustained growth over a long period. Another transitory feature is excessive reliance on foreign capital. External borrowing constitutes a safety valve that can offset a decline in exports, production failures and other mistakes. However, few states can sustain borrowing much in excess of 4 percent of GNP over long periods.

A comparison of the development plans and subsequent performance of various states indicates that groups 1, 2, and 4 do represent distinctive development strategies that are reflected by the statistical similaries in their results. This hypothesis will be developed by studying the level and composition of trade, the structure of production and investment, and the role of external capital—in which the three strategies differ most significantly. Each strategy produces a different sequence of change in these elements. In analysing these sequences, it is useful to break down the transition from the productive structure of a country producing $100 per capita GNP to one producing $1,000 per capita into two phases, early and late. The early phase may be said to run from $100 to $300, and the later from $300 to $1,000.

The early phase is characterized by primary exports, "easy" import substitution, and the availability of public capital imports on soft terms. By contrast, the later phase shows a shift to nonprimary exports, import substitution in intermediate and capital goods, and borrowing on hard terms. Similar distinctions can be drawn in production, where the major expansion of output and employment comes in primary sectors in the early phase and in nonprimary sectors in the later phase. Each strategy accelerates the advent of later-stage activities in some respects, while retarding them in others.

Primary Specialization

Most countries start to develop by specializing in exports of unprocessed or initially processed natural resources and only later develop exportable manufactures and services. The primary specialization strategy maintains this pattern during part of the transitional period so as to take advantage of favorable export possibilities. Except for Iran the 14 states following this strategy in the 1960s were all small. Usually, their exports were based on one or two items (for example, oil in Saudi Arabia, Iran, Iraq, and Venezuela; tea in Ceylon; copper in Zambia). In almost all countries the initial development of the export product and of the supporting infrastructure were heavily supported by foreign investment. This accelerated the growth of total output but often concentrated the benefits in the primary export sector. Most of the states concerned are now well beyond the initial stage of heavy investment in primary exports and have a net capital outflow representing the profits and amortization of these investments.

The desirability of maintaining this pattern depends largely on the supply of local resources, the world demand for the products exported, and the need for a better distribution of income and employment. In the past decade, world demand has been relatively strong for oil and most minerals but relatively weak for agricultural products other than meat, fruit, and vegetables. The relative growth rates of states in group 1 are seriously affected by these differences in export market conditions.

There are three major difficulties with this strategy:

1. Its initial dependence on foreign investment and subsequent requirement of heavy amortization payments.
2. Its negative effects on income distribution.
3. The difficulty of forecasting future demands and securing the necessary changes in the production structure.

Shifting from primary specialization to more balanced patterns of trade or production without disrupting the growth process is difficult. Current prices based on equilibrium exchange rates are no incentive to shift investment to nonprimary production necessary for further growth when primary exports decline. In most states, such as Argentina, Brazil, Colombia, Ghana and Ceylon, declining export earnings were not anticipated in country policies. Therefore, these states had to restructure their economies under the pressure of foreign exchange shortages and limited investment funds. Despite sound policies, it took years for Brazil and Colombia to adjust to the decline of coffee earnings by moving from primary specialization to the import substitution pattern.

Some countries, including Costa Rica, Peru, and Kenya in the past decade, managed to make this shift without seriously disrupting growth. Thailand, Malaysia, and Ivory Coast seem to be moving effectively in this direction. In all six, success has hinged on steps encouraging import substitution and new exports while traditional export earnings were still relatively high, thus avoiding a structural crisis in the balance of payments.

Primary specialization implies that industry will be developed after incomes and investment rates have already started to rise as a result of high primary output and productivity, as in Canada or Denmark during an earlier period. While the higher wage rates of states that industrialize late inhibit the development of labor-intensive exports, the high investment rates permit the country to specialize in other types of industrial or services exports to replace stagnant primary exports. However, apart from the oil producing countries, few states found it possible to maintain this strategy beyond an income level of $500 per capita.

Balanced Development

Countries in this category do not specialize. They fall into two main groups: states with normal levels of imports (group 2), and states with an import substitution policy and low levels of imports (group 3).

These strategies are adopted because the country lacks the resource base for continued primary specialization or because it desires a more balanced industrial structure so as to avoid the uncertainties of continued dependence on primary exports. When this decision is made when primary exports are still high, the measures to stimulate industry need not be at the expense of exports. Usually, however, the decision to industrialize comes after primary exports have stagnated for some time. Industrialization is then promoted by high tariffs, quotas, and direct public investments. These make domestic production more profitable than exports and, unless offset by export subsidies, constitute an inward-looking strategy.

Most states pass a period of favoring industrial production for the home market, and it is arguable that for many types of manufactures this process enables the subsequent development of exports. The main differences between normal and excessive import substitution are the length of time that this policy is pursued, the extent of the distortions produced in the economy, and the consequent obstacles to further growth.

Excessive import substitution has been particularly characteristic of large countries, though only with extremely favorable primary resources (Iran) and high external aid (South Korea and Pakistan) can a large country avoid a fairly balanced pattern of resource allocation during much of the transition.

Some big states developed initially as specialized primary exporters, but few maintained this pattern beyond the GNP level of $150 per capita. Once primary exports ceased to be a leading sector, most large states adopted import substitution strategies that persisted for several decades. In Argentina, Brazil, Mexico, and Turkey these strategies received a major impulse in the depression of the 1930s and again during the trade disruption of the Second World War. In the Philippines, Yugoslavia, India, and Pakistan the strategy dates from the early postwar period.

In the most extreme examples—Argentina and Brazil—import substitution policies produced a subsidy to industry of more than 6 percent of GNP. The extent of protection in India, Pakistan, and Turkey was comparable, though the size of the industrial sector was smaller.

During the 1960s, there was a major shift to the promotion of manufactured exports in some big states previously favouring import substitution, such as Spain, Yugoslavia, Pakistan, Brazil, Colombia, Turkey, and the Philippines. This change produced growth rates of 20 percent or more for manufactured exports in most of these states, moving the early starters (Yugoslavia and Pakistan) into the industrial specialization group. However, since exports are a smaller share of GNP in big states, export specialization has only modest effects on the structure of production. In 1968, Yugoslavia, Pakistan, and South Korea were exporting some 10 percent of their industrial output, but other big countries exported 3 percent or less.

The shortage of foreign exchange produced by import substitution was sufficiently acute to disrupt the growth process seriously in India, Colombia, Brazil, and Argentina. In Spain, Turkey, Yugoslavia, and Mexico tourism and emigrant remittances largely offset the trade bottleneck that would otherwise have impeded growth.

In small countries limited domestic markets make import substitution strategies less attractive. Only in Chile and Uruguay have they been pursued to such extremes and with such serious

consequence for growth as in some larger countries. Most of the
10 small states in group 2 followed a balanced allocation strategy.
Costa Rica, El Salvador, Peru, and Jamaica diversified their economies
and moved towards more balanced exports without going through an
inward-looking phase of restricted trade. In some small states,
foreign capital facilitated the structural transformation to a much
greater degree than is possible in large countries.

Industrial Specialization

Early industrial specialization is a response to unfavorable
resources for primary exports plus the availability of sufficient skilled
labor and organizational ability. Virtually all states adopting this
strategy so far were able to rely on significant amounts of external
capital for at least the first decade.

During the interwar years, Japan developed an outward-oriented
light industry providing the basis for export growth, while its per
capita income was still less than $200. The postwar pattern of outward-oriented industrialization was pioneered by Hong Kong, Israel,
Taiwan, and Yugoslavia in the early 1960s. Their aim was a structure
of production and trade exploiting comparative advantages in manufacturing or services. South Korea, Singapore, Pakistan, and other
states followed similar patterns, which varied according to the initial
production structure and the availability of foreign capital.

The first decade of this strategy was devoted to developing
industry for the home market as a base for subsequent exports. Until
1958 Israel followed an import substitution strategy accounting for
60 percent of the increase in industry's share of the GNP, which
was accompanied by a rapid growth of agriculture. Israel could
reduce the heavy dependence on external capital, as manufactured
exports grew at the rate of 20 percent per year for the next decade.
South Korea started five years later from a much lower base, but
expanded industrial exports even more rapidly.

The success of the industrial specialization strategy has been
quite impressive. The states in group 4 account for $6,000 million
of manufactured exports, some two-thirds of the total from all
developing countries, though they have less than 10 percent of the
total LDC population. The group has a median growth of 4.7 percent
per year in GNP per capita, as compared with 3 percent for all
transitional countries. This strategy has also produced a better
income distribution than the other three. However, it is only feasible
after a country has completed the early phase of development as
regards education and import-substituting industrialization.

As more states shift to export-oriented industry, competition will become more intense and high growth rates more difficult to attain. Even with these provisos, however, a greater movement towards industrial specialization and exports from countries in the middle and later stages of the transition seems both feasible and desirable.

EVALUATION OF STRATEGIES

Most attempts to compare the performance of developing countries assume either the validity of neoclassical assumptions of general equilibrium or that countries are faced with similar constraints and follow the same development strategy. The present study suggests the existence of many optimal routes, depending on the initial conditions of each state. Since each route involves periods when the climber is traversing as well as periods of rapid ascent, we cannot judge his overall progress by his distance from the top.

Each strategy has more difficult periods, when the growth of GNP may be a misleading measure of progress. In primary specialization and import substitution rapid growth can be achieved for a decade or so, but then a major shift must be made to new exports. In the industry-oriented strategy the difficult structural transformation takes place earlier and is followed by accelerated growth once manufacturing exports have become established.

The countries most successful in industrial specialization—Taiwan, South Korea, Yugoslavia, Israel, and Singapore—experienced a decade or so when the returns on big investments in restructuring were not impressive in growth terms. Yet this period established a productive structure later able to sustain accelerated growth without excessive reliance on foreign capital. Military requirements in Israel and South Korea distort this pattern somewhat, but with this qualification the generalization applies equally to them.

The apparent success of primary specialization is likely to be exaggerated in the early phase. Iran, Zambia, and Ivory Coast have achieved rapid growth but should be judged as much by their movement towards greater diversification of production and exports as by their increase in output. Export diversification by states such as Costa Rica, Peru, and Malaysia may be more important for long-term growth than the high growth rates of some single commodity exporters.

Brazil switched from primary specialization to a balanced growth pattern between the middle 1950s and the late 1960s. The static inefficiency due to excessive protection during this period was largely offset by the contribution made by protection in the transition to a viable industrial structure based on industrial exports. On this basis, Yugoslavia, Brazil, and Pakistan can be judged more favorably than Argentina, Chile, and India.

The early industrialization strategy has usually produced better than average income distribution, while the import substitution group is worse than average. Yet the unequal distributions of Peru, Colombia and Ecuador are associated with their earlier primary specialization, and on the whole this strategy appears most likely to produce extremes of inequality.

Import substitution tends to worsen income distribution. Its typical instruments, industrial protection and investment subsidies, create capital-intensive forms of industry and agriculture in which labor absorption is limited, besides limiting the capital and foreign exchange available to small producers in rural areas. The worsening effects on income distribution have been noted in Mexico, Brazil, India, Pakistan, and other states.

Early industrialization has some advantages for income distribution and provides a basis for later rapid growth. The type of industry encouraged by export orientation is more likely to be labor-intensive, as was true of Taiwan and South Korea, which pioneered this strategy. Several states with the most equal income distributions—Israel, South Korea, Taiwan, and Yugoslavia—belong to group 4. This appears to be partly due to their high growth rates, which led to high levels of employment. The relatively high education levels of states in this group are also conducive to economic mobility and more equal distribution of income. Poor states can improve income distribution by employment generation and asset redistribution.

DISCUSSION

SIMON KUZNETS (United States): We are dealing with patterns rather than strategies of development. Often developments came as a surprise to the governments concerned, or were different from what was planned. One must ask: "How did these patterns emerge?" Were they deliberately chosen from a number of real alternatives, or were they a natural response to the location and size of the country, the composition of its resources and so on?

Countries with a substantial surplus of valuable raw materials naturally fell into the primary exporting pattern. The Soviet Union and some other communist states exploited their comparative advantages in certain raw materials to export items like furs, minerals, and even some agricultural products to finance their initial industrialization. They did this for a very short period to accumulate enough purchasing power to buy indispensable industrial imports, and they then used their labor force and the compulsory power of their dictatorial governments to industrialize. In Argentina, on the other hand, primary exports were continued for too long, and the question must be asked: "Why?" What is there about the economic and social structure, at crucial points where a shift has to be made from one phase to another, that explains why some countries fail to make the shift, while others make it? What kind of labor force and organizational capacity are needed to enable a country without raw materials to create an industrial base with the aid of relatively short-term capital imports is another important question. Can society be mobilized to bridge the initial gap towards a higher level without the constraint of a dictatorial communist system?

The links between income distribution and different growth patterns are very weak. Any pattern of development can give a very unequal income distribution. This includes industrial specialization. In any case, income distribution data are most inadequate, especially in developing countries. Even UN publications on this subject for Latin America are unreliable. Except for Argentina and possibly Mexico, no usable data are to hand.

MARC HENRY (President, OECD, Paris): There is an obvious relationship between the level of available technology and the so-called natural resources endowment. The first proper strategy for a developing country is to know whether it has the technological capacity to develop its natural resources, and if not how it can obtain it.

In Libya, as late as 1957, planners could only produce some depressing agricultural projections for Cirenaica. Since then, highly advanced technology has led to the exploitation of oil in the Sahara. Now Libya is able to blackmail the United States with a technology it does not possess.

The distinction between types of development should be made not between capital-intensive and labor-intensive but between energy-intensive and non-energy-intensive. To advance the economy, high energy consumption is needed. One of the best criteria of the gap between developed and developing states is the consumption of energy per head.

Local sources of energy and technology available to make use of them affect strategies of development. Capital has often been lacking to develop even hydroelectric power.

Fuels and certain minerals are nonrenewable resources. Agricultural production is renewable—unless and until it exhausts the soil. Further examination of renewable and nonrenewable concepts is necessary. For instance, plantation production of sugar or groundnuts exhausts the soil and makes it impossible for normal food production to take place.

Development strategy is conditioned on a clear idea of the state's basic food production and consumption. Japan was able to start development because her intensive agriculture and very good management made her quickly independent as regards rice. But then consumption patterns in Japan changed, and now Japan is heavily dependent on food imports. They are looking for a food base elsewhere, through contractual arrangements with such nations as Brazil and Indonesia.

On the other hand, in Indonesia, the food base remains rice, though land is short, and they are trying to squeeze three crops instead of two or two instead of one on the same land. The dependence on rice has grown there, and there is no sign of diversification.

In West Africa, the dependence on food imports has been in direct proportion to the intensification of industrialization. The food dependence of West Africa, not least for rice, was growing at the rate of 10 percent per annum. Good examples are Senegal and the Ivory Coast.

A country can develop and be independent in a basic sense only if it has a certain infrastructure in energy, transportation, and food production.

SOLON BARRACLOUGH (FAO): The political and social elements of development are the key to strategy. Economic factors in development must be linked to social and political decisions, in order to produce results.

A project to raise Negro farm incomes in the Mississippi Delta was closed down, 20 years ago, because it was successful in breaking accepted norms of what wages and living standards should be. The same probelm had to be faced in Latin America and the Near East since then.

Chile tried three strategies: the first, to modernize without changing the social structure; the second, providing for limited income redistribution; and the third, a revolutionary strategy. All three failed because of political and social constraints. The income redistribution was successful and food consumption rose by 25 percent, but internal and external pressures are likely to cause failure.

If economic strategies are to have an impact on policy-making groups, they must be linked to an analysis of social class relationship within the country and to international power relationships.

Unless our discussions deal with problems of imperialism and of the social class struggle, many developing states will ignore us.

HOLLIS CHENERY (IBRD): I must say to Professor Barraclough that science consists of starting with what we have rather than taking up what is politically popular. Strategy **reflects** not only a plan but also something of what was intended and what was achieved by the states concerned.

Concerning the question whether or not to use the existing data on income distribution: In 1963, Professor Kuznets speculated correctly, on the basis of data from 6 or 8 states, that income distribution worsens in early stages of development but improves in later stages. The data from 60 states now available confirm this hypothesis. The data are not very good, but if they are used the people who collect them are forced to improve them. They should, however, be used with circumspection.

**DEVELOPMENT PLANNING:
SOME LESSONS
FROM EXPERIENCE**
John P. Lewis

Twenty years ago—even 10 years ago in most of the poor countries—national development planning had strong adversaries, little experience, weak data and technique, and great expectations. By now most of the controversy over the basic appropriateness of planning has disappeared; at least the opposition has lost its passion. Much planning experience has accrued. The data and the available analytical techniques, while still imperfect and incomplete, are much improved. And almost everywhere expectations about the benefits that planning can yield have diminished.

In short, national development planning in the poor countries is being routinized and is losing its magic. For all the diversity of experience and geography we represent, a large majority of the participants in this conference probably agree that there is need for a fresh, searching look at the radically altered condition into which development planning has evolved, and that by now there are many lessons to be drawn.

But there will be little ready agreement about what it is we are talking about. Is "development planning," as we use the term, identical with "development policy"? Is it narrower than and, in some sense, derivative from, the latter? Is it, on the contrary, broader and antecedent? Is planning necessarily or predominantly quantitative? Does it imply controls? Is it, indeed, inseparable from whatever system of controls is chosen to make good the plans? Can any reliable line be drawn between planning and implementation?

The answer to none of these questions is self-evident or commonly agreed. Thus, in trying to cite some lessons of the development planning experience one must be arbitrary not only about which lessons to select for comment but also about choosing a working definition of planning itself.

My assumption is that planning involves systematical attempts by governments to analyze the requirements, and choose the measures needed, for accomplishing selected development goals.

John P. Lewis is Professor of Economics and International Affairs and Dean, Woodrow Wilson School of Public and International Affairs, Princeton University, United States.

A number of issues implicit in this definition, including some relating to controls and implementation, will be elaborated as I proceed. However, the terrain from which I draw lessons will be arbitrarily narrowed in two ways.

First, I propose to deal primarily with the process of development planning rather than with the substance of the development problems and responses with which planning deals. This sweeping exclusion cuts out at least 90 percent of what development planning practitioners and observers do and talk about. Nevertheless, there is a certain logical priority to issues of process, and in the opening phases of a conference on the state of development planning it is appropriate to give them precedence.

Second, as regards the procedural aspects of planning, I do not propose to say much about questions of data (their availability, adequacy, quality) or about questions of modeling and analytical technique. This reflects respect for the comparative advantage that some of my colleagues on the program bring to these issues, confidence that they will not be neglected, and concern lest we neglect the rest of the procedural questions.

The points I shall be making have mainly to do with the institutional contexts and dynamics in which development planning is done. My observations derive much less from close academic study of planning than from certain working experiences—both in the nearest thing to a national economic planning agency possessed by a government that professes not to do national economic planning and as a continuing observer of and sometime foreign-aid practitioner in India. Undoubtedly, the selection and content of the observations have been skewed by the limitations of this background. But, for what they are worth, let me cite a dozen procedural lessons that can be drawn from the last couple of decades' experience.

1. What concerns us, plainly, is planning, not plans. Documents fill documentary libraries, but as such they do not accomplish much. The preparation of plan documents can constitute a very important part of the collective decision-making process that is called planning; and the periodicity with which multi-year plans are formulated and adopted helps, benignly or perversely, to determine the rhythm of the planning process. But the planning that counts is a continuing, self-revising process, interconnecting with other official and non-official decision making. It it not the documentary artifacts of that activity.

2. A government's designated planners may not be its real planners. Just as the fact that a government's plan documents are inoperative does not necessarily prove that it is not engaged in constructive development planning, so it should not be assumed that a government's consequential planning necessarily centers in its

planning commission or board simply because it has an agency of that name. The pivotal planning unit may instead be a ministry of finance, a cabinet secretariat, or even a so-called research institute. Serious analysis of planning procedures cannot be deluded by appearances. That pieces of government machinery sometimes get mislabeled and others become redundant is not proof that the systems to which they belong are ineffective, or even particularly inefficient.

3. Even when it extends to all economic sectors in the system, effective development planning always is selective, in the sense that it concerns the pursuit of only some, not all, of the goals that governments simultaneously seek. For example, development promotion as such does not attempt to alter defense postures or cope with emergencies or natural disasters. Its boundaries and parameters may well be set by these other needs, but the goals of development itself are different and conceptually specific. If the effort is to be purposive its goals need to be articulated with some precision by the governments doing the development planning. Many governments during the past four or five years have been reminded of the need to update and reorder their formal planning goals as their senses of broad social priorities shift. Under conditions of routinized planning, governments have to bestir themselves to replace the single-minded pursuit of rising (average) income per capita with a different mix of objectives that more faithfully reflects the increased concerns about inequalities and underemployment in many of the poor countries.

4. In some countries just now a kind of sour grapes, backlash attitude is building toward rigorous, increasingly sophisticated plan analytics. In view of the insensitivity that model-builders often show to the institutional and political phenomena that surround their models, one has some sympathy for this backlash—although not much, for the more sophisticated techniques are normally more powerful, and the more complex models have a greater capacity to be realistic. The basic point is that any genuinely anti-quantitative fashion in planning would be idiocy. Only number can impart the sense of proportion that is indispensable to planning, express reconciliations of needs and resources, or distinguish larger from lesser issues and policies. Development planning is not exclusively quantitative in content, but it is centrally so; and any impulse to the contrary is retrogressive.

5. A broader lesson can be derived from the experience of many countries of the comparative roles of planning technicians, on the one hand, and of bureaucrats and politicians, on the other. The lesson is mixed. Good, professionally competent, and (most particularly) honest technical analysis is invaluable. Thus any government serious about planning will establish an organizational environment that attracts and rewards excellence, gives its professional planners scope and influence, and prizes analytical candor. Yet unless these

excellent technicians are effectively wired into the politico-bureaucratic system where the nation's decision-making power lies, and unless their diagnoses and recommendations are politically or administratively authenticated, they will succeed only in writing pamphlets. Healthy planning must strive for both technical and political vigor, but of the two the latter is the more essential. It is very commonly claimed that planning, to be more responsive, needs to be more participatory. This may or may not be so. If the government's regular representative structures do not need supplementing, the regular leaders and officials of the government may constitute serviceable surrogates for the public and its various interest groups in planning as they do in other kinds of public decision making. But whether the representation is participatory or conventional, workable planning requires continuing, recurrent political validation.

6. Should planners get mixed up in year-to-year and even week-to-week policy making and operations? At a later point I shall be arguing ". . . not too much." However, some judicious contamination of the planning function with current operations may be essential for maintaining the political and bureaucratic leverage that effectiveness requires. In the United States, the National Resources Planning Board of the late thirties was admirably designed and staffed for long-term planning, but had no influence because it was not involved in consequential decision making, which determined longer run outcomes in short-term bites. In contrast, the United States' post-World War II central economic agency, the Council of Economic Advisers, has been integrally involved in critical day-to-day decisions and often has exerted substantial influence, but has had little time or perspective for long-term planning. In developing countries, unless the planning agency participates with some authority in annual budget making, its multiyear plans for resource allocation often come to little. To maintain the political viability of planning, the sole substitute for such operational involvement is the active participation of the prime minister or the chief of government in planning itself. And this, as the Indian Planning Commission has discovered, is a very difficult phenomenon to sustain. The one thing that has kept the (designated) Indian planners from becoming bureaucratically trivial has been the operational role they have as the authoritative year-by-year allocators of central-government development grants to the Indian states.

Now let me bracket two closely related lessons. One concerns how comprehensive development planning needs to be with respect to economic sectors. The other involves the relation between planning and controls.

7-8. The real-world economies that planning seeks to alter are systems, their sectors and components interact. Hence the ramifications of planning a particular sector, say, agriculture, are never limited to that sector. Planning that would rationally intervene in the economic system must take account of intersectoral and inter-industry relations, transactions, and feedbacks. It must strive for internal consistency. It cannot be satisfied with the assumption of traditional government budgeting that the relations among the subdivisions of a budget are only additive and that the only internal-consistency requirement is that the sum of the parts shall not exceed some targeted total. In short, good national planning must be conceptually comprehensive.

But none of this means that everything that is going to happen in an economy—even actions and decisions that bear on the selected goals of planning—need be purposively planned from a central point. In many instances it is appropriate to rely on the feedbacks, forward and backward linkages, and other response mechanisms that characterize the real-world system to bring behavior into line with plan design. Here is where we slip over into the matter of controls. Systematic planning does imply systematic controls—of some kind. For planning is not forecasting. It is rather an attempt, by purposive intervention emanating from government, to alter the future from what it otherwise would have been. It requires implementing mechanisms that can make the desired future happen.

Yet this need not mean overt, busy, interventionist, detailed management of all economic decisions by government. On the contrary, there are three grievous costs to such unbridled interventionism: first, the intrusion on private liberties; second, the stifling of spontaneity in the system; and, third, the inherent inefficiencies of centralized, excessively hierarchical bureaucracies. Hence, as systems of all ideological hues have been learning, the implementation of planning is furthered by optimal reliance on decentralized decision making. This involves delegations downward to lower governmental jurisdictions. But also it involves greater reliance on self-adjusting subsystems of private (or, at any rate, nonofficial) decision making, of which officially conditioned but still flexible, responsive, self-adjusting market mechanisms are the most important example.

9. It is perfectly clear, not only that planning without implementation comes to nothing but that in many developing countries implementation now is perceived to be the greater problem. Moreover, it is widely felt that the "implementation crisis" calls for the active services of a powerful, efficiency-bent centralized staff unit that closely monitors project management and other sectoral implementation efforts across the government board in a way that cannot safely be entrusted to the parochialism of regular ministerial or departmental administrations. Taken together with the need for planning agencies to keep one foot in operations for the sake of political and bureaucratic effectiveness, this may be enough to cause any red-blooded,

results-oriented planner to plunge enthusiastically into the business of implementation policing and expediting.

In fact planners should do so with great caution. In the process it is easy for a planning agency to get bloated and bogged down and to lose track of its primary function. It is important to recognize that the setting of broad social goals, the development of plans for achieving the goals, the selection of policies framing, supporting, and articulating the plans, and the administration of programs and projects implementing the plans are not qualitatively different activities. They are gradations of a seamless web. But this does not mean that the same agency has to take central staff responsibility for the whole continuum. In fact it probably cannot. The planning agency must remain highly sensitized to and closely informed about implementation. But it may be better for a sister staff agency—an office, in effect, of public management—to carry the burden of project monitoring and for the planners to stick primarily to planning.

10. Evaluation is distinctly different from implementation. Implementation is operational; it is concerned with carrying out plans and policies. Evaluation is essentially investigative and analytical; it is concerned, as a feedback into future decision making, with examining not only the quality of the implementation but the appropriateness, retrospectively viewed, of the plans and policies themselves. Few governments, whether in developing or developed countries, have sufficiently institutionalized the independence and incisiveness of the evaluative function. It is to be hoped that more will do so; and, as they do, there should be no more avid readers of official evaluations of various aspects of the development effort than the planners. At the same time, a decision to lodge the evaluation function in the planning agency is not a particularly happy one. Not only does it run the same dangers of bloating and distraction that apply in the case of implementation monitoring; it makes the evaluators administratively subordinate to what should be a principal subject of their critiques.

11. Governments should take great care not to make planning excessively realistic, for if they do so they will lose its essence. Planning is inherently committed to abstraction. It focuses on only a few of the purposes of a society and its government, abstracting from the rest. It makes conditioning and protective assumptions about, but otherwise it abstracts from, emergencies, distractions, and unexpected events. In terms of time, it tends to abstract from the short run in trying to make sense of the longer run. Planners cannot go overboard in any of these directions. They must try to keep some handhold on current decision making. And if their country is racked by drought or overtaken by war they cannot stand aloof. But governments that appreciate the usefulness of systematic attention

to longer and larger issues that lurk beneath the surface of day-to-day business will preserve some detachment for their planners and insist, nevertheless, that the products of that detachment get factored into the political process.

12. Development planning to date has been almost exclusively a national enterprise. It has been premised on the assumption that, among the various levels of political jurisdictions, only nation states possess the capacity to control their own destinies economically. But because in fact nation states vary so widely—because, in particular, they differ so radically in size—this treatment of development planning as a peculiarly and exclusively national function has produced anomalies with which we only are beginning to cope.

For one, there is the anomaly of the very large nation state where, as in China and India, there is evident need and now ongoing effort to distribute effective planning, as well as other public responsibilities, downward to lower jurisdictions.

Second, there is the anomaly of very small states that, if they have other small, contiguous, and reasonably compatible neighbors, have reasons of scale to amalgamate their economies and therefore to engage in supranational regional planning

But third, there is the anomaly that nationally bounded development planning cannot deal with many of the dominant issues of the future—environment, nonrenewable resources, trade, monetary order, global income inequalities—which are plainly transnational in character. The need, quite obviously, is for some kind of coherent, reasonably influential transnational planning. In a world still limited by the myopia of sovereign-state self-interest it is not clear how this need will be met. But part of the answer may come from the intercourse of national planning agencies that, without sacrificing their local political authority, have been allowed sufficient discretion to give sober attention to some of the larger questions of global self interest.

DISCUSSION

PAUL STREETEN (Great Britain): The need to emphasize more attention to the repercussions of national planning and actions on the people of other countries is important. At present this is done chiefly by security planners whose work is not very closely integrated with economic or social development plans. This is not enough. For instance, Ethiopia is diversifying her economy from coffee into tea, while Sri Lanka may be diversifying from tea into coffee. Crop plans should be coordinated and take cognizance of world demand situations.

John Lewis stresses need for continuity planning and flexibility. Is this compatible with fixed period planning for five or ten years? The latter helps to harness enthusiasm and political support, but tends to be rigid and inflexible. Thus flexibility may cost political support.

Finally, John Lewis warns against making planning excessively realistic. I think that most plans have erred by being excessively unrealistic, abstract, and divorced from the facts.

MARC HENRY (OECD): Natural catastrophes are not unforeseeable. For instance, the floods in parts of the Punjab or storm damage in areas on the Gulf of Bengal can be anticipated, as can drought in other regions. Even if one cannot tell during which year the catastrophe will occur, one can prepare against it.

There is little practical difference between short-term and long-term planning objectives. Fixed-period planning is normally a mistake, the period fixed being usually too long for some essential projects and too short for others.

The question of harmonizing national objectives on a global or regional scale is being dealt with by international organizations, including regional commissions for Asia, Africa, Europe and Latin America. It is surprising Professor Lewis did not mention this.

TARLOK SINGH (UN Children's Fund, New York): Medium-term planning fulfills certain political and administrative functions, governments often not being long-lived, but tends to be influenced by pulls and pressures of the moment and the immediately preceding situations. Some of the more serious development problems require a long-range view and cannot be dealt with in the context of a 5-year or 6-year plan.

On the other hand, better coordination is needed between medium-term planning and short-term economic management. More accurate and comprehensive data available at shorter intervals are needed for this purpose—and not available today in most developing countries. In many of them, there is an increasing contradiction between what is planned to happen in four or five years time and what is actually happening at the moment.

Early development plans define the major problems facing a country. Later, the dovetailing of different aspects of development, the allocation of resources becomes the vital aspect.

All organizations tend to go on doing what they are doing the way they are doing. This includes international organizations. A way should therefore be found to examine from time to time how problems are changing, how the capacity to deal with problems is changing in various states, and what improved methods could be introduced.

HUMAN RESOURCES IN THE DEVELOPING WORLD— A FORWARD LOOK
Victor L. Urquidi

To speak about human resources in the developing world is to address oneself to the major task of mankind: how to provide individuals in the countries classified as poor with a decent basic standard of living and how to enable human beings, through education and practical training, to utilize their own abilities, available natural resources, and man-made productive power for the attainment of material needs consistent with the higher aims of society as a whole.

What is the state of the Third World in this respect? Economist and many others have become development minded in the last quarter of a century. Major revisions of theory and policy have been attempted and offered. The United Nations, whatever its peace-keeping benefits to the peoples of the world, is devoted to promoting development. New and more exacting targets are proposed to induce the necessary changes.

The record, however, is not very encouraging. Per capita product in the developing nations has risen and international trade and aid have increased. Technology has been transferred through public and private means. But growth has been more rapid in the developed nations than in the less developed. The gap in science and technology has widened. The Third World has been largely marginal and has been treated marginally. It is too poor to apply massive resources to critical problems, too poor to follow the classical recommendation of thrift and sacrifice as a means of advancement. The rich countries may soon place themselves in a position where they are cut off from the poor countries—unwilling to buy from them, unable to receive cash for their exports, no longer inclined to lend or give, even confident that technology will reduce their own dependence on scarce primary resources.

There is a need to ask again: Where do we want to go? How do 2.7 billion people of the Third World think they can get there? And what do the 1.1 billion from the developed countries believe they can do to keep the world together?

The facts are staring us in the face: Close to 70 percent of the world's population, with a very low average standard of living, is increasing in numbers at a rate of 2.5 percent per year—a doubling time of only 28 years. The richer 30 percent, with more than twelve times the average standard of living, is expanding slowly. The motivations necessary to induce a considerable decline of fertility in LDCs, as has occurred in almost every industrialized nation, are neither sufficient nor widespread. Though recent contraceptive methods may enable birth control to be theoretically efficient, the economic and cultural constraints in most developing countries are still very strong. Spectacular declines in fertility are not likely to occur in the near future in developing nations. With the present age structure and increasing life expectancies, actual population is bound to grow for decades until fertility is reduced to the replacement level.

POPULATION PROJECTIONS

A recent set of projections by the United Nations Population Division attempts to bring this issue into perspective: Assuming the so-called "medium" variant in fertility, which implies that the birth rate will decline from 48 to 27 per thousand in the LDCs by the year 2000, with mortality also declining, population will still be increasing at that time at about 2 percent per annum. The present 2.7 billion of the Third World will grow to some 5.1 billion in 27 years. The population of the LDCs will increase to over 9 billion by the year 2050, by which time average fertility may have declined to replacement level. But actual numbers will continue to rise and only tend to stabilize around 10.5 billion by the early part of the 22nd century. For the world as a whole, zero growth would imply a total of 12 billion by the turn of the 21st century, with virtual stabilization of population in the developed countries, as designated today, from the year 2050. Population in the LDCs will account for 84 percent of the total by the year 2100.

In fact, because of numbers, age composition, and entry into the labor force, the problem is already quite serious. In the LDCs 40 or more percent of the population are still likely to be under the age of 15 by the year 2000. Pressure on the school system and on entry into work is already an acute problem, reflected by illiteracy, rising numbers of school dropouts, and widespread under- and unemployment. Assuming the labor force of the LDCs today to be over one billion and the rate of participation remaining close to 40 percent, by the end of the century jobs will have to be found for nearly 900 million people in addition to those already in the labor force today.

Due to the growth rate of the population, employment in agriculture alone will have to increase from about 670 to 840 million, a rise of 25 percent in thirty years. In nonagricultural activities, a more than threefold increase in employment will be required, from some

340 million to 1.1 billion, both the relative share and the absolute amount increasing.

The above assumes that the development pattern we have known in the past will remain. However, these assumptions may be wrong. Agricultural output is likely to increase mainly through higher yields on existing arable land, thus counteracting the prospective increase in employment. Weak labor absorption trends will be stimulated by more intensive use of machinery and its spread to new crops. Moreover, the industrial structure in the LDCs may develop more rapidly in the direction of capital-intensive industries, so as to meet new demands imposed by consumption standards and to substitute imports of intermediate and capital goods, as well as to compete in export markets for manufactured goods. This process will be reinforced by the increasing adoption of labor-saving methods. Consequently, the prospects for LDCs are difficult indeed in terms of employment, whatever they may be in terms of output. A serious reconsideration of development objectives, and of strategies seems to be urgently needed.

At the center of this problem lies the improvement in the distribution of income. This requires not only redistributive measures through taxation and certain public expenditure policies but a major reorientation of economic and social policies to raise substantially the share of wage earners and farmers in the national income.

REDISTRIBUTIVE POLICIES

Let us look briefly at the relevance of some of these policies to employment. The main difficulty about land distribution schemes is that the subdivision of large estates is frequently an end in itself. This resulted in the creation of minimal subsistence plots without benefit of technical improvements or the ability to obtain loans to purchase better seeds or fertilizers. As the size of the farm family increases, that is, the land-man ratio declines, intensive use of the land may take place but emigration occurs from the villages to the medium and large sized towns. Meanwhile, much land that remains in the hands of commercial farmers and plantations is underutilized. The untapped sources of rural employment and income include the utilization of uncultivated land. But perhaps more important is the need to consolidate the small holdings, in order to make them capable of receiving financial assistance for permanent improvements, high-yielding seeds, modern technical inputs, and minimal necessary equipment. This means introduction of equipment to increase productivity without displacement of labor. Larger crops will require more labor and mixed farming will require labor for additional tasks on the farm thereby providing more income. An agricultural development strategy aiming at employment and income on the small farms requires a redirection of resources, through public sector investment and long-term finance on favorable terms, to cooperative-type units. Adequate infrastructure should be provided by the public sector, providing employment utilizing labor-intensive methods of construction for idle farm labor.

However, the expansion of farming alone will not do much to create employment in rural areas unless industrial processing plants are integrated into the farm communities. Even after land distribution, not the farmer but the middleman, the owner of the drying plant, the food-processing factory, the cotton-ginning mill, or any similar processing stage, reaps a large share of the value-added. The surplus farm population ends up working for a low wage at a processing plant or migrates to underemployment in urban areas. Substantial participation of the growing labor force in the integration process can take place under different forms of profit sharing. Labor is retained in rural areas; employment results through higher wages raising basic consumption and the farmer's direct profit participation is increased.

Appropriate education and training are a high priority for such a policy. Rural education in LDCs is still at very low levels. By 1980, there will still be some 230 million children of school age not attending any school, mostly in rural areas of developing countries. Even in 1968, primary school enrollment was only 40 percent in Africa, 55 percent in Asia, and 75 percent in Latin America. Most enrollment occurs in the cities. Rural schools rarely provide education beyond the third grade, and the quality provided in relation to local needs leaves much to be desired. Such schooling encourages children to seek jobs in the cities, thus swelling the supply of unskilled unemployed. Agro-mechanical education and training are equally deficient. If traditional farming is to be transformed, and agro-industrial processing to be increased, larger allocations for rural education and training (including programs for adults) are required.

Wage protection demands the development of legal and institutional means to raise wages above subsistence levels, in both rural and urban areas. Minimum wages are hardly complied with throughout the Third World and are usually fixed barely above subsistence. A labor policy to enforce minimum wages is urgently needed. Unionization is not widespread in the developing countries and is frequently opposed by business groups or hindered by public policies in favor of such groups. Labor unions can further educational and training programs, as can business enterprises. Such programs should not be the responsibility of the state only.

Health programs are essential for ordinary economic activity and for raising productivity. However, they do not reach much beyond the large urban centers in LDCs. Resources are needed both for the programs and for training of necessary personnel, including auxiliary staff. Rural medicine and health programs, together with introduction of water supply and sewage disposal systems, should be a high priority throughout the Third World. Undernourishment and inadequate diets affect vast masses of people in LDCs.

Too often, developing countries copy the patterns of richer states. Industrialization is designed to produce consumer goods for the middle and upper classes, which in turn follow consumption patterns of the richer countries. High tariffs and other imports restrictions afford market protection, resulting in high prices. Lessons of early industrialization in developed countries, where mass-produced essentials were made available at cheap prices, are sorely neglected. Every LDC should set itself basic consumption targets and, through appropriate planning techniques, organize its production and distribution system to meet them. This may involve further expansion of public sector enterprises. In many economies, of course, production for export of less basic products would continue to be justified by possible good international trade deals.

The above implies a sector mix in the planning process, which should view employment creation as a principal target, requiring educational, training, health, and other redistributive measures. Choices of technology should be governed by employment creation instead of the traditional labor saving, whenever this is technically and economically feasible. Inertia has resulted in the adoption or continued use of industrial technology more suitable for labor-scarce economies. It is not enough to point out that tariff policies, taxation, incentives, etc., in LDCs induce industrial enterprises to use labor-saving equipment. The problem lies in the research devoted to producing equipment for the industrial needs of the richer countries. Little thought is given to the conditions in LDCs in terms of relative factor endowments, use of local materials, adaptation to smaller scales of output.

A new development strategy for better utilization of human resources must thus include more selective imports of technology and a policy for the local development of R and D. It should move boldly into the design of equipment for industrial processes requiring relatively more labor and less wastage of capital. Equally important is the design of useful durable consumer goods adapted to mass purchasing power. Expansion of R and D requires not only government support but also fiscal and other incentives for private R and D expenditures. It should be supported by an improvement of the secondary and higher education systems.

INTERNATIONAL TECHNICAL ASSISTANCE

Development involves structural change. A development policy must basically aim to reallocate resources to fulfill long-term material, social, and cultural needs. Capital is at the core of development. Technical progress is a necessary input. But human resources are also in the nature of capital and skill, and this is the ingredient most neglected by LDCs. Patterns of growth have up to now resulted in increasing un- and underemployment, which means maldistribution, poverty, frustration, and failure. Each country has to work out for itself its ultimate objectives, its international position, its life style. But an important role can be played by international cooperation.

For a generation we have been told that vast transfers of capital from the rich to the poor countries were necessary to assist the latter in their economic development. The function of capital movements and international aid was interpreted as a means of reducing the technological gap and making possible a massive transfer of technology to LDCs. It is now becoming apparent that much of the technology transferred has been irrelevant or even harmful, that private transfers of know-how have been costly to the recipient country, and that even much of the training provided under the guise of "technical assistance" has been an instrument to promote sales of equipment for which indebtedness has had to be incurred—all this alongside with growing local unemployment and, in many cases, brain drain. In addition, the donor countries are reducing the amount of aid or manipulating it politically, and the multinational corporations are complaining about local legislation that they would normally accept in their country of origin.

The whole strategy of international aid is misguided. LDCs lack not so much finance or unwanted technology but education and training. One of the fateful errors of international technical assistance has been to stress expertise rather than training. The LDCs were inundated with superannuated colonial administrators or persons unwanted in their own countries who are not up to date with recent scientific and technical developments, instead of establishing regional and national training centers assisted by outstanding international experts, thereby creating national cadres of scientific, technological, and administrative staff essential for development. Important centers were established with international support but have fallen short of requirements, and now even their continued financing is jeopardized.

Training is an endless chain. With the identification of problems at different levels, the impact of education and training can be achieved throughout the system, at many points of any given structure. Besides national efforts, we need an international plan for the integrated improvement of human resources, involving education, training, and health. The unavoidable population increment expected over the next hundred years must be better prepared culturally and technically for the development tasks that lie ahead. This should be the centerpiece of future international cooperation programs.

DISCUSSION

GLADSTONE G. BONNICK (Jamaica): I reject the thesis that labor-intensive techniques should be encouraged in developing countries in order to speed the process of more equal distribution of wealth and the growth of effective demand. Capital-intensive processes have served the developed countries very well. They save wear and tear on the human being and provide him with leisure. The distribution of wealth need not be left to the market mechanism. It can be tackled in other ways. Human beings should not be looked upon as production factors but as persons whose time has to be used partly to satisfy their material wants and partly their psychological and social wants. The main concern should not be with finding employment for them but with finding ways to maximize their sense of well being. Even in developing countries, training and planning should place greater stress on the creative use of leisure.

BRUCE F. JOHNSTON (United States): It is preferable to use techniques for expanding agricultural productivity that enable a large part of a country's agricultural labor force to participate in technical and economic change rather than to use capital-intensive techniques necessarily confined to a very small fraction of the labor force.

In Japan and Taiwan agriculture was developed by capital-saving techniques and the progressive modernization of the farm labor force. Fertility declined sharply in these two states during the last two decades. In Mexico, despite impressive economic growth, fertility has declined very little—possibly because the expansion of agricultural output was confined to a certain part of agriculture, and most Mexican farm households were not seriously affected by economic and technical changes.

FINN MUNCH-PETERSEN (UN Development Programme Representative in Israel) agreed with Professor Urquidi's thesis that over the last 25 years international aid to developing countries has been given according to incorrect priorities but insisted that these priorities were decided by the developing states themselves. The aid programs are still being prepared by the recipient states.

SHIMON AMIR (Israel): The exodus from rural areas in developing states is proceeding at the rate of about 6 percent per annum. This rate is too fast.

The cost factor of agricultural development should not be decisive. Agriculture is still being subsidized in the developed EEC countries, so there is no reason not to subsidize it in developing states. On the contrary, in these states too available resources should be redistributed by a deliberate policy of supporting the rural sector.

HOLLIS CHENERY (IBRD): Professor Urquidi stressed that the wrong kind of technology was being imported to developing states and the wrong kind of goods were being produced there. But producing the right kind of things for poor people does little good if they have no income to buy them.

In Mexico and Brazil, during the last 10 to 15 years, some 75 percent of the national income increment has gone to the 20 percent of the population with the highest incomes. The growth of income inequality in Mexico is due to its very low taxation—about 10 percent of GNP only. The willingness to tax the middle income groups and provide higher incomes for the lowest income groups is essential for the solution of the problem.

PAUL MORAWETZ (Australia): In Africa, suggestions that less capital-intensive industries should be encouraged in order to provide employment have often been regarded as almost a colonialist plot. Developing countries see no reason why they should not utilize the best technology available at the time. Our concern should be with filling the leisure of those bound to be unemployed. Education should be redirected to the environment to which these people are used. This might contribute to saving their cultures.

VICTOR URQUIDI: Certain capital-intensive techniques should be supplied to developing states, for some exports markets and local needs. But the emphasis should be on an overall strategy in terms of sector development and types of industries providing adequate employment.

The income distribution problem exists but cannot be tackled by merely raising taxes.

Mr. Urquidi disagreed with Professor Chenery that there is a link between low tax burdens and bad income distribution. In many countries with a high tax burden income distribution is very bad. The main factor in income distribution is the way agriculture is developed and the way it is integrated into industry. Tax policies should be improved but are subsidiary in this respect.

Farm modernization will not reduce fertility, unless it is accompanied by educational programs and opportunities for steady employment in nonfarming activities on the farm.

As regards the UN, the donor countries establish the basic technical assistance policies, though in theory the recipient states can ask for what they like. Over the last 25 years there has been insufficient stress on educational and training programs.

ECONOMIC GROWTH AND THE QUALITY OF LIFE
Richard Hoggart

The title given to me brings together two concepts that are now more and more seen as not necessarily compatible, as needing to have their interrelationships more carefully considered. In other words, some people now say that economic growth may not only fail to improve "the quality of life" but may positively damage it.

At one time, to say something like the above was automatically to be accused of being against economic growth and an improved standard of living. That only rarely happens nowadays. Everyone, or virtually everyone, starts by assuming the need for economic growth, recognizes that without economic growth many other things which are indisputably valuable, such as better health, are not likely to come, that millions of people who are at present living in desperately poor conditions rightly seek to have more choices, whether of goods or of ways of life, and that economic growth is the foundation for this increase in choices.

However, what one actually gets from economic development is not always what one had hoped: Choices do not always increase; and development, pursued in the ways we now usually pursue it, may have damaging side effects, which we do not always expect in advance. Development sometimes widens the gaps between countries or between different groups within countries, and distributive justice is not always increased. Besides, economic growth pursued in certain ways may mean a loss of some elements essential to a good quality of life, elements that certain nations, even though their economic state was low, nevertheless possessed. I am thinking both of physical matters such as the destruction or pollution of the physical environment by over-rapid industrialization or by the squalor of over-rapid urbanization; and of the fact that these elements, taken together, produce living and working conditions for millions of people that cannot be regarded as an improvement on what they have left, no matter how poverty-stricken that previous condition may have been. One can justify such changes only by arguing that they are unavoidable interludes towards something much better. When we talk about a loss in the quality of life, we mean that there can be damage to the internal landscape within which people live—damage to the social and cultural texture of their lives, a breaking of links that previously helped to give some coherence and meaning to their existence, without anything comparable emerging to replace these links; a loss of any sense of belonging to a community or group, a breakdown of family feeling, a loss of any sense of personal place or significance; a growth in the feeling of naked and anonymous separateness.

Changes like these do not concern developing countries alone. Developed countries are also affected by them and were affected by them first. Remember only what Europe did to itself by its headlong movement into industrialization during parts of the nineteenth century. Remember what it did to its physical landscapes and what it did to its people at the time. These costs have still not been paid off.

Because the phrase quality of life has both internal and external meanings, it is hard to define in quantifiable terms. A good many attempts have been made to define it. One lists the need for clean air, for adequate space, for decent living conditions; one notes that the availability of certain kinds of goods and services is essential, for example, different levels of education and different types of communications; and so one can go on refining and sophisticating the elements. But the phrase quality of life is an attempt to point towards elements even more crucial than those of the sort I have just listed, elements much more internal to a society or a culture. This makes it possible for some persons in rapidly developing societies to say, without being folkloristic or backward-looking, that insufficiently considered development through industrialisation is bringing a loss in the quality of life of their people.

I am not going to try to define here these other elements or the meaning of the phrase the quality of life when it is used in relation to economic growth; but I will discuss two examples in which the issue, the tensions, the possible balance of costs, are highlighted. My two examples—the impact of population policies and the impact of tourism—may at first seem marginal to the major issues. It would have been better to look more generally at the overall pros and cons of development, at both the external and internal costs, and to attempt an outline of a comprehensive balance sheet. However, this is impossible in the restricted space we have here. It needs whole books; in fact, none of the many books written on it can be said to have caught the issue in its full complexity.

Or one might have taken as an example the impact of education on societies that are moving into industrialization. Here again there is a great deal of inquiry and of disquiet. Education at all levels and very widely spread is essential if modernization is to go ahead, but taken too precipitately or in the wrong way certain kinds of education may destroy some of the integuments of the traditional life without putting anything adequate in their place. Hence the current debate on the better definition of the purposes and practice of education. This debate too concerns not only developing countries but also those that are most technologically developed.

The two examples I have chosen come from my recent day-to-day experience. Both are related to the problem of economic growth, though not so massively or directly related as some other elements in social change; their impact on the external and, preeminently, on the internal quality of life has not so far been greatly considered.
I would argue that these two issues point to the heart of the problem of the relation between economic growth and the quality of life.

POPULATION POLICIES

The problem of population growth today is enormous and inescapable; so the attempts to convince governments that they should have population policies and persuade individuals to change their attitudes towards family size are correspondingly strong. Some developing nations suspect and resent the encouragement from outside to have population policies, feeling that such pressure is exerted by the developed nations for their own ends (though some of that particular kind of suspicion may be fading now). On the other hand, some developing nations have very strong population policies. They see their growth in economic power, which could lead to an improved standard of living for their peoples, being constantly overtaken by an increasing population and making on balance no real improvement in the standard of living. And some believe they have a fundamental responsibility towards their citizens to make the means of family regulation available; they see it as a right of the people, as one of the increases in freedom of choice which technology can bring.

In most societies fertility in itself has for centuries been regarded as good, and in very complex psychological and cultural ways. That attitude was part of the sustaining fabric of community, family, and individual life. There is now a very large scale attempt to ask people to change that deep-rooted set of attitudes, to reverse them, and to do so quickly. An immensely important inner shift is being promoted; and one does not make such important shifts without disturbing much more than that one is directly aiming to change, in the culture and in the individual and in the family.

This is understood only patchily. The thrust and tone of population programs are largely operational, manipulative, persuasive, seeking to get people to behave in new, nontraditional ways, as soon as possible and as effectively as possible. Success is measured by a rise in the use of fertility control devices and a drop in the number of children per family.

But is this enough? Isn't it rather as though a doctor went headlong into very strong treatment of some diagnosed ailment but paid no attention to the likely side effects of that treatment on the organism as a whole? By now, experts in population issues are talking about a backlash against population policies. As a result they are recognizing the need for more and better social and psychological research. That research will not be easy to do properly. If it is regarded simply as a way of achieving more quickly more effective operational, manipulative, and persuasive population policies, it will both be inadequate for those ends and, more importantly, ignore the really important questions raised by the very existence of the backlash.

For perhaps that backlash is a sign of the organism protecting itself against too sudden, too massive, and too ill-considered an assault on its old cultural balances. In these matters, the anthropologists and above all the insights of the poets are better guides than the technicians of delivery systems or of mass persuasion. The poems and songs of society illuminate better than anything else the meanings for that society of the idea of the family, married love, the pride of parenthood, the respect due to old age, and all such attitudes.

So, yes, we do need more and better social and psychological research. That is a responsibility towards the people whose attitudes we presume to attempt to change, a responsibility towards them as whole human beings, living in societies often with considerable coherence, not simply a means of being more effective on our own relatively narrow front. Therefore, such research must be sustained and difficult and not always aim at an immediate, population-policy, operational target. We have to try to ensure that, whilst fertility regulation is accepted more and more, as I think it must be both on the ground of human rights (the right to choose) and on that of necessary economic growth, this change is not brought about at excessive social and psychological cost to the family and to the individual. How often, for example, in areas where crash programs of fertility control (for example, male sterilization) have been undertaken, has there been sufficient prior research or follow-up action on the impact of these processes on the communities and the individuals to whom they have been applied?

TOURISM POLICIES

Tourism raises similar questions. It is argued for, encouraged by governments, and promoted by agencies as an instrument for economic growth; and there are figures to prove the case, though even that case is not always as simple as it might look. But suppose the economic case—that each tourist means on average a substantial number of dollars per week to the national economy—is sound and uncomplicated: What then?

Tourism, not sufficiently controlled and too rapid, can destroy the very ambiance that was one of the reasons that the tourists came in the first place—the skyline, the shoreline, and the setting in general (though if most of the tourists come only for the sunshine, which can't be destroyed, there is no reason, even if the local environment has been damaged, that the boom should not continue). Here, Europe has as striking examples of spoliation to offer as any part of the world; and Europe, like other parts of the world, shows that people and their habitual ways of life can apparently survive under such rapid changes much more than one would have thought possible.

But look a little more closely at the effects of really sudden tourism on societies far removed from the manners and styles of the developed world. Tourism can inject into these societies a set of assumptions about the relationships between people that are quite different from those traditionally held—relationships based on buying and selling, on using people, on seeing people as objects from which one gets something, a whole way of seeing life as getting and spending and tasting and passing on. Even trickier, the styles of such a people, which may have been part of a complete and organic pattern of life, themselves become under tourism something offered for sale; and in that process they become something different.

Think of the kind of dance in Asia that is essentially contemplative and religious, that has no need of an "audience" in the Western sense. People have always watched it, it is true; but they are part of the ceremony and observe intensely but silently. A reaction from them is not needed because nothing is, in the Western sense, being given to them. This is not an audience-with-actors relationship as, say, Europe knows it.

But tourists want to see such things, and tourism promoters in the countries concerned want to offer them. So shows are organised. A few rows of seats are put in for the tourists, prices are charged, and the local inhabitants stand at the back outside a roughly made compound. But what happens to the dance itself? To begin with, it becomes in some ways "better," more expert and "finished," than it was before. A competition sets in between villages to provide an ever finer spectacle. It also becomes finished in another sense, because it is now no longer a contemplative ritual; it is a performance for an audience. It is turned outwards towards those people in those rows of chairs, who click their cameras steadily and—with an extraordinarily shocking (in the pure sense) effect—clap at the end. The dance has become an offering to tourists, not the celebration of a shared rite.

So much about the effects that tourism, even what we call cultural tourism, may have on a society. As to the attitude of tourists themselves and what they are getting from such experiences—that is another question that has not been much looked at.

One of the roles of the multinational agencies is to look as fully as possible at issues common to many countries, so as to help individual governments to know better the options before them when they are making their policy decisions. This matter of tourism and its promotion, with which several multinational agencies are involved, needs just such close and varied examination, and so far has hardly had it.

To sum up: nothing I have said argues against economic growth as such. Economic growth is needed both to improve the material standard of life and because it can (though it does not automatically) increase choices and freedoms. But ill-considered economic growth can arrive in ways that destroy valuable parts of a people's inheritance, parts no less valuable because they are not always tangible. So the promotion of policies that hasten economic growth should not be narrowly operational only but should be set in this larger context. By this means, the traditions of a people, external or internal, will not simply be washed away or made into showpieces for outsiders or into respected but inert museum pieces for the people themselves. They will be carried into the new, technological, and developed future as lived-into and living attitudes that distinguish that people and are still valuable to them here and now. It is a question of neither disowning the past nor allowing it to be a dead weight against needed progress. One is tempted to call it a question of finding a balance between the past, the traditional past, and the technological future. But even the image of balance is too still; the process is much more dialectical and active. For some new nations, especially those whose peoples experienced colonialization from Europe, this question presents itself in most complex forms. But it is the larger question facing all countries behind almost all of the issues related to growth, behind population or tourism or education or town planning or rural development or almost any other public issue.

DISCUSSION

LEAH PORAT (Israel) disagreed with Professor Hoggart's point that tourism or other aspects of economic development may undermine the nature or appeal of certain cultures. Cultures and ways of life should be and are dynamic rather than static. She stressed the positive aspects of mass tourism in creating understanding of other people's cultures and a cross-fertilization of ideas. The dangers of economic development stressed by Professor Hoggart can be met by education and intelligent administration.

A Participant said that Professor Hoggart appeared to define population policy in terms of fertility control only, while it should also include the distribution and composition of the population, which are more relevant to development problems.

LE BA NHON (Vietnam) suggested that there is a difference between cultural dynamism propelled from within and the application of outside influences to a culture. However, tourism can also stimulate positive cultural developments, reviving activities that have died down for lack of local interest.

WILFRED BECKERMAN (Great Britain): The alleged conflict between economic growth and quality of life largely reflects middle-class value judgments. Usually opponents of economic growth were reactionary. Growth increases the range of human choice, though some people may suffer from the changes it produces. Concerning tourism, as against the few people who liked to go to out-of-the-way places and now find them overrun by others, there are the many who like these places all the better for the modern facilities they now provide and the millions now able to enjoy a visit to them that was previously out of their reach economically.

JULIO ESTRELLA (Dominican Republic): Tourism may lead to a kind of universal culture—an ecumenical kind of culture.

RICHARD ABLIN (Israel): Good taste and modesty should be applied to investments in tourism, for example, by building low hotels that blend into the scenery of beautiful areas rather than high rise structures dominating them. The same logic applies to the problem of spoiling landscapes, pollution, and congestion. The loss of satisfaction caused to nonusers of the new facilities must be taken into consideration when making decisions.

RICHARD HOGGART (Great Britain) agreed that culture was dynamic and not something static that needed preserving. In his opinion, mass tourism does not increase understanding of other people's countries. Studies are being made of the positive and negative effects of tourism on various societies. UNESCO is committed to cultural tourism.
The more you look at different cultures, the more you discover that each culture has quite unsuspected strengths, which are elements in its quality of life. Unless the highly complex nature of these

manifold cultures is properly understood, people cannot be helped to build on their own solid foundations and create a real dynamic relationship with the new things now available. It is no service to a nation to push aside the attitudes sustained throughout its history as if they were of no value. He challenged the right of the developed world to change the cultures of others quickly for selfish ends. He does not believe in a universal culture. People should have roots though they should not be intellectually bound by their roots.

THE FINANCIAL ASPECTS OF ECONOMIC GROWTH
Felipe Herrera

Development, and national and international aspirations for it, cannot be conceived in a vacuum or fulfilled by mechanical application. The concepts of development are closely connected in a reciprocal fashion with every type of significant process of change experienced by humanity during the last twenty-five years. This applies particularly to financial aspects of development. At the end of the Second World War some fundamental concepts were defined on this subject, expressed mainly through the institutions created at the Bretton Woods Conference and through the then prevailing philosophy of free competition.

Thus important changes were witnessed during the last decade in orientation and techniques relating to the financing of the development precess. At present, the banking profession requires, more than ever, much imagination and a better understanding of what is currently happening in the world, especially as regards the international aspects of its activity.

The following comments are based on the author's experience as General Manager of the Central Bank of Chile and as Minister of Finance during the fifties, and as organizer and first president of the Interamerican Development Bank, the first regional institution devoted to international public financing, during the sixties.

The idea of "public international assistance for economic development" belongs to the period that followed the Second World War. Even if in the past, financial assistance between two different countries existed, an idea of a "developing" character such as we understand it today did not exist. It was rather assistance provided to solve fiscal or foreign trade troubles.

The "metropolis" made transfers to its colonies, with the main goal of creating an infrastructure afterwards useful in developing productive activities for the benefit of the "central country." However,

---

Felipe Herrera is Professor of Economic Policy, University of Chile and Catholic University, Chile.

colonization policies frequently exploited the resources of the colonies to increase the wealth of the metropolis.

During the nineteenth century and until the end of the economic depression of the thirties, an active process of financial transfers was performed by means of the utilization of surpluses that flowed into the capital markets, especially to London. But in the underdeveloped world the use of resources was orientated to benefit the exporting capital centers without taking into account the healthy economic development of the debtor.

NEW CONCEPTS OF PUBLIC INTERNATIONAL ASSISTANCE

The new concepts of public international assistance are expressed mainly from two different viewpoints: goals and criteria guiding it and channels and institutions backing it. The basic criterion has been that of complementing the process of capital formation of underdeveloped countries; in other words, of supplying additional savings that the internal economy of these countries is not capable of producing or that cannot be received in the form of private foreign capital.

It is a paradox that countries with greater capacity to save and with better opportunities of absorbing private foreign resources have received in the last 25 years the major part of public international assistance. Because of this the less developed countries of the Third World have demanded special treatment within the framework of public international finance. The decisions adopted in April 1973 by UNCTAD III in Santiago, Chile, specified that 25 countries would be considered as "relatively less developed"; Asian and African countries predominate in this list, Haiti being the only Latin American nation.

The quantitative concept is complemented by a qualitative concept through different criteria employed by international public financing with respect to borrowing countries, ways of lending, and so forth. This qualitative concept has drastically changed in the early sixties. The following new concepts are important:

- the expansion of the eligibility of projects requiring financial aid, starting from a strict economic development approach (especially, financing of infrastructure and industrial activities of high profitability) to projects generally termed social investment (education, public health, rural development, and other projects not characterized by a high cost-benefit ratio);
- the financing of global programs, with special consideration for the balance of payments and the fiscal and monetary situation of the borrowing country;

- a softening of lending conditions in such forms as longer payment periods, lower rates of interest, possibilities of paying in local currency, longer period before redemption starts.

INSTITUTIONALIZATION OF ASSISTANCE

Together with the transfer of resources by means of multilateral agreements, under terms specified by the founders of the World Bank in Bretton Woods, steps were adopted leading to the implementation of bilateral assistance. Since the early sixties, multilateral cooperation began to take on regional and subregional forms.

International economic institutions are created and strengthened through the accumulated experience in the fields of international public financing, either bilateral or multilateral. They not only serve as a channel for resources but also contribute significant technical capacity to the managing of development problems.

The process of reinvestment is a relatively new phenomenon in this institutional framework. The United Nations has achieved the most in this field through the utilization of the United Nations Development Program. Other national and multinational institutions have begun to act in the important preinvestment field. This helps to break the absurd vicious circle, in which LDCs were unable to receive international assistance because of the lack of adequate projects, a by-product of their backwardness.

New institutional and technical means have been vigorously developed in the Third World resulting in a better exploitation of available resources and, particularly in the last ten years, overcoming existing prejudices against planning and state intervention in the economy. One should recognize the role lenders have played in the guidance of borrower countries in the use of funds and development of projects, in particular, the role of regional banks, which have had the advantages of functional proximity to the member countries.

Another aspect of institutionalization has been greater coordination between different sources of finance. The best example of this process is the DAC (Development Assistance Committee).

It was intended to quantify, by means of recommendations, the volume of the transfer of resources, particularly through the definition of a global strategy for development adopted by UNCTAD. The limited success of this concept was due to the lack of political support from industrial countries, which are reluctant to adopt firm commitments.

In recent years, the concept of country performance, has increased in importance. Unfortunately, it may constitute a dangerous element of foreign pressure on social and economic policies of LDCs. The institutionalization of evaluation schemes of country performance has been resisted by a large section of the Third World.

In relation to this topic, it should be noted that its financial aspects may appear in different forms: creation of multinational organizations for long term financing of development; creation of mechanisms and execution of agreements related to monetary cooperation on a regional scale; promotion of foreign trade; and multinational projects, particularly related to geographic infrastructure. The last aspect does not necessarily imply that regional sources of finance participate in these projects.

REGIONAL AND SUBREGIONAL FINANCIAL INSTITUTIONS

Regional integration schemes of less developed countries that have given priority to commercial policy aspects have commonly generated regional and subregional financial institutions. In the early sixties, the Interamerican Development Bank and the Central American Bank of Economic Integration were created, parallel to the development of economic integration in Latin America (Latin America Free Trade Association, and Central America Common Market).

It is no mere coincidence that the Interamerican Development Bank commenced operations almost at the same time as the signing of the Treaty of Montevideo, under which the Latin America Free Trade Association was created. It can be argued that the participation of the United States in an interamerican institution changes its exclusively Latin American nature. In practice, however, the United States and other capital exporting countries have utilized the Bank to channel resources to Latin American countries, stimulating projects leading to integration. The Interamerican Development Bank became an important financial and technical assistance body developing into The Integration Bank for Latin America. Within the western hemisphere two additional institutions cooperate with the existing subregional integration schemes. I am referring to the Development Corporation of the Andes (Corporacion Andina de Fomento), created concurrently with the Andes Common Market (Mercado Comun Andino), with the participation of Venezuela, Colombia, Ecuador, Bolivia, Peru, and Chile. The treaty for Free Trade of the Caribbean Countries (CARIFTA) is linked to the creation of a subregional financial mechanism, the Caribbean Development Bank.

The experience accumulated during the first years of operations of the Interamerican Development Bank influenced the creation of the African Development Bank, and, later, the Asian Development Bank. The fundamental difference between these institutions is that in the first case only African countries participate, while in the second most of the Asian countries are associated with the main capital exporting states.

The East African Common Market also has a subregional institution that directs resources to the less developed countries of that area. However, the Bank's attitude has not yet been effective, because of the lack of viable projects in the industrial sector of those countries and its limited financial capacity.

The general goals of regional and subregional financial mechanisms are to promote investments in multinational projects, that is to say, projects in which two or more countries are interested. In practice, these institutions have adopted flexible criteria for this subject. The creation of projects has been one of the most serious problems in implementing financial cooperation at a multinational level. The same problem exists at the national, regional, or subregional level. Therefore, the above mentioned institutions have devoted part of their resources, through loans or grants, to the development of projects.

THE INTERAMERICAN DEVELOPMENT BANK

A short while after the Second World War, Latin American countries became critics of the existing mechanisms of multinational or bilateral public international cooperation. Latin America felt overlooked in the major programs of financial cooperation. Priority was given on the international level to European reconstruction and to economic development of Africa and some Asian areas. There were also critics of the inflexibility of the operative policies of the World Bank and the Eximbank. This dissatisfaction, together with the traditional aspiration to have their own regional financial system, proved a relevant stimulus to create a regional bank. This was resisted by the United States government, which argued that instead it was necessary to adequately utilize the facilities offered by private capital sources and by the Eximbank and the World Bank.

One of the reasons for the change in the United States attitude, which occurred in August 1958, was the crisis in Lebanon. The Eisenhower Doctrine, created as a consequence of the crisis, stated, among other things, that integrated development of all the countries of the Middle East was required; for this purpose it was necessary to create a "regional financial fund."

For the United States to justify the creation of this fund, it had to declare its willingness to cooperate with Latin America in the creation of an interamerican development bank, thus carrying out a consistent international policy. The Interamerican Development Bank was created in 1959.

We will try to summarize the most important aspects of this regional institution, which are common to other similar bodies.

1. Capacity for the mobilization of resources, not only from contributions of member countries, but also from funds collected in developed countries which are not an integral part of the institution. Presently, the Bank is exploring the means by which funds can be received from capital exporting countries, in addition to the United States and Canada. Because of this decision, the structure of the IDB resembles that of the Asian Development Bank. For many years, Latin American countries thought, justifiably, that the addition of new members to the Bank could work against the regional philosophy that was behind its creation. The new scheme was mainly promoted by the United States, as a way of sharing the financial contributions of the Bank and avoiding being the only capital exporting country among a group of 22 developing nations.

A regional entity has better facilities to assist recipient countries in the provision of local funds. The IDB experience in this field has been successful; for each unit of foreign money loaned, two equivalent units were collected in the domestic market. This process of stimulating domestic investment by means of foreign assistance tends to improve the whole domestic savings-investment mechanism of developing countries, both public and private.

2. Some areas of activity efficiently dealt with by this regional bank, would not have been covered by sources of a different character. These include:

- Promotion of balanced growth of the Continent; policies have given preference to the "relatively less developed countries", and within the particular country, priority to its more backward areas.
- The strengthening of regional physical infrastructure. Around 30 percent of the loans provided during last decade were directed to transport telecommunications and a more intense exploitation of energy resources. This was to avoid unbalanced development of centers disconnected from each other, which would have made the conquest of the interior of America and regional integration processes more difficult.
- The provision of international financing for the agricultrual sector. The approved operations for irrigation projects, diversification of agriculture, livestock development, and commercialization, turned the IDB into the main supplier of foreign capital for the development of agriculture in Latin America.

- Strong support of the industrial sector through the financing of national enterprises by global loans in favor of promoting corporations and industrial banks, and by direct financing of intraregional exports of capital goods. Latin American industry has also been helped by purchases of goods and services produced in the region with funds provided by the Bank. Some countries were their own suppliers in projects financed by the Bank.
- Support for urban development was required to face the intense concentration in Latin American cities due to modernization of the productive process in agriculture and industrialization. The Bank has attached great importance to financial, technical, and institutional cooperation in promoting the improvement of the urban infrastructure of the member countries.

As in other underdeveloped regions, the urban problem in Latin America is the inadequacy of existing services and institutions in the large metropolitan centres, and their total absence in the new population centers. Cities are not only incapable of providing for the social needs of their inhabitants, but are unable to absorb them. Hence, new residents settle on the outskirts of the most dynamic economic centres, in slum dwellings. The new forms of urbanization are characterized by a better adjustment to the environment and a greater ability of the inhabitants to create their own social institutions.

- Financial assistance to education and advanced training programs, since technological capacity constitutes one of the most dynamic development factors. The Bank has helped Latin American countries to increase the volume and improve the quality of technical and university education. It has encouraged academic fields effective in the development of human resources for productive activities. Another goal has been to introduce substantial modifications in the organization of teaching institutions, teaching methodology, and scientific research.
- A regional bank helps the creation of an institutional infrastructure for development. The granting of loans stimulates the creation and improvement of promoting institutions and the planning process.

A regional organization also aids the interchange of experience between people working for it, not least by the strategic positions they occupy in their respective countries on leaving the Bank.

3. The criterion used in this section has been pragmatic, the intention being to lessen the disequilibrium between countries with varying levels of development, and between different developing regions within a country.

WEAKENING OF MULTILATERALISM BY U.S. INTERESTS

Unfortunately, in the IDB the diversity of interests in an interamerican system presently in a state of crisis caused some difficulties. Paradoxically, multilateral organizations have increased their importance as a channel for public funds from the United States to the detriment of bilateral public sources. This has weakened the multilateral philosophy of international financial organizations and other multinational entities. Recently, for example, bilateral problems between the United States and some Latin American countries were presented to the IDB and World Bank forum.

A significant issue is: To what extent is multilateralism multilateral? The answer depends on the rules of the game and on the intentions of countries participating in multilateral organizations. It is evident that such organizations deviate from their role if their member countries bring their policies and bilateral problems into the multilateral framework. Nor is it sufficient that the Bank's principles be proclaimed within the organization. The Bank depends on public opinion and on the governments of its member countries. In order to achieve its goals, it needs the understanding and respect of various organizations and the mass media of the entire American community.

THE EFFECT OF PEACE

A greater amount of resources may well be available in future under more flexible conditions to assist the Third World in overcoming its difficulties.

Without peace there is no development in its full meaning. International peace may represent a new and significant opportunity for the necessary process of a massive transfer of financial resources to developing countries, centered on resources that should be freed as a result of a lessening of international tension. In 1972, the world spent more than 200,000 million dollars on arms and for military purposes; over 80 percent of this amount was spent by the big powers.

STRUCTURAL CHANGES IN LDCs

Many countries belonging to the Third World tired of their educational and material poverty, are effectively trying to act within their own structures, using different methods and achieving different results. The revolutionary goals of many developing countries are formulated, creating a new economic and political reality reflected in the relations between those countries and the industrial world. The rules of the game honored during recent decades with respect to foreign, public and private investment processes have changed. It is difficult to systematize this new reality, because of its heterogeneous character, but it requires a new historic attitude.

The recent Annual Report of the Economic Commission for Latin America states:

> When in executing a development strategy a country simultaneously tackles every aspect of development, and promotes the required structural changes in order to achieve integral development, the accumulated experience shows that, in the early stages, a lack of adjustment is observed which restricts the continuation of the process. The historically accumulated injustices and social tensions are translated into demands that cannot be satisfied with existing internal resources. In order to be able to positively reply to these demands, international cooperation with the particular country should not be subjected to limitations, as has frequently occurred. Some countries that are involved in structural changes, consistent with the International Strategy for Development, are sometimes faced with foreign hostility and economic aggression. This is particularly serious because, through commitments specified in the "Strategy", countries which transform their structures should receive international backing.

Thus, we need a new language and new techniques in order to foster understanding between developing and industrial countries. This responsibility rests not only with advanced countries but also with the Third World. The problems communities have to face, such as social justice, unemployment, and the removal of privileges, are part of any integrated plan leading to full development. Unfortunately, it takes a long time for these plans to be translated into reality and to be disseminated among wider groups.

FOREIGN DEBTS OF LDCs

Though a certain softening in the conditions under which international public assistance is granted may be observed, the problem originating from accumulation of debts has become extremely serious for many underdeveloped countries. This necessitates painful renegotiation processes where, unfortunately, political intervention is a determinant factor. Developing countries point to the limiting conditions of international trade as a disrupting factor and to the lack of regular and stable transfers of financial resources.

The total public foreign debt of countries of the Third World has increased from 21,600 million dollars, in 1961, to around 66,700 million dollars, in 1970; this implies high periodical payments in terms of capital and services. In 1970, the Third World paid 1,800 million dollars in interest to industrial countries. Such reality continues to highlight the relevance of the so called "Horowitz Plan"; this plan would be a valuable instrument if it were generally accepted.

SPECIAL DRAWING RIGHTS

Another factor that arouses deep concern is that the creation of the special drawing rights (SDR) has not been utilized to improve the external position of developing countries; in particular, in employing part of the newly created international liquidity for the financing of growth in the Third World.

Further progress has not been achieved in this area since this is a difficult period for the world economy, characterized by a deep monetary crisis, which, although at first seeming to affect only advanced countries, in fact affects the whole structure of international economic relationships, and certainly the situation of developing countries.

The creation of the Group of 20 and UNCTAD recognition that present problems of the international monetary system involve aspects other than those relating solely to advanced countries facilitate a dialogue between industrial countries and developing states.

ACCESS OF LDCs TO CAPITAL MARKETS

Developing countries face a new situation with respect to capital markets. During the sixties, regional financial organizations have been forced to make loans at higher interest rates, which is not consistent with the development goals and the indebtedness position of the Third World.

More recently, a trend has been observed in providing some of the developing countries with direct access to capital markets. This is not due to a more positive attitude towards the Third World but mainly to the resources available in the Eurodollar market or in the European capital market.

Developing countries that received only a little more than 70 million dollars from capital markets in 1960 received 444 million dollars in 1971.* Over the same period, the World Bank and regional development banks increased their bond allocations from 455 million dollars to 1,854 million dollars.

---

*The countries that mainly resorted to capital markets in 1971 were Israel, Spain, and Mexico (80 percent of the total).

PART II
RESOURCES, TECHNOLOGY, AND INCOME DISTRIBUTION

**DISTRIBUTION OF
INCOME, WEALTH,
AND POWER**
Gustav F. Papanek

The cliche of the 1960s was that it is undesirable to distribute poverty; economic growth was therefore the overriding objective in poor countries. The cliche of the 1970s is that growth in average income is meaningless, what matters is the well-being of the poor majority; therefore equity is the overriding objective. Both cliches are obviously right. If the objective of development in LDCs is to increase the income of the poor, then a highly egalitarian distribution of a yearly income of $100 or even $400 is unsatisfactory. Rapid growth in average income may be equally unsatisfactory, if it leaves the majority in poverty. Economic growth with equity is the stated objective of most countries.

But growth and equity—the distribution of income, wealth, and power—are related in a variety of very complex ways. To clarify the different ways in which they can be said to conflict may avoid confusion.

1. Capitalist economies have seemingly higher growth rates but less equitable distribution than socialist ones. The conflict in choosing the basic political-economic strategy of a country is thus between the degree of equity and the rate of growth.
2. Closely connected is the issue whether, once it is decided to adopt a capitalist or socialist strategy, policies to achieve a higher rate of growth worsen income distribution.
3. Also important is the effect of economic growth on income distribution over several decades. The Kuznets hypothesis is that as the average income rises in private enterprise economies, distribution first becomes less and then more equitable. The conflict would be between levels of per capita income and degree of equity.
4. Inequality may contribute to growth. If a small minority owns much of a country's wealth and receives much of its income, it may be able to achieve very high savings rates and therefore rapid growth. But the high growth rates in South Africa, Rhodesia, pre-independence Algeria or Zambia clearly did not cause inequality. The two objectives conflict only in the sense that a more equitable distribution may reduce the rate of savings and the availability of technical manpower.

5. Usually only one dimension of equity is measured: the distribution of income. If the poor receive a smaller share this is considered less equitable. But three other aspects of equity should be taken into account: the absolute level of income of the poor—moral concern may be less if the poorest 20 percent have an average yearly income of $1,000 than if it is $40; changes in the absolute income of the poor—regardless of absolute level of distribution, if the income of most of the poor is increasing, they are presumably better off; the change in income distribution—if the income of the rich increases more rapidly than that of the poor, the latter may feel both envy and hope.

6. The relationship over time between growth, equity, and politics is complex. Rapid growth may strengthen pressure for equity.

A caveat: In cross-country analysis various reasons for negative association between growth and equity are examined together. Conclusions can be quite wrong, if one does not clearly distinguish between countries where rapid growth caused unequal distribution and where it did not, or between the degree of equity and changes in equity. For instance, the existence of resource-rich countries with unequal income distribution does not demonstrate that growth caused inequality.

CAPITALIST GROWTH, SOCIALIST EQUITY

The few data available indicate that capitalist economies are generally more successful than socialist ones in raising average per capita income, but at the cost of a very inegalitarian distribution of income, wealth, and power. In the Adelman and Morris sample of 18 countries poor in natural resources the wealthiest 5 percent of the population received 28 percent of national income in predominantly private enterprise countries, while in states with a larger role for government they received only 18 percent. The greater equality of income in socialist economies is generally accepted on an impressionistic basis, although income distribution data are not available for most of these countries.

A comparison of growth in private and public enterprise economies is shown in Table 1. Both groups include countries at very different levels of development in Asia, Africa, and Latin America. Some of the growth data are suspect. But at least superficially the private enterprise countries have grown more rapidly. A simple average shows them growing at roughly 7 percent, while public enterprise countries grew at 4 percent.

The classification of countries is inevitably somewhat arbitrary. The proportion of government investment is perhaps the best indication of the government's role in the economy (for example: 90 percent for the U.A.R., 30 percent for Israel, 20 percent for Venezuela).

TABLE 1

Growth in Private and Public
Enterprise Countries
(in annual percentages)

Country	Percentage	Country	Percentage
Public Enterprise			
Algeria	0-2.6	Iraq	5.9
Burma	3.7 or less	Mali	2.8
Ceylon	4.1	North Korea	8.5
Cuba	0.3	Syria	6.7
Ghana	1.9	Tanzania	4.3
Guinea	5.2	U.A.R.	4.7
Indonesia	2.4	Yugoslavia	7.05
India	3.7		
Private Enterprise			
Argentina	3.6	Lebanon	9.9
Bolivia	5.4	Malaysia	5.8
Brazil	6.5-8.8	Mexico	6.65
Chile	4.7	Morocco	4.1
Colombia	5.3	Pakistan	5.7
Central America	6.1	Peru	5.05
Ecuador	5.1	Philippines	5.9
Greece	7.8	Singapore	7.2
Hong Kong	12.5	South Korea	9.5
Indonesia	7.0 to 7.5	Taiwan	10.1
Iran	8.8	Thailand	7.4
Israel	8.4	Tunisia	4.6
Ivory Coast	8.4	Turkey	5.7
Japan	11.15	Venezuela	4.5
Kenya	5.0		

However, when government completely dominates the economy (for example, in Tanzania, Burma) the country has been classified as public enterprise even if public investment is recorded as less than half of total investment.

Indonesia is classed as public enterprise for 1960-66 and as private enterprise for 1967-71. For Brazil the lower figure is for 1960-71 before the all-out shift to private enterprise; the higher figure is for 1966-71 after the shift. For Algeria the lower figure is for 1960-65; the higher figure is for 1965 to 1969. The figure for Central America is a simple average for Costa Rica, El Salvador, Guatemala, Honduras, Nicaragua, Panama.

There is a great deal of dispute about the growth rate of China. For 1957 to 1970 the estimates range from 1.4 percent to 4.8 percent. The addition of China to the public enterprise group would not change the conclusion, nor would the deletion of India.

Some additional evidence comes from a comparison between India and Pakistan, countries that are similar in many respects but followed somewhat different strategies in the 1960s. Pakistan* shifted from direct government intervention to the partial use of taxes and subsidies in this period. Rising conspicuous consumption by the wealthy was one consequence; increasing aid and more rapid growth were others. Particularly striking is the more efficient use of capital by Pakistan. With roughly the same investment rate as India, Pakistan achieved a rate of growth 50 percent higher. (See Table 2.) That this difference was not due to any inherent advantage of Pakistan's but was largely the result of differences in policy is suggested by the fact that in the 1950s its growth rate was about 30 percent lower than India's.

The greater efficiency of investment and more rapid growth in capitalist economies is what one would expect. Public enterprise economies have difficulties in providing noneconomic incentives for effort, risk taking, and willingness to change. They face problems in decentralizing decisions if economic incentives and market prices

TABLE 2

Growth and Investment in India and Pakistan
(as percent of GDP)

	India		Pakistan	
	Investment	Growth	Investment	Growth
1949-59	12	3.8	10	2.6
1959-69	17	3.8	15.5	5.8

*All references to Pakistan are to a period ending in early 1970 and therefore refer to an area that has since become the two states of Pakistan and Bangladesh.

are not used, and equally serious problems of avoiding inefficiency if decisions are highly centralized.

In choosing a basic strategy there appears to be a conflict between growth and distribution. Pure capitalism is rare among less developed countries. The hybrid form adopted by Brazil, Japan, Korea, Ivory Coast, Taiwan, Thailand, and Indonesia (since 1967) seems to be highly favorable for growth but, during early development, less favorable for equity.

It is perfectly possible to design an efficient and equitable economic system combining the best features of capitalism and socialism. From capitalism would come decentralized decisions, guided by market prices, and economic incentives to stimulate innovation, effort, savings, and some willingness to take risks. Socialism would contribute limits on the consumption of the upper income groups, to improve equity and channel resources to savings, subsidized (or free) services for the poorer groups, again for equity reasons, and greater equality of opportunity. Such a utopia of rapid growth and substantial equity can be approached from either direction.

Socialist economies can decentralize decisions to factories, cooperatives, local government units, and even small private firms, operating in the environment of a price system rigged by government to assure that decisions are socially desirable. Some economic rewards can be provided to units and individuals that perform efficiently in economic terms. But the greater the reliance on economic incentives, the greater the disparities in income distribution.

Yugoslavia and China have gone further in this direction than other countries. Yugoslavia has achieved quite rapid growth, but with constant strains because decentralization and economic incentives resulted in growing disparities between regions, firms and individuals. In China the decentralization of decisions in the early 1960s by delegating them to smaller collective units and to families on their private plots stimulated agricultural production. Foodgrain output increased at an annual rate of over 8 percent during 1961-65. Even if the banner year of 1961 is excluded, the rate of growth was still over 5 percent. This was the period of decollectivization, when private plots reached nearly 9 percent of cultivated land and showed a productivity double that of collectivized areas. The Cultural Revolution followed, designed in part to reassert the objective of equity over that of growth, with serious setbacks to output. Until recently China seemed prepared to sacrifice growth in order to avoid substantial reliance on economic incentives and the inequality they bring.

The governing group generally tends to resist decentralization because it limits the power and privileges of the central bureaucracy. Moreover, decentralization without material incentives is difficult to manage, while with economic incentives it inevitably is accompanied by disparities in income. The growth of such disparities can serve as a reason for the central bureaucracy to oppose decentralization.

A satisfactory combination of growth and equity is equally possible in a capitalist system. Heavy taxes on goods consumed by the rich can encourage savings and limit conspicuous consumption, while generating the resources needed to provide services to the poor. Commodity taxes, unlike those on income, can usually be collected. To assure greater equality of opportunity, commodity taxes can be supplemented where necessary by heavy inheritance taxes and land reform. Inheritance taxes are more difficult to collect than taxes on commodities, but if they are imposed on the really rich, as they should be, the administrative problems are manageable. Much evidence has accumulated that if agriculture is carried out by smallholders, as in much of Asia, Africa, and South America, productivity may increase if land reform gives ownership to the smallholder who actually works the land. The resources available from commodity and inheritance taxes can finance access to education for poorer groups. Such access is a powerful factor in greater equality of income distribution and in improving equality of opportunity.

Fortunately, there is evidence that many businessmen in LDCs, like their colleagues in the developed world, work hard to expand their enterprises and increase profits, even if consumption and inheritance are restricted. Taxes on consumption and inheritance do not seem to affect incentives as much as does a hostile climate, government regulations, and uncertainty about government policy.

One can add other elements in designing a modified capitalist system favorable to growth and not too unfavorable for equity:

- a pattern of government investment, taxes and subsidies that favors production of goods consumed by the poor over those consumed by the rich;
- the concentration of government investment in poor regions and on the provision of services for the poor (water supply, health, housing, scholarships, education in poor regions);
- government programs providing employment to unskilled workers. This can raise the income of the poorest group in the population, since the biggest gap in income is often between those with steady employment, including industrial workers, and those without regular jobs.

Governments of many countries have adopted some of these policies. Taxes and government expenditures are widely used to improve equity.

Some countries, usually relatively wealthy ones have the great majority of children in school, and in nearly all countries enrollment is increasing. There is a strong correlation between children in school and equitable income distribution, so increasing enrollment is likely to be a powerful force for equity. (See Table 3.)

A few governments have financed programs to provide productive employment. One such program in Indonesia has provided half a million man-years of supplementary employment (of 100 days per year).

Such measures, including a highly progressive tax system, widespread education, and other socialist principles enabled Israel to achieve a high rate of growth and, in 1957, a quite egalitarian income distribution. (see Table 4.) Particularly striking is the low share of the upper income groups in the national income. At the bottom of the income scale the system is less egalitarian, though still better than in most countries, presumably reflecting the low incomes of recent immigrants not yet integrated into the economy and of the Arab minority.

While some private enterprise economies have adopted policies to improve equity, politics usually intervenes before such policies can have very far-reaching effects. Government taxes and expenditures, potentially a most powerful weapon, have had a very small impact on income distribution in many countries. Education is a significant force for equity only in the wealthier of the less developed countries, where over 70 percent of children are typically in school. In the poorest countries, with enrollment typically below 50 percent, the impact will obviously be less.

India, a country concerned with equity, had 44 percent of its children in school, Pakistan only 27 percent in 1965. India had more than doubled its percentage since 1950, while Pakistan had increased it only by a third. Labor-intensive works programs have been carried out in only a few private enterprise economies. Even there, the effect

TABLE 3

Education and Income Distribution
(percentage of total income)

	Countries Whose School Enrollment Is:	
	Higher	Lower
Income of poorest 60 percent	30	23
Income of middle 40-60 percent	13.5	10.3
Wealthiest 5 percent	31	42

Source: I. Adelman and C.T. Morris, "Who Benefits from Development" (mimeographed, January 1972).

TABLE 4

Income Distribution in Israel—1957
(rounded percents)

		Israel	Average for 45 Countries
Poorest	20 percent	7	5.5
Low	40 "	20	14
Middle	40 "	40	30
High	20 "	39	56
Highest	5 "	11	30

Source: I. Adelman and C.T. Morris, Economic Growth and Social Equity in Developing Countries (Stanford, 1973).

has been small. The Indonesian program, one of the largest, was in its third year providing partial employment to perhaps one percent of the labor force.

The reason for the limited impact of measures to improve equity in private enterprise economies is clear: an economy dominated by private enterprise usually means a government heavily influenced by the wealthy. The wealthy are understandably unenthusiastic about high taxes on their consumption and inheritance to finance services and jobs for the poor, and use their influence to avoid this.

While it is possible to design a public enterprise system that relies on decentralized decisions guided substantially by economic incentives, or a private enterprise system with taxes, subsidies, and other measures to redistribute income, in fact, countries find it extremely difficult to achieve rapid growth and equity simultaneously. In part this is because economic incentives facilitate growth but harm equity. More important, decentralization runs counter to the interests of the elite in public enterprise economies, redistribution counter to those of the elite in private enterprise ones. Therefore, there appears to be a significant conflict between growth and equity in decisions on a country's basic development strategy.

THE EFFECT OF DEVELOPMENT ON EQUITY

Another question is whether over a period of several decades economic growth tends to increase income inequality. The Kuznets hypothesis is that as development proceeds, inequality first increases, then declines.

There are good logical reasons for supposing that development initially leads to increased disparity in incomes, subsequently to decreased disparity:

- In economies with very low per capita incomes, the lowest income groups could not survive with a very small share of the national income* Subsistence economies therefore tend to be relatively egalitarian. As development begins, the lowest income groups in labor surplus economies may remain close to subsistence. If their absolute income does not increase as average income rises, their share of national income declines and inequality increases.

However, as development proceeds, additional workers can be obtained by manufacturing, construction, or other nonrural activities only if they pay more than subsistence wages. The absolute income of the lowest income groups would then rise, and the deterioration in equity characteristic of early growth would come to an end.

- Economic growth also means a shift from rural to urban areas and from traditional to new activities. Income disparity is usually greater between the average income in the cities and in the countryside and within the cities, than within the rural areas. Therefore, as the proportion of urban population increases, the disparity in incomes may also increase even if there is no change in income distribution within the cities and the rural areas.

But if growth continues, the rural population will no longer represent the norm. As additional families then move into urban, nontraditional, occupations income disparities will decrease, because they will be moving to the new norm.

- Development is uneven and the income of some regions or occupations will rise more rapidly than that of others. In a slowly growing economy, people in different regions and occupations can continually adjust to earning opportunities and great income disparities do not arise. But if growth is reasonably rapid, and concentrated in particular areas or occupations, the shifts of the labor force may not catch up for a long time and income disparities will increase, especially in early development when labor mobility is low.

Eventually, however, if growth continues, mobility of labor will increase and regional-occupational disparities are therefore likely to decline.

---

*For instance, in a country with a per capita income of $70, if the poorest 30 percent had only 5 percent of the income, which is typical for all countries, then their income would average $12 a year. This is probably not enough to survive even in a subsistence economy.

- Economic growth requires changes in customary behaviour. Strong incentives must be provided to achieve such changes as from subsistence to cash crops, from petty trade and handicrafts to international trade and large scale industry, and from the use of traditional to commercial inputs. The inevitable concomitant of economic incentives is high financial rewards to those who respond. Growth also increases the opportunities for high rewards for some groups and individuals.

Of course response to incentives and opportunities is not uniform Those with better education, greater experience and knowledge, more capital, more ambition and willingness to take risks, fewer scruples, better access to government, and so on will respond disproportionately They will reap high rewards that in turn provide them, and their children, with still better education, more capital and experience, better access to government, and so on. Their income is likely to keep growing, while some of those who did not or could not respond to incentives or opportunities originally are likely to become actually worse off. For instance, with increased agricultural production prices of agricultural products will drop and farmers who have not increased their output will be worse off. Protection for new industry means high profits for industrialists but higher costs for consumers. The development of modern industry is likely to drive more traditional firms out of business.

If growth continues there are offsetting factors. Incentives and rewards for entrepreneurial activities may diminish, as innovation becomes less of a rarity. As capital becomes less scarce, its rewards decline. Moreover, the offspring of some well-established, wealthy families may tend to be less enterprising, less eager to pursue economic rewards.

Available data do not permit very firm conclusions, especially since data for a number of countries are obviously incorrect. However, from cross country data it appears that, as development takes place over several decades: the lowest income groups may receive a slightly smaller share of income as average income rises initially but their share probably rises again once income exceeds $300; the share of the middle income groups probably remains unchanged in the early stages of growth, and increases subsequently; and the top income group probably has a rising share initially, a declining one subsequently.

In general, the quantitative evidence also tends to support three conclusions: First, if a small, foreign-dominated enclave is responsible for most of the increase in average income, growth is usually accompanied by a severe deterioration of equity. Second, if growth continues and higher levels of income are reached, income distribution seems to improve. Third, with some exceptions, the poorest groups in less developed capitalist countries have a very low share of income. In less developed countries with average income above $300, the lowest 40 percent have only 14 percent of income, the lowest 60 percent only 30 percent. The poverty problem remains in most less developed countries. In the wealthier group of countries the middle income groups seem to gain a larger share, while the share of the rich declines.

RATE OF GROWTH

Once a country has started to develop and has decided to adopt a basically private enterprise economy, the short run impact of different growth rates depends to some extent on its stage of development. If it is beginning the growth process from a stagnant, but relatively egalitarian subsistence economy, the more rapid the growth, the more likely that income disparities will increase. If, on the other hand, the country has nearly exhausted its surplus labor, more rapid growth means rising wages for unskilled workers and decreasing income disparities.

But more important are the policies adopted to achieve growth. In private enterprise economies, steps that reduce consumption of the wealthy, eliminate windfall profits, or increase competition, are generally favorable for both a high rate of growth and equity. Examples of policies of this kind include cuts in import controls, investment licenses, and restrictions on the movement of foodgrains. Generally such controls fail to assure supplies to poorer consumers or smaller firms, reduce investments, raise costs, and give windfall profits to already wealthy groups—senior civil servants and businessmen who receive licenses. If the opposition of the beneficiaries can be overcome, abolition of controls can improve both equity and growth. On the other hand, steps that shift income to the rich may increase the rate of savings, and therefore of growth, but at the cost of equity.

The previously quoted comparison of India and Pakistan is again relevant. There is no doubt that the Indian government was more concerned with equity in the 1960s. Despite more effective policies and programs to promote equity, India's income distribution may have worsened and Pakistan's may have improved. (See Table 5.) The reason almost certainly was that Pakistan's economic growth rate was about 50 percent higher than India's. As a result:

● Monopoly and windfall profits diminished, partly because increased competition drove down prices, partly by the reduction of government generated windfalls from licenses and permits.

TABLE 5

Income Distribution in India and Pakistan
(Gini Coefficient)

	Consumption	Income
Pakistan		
1963/64	—	.38
1966/67	.337	.36
India		
1951-55	.371	—
1955-60	.392	—

Source: Javaid Azfar, unpublished Ph.D. dissertation, Harvard University.

- The rapid expansion in industry and construction (in West Pakistan primarily) made it easier to find jobs and raised wage rates.
- Most important, increased production of foodgrains, cloth, and similar goods lowered their prices and therefore raised real incomes for poorer groups. The data on Pakistan (and, to a lesser extent, India and Indonesia) show that money wages lag behind price changes, at least in countries without experience of persistent inflation and without strong labor unions. When prices rise because output lags behind population growth, real wages decline; when prices drop because output is rising rapidly, real wages increase.

A rapid rate of growth seems to have been favorable for equity in Pakistan, once the basic decision was made to pursue an essentially capitalist strategy.

The evidence from Brazil seems to tend in the opposite direction. Between 1960 and 1970, GNP increased by an average of 6 percent a year, but income distribution became less equitable (the Gini coefficient increased from .59 to .63 and the share of the richest 3.2 percent increased from 27 percent to 33 percent of national income). However, since the period of rapid growth began only in 1968, the 1960's included only 3 years of rapid growth (over 9 percent per year). Moreover, the period 1964-67 was dominated by a successful program to a stop runaway inflation and for the "destruction of the urban proletariat as a political threat." A central feature of policy was government imposed wage restraint. Brazil may therefore provide better evidence that policies affect equity than on the effect of the growth rate.

In short, it may be possible to step up the growth rate in capitalist economies without undesirable effects on income distribution. But the relationship between growth rates and equity is complicated and dependent on circumstances and policies.

THE ABSOLUTE INCOME OF THE POOR

Generally development improves the absolute income of the poor majority, and the more rapid the growth the greater the absolute increase.

Pakistan again provides useful evidence. In the 1950s per capita income decreased in East Pakistan (now Bangladesh) and barely rose in West Pakistan, while real wages declined. From 1959 to 1965, on the other hand, per capita income increased by more than 3 percent per annum. During this period of rapid growth rural wages increased by over a third in East Pakistan and industrial workers' wages in both provinces rose by over 10 percent. Similarly in India, wages declined during the period of slow growth in the 1950s but rose with more rapid growth in the early 1960s. (See Table 6.)

TABLE 6

Real Wages in India and Pakistan
(averages—to reduce effect of yearly fluctuations)

Rural Workers—East Pakistan (index)		
1949-50	110	
1958-59	95	
1963-64	130	

Industrial Workers—Pakistan (Constant rupees)		
	East	West
1954-56	713	1015
1957-59	632	973
1960-62	745	1079
1963	787	1032

Wage earners—India (index)		
1950-52	104	
1958-60	100	
1962-63	113	

In Brazil real wages in industry declined during the period of slow growth, 1964-67. They rose with rapid growth after 1967 and by 1970 were 10 percent higher than in 1964. In 1960 over 60 percent of the population had a monthly income of NC $150 or less, but by 1970 the proportion of poor had declined to 56 percent.

In Colombia workers in industry and commerce, and domestics, had increases in real wages over a decade or fifteen years that ranged from 20 percent to 60 percent. The real wage of unskilled construction workers (in Bogota) also increased over 60 percent from the early 1950s to the early 1960s and rose by another 5 percent to the late 1960s (Berry). However, between 1965 and 1970 construction workers' real wages declined, despite rapid growth. The causes are not clear.

If one uses cross-country data for conclusions about changes over longer periods of time, the conclusion about absolute levels is strengthened. If data for all 44 countries are averaged (Adelman-Morris), the poorest 60 percent of the population seem to benefit from an absolute increase in income of about 55 percent when moving from the lowest to the medium income groups, although their share of income drops by a quarter. Moving from the middle to the wealthiest group, with both their share and average income increasing, the poorest 60 percent seem to benefit from a more than tripling of their average income. (See Table 7.)

In short, to the extent that readily available time series and cross-country data permit any conclusion, it is that with growth the absolute income of the lower income groups rises. The more rapid the growth presumably the more rapid the rise, other things equal. In this respect no conflict between growth and equity seems to arise.

TABLE 7

Average Income of Poorest Groups at
Different Levels of Development
(in dollars unless otherwise indicated)

Unweighted Income Ranges	Average Income	Share of Lowest 60 percent (in percent)	Average Absolute Income of Lowest 60 percent
145 or less	94	28	44
146-300	194	21	68
300 or more	502	28	234

Source: Calculated from Adelman/Morris, 1973.

THE POLITICS OF DEVELOPMENT, THE DEVELOPMENT OF POLITICS

The relationship between growth and equity is not entirely an economic one. Politics enter in a variety of ways.

Improvement in the income of some persons or group can arouse envy or hope on the part of those whose income has remained unchanged. Whether envy or hope predominate obviously influences how groups that are left out in the development process react politically.

The groups and individuals left out can either be totally or partially left out. When the distribution of income deteriorates, the lower income groups may experience an increase, deterioration, or stagnation of their real income.

Moreover, the lower income groups can change, regardless of what happens to income distribution. For instance, Brazil's stabilization program may have reduced the income of industrial workers, while investment in the northeast may have raised the income of construction workers in that poor area. The low income group, as a result, may have more industrial workers and fewer people from the poor region. Peru's land reform is another example. The workers who happened to be on sugar estates, taken over by the government and transformed into cooperatives, are experiencing a substantial increase in income that may raise them into the lower middle class. At the same time some owners of smaller firms are experiencing difficulties and may drop to the lower income groups. The Indian smallholders in the mountains remain the majority of the lowest income group. Income distribution may remain unchanged, but the class composition of the different income groups can change and with it the politically disaffected.

The experience of India and Pakistan in the 1960s suggests factors that may be of crucial importance in determining the political consequences of inequality. The absolute level of income of the lower income groups in Pakistan improved more than in India. Their relative position was no worse and may have been better. But the history of the two countries clearly indicates that they were more dissatisfied than the comparable groups in India.

One factor in India making for greater political stability was that each succeeding Indian government took more radical steps to make clear that it wanted to help the poor and restrain the rich. Some of the steps taken were largely cosmetic—nationalization of banks and insurance companies—and some were counter productive—the expansion of a costly and in many cases inefficient government industrial sector. However, others made an obvious, though small difference, notably more effective restrictions on luxury and conspicous consumption than in Pakistan. Conspicuous consumption by the rich brings home to the poor the miserable nature of their existence and the lack of concern both the government and the rich feel for that misery. It seems that a government and society may be forgiven a great deal, even a lack of improvement in the absolute and relative position of the poor majority, if it is seen to curb the extravagance of the rich and is believed to be trying to improve the lot of the poor.

The problem in Pakistan was aggravated by a sharp drop in income for crucial groups after 1965. Urban and rural workers saw their real income drop 15 to 25 percent in the course of the year. Some students, professionals, and technicians also faced much poorer prospects, as the investment program was cut back. Continued conspicuous consumption can be especially offensive, and politically dangerous when less favored groups have experienced a sharp decline in income.

Pakistan also showed the political consequences of another important aspect of equity: regional distribution. The absolute income levels and growth rates were less important than the political context in which they occurred. The breakup of Pakistan did not occur in the 1950s, when income per capita in East Bengal was probably declining, but at the end of the 1960s, when it was increasing at over 1 percent per year. The main reason was political: by the mid-1960s it became increasingly clear that the ruling elite of West Pakistan was not disposed to give the Bengali majority a significant share in political power. The disaffected Bengali elite mobilized support around the issue of economic neglect. Since East Bengal was and is desperately poor, blaming that poverty on neglect by the central government was a powerful political issue.

Pakistan demonstrates the political consequences of neglecting the political dimension of equity. It was not enough to have quite rapid growth, improvement in the absolute income of the poor, and no obvious deterioration in their relative position. In a really poor country with a 6 percent rate of growth, many groups and regions inevitably remain poor and their concrete improvement is slow. To some extent they live on hope. Sharp temporary setbacks are inevitable. If, then, the government conveys the impression that it is prepared to tolerate conspicuous consumption for the rich while ignoring the needs of the poorer groups and regions, this can contribute to political tensions.

While Pakistan's experience shows that poor countries cannot neglect equity and the politics of development, India demonstrates that they cannot neglect growth. A year after winning an unprecedented electoral triumph and a war, the government of India is in serious difficulties, owing to mounting economic problems. For 25 years the Indian political leadership retained support by promising improvements to the poor and curbing the conspicuous consumption of the rich. But given India's low rate of growth, the government was unable to keep its promises. Some potentially powerful political groups could not be provided with economic improvement. There just is not enough to go around. Some politically attractive steps, which maintained support for the leadership, simultaneously discouraged private savings and investment (for example: nationalization; restrictions on large enterprises) or reduced efficiency (protection for handlooms; control over imports and investment). They thus contributed to slow growth, with political costs in the long run.

India and Pakistan are examples of the difficulty faced by poor countries in neglecting either growth or equity. Wealthier countries have an easier time, as long as they do not go to extremes. Thailand has not been noted for great concern with the distribution of its rapidly growing income, and some outsiders have long predicted disaster. But growth has been rapid, cultivable land has been reasonably freely available until recently, and most groups seem to see a sufficient improvement for the system to survive. Malaysia has a particularly severe problem, since class differences are worsened by some overlap with ethnic differences. However, economic improvement and the government's expressed concern for some economically disadvantaged groups seems to have been sufficiently great to avoid serious difficulty.

Uruguay, on the other hand, had a stagnant income for many years. But social welfare measures and the high absolute level of income helped in maintaining it as a model of stability. Recently, the political fabric seems to have unraveled, providing another example that even wealthier countries run into problems if growth is too long neglected.

The same seems to be true of Indonesia and Ghana. Outsiders predicted political problems for years, as the economies of the two countries stagnated. Both countries could more readily tolerate stagnation than India and Pakistan because of greater wealth, and the governments of both were helped by the populist, egalitarian impression they created. Eventually there was a major change in government in both countries, although some would dispute that economic stagnation was a major force.

The picture is complicated further by feedback. Growth itself increases the importance of different groups in the political process. Three groups, mentioned with respect to Pakistan, have played an important role in political change in some other countries: regional or ethnic political leadership (or elites); urban workers in industry, transport, construction, and so on; and the students and professionals, often from the lower middle class. In some states the last group also includes bank employees, junior officers, and junior civil servants. It seems to be an inevitable concomitant of development that these groups increase in importance, and, usually, in number. Regional and ethnic elites see greater economic rewards for the effor at organization, when more government resources are available for allocation as a result of growth. The urban labor force, organized in large units, invariably becomes more important with growth in the industrial sector and investment. The explosion in secondary and higher education has been nearly universal, even in slowly growin economies. Economies that grow rapidly may also experience a rapid growth in demands for equity, as students, workers, and other groups of little significance in traditional economies reach numbers that make them a significant political force.

Again Pakistan provides an example. Over 15 years the labor force in modern industry increased from less than 100,000 to over 600,000 and students in colleges and universities rose from about 30,000 to about ten times that number. The Bengali movement obtained much of its support from students, teachers, traders, and industrial workers. The same groups, except that professionals substituted for traders, were also at the forefront of political change in West Pakistan. Rapid growth in the 1960s also strengthened the political position of the businessmen and industrialists. Conflict resulted when they used their enhanced political power to shift the burden of the severe economic setback in the mid-1960s to the lower income groups and the poorer region. Two decades earlier urban workers, students, professionals, and the Bengali elite might not have had the numbers to challenge the upper income groups.

Another interesting example is Venezuela. In the 1950s its income from oil accrued to foreigners and a wealthy oligarchy. It was charged, with considerable justice, that the country would end with a hole in the ground, a few families with foreign bank accounts, and little else to show for its oil. But the process of oil development itself helped to open up the country and expand the number of skilled, trained, and organized workers. This in turn affected the political process, increasing the importance of lower and middle income groups. By 1970 Venezuela was a functioning democracy, with rapidly rising expenditures on services for the poorer groups and not too unfavorable an income distribution. For instance, school enrollment practically doubled (41 percent to 79 percent) from 1950 to 1960. By 1961 the middle income groups (40 percent to 80 percent) had 41.5 percent of income, as compared to only 30 percent for the average country, while the share of the upper 20 percent of the population was well below average.

In short, a strategy based on private enterprise may favor growth, but can over time run into severe problems:
- Income distribution can worsen. With satisfactory growth and unsatisfactory distribution, emphasis is likely to shift to equity as the primary goal.
- Meanwhile some upper income groups will have gained wealth translatable into political strength, which will be used to oppose steps to increase equity.
- At the same time, the political importance of the groups to whom greater equity is a matter of rice and fish, not of an abstract belief in social justice, will increase. Conflict between them and the rich is likely, especially if the country is poor and the improvement for the lower income majority is small.

On the other hand, a strategy based on public enterprise may favor equity, but can also run into severe problems:
- Growth can be slow. With satisfactory equity and unsatisfactory growth, emphasis is likely to shift to the latter.
- The bureaucracy which controls the economy has gained political strength from that control. Without checks, absent in authoritarian centralized regimes, it may also have gained material benefits. It is as unwilling to give up power and its higher standard of living as its capitalist counterparts in a private enterprise economy. Attempts to decentralize decisions to improve efficiency and raise growth are thus difficult to carry out.
- At the same time the majority of the population becomes disenchanted with relative equity if there is little increase in absolute economic well-being. Tension between the leadership and the masses is likely to increase, especially in a poor country where improvement in absolute levels is especially important.

As a result of the problems experienced by stagnant economies where governments have stressed equity a radical change in the political leadership has sometimes taken place. The new governments tend to emphasize growth. (Examples include Brazil, Ghana, Mali, Indonesia, Tunisia.) There are instances of equally drastic change in countries that emphasized growth at the cost of equity (for example: Pakistan, Burma, Algeria, Peru, Cuba, Libya, Philippines, Venezuela).

How long stagnation with equity, or growth with inequality, is tolerable is obviously a complex question, which has at least as much to do with political, social, and historical aspects as with economic factors. But in the economic realm, very rapid growth may help (as in Japan, Greece, Mexico, Thailand, Hong Kong) and so may a radical redistribution (as in Cuba, Burma). Countries wealthy in natural resources, people, aid, or institutions obviously find it easier to achieve a high rate of growth. Those with widespread participation in the political process are more likely to achieve a degree of equity.

But only a handful of countries have achieved simultaneously a high rate of growth and a high degree of equity. The conflict in objectives seems to be a real one, but what trade-offs a particular country chooses at a particular time clearly depends on a variety of factors including its growth potential, level and distribution of income, political system, and values. The widespread emphasis on equity, even at the cost of growth, of the 1970s can be as wrong for a particular country as was the widespread emphasis on growth, even at the cost of equity, of the 1960s.

DISCUSSION

BEN AMI ZUCKERMAN (Israel): The quality of statistics relating to rate of growth and the national product in less developed countries has improved in recent years. This does not apply to statistics about income distribution which are poor the world over. Even in Britain, income distribution based on tax statistics is quite different from the effective income distribution. This problem is likely to be more severe in less developed states. Present income distribution statistics should be used very carefully, and a big effort must be made to improve them by various international organizations. Within each country, the quality of these statistics today varies from branch to branch.

When measuring the relationship between the share of government activity in an economy and the gross national product per capita, it becomes apparent that when per capita income is low the government's share of the economy declines until a certain higher income is reached. Then the government's share begins to increase. Hence it is sometimes larger in developed than in poorer countries.

The role of taxation policy in changing income distribution is limited, even when taxes are high. There should be a shift to the expenditure side of the budget, which through services, subsidies, and so forth can play a major role in changing income distribution. More attention should be paid to the effect of various expenditure policies on income distribution, which is not obvious at first glance.

Dr. Papanek's slightly pessimistic conclusions concerning the possibility of having both growth and equity in developing states seem contradicted by the case of Israel, which achieved substantial growth without a noticeable worsening in income distribution.

IRMA ADELMAN (United States): I believe that the relationship between growth rates and levels of absolute income is U-shaped. Low and moderate growth rates reduce the absolute income levels of the poor, but rapid growth rates cause a sustained improvement in these levels. This conclusion, however, is affected by the kind of development strategy adopted, as well as by the level of socioeconomic development in the economy where the policies are applied.

Data from India show that the income of the poorest 20 percent there fell slightly in the 1960s. It should be noted that when wages move one way, fringe benefits tend to move the opposite way. In Brazil the improvement occurred only between 1968 and 1970, too short a period to base conclusions on. On Colombia there is conflicting evidence. The evidence, therefore, is not as clear as Professor Papanek implies.

SOLON BARRACLOUGH (FAO) objected to Professor Papanek's oversimplification in classifying states into socialist and nonsocialist. In Chile, classified as capitalist, over 60 percent of net investments since the mid-1950s emanated from the government. In Brazil during the present period the proportion is 50 percent. Israel, classified as capitalist is much more socialist than any country on the socialist list. Moreover, socialist states like Rumania, Bulgaria, Poland, and Hungary, which achieved very fast rates of growth in recent years, were not considered at all by Professor Papanek.

Data are often lacking. In Peru it is not even clear if the population numbers 15 million or 21 million, and nobody can say whether its income is going up or down. In Brazil, there are no data for rural incomes. In Ecuador some census takers were shot by Indians, and then most of the rest did not even visit the countryside. In Mexico where data are about the best, they show that there was a drop in the income level of some 40 percent of the rural population, though this conclusion is unclear. In Cuba no statistics at all are available for incomes, but Cuba has been investing heavily in education and health, which would not show up in income data anyway. The statistics cited by Professor Papanek simply don't mean anything.

TARLOK SINGH (UNICEF): A country beginning development seriously starts with a certain production apparatus and techniques. Income distribution is influenced by the government's expenditure policies but more so by the production system itself and its ownership. In some economies, changes involve a complete break with the past. Elsewhere, a gradual approach is necessary. In all underdeveloped countries, it is necessary to create a modern infrastructure. There is also the question of how to deal with the distribution and use of land.

We should think in terms not only of income distribution but also of production instruments and skills available. For an undeveloped state, development strategy, the technologies to be adopted, the directions that the production effort should take, and the consequent impact on distribution—all these must be closely related to available manpower and available skills.

FANNY GINOR (Israel): Social tensions arise when the poor become aware of their situation and more politically articulate, rather than when income distribution deteriorates. Economic growth and improved income distribution together with greater awareness of equality can thus increase internal tensions. The employment situation can, however, be a key factor in this connection.

GUSTAV PAPANEK (United States): The statistics are indeed very poor, but since they are used by policy makers to guide their decisions, they have to be taken into consideration. Economic growth does not cause the absolute income of the poorer sections of the population to fall in the long run. A rapid growth rate may help the poorer parts of the population. In Pakistan, real wages first declined but then rose.

As regards Mr. Barraclough's comments, data are bad in some cases, but by combining global income distribution data with data describing developments in the real income of particular groups from a variety of states, one can do slightly better than by dealing with a single state. The classification into socialist and non-socialist states was made on the basis of the proportion of government investment. Some faulty data would not affect the conclusions.

What instruments are to be used to achieve a rapid growth rate together with an improvement in income distribution must largely depend on who is to wield these instruments and on the basic economic structure with which you start. Starting from an egalitarian land tenure system, it is easier to improve productivity without worsening income distribution.

Another important question is how to obtain investment capital for a faster rate of growth. This can be done by squeezing peasants who are also exporters, like the jute growers of East Pakistan, the rice growers of Thailand, and the cocoa growers of Ghana. It can also be done by checking the consumption of the rich. The method adopted makes a high difference to income distribution.

Real wages will begin to rise when economic growth has reached a level at which the reserve of unemployed is exhausted.

Some facts and figures cited in this paper were obtained from works by I. Adelman and C.T. Morris, A. Fishlow, A. Berry, and Javaid Azfar.

INCOME DISTRIBUTION AND REFORM OF RURAL INSTITUTIONS

Thomas Carroll

Too much importance is attached to the questions of how much equity can be achieved at various stages of development and how much it costs in terms of equity when economic growth is accelerated. In rural areas, growth and equity can be achieved simultaneously. And most poor people belong to the rural sectors. In developing countries, probably as many as three-quarters of rural households are poor.

There has been a certain static concept of income redistribution. It includes welfare transfers through government channels and the skimming off of high incomes or commercial profits beyond a certain level and reinjecting them in the poor sectors. This can be done over a long period but contributes little to development. Nevertheless, governments like to do it for political reasons. It would be more advisable to concentrate on a long-term, dynamic concept of income redistribution.

Land reform, though more or less violent when seriously tackled, is also a static concept. It is a nonrecurrent redistribution of existing assets with a very limited developmental effect.

Rural development involves the injection of resources among the poorer rural strata, but has often proved disappointing in the equity-cum-growth context. When it concentrated on growth, it had serious economic weaknesses. There were serious equity problems accompanied by stresses and strains whenever a limited breakthrough in the technological sphere was achieved.

Our major redistributive mechanisms ran into serious difficulties too. The land reform approach tended to stimulate a limited income redistribution in favor of the middle income groups rather than the poor. In time, land reform communities developed serious inequalities. Large masses of rural dwellers seem hard to reach on an individual basis. Whenever rural development programs were reasonably successful, there was an equity problem.

Consequently, I want to recommend a new type of rural organization. It is a group-based system. It provides for joint ownership of an important proportion of productive resources, as well as for a substantial degree of peasant organization and participation in decisions.

Two major types of such organization exist: One in which land and other productive resources are owned jointly and another in which land remains wholly or partly in individual hands but input and output are dealt with collectively. I recommend the second.

At present, we either have a strongly individualistic approach, saying that peasants know best, small peasant holdings have been successful, therefore this must be the model; or else organization into large units (it makes little difference whether these are private, capitalist plantations or government-owned farms). I believe that we have to aim at something between these two systems.

The theory of economies of scale in agriculture has recently been attacked, with good reason. Scale is now much less important for agriculture than it used to be. Efficiency has proved to be similar on smaller and larger farms.

However, scale has still meaning in a context of dynamic development. New assets, new opportunities created by rapid technological changes give scale a certain importance, not only in the production process. Scale is also important during the period of emergence from colonial and semifeudal patterns. The most efficient types of plantation systems in Africa and Latin America are enclave systems. These are now being taken over by the state or transferred from private to public hands. The physical redistribution of plantation systems is not only difficult but often unwise. Once such a system has been organized, irrigation canals have been laid out, and the infrastructure for large-scale exploitation provided, subdividing such plantations can only do harm.

Finally, there is great scope for economies of scale in the delivery system and the marketing system, even when a small farm pattern is convenient. This applies to extension services, credit, transportation, and various processing services.

Economies of scale in the use of manpower and its training can also be important.

In peasant systems, the injection of resources has tended to create serious inequalities, as already mentioned. Even if the land-holding system is reasonably uniform, as in some Asian states, the village structure is economically and socially heterogeneous. Rural development programs not allowing for this have increased inequality and created serious tensions. Besides, land reform concentrating on injection of resources or redistribution of productive assets has tended to neglect the local power structure. A great deal of income created by such programs found its way to merchants, moneylenders and other nonpeasants living in villages or small towns in rural areas.

Consequently, those for whose benefit the development or land reform programs are framed must be given control not only over land and other production assets but over access to the capital market and to the marketing systems. This is much easier to do for groups than for individuals.

In the more formal type of production cooperative, where land is pooled, the labor income of the members accrues to them in greater measure than in an individual system. It is also easier to capture more of the surplus.

In Chile, they seem to be caught between a situation where large farms captured the labor output of the peasants and a state farm system in which all the surplus was captured by the state. This dilemma faces many countries willing to undergo a structural change. Hence, I recommend a group system giving peasants much greater influence through their ownership of assets and control of markets, allowing them to capture a much larger share of the labor income, and vesting them with some control over the surplus being produced.

In this kind of system, it is much easier to provide an income floor. In practically all collective systems in which membership is universal and land is pooled, there is a decent minimum of family living provided, which claims priority over creating a surplus. Moreover, these are usually the most productive systems, which create surpluses sooner or later.

Another great advantage of these systems, when properly adjusted, is that there is greater social control over the surplus produced for consumption and investment.

Redistribution through taxes deserves comment: In socialist systems there is a very strong tendency to extract surplus and reinject them in other parts of the economy. From the viewpoint of regional rural development, such a policy is counterproductive. Regionally linked cooperative enterprises can redirect a surplus to regional development much more efficiently than when it is channelled through the national system. In the latter case, the surplus may not even return to the regions.

A second major system is the service cooperative. The main argument for service cooperatives is that they have proved their viability. At higher levels of development, in particular, important portions of the surplus come from the marketing rather than the production system. This surplus can be captured through the control of the marketing system by cooperative arrangements.

It is possible to combine the two systems very successfully, land being pooled to some extent only, while part of the production process is collective and part individual. This was done in Israel's moshavim. The mixed system has advantages of flexibility and adaptability, which are important in rural development. Once organized, local groups can manage or influence programs effectively because they know their members and local conditions. They can adjust to changes better than large farm systems, such as state farms directed from the center. The intimate knowledge of their members facilitates credit programs where repayment capacity is based on trust rather than the individual's assets. Besides, the mixed system can be an excellent compromise between efficiency and equity, since resources can be effectively used and greater social justice can often be achieved

One should not be dogmatic applying the system in practice. In Peru, for instance, three different patterns were followed: On the coast, large sugar plantations were taken over from private owners and large, integrated cooperatives were established—a sort of worker-managed agricultural-industrial complex. In the sierra, where most of the Peruvian peasants live, a mixed type was created, based on small and large peasant cooperatives involving the enterprises directly affected and the local communities. In the jungle, newly colonized, they have established marketing and credit cooperatives, with more emphasis on private initiative and private reward owing to the very trying environment.

The countries of Eastern Europe, after a period of ideological rigidity in the late 1940s, have grown rapidly, and their income is well distributed. This applies particularly to the rural areas. Each state tried to adjust its agrarian system to its own conditions. Bulgaria is operating mostly collectives of a heavily centralized kind. In Poland, most of the land has reverted to individual holdings, though there is a cooperative superstructure. In all communist states, the original estates were not restored. Their main interest is in a decentralized type of worker-management with more voice for the individual participant. Hungary has gone furthest with decentralization. These are interesting experiments to which developing countries should pay special attention.

Socialist rural systems often encourage rural industrialization. Israel has a lot of experience in this. In a modern kibbutz in Israel landless people can acquire shares of interest in land and agriculturalists can acquire shares of milk processing plants and may soon come to own electronics factories. Basically, even with the best cooperative system, one cannot solve the employment and income distribution problems in rural areas.

My conclusions are as follows:

First, economic growth and equity in rural areas can be achieved. Economies of scale in rural areas should be reconsidered and concentrated in the delivery and service sectors, or where a technological jump takes place.

Second, when considering redistribution, serious attention should be paid to the distribution of assets and productive capacity in a dynamic framework.

Third, cooperative and group systems are of great importance, but should be accompanied by less dogmatism and more pragmatic thinking. A new ideological basis is required. Where large-scale land reform or plantation systems are introduced, there should be a joint production basis, especially where labor has peasant experience. But there are greater possibilities for cooperative or group systems in services and marketing.

If the underprivileged rural classes are not organized, benefits from rural development and poverty elimination programs will be captured by dominant local groups—those who own more assets, have a better education, and control the marketing system. Such organization is best done through economically meaningful cooperatives. In this manner, the painful dilemma of equity versus growth can be avoided and policies can be designed to achieve both. The Israeli experiments with the kibbutz and the moshav may have a great deal more to offer other countries than was hitherto believed.

DISCUSSION

JOSEPH SHATIL (Israel): In the kibbutz sector of the Israel economy above-average rates of economic growth together with extreme equality have been achieved over a very long period. The motives enabling a state or community to achieve rapid growth and equality must include ideology. The promise of material advantage alone is not sufficient to maintain good cooperatives. There is no contradiction between noneconomic and material incentives. When there is a gap between what is promised to the poor and what they actually receive, they can react either by losing hope or by political opposition.

The decision-making process within the economic units themselves is important. Participation in decision making is again a question of ideology—not only in developing countries.

YITZHAK ABT (Israel): What do we mean by "equal incomes"? Equal to other parts of the same agricultural sector? Or equal to other sectors? If efforts in rural development are aimed at an income level for farmers similar to that in other sectors, this has grave implications as regard investment. In Latin America, Asia, and Africa, where most people live in rural areas, such an objective is almost impossible to attain.

We should think rather about greater parity of services offered to rural folk. The problem is how to push people from the subsistence level to a level of income high enough to induce in them a desire to earn more.

IRMA ADELMAN (United States): We know little about transplanting institutions, but the response to this process depends on the social and economic structure into which the transplanting takes place. Attempts to create cooperatives in India yielded disappointing results. Existing social institutions inimical to equality tended to subvert the new social structure set up.

YEHUDA LANDAU (Israel): Redistribution of resources for large rural populations sometimes reduces productivity and checks growth.

Mr. Landau asked Dr. Carroll if he was speaking against individual production units as such, and against the individual family's motivation to be independent in its production and obtain a big part of the surplus. We should not give up the idea that the farming family should have its own balance sheet.

THOMAS CARROLL (Inter-American Development Bank): The first priority must be to raise subsistence incomes. This is a political decision, and many governments have not been very determined in doing this. Many middle incomes but very few of the really low incomes are normally being raised. A certain social minimum income specific to the country or region concerned should be the first target. There is much to be said for improving subsistence incomes in a subsistence setting. There is often no need to push people out of subsistence.

We are dealing not only with redistribution of incomes but also with redistribution of power. This is a deeply political issue and one to some extent subversive. If a country like India is not ready to face it, little can be done to push it in this direction.

I am not advocating individualism, but a closer look at group systems—either collective or based on individual peasant proprietorship. Where collectives are desired or work well, we should consider them. Where the cooperative is a superstructure and individual peasants do a good job, we should consider this system.

ECONOMIC AND SOCIAL COSTS OF MODERNIZATION AND DEVELOPMENT

Tarlok Singh

This paper explores some problems involved in choosing a strategy for development such as could minimize the economic and social costs borne by the population concerned.

The two expressions, "modernization" and "development" are generally interpreted in different ways according to the context. Thus, the economist may focus attention on increase in per capita product with which important structural and technological changes may be associated over a long period. The student of history may stress the evolution of institutions and their adaptation to the far-reaching developments in science and technology over the past two hundred years or more. The development planner may see in modernization ideals a frame of reference for the systematic choices that countries increasingly attempt through their long-term and medium-term plans.

Speaking of modernization, we have in view, in relation to industry, agriculture, and other segments of the economy, the following features of economic and social change:

- expansion of technical production capacities,
- application of scientific techniques,
- changes in traditional social structures in keeping with new economic and social needs,
- creation of new economic organizations and instruments, and
- development of innovative, managerial and technical skills.

These components of development support one another. Any of them could provide the initial stimulus to modernization. However, in underdeveloped economies functioning at low levels of production and productivity, measures aimed at expansion of production capacities in industry, agriculture, and related services have often provided the incentive for manpower planning, establishment of new institutions, and innovations in science and technology.

Expansion of existing production capacities is an essential component in planning for development. The utilization of human resources should rank as an equally important component, though hitherto this aspect has usually been given a subordinate place.

Attention to human resources would lead to changes in the intersectoral priorities on which resource allocations are based. It would also require a more clear-cut approach to structural and institutional changes. In the short run, there may be conflicts between emphasis on economic growth and the development of human resources, but this need not be the case if comprehensive modernization and development are gradual, cumulative processes spread over long periods. Wherever we may start, before long each must become the means and the condition for the other. In the modernization and development of an economy, progress towards integration of the modern or the organized sector with the presently unorganized segments of economic activity, such as agriculture, household industry, and local trade, has a crucial role.

All underdeveloped countries are under compulsion to seek appropriate paths of growth, modernization, and development. If a long enough view were taken, they would choose strategies that, in their given circumstances, might:
- maximize the use of resources available in relative abundance,
- minimize the use of resources which are relatively scarce,
- raise the productivity of available human resources to the highest levels feasible, and
- reduce social costs to the minimum.

In practice, the choice of modernization and development strategies is influenced by short-term problems and by considerations of quick economic growth. Insufficient thought has been given to the long-term economic and social costs involved.

The economic and social costs relevant to the formation of strategies for modernization and development may be grouped into the following categories:
- Investment costs in terms of domestic and external resources;
- Costs to the economy, in terms of accounting prices, labor, capital, and foreign exchange;
- Opportunity costs related to utilization of human resources and increase in general productivity; and
- Social costs involving sacrifice on account of (a) effect on the environment and (b) impact on human well-being of changes in political and social values and institutions associated with the goals and methods adopted in any given situation.

Social costs might also include costs attributable to national security considerations, which now exert a disproportionate and on the whole negative influence on policies for modernization and development in many countries. Costs arising from the efficiency with which the available human resources are used and some kinds of social costs deserve to be considered separately.

Any detailed consideration of investment costs and costs to the economy would require an item by item examination of the actual investments undertaken in a given country during a specified period. In this paper, at best, attention can be drawn to factors that, especially in the Indian experience over the past two decades, have tended to raise the economic and social costs of development, both in the planning stage and in subsequent performance. Similar problems have arisen in other countries although, it should be stressed, each country and even each phase of development represents a unique situation.

Economic and social costs are intimately related to: the scope of modernization and development in a country at its particular stage of development; the period over which the changes occur; the institutional means that are adopted and their effects on existing institutions; and the means by which modernization and development are financed.

THE SOVIET FIVE-YEAR PLANS

Although Russia had already a fairly developed industrial and commercial economy before the First World War, by comparison with Western countries it was socially and technically a backward country. The period of the earlier Soviet Five-Year Plans still provides the example par excellence of a determined effort to achieve modernization and development within a comparatively short period of barely twelve years or so. This effort raised the issue of economic and social costs more sharply than in any earlier period. The statistics of industrial growth, of changes in agriculture, and developments in education and other sectors are well known. What makes it difficult to relate these changes to the economic and social costs involved is their colossal institutional import, then and in the future, for the entire economy and society of the Soviet Union. The issues here are by no means confined to the evaluation of costs and benefits. They suggest that present concepts for analysis of economic and social costs are less than adequate. The Soviet Five-Year Plans were an expression of fundamental political and social strategy, which excluded every consideration that could point in a different direction. In its economic aspect, the entire development was financed from internal resources. The structure of the Soviet State made it possible for the mass of the people to bear the cost through restraints on consumption and lowering of living standards, especially in the rural areas, which then held 70 percent of the population.

Few countries are likely to have the option to follow the strategy, scale, and tempo of the first Soviet Five-Year Plan. Save for China,

Mongolia, North Korea, North Vietnam, and Cuba, underdeveloped countries are attempting to modernize and develop initially against the background of a market economy and of a high proportion of land, capital, and means of production in private hands. The modern sector in their economies first came into being through economic activities undertaken by foreign private companies, with the support of the colonial powers concerned. These activities included trade in primary agricultural and mineral products and the development of communications, agriculture-based industries, plantations, port towns, and urban commercial and industrial centers. In turn, they stimulated indigenous enterprise in trade and industry and the growth of market economies. In these circumstances, it was natural for most underdeveloped countries in Asia, Africa, and Latin America to accept the principle of a mixed economy and to extend the scope of the public sector. Their state interventions, including fiscal measures, have been addressed mainly to the modern industrial and commercial sector and have barely begun to reach out to the rural sector that holds the larger part of the population.

MODERNIZATION AND DEVELOPMENT IN INDIA

The experience of India may be cited in seeking a strategy for modernization and development that might minimize economic and social costs. India has enjoyed exceptional continuity in her planning process. The main period of intensive construction was from the mid-fifties to the mid-sixties. In the most recent period, there has been a measure of stagnation associated with underutilization of industrial capacities, which has tended to lower the long-range performance of the economy. Briefly, accompanying a population increase of 187 million between 1951 and 1971, national income has grown at nearly 4 percent per annum, industrial output at about 6.5 percent per annum, and agricultural output at slightly less than 3 percent per annum. Of the public outlay on development, about 60 percent has been devoted to industry, transport, and power, about a quarter to agriculture and irrigation, and the balance to education and social services. Of the external assistance received by the economy, 72 percent went to industrial development and 18 percent to economic overheads. Since the mid-fifties, basic and heavy industries and machine-building industries have held the first place in industrial priorities and, in spite of unutilized capacities, during the sixties, the output of basic and capital goods industries increased by some 120 percent.

At the stage now reached, there are some conspicuous lags that indicate the need for radical changes in the scheme of development:

The organization of agriculture and the structure of land ownership have not yet changed. The problem calls for much more than effective implementation of agrarian reform measures already legislated, which is of course essential. A large proportion of the agricultural holdings are small, uneconomic, and unable to generate resources for their further development. Some degree of cooperative management has now become indispensable for the technical development of agriculture, efficient use of the available manpower, and greater integration between the organized and unorganized sectors within the economy.

In deference to the priority given to economic growth and the creation of new industrial capacities, agriculture has received less than its due share of scarce capital and foreign exchange resources. For the same reason, employment generation has fallen behind, and measures calculated to utilize available human resources in productive employment and to raise the general level of productivity have been somewhat neglected. This bears also on the place given to education, adult literacy, and health within the scheme of development.

Efficient short-term management of the economy and maintenance of price stability are essential if the country is to utilize available industrial capacities, expand investment, save at rates approaching its present savings potential, and secure rising levels of exports. Besides fiscal and monetary policies, economic stability is now a reorientation of priorities in the direction of agricultural development and structural changes in agriculture, employment and human resources, and attack on the problems of poverty and low productivity.

If the Indian economy had grown entirely from its own resources without significant support from abroad, it would have been necessary to put the entire reserve of manpower to work. Structural and institutional measures for generating the necessary investment resources and creating appropriate local organizations might then have assumed a certain urgency. The availability of external resources for industrial development and of cheap food imports removed some of the pressure from the immediate requirements of agriculture and manpower utilization. This should be reckoned as an element of cost in the development pattern adopted in India.

Industrialization through import substitution was well under way in the early fifties, even before basic and heavy industries and machine building were accorded the first place in the industrial pattern. The priority given to them fitted well into the picture of natural resources and rising levels of imports. However, the growth of capital goods industries was not accompanied by a parallel effort to transform and reorganize agriculture. Likewise, import substitution led to the production of a wide range of consumer goods for which the main demand came from the urban areas and the better-off sections of the rural population. From the aspect of modernization and development, the provision of basic necessities for the bulk of the population should have come first.

Thus, of two possible strategies for modernization, India chose the one that seemed more feasible at the time. The implicit expectation was that, with substantial growth and industrial capacities achieved within a relatively short period, the country could turn to the solution of the longer-range problems of agriculture, rural employment, and social change. The pattern of industrial and economic development built on these assumptions was more capital-intensive and demanded larger foreign exchange resources than seems, in retrospect, to have been appropriate to the underlying conditions of the country. It is difficult to say if the cost to the economy was excessive. However, it is legitimate to suggest that a different pattern of modernization and development might have economized on scarce resources to a greater extent, utilized internal resources more productively, and probably achieved higher overall rates of growth and domestic savings.

In the scheme of development followed, three sets of factors tended to raise costs: First, large investment projects invariably took longer to execute than was planned; and, almost always, cost estimates were exceeded by large margins. This happened in both the public and the private sectors; but, because of the size and complexity of projects undertaken by the government, the former was affected to a much greater degree. Second, the lengthening of gestation periods in the sectors where the main investments were concentrated caused shortages and imbalance at several points in the economy, such as steel, fertilizers, power, and transport. These imbalances accentuated inflationary trends already inherent in the situation, creating additional costs. Third, in recent years, after a prolonged underutilization of available industrial capacities and other shortfalls within the economy, prices and costs rose still more sharply, with little to counter them except the prospect of a good harvest. Under these circumstances, fundamental changes in the direction of the economy along the lines indicated become even more necessary.

In the discussion so far, we have looked at development, economic costs, and possible changes in strategy from the viewpoint of the economy as a whole. Similar questions arise at the level of the enterprise and around every significant investment directed towards increase in production capacity or application of new techniques. Two examples may suffice.

A number of large public sector enterprises in India have come to be located in regions inhabited by tribal communities, which are among the most backward in the country. The three major steel complexes at Durgapur, Rourkela, and Bhilai and the heavy engineering complex at Ranchi can be cited as examples, but there are also others. In each, the investment project entailed large-scale acquisition of land belonging to tribal groups, payment of compensation to them (generally in money), and opportunities for work during the construction phase, followed by unemployment (for lack of skills) and disruption of the traditional economic and social life of the population in much of the surrounding area. Thus, the heavy engineering industry in Ranchi led to the acquisition of 25 tribal villages involving some 2,200 families and a total population of about 13,000. The social costs of development fell heavily on this population. A regional approach to economic and social development, which took proper account of the human element, prepared the local population (and especially the young) for the change, and assured agricultural settlement for the displaced population, could not only diminish the costs, but also enhance the gains. Even among those who entered new occupations, there was need for social and psychological adaptation. This aspect had received no attention.

To take another example, the introduction of high-yielding varieties of cereals in several parts of India, coming at the end of a long period of development of credit and marketing services, greatly increased the profitability of agriculture for farmers who had the necessary resources in land, irrigation, and capital. For them, even more than before, agriculture became an industry subject to the calculus of costs and profits. Therefore, from the standpoint of the individual, substitution of capital for labor was justified if this increased his returns. In a labor-surplus economy, where there is no protection against loss of work, situations could arise, and have indeed arisen, in which economic and social burdens fall on those least able to sustain them.

CONCLUSIONS

The economic and social costs of modernization and development should be minimized. In each underdeveloped country patterns of modernization must be adapted to its natural endowments, human resource situation, and stage of development. Different concepts of development gained wide acceptance during the past two decades and were later found wanting. To propose concepts that are authentic and within the capacity of each country calls for objective analysis and understanding of all the relevant facts.

Growth of population, improved living conditions and opportunities for small groups already within the modern sector of the economy, and the meager existence of the bulk of the population, have made an effective modernization and development strategy essential for every underdeveloped country. The basic features of such a strategy have to be evolved independently of the possibilities of additional resources becoming available from abroad. With the foundations thus established, such external resources as may be available should then serve to fill essential gaps and accelerate development along the desired lines rather than to deflect from the natural priorities. Modernization and development are dynamic processes. Therefore the initial assumptions and measures proposed for their fulfilment should be reconsidered from time to time in the light of actual developments.

The purpose of modernization and development is to influence the life and attitudes and raise the productivity of the population. This implies the modernization in depth of the entire economy, of industry and agriculture alike, as well as of social institutions. Although an important component, industrialization by itself is not to be equated with modernization. The modern sector, already in existence, is to be viewed as a starting point and a means for tranforming the technical and social basis of the rest of the economy.

The crux of the problem is to achieve a satisfactory blend between the expansion of technical production capacities, which has dominated development planning in the past, and human resources development accompanied by a steady rise in productivity. The major condition is the readiness to bring about the necessary structural and institutional changes. In particular, the structure of agriculture has to be so reorganized that there are no permanently deprived and disadvantaged groups, that efficient production units can be established and that a measure of pooling of land and labor can be realized to assure intensive development and effective use of human resources.

Modernization implies a continuous effort to apply and adapt new technologies, to modify economic and social institutions in keeping with the needs of the people, and to prepare the population of each region and area for prospective changes. In the last analysis, the conditions of change and the capacity to harness potential resources have to be strengthened within each socio-economic group.

DISCUSSION

EMILIO CASTANON (O.A.S.): In Latin America, there is a problem of harmonizing economic and social development, which is uppermost in the minds of many.

ELIHU BERGMAN (United States): What are the political, ideological, and cultural conditions that have influenced economic policy choices? Why is an oil refinery selected rather than a beer factory? Why a crash program of agricultural development rather than a gradual one? Why has Mexico neglected the part of the agricultural sector where most of the rural population is concentrated? Why has a better income distribution been achieved in Korea than in Brazil, though both are authoritarian regimes with planned development programs?

FANNY GINOR (Israel): How can economic and social costs be assessed? There has been a breakdown of the large family into small units. The mental attitude changes so that modernization may proceed. In a sense, the more developed developing states have become achieving societies, which means less peace of mind and more stress. How can this be avoided?
There is a danger of loss of cultural values during modernization. How can one retain at least some of these values and reduce the imitation of foreign cultures?

TARLOK SINGH (UNICEF): The actual decisions taken and the manner of allocating resources in Latin America leave room for greater application of the present thinking on harmonization of social and economic aims.
The issues raised by Dr. Bergman require two kinds of analysis, one broader, the other dealing with specific institutions, personalities, and forces. The outsider can best contribute by seeing the problems within a larger framework including social, political, and cultural components and by aiming to understand the interactions.
Dr. Ginor's point about assessing changes is important. For this both statistical and other indicators are required. Behind development policy lie values and judgments, and it requires a great variety of tools. Some of our difficulties are due to the fact that different ways of looking at development have not been brought together. Questions on development policy have to be asked at intervals, and each new combination of circumstances may yield different answers. We have to be ready to learn from other countries' and our own experience.

ECONOMIC AND SOCIAL COSTS OF MODERNIZATION AND DEVELOPMENT

Wilfred Beckerman

INTRODUCTION

During the last few years there has been a growing concern with the environment in the advanced countries of the world. This has provided further ammunition for those who have questioned the desirability of further economic growth in these countries and even the feasibility or desirability of economic growth in the less developed countries.

Recently the antigrowth movement has become very fashionable, on account of its simultaneous appeal to various forces in society, some of which make strange bedfellows. It appeals to extremist radical youth, who identify the evils of economic growth with the soul-destroying effects of capitalist greed (in spite of the well-known serious pollution in the noncapitalist world). It appeals to the middle classes—at least in advanced countries—who fear that further econom: growth may destroy many of their privileges. It appeals to a few scientists, who find that they can best demonstrate that scientists have a sense of social responsibility by warning society of the evils of further scientific and technological progress. It appeals to certain media of mass communication that find that doomsday prophecies are always good news.

While previously the antigrowth movement was based largely on the alleged soul-destroying effects of the pursuit of "vulgar" material goods, it was given a boost by the recent increase in awareness of the possibility of environmental disruption and damage. Fears of environmental catastrophe or severe declines in the quality of life due to increasing pollution rose to a peak a few years ago and were partly responsible for the UNO 1973 Conference in Stockholm on the Human Environment. Thus, the environmental impact of economic growth has been added to the other costs of economic growth that are widely believed to be inadequately allowed for in growth policies.

THE ECONOMICS OF THE GROWTH PROBLEM

The growth problem is a problem of how resources should be allocated over time. In order to grow, an economy must invest in physical capital, human capital, or in research and development. Resources used for investment cannot be used for current consumption. To the economist, therefore, the costs of growth consist of the current consumption foregone. The optimum growth rate is the one at which the additional sacrifice of current consumption is just worthwhile, given the addition to future output obtained by the extra investment and society's preference as between present and future consumption. Until recently it was fashionable to maintain that because the free market economy failed to devote adequate resources to investment, the free market growth rate would be below the socially optimum growth rate. This view was generally based on the proposition that the investment costs to private enterprise included many elements, notably a risk allowance, that were not true social costs, and thus, in the absence of special government measures, investment would be below the social optimum. Nowadays the mood has swung to the opposite extreme; and it is maintained that, in the absence of special government measures, growth rates will be too high, since growth involves many social costs not adequately allowed for in the calculations of the private enterprise firms.

The earlier view that growth was too slow did at least rest on a coherent analysis of the divergence between the private and social costs of investment. The opposite view, that growth is too fast, does not rest on any such clear theoretical basis. The external costs quoted in support of this view are costs such as environmental pollution, which are not costs of investment, but costs of production in general. This only implies that resources are misallocated at any given point of time, through too much output of pollution-intensive goods and too little environmental protection in general. It has no implications at all for the growth rate, since it does not necessarily imply that the resource misallocation takes the form of inadequate or excessive investment.

It is true that there is too much pollution, and too much congestion of cities, and too many cars on the roads, and so on. These forms of resource misallocation exist in the unregulated economy because of their associated external diseconomies—because, for example, the smoke from a factory chimney damages neighbors and imposes costs on them that are not reflected in the costs of production of the firm that owns the factory. But the misallocation of resources at any moment of time on account of failure to correct for such externalities does not necessarily mean that the growth rate is wrong. To prove that the growth rate is wrong it is necessary to show that the resource misallocation at any point of time takes the form of suboptimal investment.

ECONOMIC GROWTH AND ENVIRONMENTAL POLLUTION

A brief review of the main trends in environmental pollution suffices to demonstrate that in some of the advanced countries the most important forms of environmental pollution have been declining, not increasing. There are quite enough data to refute the assumption that pollution must rise with economic growth to such a level that, even if mankind is not first struck down by starvation or the exhaustion of raw materials, it would be nearly killed off by the polluted environment.

Far from it's being true that the few kinds of pollution that have been measured are increasing, they have been decreasing for some time in Britain, and their rise has been checked in the United States during the last few years. In Britain the dramatic reduction in air pollution is well known: the total smoke produced in Britain fell from 2.3 million tons in 1953 to 0.9 million in 1968. The total quantity of sulfur oxides emitted in the air in Britain has been falling since 1962, and there has been a sharper fall in ground level concentrations of sulfur oxides. Over the decade 1961-71 average smoke concentrations in urban areas in Britain fell by 60 percent and SO_2 (sulfur dioxide) concentrations fell by 30 percent, despite increasing population and industrial output.

There has also been a fall in the pollution of rivers in Britain, though less dramatic than that of air pollution. But this is merely because, on account of other pressing needs in the public sector, such as housing, schools, roads and hospitals, the necessary authorizations for the very heavy expenditures involved in reducing water pollution have only been granted during the latter part of the 1960s.

The reduction in pollution in other countries, particularly air pollution, has not been so dramatic, but this is not because Britain is favored by some exceptional technical circumstances which enable this country alone to achieve such great reductions in pollution. It is simply because antipollution legislation has been introduced in the other countries later than in the United Kingdom. Claims that all measured pollution has been rising are simply factually untrue, and flagrantly so since the improvement in air pollution in Britain has been widely known for many years.

Even in the United States, where tough antipollution legislation has only been introduced during the last few years, there was some reduction in measured pollution in the 1950s and 1960s as a result of various autonomous changes associated more with economic growth than with legislation. For example, smoke concentrations in urban areas have declined slightly between 1957 and 1970, largely on account of the dispersion of industrial plants and the movement of population out of cities. But already there has also been a decline in carbon monoxide emissions, which is partly due to the installation of antipollution devices in new automobiles since 1968. Much greater reductions in this and other forms of pollution from all sources will take place over this decade as a result of the policies now being introduced in the United States and in many other countries. A general move during the last few years in Britain and the United States to introduce much tougher antipollution policies means that the favorable trends described above may be accentuated rather than reversed in future. Most other major industrial nations have also introduced antipollution policies during the last few years, and in Japan, Sweden, and Germany considerable amounts are to be spent on pollution abatement. A Japanese ten-year plan to reduce pollution is expected to cost about 3,500 million pounds sterling over the ten-year period from 1971.

Sweden set up a government agency to tackle pollution in 1967. Germany is compelling industry to pay for cleaning up its pollution, the legal penalties for breaches of the regulations being ten years in prison or very heavy fines in some cases!

The examples of these states provide a second reason to reject predictions that economic growth must eventually be halted on account of the inevitable increase in pollution. Even had it been true that all pollutants had been increasing in the past, this could not provide the basis for any sweeping predictions about the future, since the main industrial countries have only relatively recently begun to adopt tough antipollution policies.

OTHER ELEMENTS IN THE QUALITY OF LIFE

One of the most important of elements in the quality of life is health, which has steadily improved over the decades, quite apart from any health benefits obtained from the reduction in pollution. The general health improvement is measured by a rise in the health expenditure component of the much-despised GNP. There have been enormous reductions in the health risks from many of the diseases that still plagued society earlier in this century. Deaths from respiratory tuberculosis were still running at about 25,000 per annum in England and Wales as recently as the 1930s, but they have now been reduced to about 1,000 per annum. In the United States, deaths from tuberculosis declined over the same period from a rate of over 50 per 100,000 population to about 3 per 100,000. In England and the United States there are now virtually no deaths from diptheria. The elimination of acute anxiety and strain from hundreds of thousands of families as a result of the virtual eradication of these and other potential killer diseases reflects an incalculable increase in their welfare.

Other components of welfare include the output of public capital, such as schools, hospitals, roads, libraries, parks, and other public buildings or installations. Unlike private capital or the capital equipment of nationalized industries, the output of these forms of the community's capital stock is not included in GNP but it has certainly been increasing.

The same applies to numerous leisure activities, not to mention housewives' services. Perhaps the most important elements of welfare not reflected by GNP are the conditions of work and the degree of leisure enjoyed by the working population. The sort of work that men do and their attitudes toward their work are among the chief components of human welfare. The problem is to find quantitative indicators of working conditions. One obvious indicator in industrializ countries is the number of factory accidents. And in spite of a large increase in the industrial work force in Britain during this century, the number of fatal industrial accidents has fallen steadily to an alltime low. It is now, at about 800 per annum, half of what it was 20 years ago and only one sixth of what it was at the beginning of the century. In the United States, although no further improvement occurred during the last decade, the previous years had witnessed a similar steady fall in the number of fatal work accidents.

Furthermore, the hours of work have decreased sharply in the course of the century. Other things being equal, this would reduce GNP while increasing welfare, for in advanced countries, greater leisure time is one of the most important components of welfare.

There are still pockets of poverty and squalor in the advanced countries and widespread poverty in the rest of the world. It is difficult to see how further progress to reduce this poverty will reduce the importance attached to the quality of life. Indeed, it is much more likely that the greatly increased concern with the quality of life in the advanced countries is the direct result of greater economic prosperity and hence a decline in acquisitiveness and obsession with material goods.

A MEASURABLE CONCEPT OF ECONOMIC WELFARE

Increasing concern during the last few years with the alleged excessive social costs of economic growth caused a revival of interest in the degree to which the conventional concepts of GNP used in most countries could be adjusted, so that changes in GNP over time would more closely reflect changes in welfare. Various estimates have been made during the last few years of the value that could be placed on the rise in leisure and on the increase in some social costs of growth, such as urban congestion. Comprehensive estimates of a welfare-oriented measure of national product were prepared by William Nordhaus and James Tobin, who set out to adjust the conventional GNP measure for both the favorable items now excluded (such as leisure, or nonmarketed services) and the unfavorable excluded items, such as the costs of urbanization. They also took account of some items that are included in GNP but, in their opinion, ought not to be included in any measure of welfare. These comprised expenditures on some government purchases, such as police services, sanitation services, road maintenance, and national defence.

Their estimates show that the rate of growth of what they call "Measurable Economic Welfare" (MEW) over the period 1929 to 1965 was slower than the growth of net national product (NNP) as conventionally measured. But this does not prove that all the "bads" omitted from GNP have now been shown to be very important. Indeed, the opposite conclusion emerges: The reason that the growth rate of MEW has been slower than the growth rate of NNP is that the value of the desirable leisure and nonmarket activities excluded from conventional GNP is so high that, if they are brought into the picture, the starting level of MEW (in 1929) is very much higher than the starting level of the conventional NNP. As a result, although in absolute terms the "goods" added to NNP to derive MEW have been rising much more than the "bads" that have to be subtracted, the proportionate rise in the total is smaller after both adjustments have been made. This can best be seen from Table 8.

It must be conceded that these estimates, particularly of the rise in leisure, should be treated with reserve. They are pioneering efforts in a virtually uncharted field.

One of the qualifications to the Nordhaus and Tobin estimates arises from their subtraction of the so-called "regrettable necessities" from the conventional net national product. This is linked to the extent to which the rise in output included in conventional GNP measures is offset by an increase in wants or needs (perhaps artificially stimulated) and so cannot reflect a genuine net rise in welfare. This has been a major issue in the debate about the desirability of growth. In the advanced countries, it is often alleged that consumers are caught in an absurd rat race to supply artificially induced desires; and in the developing countries it is often argued that they fall victims to the externally induced "revolution of rising expectations." This argument is dealt with separately in the next section.

TABLE 8

Changes in Adjustments to Net National Product to
Derive Measure of Economic Welfare—United
States, 1929-65
(billions of U.S. dollars at constant 1958 prices)

	1929	1965	Absolute Change	Proportionate Change (percer
Conventional net national product (NNP)	183.6	563.1	+379.5	+206
Leisure plus nonmarket activities and so on	454.9	1001.2	+546.4	+119
"Regrettable necessities" plus "disamenities," and so on	-94.9	-323.2	-228.3	+240
Total above adjustments	+360.0	+678.0	+318.0	+88
Adjusted measure of economic welfare	543.6	1241.1	697.5	+128

NEEDS, SATISFACTIONS AND WELFARE

Nordhaus and Tobin deduct from the conventional GNP an estimate for what they call "regrettable necessities," of which a major item is defense. They argue that ". . . we see no direct effect of defence expenditures on household economic welfare. No reasonable country (or household) buys 'national defence' for its own sake. If there were no war or risk of war, there would be no need for defence expenditure and no one would be the worse without them."

But the same sort of reasoning applies to any other component of GNP. Nobody would want hospital accident wards, or even home first aid kits, for their own sake! They are required to meet the possibility of accidents. Automobile seat belts are required, not for their own sake, but to prevent injury in accidents. It is not possible to draw logical distinctions of the Nordhaus/Tobin kind between the purposes served by various goods. If they are wanted, they are wanted and that is the end of the matter. If there were no winters, there would be no need for winter woolens or heating expenditures; if one never had toothache there would be no need to visit the dentist. For very poor people, even food, after all, is merely required in order to offset the pain of otherwise being hungry and dying of starvation. Surely it cannot be argued that, in such cases, the food should not be included just because it is a regrettable necessity and that we should include in GNP only the more frivolous inessentials. If so, this runs counter to another popular view, to the effect that much of the growth of GNP as measured is misleading because it includes many items that are not really necessary, for example, the artificially advertising-stimulated needs. In other words nothing should be included in GNP, for either (a) it is not really necessary, and so we would not include it since this would give the false impression that the increase in its consumption is making a genuine contribution to welfare, when it is really merely offsetting an imaginary or artificial need, or (b) it is really necessary, and so is not consumed because it gives pleasure and hence adds to our welfare but is just a regrettable necessity.

It is now generally accepted that no useful distinction can be made between the two alternative ways of increasing utility, namely reducing needs or increasing the extent to which they are satisfied.

If I have a "need" to listen to music but do not have the time or the money to go to as many concerts as I would like, I will be unable to satisfy fully my need for music listening. But I would not accept that on account of this gap between my needs and their satisfactions, I am worse off than if I did not have this need. I would maintain that, though I cannot completely satisfy it, as a result of this particular need I lead a fuller and richer life.

Of course, a person who feels a need to listen to music and who is then completely deprived of opportunities to do so might suffer greatly. This is a risk that has to be accepted as part of living. To reduce this risk by reducing man's needs is to avoid some of the risks of life by living a little less. The greater a person's education and sensitivity, the greater his capacity for the "higher" pleasures and therefore for a richer life; yet more education and sensitivity bring with them more desires, and a corresponding lesser likelihood of their satisfaction. Instruction and emancipation in one way favor happiness, and in another militate against it. To increase a person's chances of happiness, in the sense of fullness of life, is eo ipso to decrease his chances of happiness, in the sense of satisfaction of desire.* As it says in the Bible, "For in wisdom is much vexation, and the more a man knows, the more he has to suffer."† But it may be argued that an individual feels positively happier when he experiences an increase in desires that he cannot fully satisfy. Bertrand Russell asserted that "to be without some of the things you want is

---

*Anthony Kenny, "Happiness," Proceedings of the meeting of the Aristotelian Society, 28 February 1972, p. 102.
†Eccles. 1:18.

an indispensable part of happiness," a proposition many people might well accept.

It is necessary to distinguish between the objective question of to what extent people feel happier when they have more needs and the subjective question of how one defines good or bad in relation to changes in peoples' needs. Even if we were to agree that a rise in needs made people unhappier, somebody can still say that people are better off and that welfare has risen, given his particular concept of what constitutes human welfare.

What constitutes being better off is a value judgment that can take the form of believing that what distinguishes man from other forms of life is precisely the multiplicity of his needs, so that, without excluding the right to pass moral judgments on these needs, the more needs man has the better he is a man. The irony of the current attack on the way that the capitalist system creates additional needs is that part of Marx's original attack on the soul-destroying nature of capitalism was that capitalism destroyed man's basic needs! Nowadays, the trendy doctrine amongst extreme critics of economic growth is that growth does not add to welfare since it is merely the response to an increase in needs! In other words, whether needs rise or fall, economic development makes man worse off!

It is often argued that whether an increase in needs implies more or less welfare depends on whether the needs are artificially induced. One may approve of some needs and disapprove of others. One may believe that an increased need to worship God or listen to music is morally good, or that it makes people happier, but that an increased need for drugs or drink or women is morally bad, or makes people unhappy. But it is difficult to see how the artificiality of the need in question determines whether it is classified as good or bad. I was certainly not born with my need to listen to music.

Even were it possible to draw a dividing line between artificial and natural needs, what is so moral about natural needs and so immoral about artificial needs? Would some persons' artificially induced need to listen to music or to acquire knowledge be less desirable a component of welfare than some other persons' natural instinct to rape all the women in the world? The rival views on this subject are simply rival definitions of good and bad.

CONCLUSIONS: ECONOMIC GROWTH AND EQUALITY

There is little substance in the view that the alleged social costs of economic growth bring into question the desirability of economic growth as an objective of policy in the advanced countries, let alone in the developing countries where the immediate need for increased economic output is glaringly obvious. The argument is based on the following points:

First, many alleged costs of economic growth, such as excessive pollution of the environment or inadequate attention to the public sector, have really nothing to do with the costs of growth. The growth issue is a problem of the allocation of resources over time, not of the allocation of resources at any moment of time (except insofar as the optimum growth rate requires the optimum allocation of resources to investment at any moment of time). Pollution and the like are instances of misallocation of resources at any moment of time, and there is no reason to believe that slower rates of growth would help eliminate this. Indeed, the reverse is likely. For it is easier to improve resource allocation in a growing economy than in a stagnant one. A change in resource allocation invariably means a change in income distribution. It is hence easier to carry out the former if the inevitable change in income distribution can also be carried out in the context of a growing economy, since this makes possible the reduction of the relative shares of some members of the society without the reduction of their absolute levels of income.

Second, the most important ingredients in the quality of life in advanced countries—such as the environment, health conditions, leisure, and working conditions—show a dramatic improvement during the last few decades.

Third, it is argued that one of the popular criticisms of economic growth—namely that increased consumption is merely the response to rising needs (many of them artificially induced)—is based on an oversimplification of the philosophical issues involved.

If the above arguments are correct, it may be asked why the concern with the alleged harmful effects of economic growth has reached such proportions. There seem to be two main reasons for this. The first is that, as society becomes richer and so increasingly satisfies its basic and more urgent needs, it is natural that it should attach more importance to other aspects of total welfare. And clearly some of these, such as a clean environment, are not automatically protected by the unaided workings of a free market mechanism and require appropriate government policies.

But this hardly explains the pressures to reduce the rate of economic growth, which could only have acquired their substantial following by reflecting a genuine fear among influential groups in society that further economic growth would reduce their welfare. And there are obvious reasons why certain groups in society, or certain countries in the international society of nations, should fear that they will lose from further economic growth. These fears may be partly unfounded, but there is enough truth in them to explain their presence and impact.

The middle classes in most advanced countries will lose certain privileges as a result of economic growth. The loss of domestic servants is one of the earliest examples, but in the past two decades this has been followed by many others, such as the increasing congestion of the roads with the cars of the poor, or the difficulty of finding holiday resorts in interesting but accessible places that are not swamped by millions of people on cheap lightning package tours.

At the international level it is also not difficult to imagine the sort of motives and fears subconsciously promoting the view that it would be better for the developed states if economic growth were not given a high priority in the rest of the world. The economic growth of the developing countries may help by providing greater markets but can be a nuisance in other ways. Such countries will compete with some domestic industries (even though this will benefit domestic consumers); they will no longer provide cheap sources of labor and raw materials; they will have a voice of their own in matters of foreign policy; they will compete for what is often believed to be a limited supply of world resources; and so on. Hence there is fertile ground for the doctrine that the poor countries should not be encouraged to believe that they too can aspire to the same levels of prosperity that the richer countries have already attained. They are expected to give less priority to economic growth in order to give more to the preservation of the environment or of old social customs and traditions and to cherish the simple way of life, in which people could, on the average, expect to live to the age of about thirty provided they didn't die in childhood from malaria, malnutrition, and a host of other diseases associated with poverty.

Of course it is bad luck for the developing countries that they are advised to abandon the growth objective just about 1970 when some states had achieved affluence; but they need not feel cheated or envious since another useful argument can be brought to play here, namely that the richer countries are not really happier on account of their affluence, since it is all an illusion created by the consumer society.

This is all nonsense, and dangerous nonsense at that. For the debate about the desirability of growth diverts attention from what are still serious economic problems. In the rich countries these include how to use the growth that they should still experience and also how to maintain economic growth, since growth is a necessary condition for the solution of the advanced countries' problem of improving the distribution of income. In the poorer countries getting the growth is still the primary problem. The more economic growth they succeed in obtaining without an excessive sacrifice of current consumption, the more the world's income distribution will also be improved.

DISCUSSION

URI MARINOV (Israel): There is probably more carbon monoxide in industry than in the streets; but the carbon monoxide in industry affects only the workers, while the carbon monoxide in the streets affects children and old people too.

The fact is that we have marine pollution we did not have before. We have people dying of toxic chemicals, which they never died of before. Maybe they died from other causes, but this does not justify their dying of chemicals found in their food.

We should not oppose environment to development. But Professor Beckerman's reasoning is damaging the cause of protecting the environment. In many states people still talk about growth at all costs and "environment" is a dirty word. If we say: "Let us worry about growth, not about the environment. The past was much worse than the present," we will not get the laws and investments required to protect the environment. For this, one needs pressure of public opinion.

In Israel we have an irreversible change in the quality of our water. Anyway, to clean this water would require very large resources. Perhaps air pollution and noise pollution can be improved, but once we make an irreversible change nothing can be done about it. So only a delicate balance, taking into consideration both growth and the environment, can bring us the way of life we want.

PAUL STREETEN (Great Britain): One must have value judgments in economics. That we have to spend money on defense in a world with tensions and conflicts is bad; that we spend money on food to keep people alive in starving countries is good.

My second point is that if there is even a small chance of a disaster resulting from our present productive system or activities, we must take measures now to prevent this chance.

ARTHUR EISENBERG (Israel): Professor Beckerman has put problems of growth under what he calls "misapplication of resources." Thalidomide was such a misapplication, and, though it has taken us 400 years to discover this, tobacco may be another. But the real problem is that we have come to regard problems of pure quality as secondary to achievement of quantities. This is a very real danger.

I think the argument should be between growth and considered growth, rather than between growth and no growth. There should be limits to new "needs." Travelling at 4,000 miles an hour may not be better than travelling at 2,000 miles an hour.

The cleaning up of air, rivers, and other pollution Professor Beckerman mentioned may well have been due to pressures from environment faddists, even if they may overstate their case.

ELIHU BERGMAN (United States): In the United States there was an environmental movement demanding zero population growth (Z.P.G.). There were some 15,000 members of this movement, mainly on college campuses, with a few lay chapters in cities. This group was involved in an environment conference in Chicago in 1970, where some black participants criticized it for being more concerned with preserving the blue whale or the bald eagle than about eradicating rats in the ghettoes. In general, the environmental issue has become a major issue in the United States and sometimes affects political elections and actions. The environmental movement delayed construction of the Alaska oil pipeline for two years, increasing U.S. dependence on Middle East oil. Yet there is no real conflict between growth and a healthy environment.

FANNY GINOR (Israel): Is there not a substantial difference between developed and developing countries as regards environmental problems? And does modernization disrupt the social fabric in developing states?

WILFRED BECKERMAN (Great Britain): I do not take the view that we should not worry about the environment, the environment will look after itself. Far from it. We should introduce the right policies to look after the environment, but this has nothing to do with growth.

Once they were about to spend 20 million pounds sterling on a vast scheme to reduce pollution along a nice beach near Southampton. When we asked the Medical Officer of Health how much damage the sewage in the water actually did, we were told it did no damage at all. People still swam in the water and nobody was seriously ill. He agreed that if we gave him 20 million pounds sterling he would spend it on a new maternity home, better geriatric treatment, and so forth, not on the water pollution. Sewage came nowhere on his list. So environment extremists can cause misallocation of resources, even from the health viewpoint.

Resources should not be treated as something static. They are dynamic, they can be changed by human skill and endeavor. In Israel, the initial resources proved to be negligible in comparison with what the country's resources later turned out to be. And new resources are constantly being developed. I have seen estimates that in the top mile of the earth's crust there are enough minerals to last us 100 million years. Aluminum was scarce; new technologies have made it cheap and plentiful. As recently as 1949 the Pailey Report estimated that there was only a 15-year supply left of a particular mineral. Now, 20 years later, we have a 30-year supply of it left. There have been plenty of such dire predictions about resources. None have materialized. So I am not really worried about resources.

There are complaints about DDT and carbon monoxide from environmentalists. In Ceylon they banned DDT under such pressures, and the death rate from malaria leapt up again. In Oxford students have been chalking slogans about carbon monoxide with cigarettes hanging from their mouths. The carbon monoxide concentration in the lungs of anyone smoking a cigarette is 200 parts per million, or 10 times what it is in the lungs of a policeman on traffic duty in the center of Oxford Circus in London. Stopping smoking would do more for health than stopping carbon monoxide emissions from traffic.

I want to ask the gentleman who wanted "considered growth": "How much slower do you want the growth rate to be?" If 5 percent per annum is too fast, then should it be 4 percent or 3 percent or 2 percent? Why not zero, after all? One cannot say that growth is too fast or too slow unless one can define optimum growth. In the economic theory I was describing there are clear criteria for an optimum growth rate.

I agree with Professor Streeten about the need for value judgments—not only about food and defense expenditures, but also about what needs have to be satisfied one way rather than another way, or what constitutes being human. The simple argument of "needs versus satisfactions" confuses the issue, because it does not make it clear that what is involved are value judgments.

There is a nonzero possibility of all sorts of catastrophes happening, not only in the distant future but today. I can walk out of here and be run over by a bus. There may be a pollution catastrophe. But one has to weigh these possibilities against the cost involved in avoiding them. If the cost means stopping growth, it may well be excessive in terms of the probabilities of a catastrophe in the distant future.

There is a difference between the attitudes of developing and developed countries to environmental problems. The relative cost of the environment and the relative weight that should be attached to environment are lower in developing states, and these should attach less weight to this issue in their considerations than developed countries. There is no case for uniform pollution standards for all countries.

**FINANCIAL INCENTIVES TO
REDUCE FERTILITY**
Stephen Enke

BACKGROUND

Low-income and less developed countries (LDCs), as compared with the more developed countries, are notable for their higher fertility rates. The LDCs have crude birth rates of around 35 to 45 where the more developed countries (MDCs) have crude birth rates of around 20 to 30 per 1000 a year. Among the nations, high fertility and low income are associated, each being both a cause and an effect of the other. Presumably, given enough investment and time, higher incomes may lead to reduced fertility, in part because of reductions in mortality rates. Some demographers believe, however, that it is quicker and cheaper to reduce fertility rates as a means of raising per capita incomes. Several LDC governments in Asia have accordingly introduced publicly supported family planning programs, which supply contraceptive information and devices; and a few also offer incentives to women who accept IUDs and to men who volunteer for vasectomies. Because of such programs an increasing proportion of women of fertile age are practicing birth control—about 15 percent in India and perhaps 30 percent in South Korea. However, if LDC population growth rates are to fall from about three percent to about one percent, approximately 50 percent of women of every age from 15 to 45 who are fecund and exposed should be practicing effective birth control. It is improbable that this will occur during the next decade or so unless family planning programs use financial incentives.

WHY REDUCING FERTILITY IS IMPORTANT
FOR DEVELOPMENT

There can be controversy over what constitutes development. Some LDC governments are gravely concerned about reducing unemployment and income inequalities; others are concerned with urban overpopulation. All these interact with high fertility, for it slows increases in per capita income over time, makes labor cheaper relative to capital, and provides urban overpopulation from natural increase.

In many respects, increasing income and output per head can be considered a proxy for economic development. Development is certainly not more people living in the same degree of misery. Moreover, if each individual is producing and receiving more, there is more real income to be redistributed by government.

There are three conditions in which population can affect economic well-being. First, there is <u>overpopulation</u> which means too little capital or land (natural resources) per person: This means low output per worker, which is the situation in the Nile Valley, the Ganges Valley, and Java. Second, there is rapid population growth, with populations doubling every 25 years or so. Since improvements in technology and investment of capital can barely stay ahead of population, output and income per head rise very slowly: this is the situation in most Latin American countries, where death rates have fallen dramatically but birth rates have not. Finally, there is high fertility which makes for high child dependency rates, reduced savings and investment, and less output and income per capita: it is characteristic of almost all countries of the Third World.

In some situations, because of extreme poverty and high death rates, rapid population growth does not result from high fertility. In others, because both birth and death rates are low, there is little population growth. Economic well-being is greater in the latter, not only because capital and technology can keep ahead of population, but because dependency rates are lower.

Paradoxically, high fertility inhibits higher real incomes per capita, even though there is no population pressure and the country includes large undeveloped areas. It may seem that these empty lands call for high birth rates to develop them. However, it takes capital rather than babies to develop empty lands, and high birth rates reduce savings rates. That certain areas remain empty ordinarily means that existing savings are insufficient to make productive investments in the developed areas. If a larger labor force did in time migrate into formerly empty lands because of high fertility rates, it would be with very little capital. The development of these lands would then be more an indication of population pressure than of anything else.

There are some unfortunate areas of the world that combine extreme population pressure, rapid population growth, and high fertility. It is almost impossible for them to achieve improvements in real per capita output and income exceeding two percent or so a year. They may have GNP increases of five percent a year or so, due partly to the larger labor force that accompanies larger populations, but it is output and income per capita that count in the last analysis. For all LDCs there is no way to rapid economic development, as here defined, except through reducing fertility rates by almost a half.

DEPENDENCY RATES AND SAVINGS RATES

A population with high fertility rates will have an abnormally large proportion of children in its midst. Very roughly indeed, a crude birth rate of 45 per 1000 a year may mean that 40 percent of the population are under 15 years of age. A crude birth rate of from 20 to 25 may mean that only 20 percent of the population are under 15 years old.

Children may be wanted by their parents, they may be valued as a sort of parents' "consumer good," but they ordinarily consume rather than produce. Their consumption may be small while still breast fed and running naked, but within a few years they use resources more obviously for food, clothing, and shelter. In LDCs that are attempting to educate most youngsters there will be significant costs for school teachers, school rooms, and school materials. In even more advanced LDCs, where a reasonable fraction of deliveries are in hospitals, there are obvious medical costs. As regards "production," children in rural areas can be helpful, watching domestic animals or chasing away others that eat crops, but on the whole they remain economic parasites until they are 15 or so.

Private and public saving is low in a country that has high fertility and hence high child dependency rates. Lower saving means lower investment. Less investment per capita means less output and hence income per capita.

FERTILITY AND GNP PER CAPITA

Absolute GNP growth over several decades is extraordinarily intensive to changes in fertility rates. Reduced fertility eventually results in a smaller-than-otherwise increase in labor force, and this is "bad" in that it means a smaller-than-otherwise increase in GNP. However, for a given sized population, reduced fertility means a larger-than-otherwise increase in investment and capital stock: this is "good" because a larger-than-otherwise increase in GNP results. Ordinarily these two effects tend to cancel each other. The result is about the same growth in GNP being distributed among a slower-growing population.

Special advantages accrue while fertility is falling. This is because fewer children for a while mean less consumption and more saving. Concurrently, there is no impact on labor force, though an unaffected GNP is being shared by fewer people.

Other benefits result. Women with fewer children can spend more time in employment outside the home. A country with higher real income per family is likely to have more educated people who produce more and procreate less.

Under high fertility, 40 percent of the population or more will be children, and children are largely consumers rather than producers. Therefore, a young age distribution means less output per head.

GNP VERSUS POPULATION

Governments desiring to raise per capita output and income rapidly normally try to accelerate GNP growth through massive investments in industry and agriculture. Few of them in the past decade attempted to retard population growth. Yet population logically is as much a variable in the situation as GNP. Output per head is only a ratio, GNP divided by population, and governments should feel as free to influence the denominator as the numerator. It is the quotient that matters most.

Quite simple statistical comparisons are possible:

Consider 1000 babies, representative in the distribution of sex and abilities, that might be born or prevented. What would it cost to give these marginal 1000 babies a typical per capita income through life? What would it cost to prevent their being born? In all countries, MDCs more than LDCs, it costs many times more to support extra population than to prevent it.

If an LDC has a typical per capita income of $200 a year and the average rate of return on new investments is 20 percent, it will take an investment of $1,000,000 to provide this extra income for 1000 extra or marginal people. To prevent 1000 births requires 5000 acceptor-years of effective contraceptive use if typical fertility rates are .2 (that is, a woman has a child every five years on an average). The out-of-pocket costs of 5000 acceptor-years depend upon whether contraception is achieved through pills, condoms, IUDs, or sterilization, but probably average not over $2. The cost comparison is then $1,000,000 as against $10,000, a ratio of 100 to 1, in favor of preventing rather than supporting extra population.

This result obviously depends upon the rate of return assumed on capital, the rate of fertility assumed for women, and the cost assumed per acceptor-year. If each of these assumptions was changed by a factor of two, against the argument, the superiority ratio would still be 12.5 to 1. However, capital rates of return may really be 15 percent rather than 20 percent, and the UNFPA estimates out-of-pocket contraception costs at 65 cents per couple a year.

Extra children produce extra GNP because they become extra labor force. On the other hand, they also become extra consumers. The rest of the LDC population, considering these 1000 marginal children, must consider whether they will add more to output or add more to consumption. In countries where overpopulation exists already, the marginal product of extra workers is less than the average product of all workers. However, within a family, the marginal consumption of an extra member tends to be the same as average consumption.

OFFICIAL PROGRAMS TO REDUCE FERTILITY

Governments of LDCs are becoming ever more aware of how high fertility and rapid population growth threaten their social and economic aspirations. Some of them now have official family planning programs. In most cases these coexist with private programs. All official programs emphasize clinics, where women and sometimes men can be advised about contraceptive use, where a woman can have an IUD inserted, where a man can have a vasectomy, and where wife or husband can obtain pills, condoms, or other devices.

Most of these programs have grown quite satisfactorily during their early years. In most LDCs many women, especially older women who have already many children, want to prevent additional pregnancies. There are enough of these women in the urban areas to fill the increasing number of clinics for a while. Although statistics are unreliable, in many LDCs having official family planning programs, the acceptance rate among women aged 15 to 45 seems to be at least 5 percent. In South Korea and Taiwan this rate may be as high as 30 percent. In India it is around 15 percent perhaps. But acceptance rates of up to 50 percent are needed.

Some experts feel that a great unsatisfied demand for contraceptive devices exists in LDCs, especially in the rural areas, and all that is required is to establish more clinics, train more doctors and paramedics, and distribute more contraceptives through these outlets. Others hold that the problem is not lack of contraceptive supply but lack of contraceptive demand, that only a small fraction of relatively emancipated women wish to have fewer children, and that the real need is for changes in demand.

Like most controversies, there is a lot of truth on both sides, and all the evidence is not yet available. However, in several LDCs with programs acceptance rates seem to have reached a plateau of around 15 percent. Additional clinics do not seem to service more accepters so much as they occasion higher costs per accepter.

Some experts hope that new contraceptive technologies, such as the once-a-month prostaglans pill for women, will increase the number of accepters, or at least reduce pregnancies. Nevertheless, if it is motivation that is lacking among most women, a simpler-to-take contraceptive will make little difference. If distribution is the problem, clinics being too few and far between, a better pill will accomplish little.

THE CAUSES OF FAILURES IN FERTILITY REDUCTION

Why has fertility, by and large, not been reduced in the less developed world, especially in the poorest countries?

First, because most statesmen and administrators think the results of fertility reduction are too far in the future and prefer to concentrate on programs having a high impact over the next three to five years.

Second, because in states where there are rival religions, rival languages, or rival ethnic groups family planning in national programs always seems to be viewed by each group as a device aimed against the others.

Third, because most family planning programs are run by the ministry of health and public health doctors, on a clinic basis. Not only are there far too few doctors and clinics in less developed countries, but these obviously concentrate on treating the sick and give little time to birth control, sometimes even using funds allocated for family planning for their other urgent medical needs. One cannot expect clinic doctors and nurses not to treat sick people, but to spend time discussing birth control with healthy women, especially when there are many sick and few clinics. Therefore, no family planning program will ever succeed if medical doctors are in charge of it. There must be some clinics and doctors, but also the commercial distribution of condoms and pills must be subsidized. It is much easier to go to a nearby store than to a faraway clinic crowded with sick people.

Thus our supply side is not properly organized, but, even if it were, only some 20 percent to 25 percent of eligible women would practice contraception. If you want to get 50 percent of women aged 15 to 45 doing this, you must create demand either by advertising, propaganda, and education or by some kind of financial incentive.

FINANCIAL INCENTIVES TO REDUCE FERTILITY

Many LDC circumstances are pronatalist. Lack of government old-age insurance may erroneously appear to make extra children necessary. Free schooling, when it exists, reduces the cost of children to their parents. The entire culture may glorify fertility. The mother of the young bride may await the first grandchild with impatience. Offsetting all these pressures towards childbirth is difficult indeed.

One possible solution that often arouses considerable revulsion is to pay people bonuses for certain acts leading to reduced fertility. The bonus may be for an IUD insertion or a vasectomy, or for referring a person to a clinic for an IUD or sterilization. Or bonuses might even be paid to women for remaining nonpregnant over prolonged periods of time.

A bonus can be viewed as a bribe or as compensation. Couples who practice contraception do pay a social or psychological price. The man and wife may have to visit a distant clinic and wait in line. IUD insertions and vasectomies performed by strangers are not pleasurable. Relatives may scorn at a couple's modest procreativity. Parents may worry needlessly about not having old age insurance through children. Perhaps a bonus for remaining nonpregnant is more compensation than bribe.

A financial bonus system to encourage family planning is not simple to design. It must not be extravagant, giving bonuses to couples who would probably not have children anyway. It must be cheatproof, for otherwise it may be destroyed by ridicule.

Theoretically, there is a positively inclined accepter supply curve. Some women or men would be prepared to use contraceptives without a bonus, more with some bonus, and others would do so only for a very considerable bonus. If this supply of accepters is not very elastic, the marginal costs of a bonus system will rise very rapidly as additional accepters are gained, and some of the intramarginal accepters will obtain a considerable unearned surplus.

To reduce unnecessary bonus payments, a government program will have to discriminate. Older men and women, although still fecund, are less likely to want children or be able to have them: they should be given less for accepting, say, an IUD or sterilization. Unmarried women in some cultures suffer a stigma if they become pregnant; they too should be given a smaller bonus for remaining nonpregnant.

Some people will always try to "game" a government program, especially if money is involved. If bonuses for IUD insertions are too high, women may have them removed soon after insertion and then qualify for another bonus. Hence sterilization, male or female, is often stressed by programs that offer bonuses. Cheatproofing a bonus system usually depends upon registration procedures and record keeping. In LDCs this is not usually simple.

If granting money bonuses is too crass, other inducements can be tried. Script might be given to women who remain nonpregnant, with various consumer products being available at different script prices. At some Indian vasectomy festivals a sari and a bucket were given in addition to money. Old age bonds have been suggested, but most simple people fear inflation and mistrust their governments. Where schools are crowded, families might be guaranteed space for only one son, threatening the education of extra children.

WHAT SIZED BONUSES?

There are various ways of estimating the maximum money bonus that a government, as representative of all the people in a country, might be able to pay couples for preventing births.

In a typical LDC with a per capita income of around $200 a year, the maximum value of preventing a birth permanently may be around $500, this being the total worth to everyone (including the parents). In this case the maximum worth of a vasectomy for a man of around age 35 may approximate $1000. The maximum value of a woman in her 20s not having a baby for five years may be as high as $100 a year.

However, these are not the sums that can be offered as bonuses, for two reasons. More than half the net cost that marginal births occasion falls upon the immediate family and parents: it makes no sense to compensate them for saving themselves a net burden. Moreover, the government does not wish to pay as bonus the entire value to everyone (excluding the parents) of a couple's not having children. Thus the bonus that can be paid is at most about one quarter of the sums cited above. Even so, however, these reduced amounts are many times greater than the bonuses paid in the few countries that give them.

BONUSES FOR REMAINING NONPREGNANT

The most promising bonus-for-contraception scheme, in theory, is one that pays women of fecund age a sliding bonus for remaining nonpregnant.

Under this system a woman would register at a clinic, receiving a very small fee for her inconvenience. Subsequently, every six months, she would visit the same clinic for a superficial check of pregnancy by a paramedic, requiring a minute and no laboratory costs. If found nonpregnant, she would receive a cash payment on the spot of around $15. At successive six months visits, if she remains nonpregnant, this sum would be increased to around $25. The twice-a-year fee would be slightly less for older women and perhaps slightly more for women of around 20. If age records are lacking, age can be settled by fiat. A woman who missed a visit would revert to the lower fee scale on her second set of visits. Cheating, through registering at several clinics, could be substantially lessened by location of a tatoo that ordinarily does not show.

One great advantage of such a system is that it rewards performance—remaining nonpregnant. The payment of the fees also serves to finance a private market for contraceptives. Without such a market demand the growth of commercial delivery systems will be slow.

RESOURCE COSTS VERSUS TRANSFER PAYMENTS

Other ways of increasing the demand for contraceptives are radio information programs, billboards, pamphlets, and adult classes. However, these use labor and material resources that might otherwise be contributing to the goods and services that comprise GNP.

Bonuses, except for certain administrative expenses, do not occasion resource costs in this sense. They are really transfer payments. They transfer real purchasing power from taxpayers— or holders of money if the government inflates rather than taxes— to those who receive the bonuses for services rendered.

This distinction may not mean anything to the administrator of a family planning program who has a limited budget. It may mean little to the minister of finance who must find the money. But to the president and the economy this distinction should be important.

CONCLUSION

How effective bonus systems will be in reducing fertility cannot be known in advance. The only bonus plans to date have paid very small amounts. The supply schedule of contraceptive volunteers is unknown in every country. Without experimentation it will never be known. All that does appear certain is that, without bonus systems, fertility will not be reduced rapidly enough for LDCs to achieve their economic and social goals.

DISCUSSION

ZENA HARMAN (Israel): Population policy must relate to the need for sustained development, which means to the increasing of the well-being of the individual in the society where he lives. We are dealing with a long-term process that cannot be easily shortened, and we must focus on the total family as the objective of population policies. Thus family planning must be put in the context of a comprehensive approach where capital investment, fertility rates, value judgments, and social betterment converge and are correlated.

In Israel, we have been concerned with incentives to increase the size of families that are not reproducing themselves, while bringing down the size of larger families, in order to reach optimum family size. Most incentives were effective only for short periods. The real problem was that of culture, attitude, motivation, and so on.

I hope our government will adopt a social welfare policy seeing the family as an entity and providing all the services likely to influence family sizes. This means coordination between the ministries of health, education, housing, labor, and finance on such matters as health services, social insurance, taxation, and employment.

The question of family size must be tackled by a frontal governmental attack incorporating all factors that influence the quality and nature of family life, while also taking into account economic needs, manpower needs, and social purposes.

ROBERT RENOMBO (Gabon): Africa is underpopulated, despite some overpopulated areas. In Gabon there are fewer than one million people on an area of 267,000 square kilometers, though the country disposes of enormous natural resources. Consequently, our government is encouraging, not discouraging, a high birth rate. Incentives are given to women with the largest number of children, and we have forbidden the sale of contraceptives. Does Dr. Enke feel this policy is right or wrong?

N. FISEK (Turkey): Are women in the United States given incentives to reduce fertility as part of the war against poverty? And what is the reaction of the American Medical Association to the commercial distribution of contraceptives?

I. S. BANGURA (Sierra Leone): Politicians in less developed states do not dare to legislate against having children, because this is part of the cultural practices of the people. Especially in Northern West Africa, which is predominantly Moslem, men may have four or five wives, and the only way these can get attachment to their husbands is by bearing children. Each one would like to give birth to one or two children if not four. You cannot give them monetary incentives not to do so.

The only way is to educate, to go into the interior, talk to them, let them appreciate a way of life different from the one they now enjoy. As far as they are concerned, their only enjoyment now is in their children. They see them grow up and say they will take care of them tomorrow. Their children are their only insurance.

I come from a very large family. I was the only child to my mother, who died, but my father has many wives. When I grew up, I was able to earn enough and went to school. I had to raise the standard of my family before thinking of getting married, because this was my duty to my father for educating me and bringing me up. I advocate fertility control because I know exactly how much I am spending on the upbringing of my half-brothers and half-sisters. I spent too much on this. I do not want to bring up many children of my own. I cannot even afford to marry one wife, let alone many.

J. ADLER (I.B.R.D.): The cost/benefit ratio of birth prevention as compared with economic development aid was not agreeable to many developing countries and caused misunderstandings.

I also wonder why nobody has related the question of fertility control to income distribution of the benefits of economic growth. When 40 percent to 50 percent of the population do not share in these benefits, population control programs are unlikely to be effective.

STEPHEN ENKE (United States): Even if the fertility rate fell, the reproduction rate of the population will probably double in the next 75 to 100 years. Capital accumulation will increase with lower fertility. Thus fertility reduction does not jeopardize sustained development.

My idea of incentives is that you pay a woman a very small fee for coming to register at the center. She has to be examined there every 6 months. You give her little or nothing if she is not pregnant after the first 6 months. After 12 months, you give her a small amount, after 18 months, a larger amount, and so on. One should pay younger women more than older women.

To the gentleman from Gabon, I would say that even in states with a high ratio between land area and population high fertility is not desirable because it means that the output per head of population declines. What percentage of the children of Gabon get six or eight years of good schooling? The need is not so much for children but to have only as many children as you can reasonably well educate.

There is no incentive scheme in the United States for women to reduce fertility, though about $150 million per annum are spent to let the poor know about birth control. This is a pity.

The American Medical Association is against contraceptive pills without doctors' prescriptions, but one could hardly expect a different attitude from them. A woman who has side effects from taking the pill should see a doctor, but no doctor can tell in advance whether there are going to be side effects unless the woman suffers from high blood pressure or some other clearly defined things that anyone with very little training can ask her.

I agree with Mr. Bandura that in some countries politicians do not dare to back drastic family programs. As regards polygamy in Moslem states, since the total number of men and women is nearly the same, for every man with four wives, there must be three men with no wife. I can see why a young wife wants to get an attachment through a child or two, but I am not talking about having two or three children but about the fifth, sixth, or seventh, and I do not think having seven children multiplied by four will make the husband happy.

As regards allocating more money to education, we made a new model reallocating funds between health, education, infrastructure, productive investment, and family planning. It showed that if one takes funds from the ministry of education's budget and transfers them to the family planning budget, the percentage of school age children in school increases enormously within 10 years. So it depends on what you want: lots of children at school, or few children not at school.

POPULATION POLICIES
Nusret H. Fisek

POPULATION POLICY AND ITS SCOPE

Population policy, in its narrower sense, may be defined as the decision of policy makers to promote or to restrict fertility in their society. The more liberal and comprehensive interpretation of population policy may include policies that affect population growth directly or indirectly such as policies of migration, health, eugenics, abortion, housing, social security, taxation, and so forth, in addition to natalistic policy. Defined in this way, population policy overlaps to a great extent with the general socioeconomic policies of a government.

The scope of this paper will be restricted to examining natalistic health, and abortion policies.

THE HISTORICAL DEVELOPMENT OF POPULATION POLICIES

The population policies of different societies at present are better understood when they are viewed within their historical and cultural context.

The establishment and maintenance of a proper balance between the level of population and the means of subsistence available to that population has been a problem for all societies, from the most primitive to the most developed. The attitude adopted towards the problem may take the form of traditional behavior as in paleolithic societies, or planned policy, as in countries where a policy-making machinery has been created. Since food resources were limited in hunting and food gathering societies, the smallest increase in population could greatly disturb the population/resources balance and create a need for immediate curbing measures. Since these societies were unable to control their fertility effectively, one course of action taken to control population growth was to increase the level of mortality. Some of the traditional behaviors still observed could be interpreted as measures or practices of population control. Killing two-thirds of the children born to the family, allowing only children who are born in certain presentations to live, killing all newborns and then adopting a commensurate number of boys and girls of thirteen or fourteen years of age from rival tribes whose parents had been killed/or eaten, not qualifying for marriage before killing so many men, infanticide (especially the killing of female babies), the suicide and deliberate death of grandmothers among the Eskimo, and the banishing of the disabled and chronically ill may be cited as examples of the measures taken to keep the level of the population low enough to provide sufficient means of subsistence for survivors in these societies. The above mentioned mores cannot be generalized to include all preagrarian or low-energy societies.

Similar courses of action were taken against nonproductive segments of the population in some agrarian societies as well. For instance, a Spartan was obliged to kill his father. Failing to do so would bring shame to him and his family.

The traditional antinatalistic attitude of paleolithic societies gradually changed and was eventually replaced by a pronatalistic attitude in neolithic cultures, which has been a feature of every agrarian culture for more than 10 millenia. The pronatalistic urge was so strong during this period that antinatalistic measures were considered to be sins by some religions. Cippola, who studied fertility behavior in different cultures with respect to energy requirements, states that the main reason for pronatalistic attitudes in neolithic societies was the ever increasing need for biological energy and the lack of any other source of energy. He estimated that in agrarian cultures 80-85 percent of the energy consumed for different purposes was obtained from the muscular force of men and animals.

The need to have more soldiers in order to dominate other societies also supported pronatalistic attitudes or policies. Since the death rate in agrarian societies was very high in the past, antinatalistic measures affected population growth only slightly. During the paleolithic period the total population grew by 2 percent every 1,000 years, whereas during the neolithic period the total population grew by 2 percent every 100 years.

The Industrial Revolution profoundly changed social environment once again. Under the pressure of the changing conditions, fertility gradually declined. Antinatalistic attitudes became a cultural feature of industrialized societies. The main reason for this profound change was the discovery of new sources of energy, such as the steam engine, the turbine, and gas combustion machines, that replaced the muscular force of men and animals. Other changes that came about concurrently with the Industrial Revolution, such as the rapid advances in medicine and public health, mass communication, and the betterment of transportation (which made the control of famine possible), have also influenced the demographic patterns of societies, causing a pronounced decrease in death rates.

The prediction of Malthus has not been born out for Europe: the death rate declined simultaneously with the fertility rate. The transition, therefore, from a population equilibrium at a high level of fertility and mortality took place without an extended period of disequilibrium. Emigration from Europe and the active campaigns of voluntary organizations to propagate knowledge on contraception also facilitated the demographic transition in Europe.

Rapid population growth has never become a problem for industrialized countries, but the situation has not been as fortunate for the agrarian societies of our time. These societies have benefited from the advance of medicine, public health, and transportation realized in industrial countries and, therefore, their death rates have decreas rapidly. Since the social determinants of fertility have not changed, population growth has been too rapid and a great obstacle to their socioeconomic development. For this reason, governments in many developing countries have had to pursue an active antinatalistic policy

HEALTH POLICIES

The 132 nations that signed the constitution of the World Health Organization (WHO) agreed that "The enjoyment of the highest attainable standard of health is one of the fundamental rights of every human being without distinction of race, religion, political belief, economic or social condition." Although every government agreed to have a positive health policy, health activities have not been beyond criticism Hanlon summarizes the arguments of the authors who are against public health measures as follows:

> ... public health and preventive medical measures serve to protect and promote the unfit at the mental, moral, physical, and financial expense of the fit. This jeopardizes future generations by interfering with the process of natural selection ...

The treatment of patients is also against the beliefs of some religious groups.

It has been observed that health programs have lower priority than many other social and economic projects in developing countries. This is mostly due to limited resources. If more emphasis can be given to health projects and if every person in developing countries can enjoy a high standard of health as pledged in the WHO constitution, the mortality rates will drop to a far lower level and the population growth rates will increase further unless fertility drops. At first sight a positive health policy appears to work against the projects aiming to curb population growth. In fact, some economists believe that the betterment of health will further aggravate the population problem in developing countries and that the overall result will be detrimental to these countries' economies.

There are many arguments rejecting this view. One is that a decline in mortality is concurrent with economic growth. For example, Fredriksen showed that a malaria control program was the main reason for the rapid population growth in Ceylon. But, at the same time, the control of malaria opened new fields of cultivation and the wealth of the country increased as well.

The other argument is based on the relationship between child mortality and fertility. Accumulating evidence shows that a drop in child mortality precedes a decline in fertility. If this is proved, the betterment of health and the control of child mortality will be a required component of any fertility control program, and governments that give high priority to the control of population growth will have to build a network of health centers throughout their countries to render comprehensive health care and family planning services to their citizens.

ABORTION POLICY

The liberalization of restrictive abortion legislation has had striking effects on birth rates, and the abortion policy of a country should be considered and studied as one of the essential components of its population policy. For instance, the birth rate in Romania was 22.9 per thousand before the liberalization of abortion legislation in 1957. It started to decline steadily following the liberalization of abortion legislation and dropped to 14.3 per thousand in 1966. The Romanian government decided to restrict abortion in 1966, and the birth rate jumped to 38.5-39.9 per thousand between July and September 1967. Then it started to decline again, but it did not reach the level of when abortion was induced on request.

The effect of abortion policy on birth rate is also exemplified by the drop in the birth rate of Japan, from 33.5 per thousand before the Eugenic Protection Law was changed in 1948 to 17.2 per thousand within ten years.

Countries may be classified into three groups according to their abortion legislations:
- Countries where a woman may abort her child upon her demand, such as the USSR., Hungary, and the States of Alaska, Hawaii and New York of the United States.
- Countries where abortion is unconditionally prohibited including Spain, Ireland, the Philippines, Portugal, and the Dominican Republic.

- Countries where abortion is legally allowed in special circumstances: Grounds for legally allowed and medically induced abortions differ from country to country. In some countries, medically induced abortions are permitted only if the operation is necessary to save the life of the pregnant woman. In some countries where very liberal policies exist social reasons such as the number of surviving children, the age of the pregnant woman, and consideration of her social well-being entitle her to have a medically induced abortion as well.

The attitude of the public is more significant than the legislation of the government. The so-called criminal abortions by abortionists are very common in countries where abortion legislation is too restrictive. If socioeconomic conditions force families not to have too many children, women have abortions, whether prohibited or not. The religion of the woman certainly affects her decision, but its influence varies from one social group to another and, of course, from one woman to another.

The physicians' attitudes are also factors influencing the implementation of a liberal abortion policy. It should be remembered that abortion is against the Hippocratic oath. This attitude influences not only the practice of abortion but also the practice of contraception. It is fortunate that many physicians do not feel themselves bound by an ethical rule that was established 2,300 years ago and feel free to adapt themselves to the changing needs of their society.

FERTILITY CONTROL IN DEVELOPING COUNTRIES

The first developing country to realize the necessity of curbing its population growth and taking measures to control fertility was India.

No other developing countries started a fertility control program until the sixties. In the sixties it was observed that many developing countries, especially in Asia, had accepted antinatalistic policies and initiated family planning programs. Their number reached 28 in 1972. If countries that had no formal population policies but that supported family planning programs are included, the number becomes 54.

The majority of developing countries still have no policy and do not support family planning programs. Some even want to promote fertility. Most of the countries that do not have a population policy are Latin American and African. In African countries the major reasons for lack of interest in population control may be summarized as follows:

- Population growth is slow because of the high mortality rate. Hence, rapid population growth is not an actual problem for these countries.

- Most African countries have vast underpopulated territories. Therefore their governments believe that population growth will not affect their socioeconomic development adversely.
- The small family norm has not been accepted in African countries as yet. Even the elites who are in a position to formulate the policies are in favor of large families for themselves. For instance, the results of the KAP study in urban centers in Ghana show that 67 percent of the elite male population want to have five or more children.
- Some African leaders believe that population control is a new method for imperialism to hinder the struggle of the African countries to free their countries from economic and cultural backwardness.

Although most African countries are not in favor of population control, even today, there is evidence of change in government attitudes. Gwatkin, who recently reviewed the population policies in the West African countries, concludes his paper thus:

"West African policy makers have largely ignored the population aspects of development. But their concern about population is growing. Four years ago, few would have predicted that Ghana and Nigeria would have adopted population policies or that Dahomey or Gambia would have commissioned studies of their population situations. The trend is clearly with those who believe that population questions are too important to be ignored."

On the other hand, the most important factor that prevents Latin American governments from starting family planning programs to control the rapid growth of population is the attitude of the Roman Catholic Church. The permission given by Pope Pius XII to use the rhythm method to regulate fertility, the majority report of the Papal Commission in 1966, and the permissive attitude of some bishops has encouraged some of the Latin American countries to start family planning programs in their countries. But most of these countries had to cancel their programs after the Encyclical of Pope Paul VI.

More so than in the African countries, some government officials and influential leaders in the Latin American countries consider the population control movement as a political maneuver of the U.S. government to divert the attention of developing countries from economic investment to the less important problem of population control.

Interest of the governments of developing countries in fertility control, is increasing steadily. Two major obstacles hinder the universal acceptance of fertility control policies at present: the attitude of the Roman Catholic Church and the existence of more urgent social and economic problems than population growth in developing countries especially in the newly independent ones. Although the Roman Catholic Church does not underestimate the importance of rapid population growth and always reminds families not to ignore their responsibility towards the children to be born, the restrictions imposed on the choice of the contraceptive method become a major obstacle in starting family planning programs in developing countries with predominantly Catholic populations.

In the newly independent countries the lack of interest of the governments in population planning is due mainly to the long range nature of population planning programs. Since rapid population growth is not their primary problem, it is difficult for them to decide to allocate their limited resources to family planning programs that may show their major beneficial effects on the social and economic life of their countries after a decade or so.

THE NATIONAL POPULATION POLICIES OF DEVELOPED COUNTRIES

Governments in countries where the population growth rate declined to a minimum, or where a decrease in the size of the population was predicted, have taken measures to increase fertility. The social policies of the Swedish government—such as its programs for child allowance, children's pension, children's nurseries and leisure centers, maternity benefits, housing allowances, and free care for infertile and subfertile families—illustrate the social approach to promote fertility in developed countries.

In addition to social measures, some countries have also taken direct measures to increase fertility. For instance, in 1920 in order to increase the number of births the French parliament promulgated a law prohibiting induced abortion, the use and sale of contraceptives, and the dissemination of information on birth control. It should be noted that the French government had to change its policy, except for that on abortion, under public pressure in 1967.

The abortion policies of the USSR are another example of the direct measures that are taken to control fertility. According to Lenin, the decision on whether or not to have a baby was the prerogative of the pregnant woman. In adherence to Lenin's point of view, there was no restriction on abortion in the USSR until 1936. In 1936, in order to increase fertility, the Soviet government stopped the practice of abortion on request and allowed abortion only for medical reasons. Although the birth rate increased slightly, self-induced abortion became a public health problem, and the Soviet government liberalized abortion regulations again in 1955.

The population policy of the United States is somewhat different from those of other developed countries. At present, federal and state governments support family planning services throughout the country as a part of the program on the War Against Poverty. Considering the interdependence between high fertility and poverty, Congress accepted a resolution in 1967 to allocate federal funds for family planning services.

The governments of developed countries have had to maintain a balance between the measures taken to have a stable population and the rights of families to decide on their family size. Usually the latter has more weight in policy decisions. Consequently when governments decide that there is a need to increase fertility, pronatalistic measures are limited to social programs and propaganda for high fertility.

INTERNATIONAL COOPERATION IN THE FIELD OF FAMILY PLANNING

The first official international document that noted the worldwide importance of population growth and requested governments to take action to control the population explosion was the resolution accepted in the 17th General Assembly of the United Nations in 1962. Other UN agencies such as the FAO, WHO, the ILO, and UNESCO also recognized the importance of the problem, and their responsible bodies decided to initiate programs in family planning and population control in order to assist member countries. The main principle of the policies of international agencies is not to impose, not even to suggest any policy to member countries, but to assist them upon request.

In addition to international agencies, Sweden has extended assistance to other countries to help develop their family planning services. In 1965, the U.S. government started to assist other countries in the field of population control and has become the major promoter of family planning programs throughout the world.

THE PROSPECTS FOR THE FUTURE

How will the population policies of nations develop in the future? The present trend clearly indicates that the world population will keep growing rapidly during the coming decades. Therefore, the population problem of the world will be a more important issue in the future than now. Thus it is likely that antinatalistic policies will be accepted by nations on a more extensive basis and will be enforced more vigorously.

The target of family planning programs at present in countries with high fertility rates is to establish a balance between population growth and economic development. It is unlikely that such a modest goal will be sufficient in the future. The target of population policies in the future must be to reduce fertility to keep the world population stable. The concept of a stable population is already known through the slogan "Zero Population Growth." This is the first sign of future policies. World population, unless adequately controlled, is likely to reach a size too large for the well-being of its members before a "natural" dynamic equilibrium is established between birth and death rates.

Biologists know that population growth in a closed environment is not unlimited and follows the pattern of an S-shaped curve. The growth of bacteria is the best illustration of this universal law. It is slow at the beginning, similar to the growth of mankind until the seventeenth century. Then it accelerates and starts to increase geometrically. The growth of the bacterial population slows down during the next growth phase and becomes stable. The reason for the stopping of growth is twofold: the exhaustion of the nutrilites in the media and the accumulation of detrimental substances in the environment. Generalizing the law of population growth, a safe prediction might be that human population density will reach a maximum level and world population will be stable because of environmental pollution and a limitation of resources. The size of the naturally obtained stable population is quite likely to be too large for the quality of life to be at an acceptable standard. Therefore, the problem in the coming years will be to stabilize world population at a level below the level of natural equilibrium.

One of the characteristics of present population policies is their liberality. No family is forced to limit the number of their children against their wishes. This freedom is regarded as a human right. Is there a possibility of changing this liberal policy and of taking drastic measures to stop population growth? What could be done if the shortage of all kinds of resources such as food, energy, and raw materials becomes an acute problem, if population density reaches a point where we fail to control environmental pollution, and if the full liberalization of abortion and socioeconomic achievements do not reduce fertility to the desired level? If environmental conditions cannot be controlled and go from bad to worse, policy makers cannot hesitate to change their liberal policies and impose restrictions on the number of births. These measures could take the form of postponing the age of marriage and establishing legal provisions in order to discourage families from having more children than necessary to replace those who die.

DISCUSSION

ELIAHU SALPETER (Israel): Much more attention should be given to existing differences among cultures in their attitudes towards fertility. There are four cultures in which fertility rites and the fertility concept are fundamental, and giving $25 will not counteract a cultural factor that has existed for centuries.

In Israel there are very different fertility ratios for Jews of Afro-Asian origin and Jews of European or American origin. Inside each country fertility is an issue among classes, groups, and sub-groups—and very much a question of domestic politics. Hence politicians dislike to talk about it.

To bring the acceptance of birth control from the existing 15 percent plateau to the desired 50 percent of the population will require financial incentives of a size politicians are unlikely to approve.

On the other hand, our Israeli statistics show that fertility, regardless of the ethnic background, decreases as the educational level rises. Education seems to have a greater impact on fertility than is generally assumed.

ROBERT MUSCAT (AID., Washington, D.C.): There is evidence that more education for mothers is associated with lower fertility, but to lower fertility by educating would cost many times more than Dr. Enke's incentive proposal. This does not mean that education is not desirable on other grounds. The same reasoning applies to the provision of health services.

Most cultures in Western Europe valued fertility highly. It is a mistake to assume that these cultural factors are stronger in Asian or African societies. For a long time the Chinese had absolutely ferocious desires for large numbers of sons. Yet within the last 15 or 20 years this desire has been overwhelmed by other considerations. For instance, all over the world, people like television. More children mean more doctors' bills, more school fees—and fewer television sets.

TARLOK SINGH (UNICEF): Population policy must refer not only to numbers but also to well-being. The policy on numbers must be coordinated with policy on the productive use of manpower, health policy, education policy, and so on.

There is a very close connection between the development of national population policies and the development of international policies. However, UN efforts in this sphere tend to come in bits and pieces. The most important thing is for each state to develop its own population policy, relate it to the objectives that it has set and the well-being of its population. It must be a long-term policy.

We must consider how measures attempted within the context of a country's conditions can be applied systematically over a longer period.

GUSTAV PAPANEK (United States): I wonder what the fertility rate would be in Washington, D.C., if women had to get their pills and men their condoms at some little public health clinic on 14th Street and could only get a month's supply at a time. I am sure the fertility rate would go up. The way to reach people is by advertising on the radio and selling through normal commercial channels. Yet most fertility programs fail to do this because of cultural inhibitions on the part of their administrators.

It has been argued that the only economic reason for having more children is as a social security device in old age. But a study just completed for Indonesia shows that while Java is very overpopulated from the government's viewpoint, from the viewpoint of the individual family in agriculture it is desirable to increase the number of children, because each child brings in more income than it consumes. This is a problem we often have to face.

NUSRET FISEK (Turkey): The cultural pattern is important, and in many countries it is studied before family planning programs are introduced. The educational level should be raised, and this will affect fertility quite often. But experiments showed that when family planning workers got their message through, the gap between the fertility behavior of the educated and the uneducated was closed.

Family planning services have to be planned for each country individually, to fit its resources and its culture. In Turkey there is one auxiliary nurse-midwife per 2,500 persons in the rural areas, and the basic idea is to create close personal contact between her and her community. Such midwives should be charged with family planning programs and paid a fixed salary. This is a good incentive, because if they are successful their work load decreases. The successful ones may have only 1 or 2 pregnant women to follow up, the less successful ones, 15 or 20.

THE EVALUATION OF POPULATION POLICY— SOME MISSING LINKS
Elihu Bergman

Two related issues in population policy formulation have not received adequate attention. One is the establishment of an adequate working definition of population policy. The other is the proposal of a framework for evaluating population policy choices, potential and actually made. This framework must be sensitive to the requirements of those who have to make the choices—namely politicians and other decision makers.

First, what is population policy? It is commonly defined as a fertility control or fertility limitation policy, but there are some serious problems in this narrow definition. There are political problems: some societies are simply not prepared to accept the notion of fertility limitation for political reasons. There are religious problems: certain religions in certain societies regard fertility limitation as inconsistent with religious norms.

To create a realistic framework of discussion, we need a more comprehensive definition of population policy, which in addition to considering population size and population growth also considers the distribution and composition of the population.

All these variables have a mutually reinforcing relationship. As the composition of the population changes, its fertility behavior also changes. As the location of population groups changes, so their fertility behavior may change in response to new opportunities or advantages accruing to them from their new environment.

To my mind, population policy must deal with the interaction between population characteristics (size, growth, composition, and location) and the conditions governing the well-being of the population (health, nutrition, employment, and so on), as well as with problems of opportunity and mobility.

If we confine the definition of population policy to fertility limitation policy and seek to evaluate its success or failure by measuring the impact of programs designed to reduce fertility, the result would be disappointing. There is no evidence that fertility control or family-planning programs reduced fertility among populations they were designed to affect. In fact, family-planning programs are associated with lower fertility only in societies where fertility was already declining for other reasons. Such programs are said to have succeeded in Korea, Singapore, Hong Kong, and Taiwan, but in each of these states other factors played a decisive role.

Significant fertility decline has been achieved in situations where populations were experiencing better living conditions—rising per capita income, better health, more education, better employment opportunities, lower infant mortality, and a more even distribution of such advantages among all sections, especially the poor. Where people enjoy these advantages, they tend to make more choices about their own fertility, and their choice is usually to lower it. Family-planning programs are at best an auxiliary factor. They have made no independent contribution to reducing fertility. To quote Professor Hauser: "I have yet to see an example of a nation mired in illiteracy and poverty where the family planning movement has initiated a decline in fertility."

The classic cases of dramatic fertility reductions have been in Taiwan, Korea, Singapore, Hong Kong, and Costa Rica, where there is evidence that social advantages have been better distributed over the past 10 to 20 years. In countries where this has not happened, such as Brazil and Mexico, the fertility rates have remained very much the same.

I would define population policy as government action influencing population characteristics taken with reference to other conditions in which change is sought, such as the expansion of opportunities for employment, education, shelter, and health, the contraction of such opportunities, and the security of the community. These actions can be taken either to the advantage or to the disadvantage of specific groups, such as the young, the old, the rich, the poor, ethnic majorities and religious minorities. Direct or indirect manipulation can be involved. In the case of fertility reduction, for instance, the emphasis can be either on contraceptive programs (direct) or on programs to expand education and employment opportunities for females (indirect).

Population policy requires an evaluative mechanism to facilitate its assessment for policy makers and scientists in the country concerned. This evaluation system must respond to issues and options involved in the process of development, but besides facilitating an assessment of what has happened it should provide material for a pre-study of policy options on the lines of "What might happen if. . . . ?

Political leaders need a more global perspective on their population policy. They need to know how it will interact with policies and programs inspired by national development goals. They need to know the costs and benefits of alternative mixes of policies and programs for the achievement of population goals. And they need to know the costs and benefits of the alternative mixes in respect of their political goals, personal and national.

There is a need to consider the role of population policies in achieving both population and development objectives against alternative policy options not aimed directly at influencing population characteristics. Finally, the political costs and benefits must be considered, for the political assessment finally determines whether something happens or not.

I therefore propose the following framework for evaluating population policies.

Program	Development	Policy	Politics
Impact of population program on a specific population objective, that is:	Association of population program with development goals, that is:	Effectiveness of population program in terms of alternative policy choices, that is:	Role of program in achieving political objectives, that is:
Suppression of fertility	Increasing individual income	Alternation in economic system	Regime stability
Dispersal of population groups	Improving income distribution	Income redistribution	Policy loyalty
Homogenization of population group	Providing more employment	Expansion of elementary education	Leadership support
	Reducing mortality	Improvement of health care facilities	Ideological conformity
	Increasing access to education		National unity
	Decreasing dependence on external assistance		

The political factor is vital. Scientists and intellectuals who deal with population issues understandably employ standards of theoretical soundness, rational assessment, and scientific modesty. But political leaders function in a different sort of world, where rationality cannot always serve as an effective working tool. Their choices are based on the answer to the question: "Does it make political good sense?" And the standard of political good sense is often a highly subjective one, involving personal values and judgments. Political choices are based on a special cost/benefit calculation, based on the certain assumption that every push requires a pull, every take requires a give, every favor requires an obligation, and every credit requires a debit. The evaluation of these dynamics in every political system may be attempted by rational means, but judgments may well be based on instinct and prove no less valid.

The political cost/benefit calculus has been neglected within the evaluation framework of population policy making. It can safely be assumed that economic considerations do not always govern the political choices of presidents, prime ministers, cabinet ministers, legislators, and party leaders, whatever the quality of their civic commitment or public spirit. Politicians everywhere are interested in getting re-elected (where elections are relevant) and always in staying in power. They are most likely to respond to propositions helping them to stay in power. As regards population policy, there has been little interest in creating a perspective that might supply such propositions.

Early this year, the U.S. Population Council organized a conference designed to expose state-level political leaders in the northeast United States to population scientists and specialists. The idea was to confront the politicians with population problems that the experts considered relevant to the well-being of the states and thus to motivate the leaders to initiate the necessary policies and actions. A political leader from Massachusetts expressed frustration at the outcome of the conference. He complained that the experts arrived with a policy agenda based on a rational and scientific assessment of the issues, which was completely unresponsive to the political realities leaders had to face, and thus unlikely to provide convincing grounds for political action. In Massachusetts, for instance, talk of "population" is equated by many voters with talk of abortion, and the abortion issue is almost lethal to the aspirations of a politician. Any Massachusetts politician advocating issues labeled "population" thus does so at his peril. Hence, in this state population policy making requires sensitive selection, packaging, and labeling of issues to enjoy any prospect of success. This requirement was not accepted by the experts, to the discomfort of the legislator, who sincerely desired to act on population policy requirements in Massachusetts. Some experts, on their part, complained that the politicians were dense, timid, and insensitive to their public responsibilities. There was, therefore, little communication between the experts and the politicians. They, so to speak, passed each other in the night.

The episode described above, perhaps in a slightly different form, has occurred in many places outside the United States. It is significant because it demonstrates the limitation of scientific analysis in the political decision-making process. Ultimately policy is a product of politics, not of science, however unfortunate this may be. Scientists interested in policy making must therefore support politicians on political terms, even when this requires a departure from their accustomed procedures and intellectual processes. Such support may require dealing with issues and responding to problems of marginal interest to the scientists, but critical for political leaders.

Unless the evaluation process in population policy making is expanded to cover nonscientific issues, the experts will merely continue to talk to each other—at best about increasingly interesting subject matter. Under such circumstances, scientific output is unlikely to affect policy making either by providing an improved base for policy choices, or in initiating policy choices where none have been made.

DISCUSSION

STEPHEN ENKE (United States): It is unfortunate that most large family-planning programs have not been seriously evaluated. Since 1965, about $500 million have been spent on family-planning programs of various kinds, but during the same period almost 75 times as much has been spent on trying to increase output rather than slow up population growth.

If you make population policy include everything that affects people, you are never going to find out very much about what makes for fertility reduction. But it is true that fertility reduction is a political as well as an economic question. Economists, political analysts, and demographers should work together to produce suitable programs.

ROBERT MUSCAT (AID): The need for something beyond family planning is now recognized by most of the donor agencies. Available resources are still going into the type of programs Dr. Bergman mentioned because the social scientists have as yet had little useful to say. It is pointless to tell a government that there is an inverse relationship between female participation in the urban labor force and fertility rates, when the government is struggling against overemployment.

In Asia, some interesting experiments were made in policies designed to induce people to desire a smaller family. For instance, Singapore is experimenting with a housing policy recognizing that pressure on limited housing is a major factor reducing fertility. Financial and educational incentives must be based on the motives deciding parents of three or four children to have, or not to have, another one or two. One can extract specific factors relating to the economic and social costs and benefits of children.

GUSTAV PAPANEK (United States): Why was there no attempt to evaluate whether family planning programs were effective or not? Why is money being spent on programs that do not succeed? Does this reflect our willingness to fool ourselves that we know how to spend money, or our reluctance to be faced with a problem for which we have no solution?

LORETTA GOLDBERG (United States): There is a relationship between the growth of the use of material things and the rise in the status of women, which is relevant to decreases in fertility rates. Not enough emphasis in this conference has been placed on the role of women consumers in setting consumption patterns and thus determining their present and future living standards.

JEK YEUN THONG (Singapore): Our experience in Singapore has been that there are two aspects to the controlling of fertility. First, we liberalized the attitude to abortion, and this produced some good results. Second, everyone is encouraged to have small families of two or three children. If they have more, they have to pay a higher hospital fee, and do not receive the normal state subsidies for education, housing, and so on. The response, in many quarters, has been good.

ELIHU BERGMAN (United States): The evaluation of fertility control programs is very difficult, but this does not mean that we should not try to find out what reduces fertility. Funds to finance training and research of talented U.S. students in population studies have been cut off by the U.S. government. Restoring them might prove more fruitful than spending the corresponding amounts on certain fertility control programs the success of which is doubtful.

Singapore is a classic example of success in family planning, but if one studies what has happened there during the last 20 years, it seems to confirm that the broader distribution of benefits among more people reduces fertility. I think that people in Singapore take advantage of the very effective family-planning programs there for reasons other than things like psychedelic-colored condoms. If people don't know what condoms are for, or are not moved to used them, it does not matter what color they are.

The failure to evaluate is built into the way programs and the policies behind them are framed. Two problems are involved. One is a "panacea syndrome" prevalent in the United States, which says that if you spend more money on a problem the problem will be ameliorated. For five years agricultural development may be the panacea for foreign assistance, for another five years, investment in capital enterprises. Nowadays population control is the panacea. It has been sold this way to the U.S. Congress, and there is about a 10 year time lag between the time Congress decides something and the time that it starts to audit its decision. Eventually it will start asking what has been accomplished with the $500 million investment.

The second problem arises when a coalition of scientists and policy makers begin to have a stake in a certain approach to the solution of the problem. They then become impatient with questions asked by outside people.

I wish to stress that I am enthusiastically for the provision of family planning programs and for greater investment in them in developing countries where there is a demand for them, or the people are conscious about the opportunity of making choices about the number of children they should have. But I don't think we can automatically create the demand, or the consciousness about family planning, family size, or fertility limitation simply by supplying the technology.

EMPLOYMENT AND LABOR ABSORPTION IN DEVELOPMENT
Gustav Ranis

The problem of less developed country unemployment or underemployment has, in recent years, taken the center stage of public attention. The problem is one of examining the extent to which LDC output and employment generation are competitive in nature and to what extent they are complementary.

The majority of contemporary observers on both sides of the "poverty curtain" have become more and more concerned with the fact that, whatever leaky and imperfect indicator of disguised or open unemployment may be currently in use, it is likely to be on the rise in most countries—and with it formidable social and political pressures.

The identification of a major social problem of this kind, not necessarily equivalent to growth and not necessarily solved by it; is, of course, only the first, though necessary step. What is badly needed is an accurate diagnosis and workable prescription. Both of these, in turn, depend on place and time, that is, on the type of LDC under consideration as well as on the historical context.

Employment creation is not a new concern for either analyst or politician. Few five-year plans produced in the postwar era failed to list it near the top of enumerated plan objectives. (Some, for example, Ceylon, even accorded it pride of place from the beginning.) But what usually was absent was its full integration into the analysis of the growth process in a general equilibrium context. This remains true, by and large, to this day.

Increasing unemployment and underemployment, side by side with growth rates exceeding UN targets, lead some to recommend raising these targets (say from 5 percent to 8 percent) so that countries, without having to change their structure or growth path, can solve both problems simultaneously. It leads others, for example, the Indian Planning Commission (at least until recently) to support a "secondary strategy," mainly public works, to mop up the unemployment left in the wake of the pursuit of a basically unchanged primary development strategy. Still others point out that the old (and slightly tarnished) "growth now, distribution later" argument can be given new life by substituting employment for distribution. Finally, some politicians, and also technicians, have been increasingly heard to say that LDCs must now be willing to give up growth for the sake of more employment and better distributive outcomes, but without much investigation of the need for such a trade-off or the approximate terms at which it would have to be negotiated. Given the importance and enormity of the problem—and the large number of institutions and individuals currently worrying about it—relatively few attempts have been made at integrating the employment concern into a comprehensive analytical view of growth, which might then permit technicians and policy makers to view it as part of the primary strategy of development.

A satisfactory analysis of the employment problem—and therefore prescriptions for solving it—must increasingly be imbedded in a general equilibrium* growth-theoretic framework.

Most contemporary LDCs find themselves with an initial stock of unemployed or underemployed labor; moreover they are faced with labor force explosions, resulting from prior population explosions, which threaten to substantially augment this stock over the decades ahead, even if (to take an extreme case) planned parenthood programs were to be instantaneously successful in achieving zero population growth as of tomorrow.

In response, some of the literature has argued that since employment and labor productivity are at loggerheads, countries are immediately confronted with an output/employment conflict and can "solve" their employment problem only by making inefficient output mix and technologies choices. Elsewhere the dual nature of LDCs has been recognized and the employment problem defined in terms of the need to reallocate labor from low (or even zero) productivity occupations in one sector, subsistence agriculture, to higher productivity employment in another, modern industry.

Such analysis does not go far enough. For one, it fails to recognise that there are usually two agricultural sectors, a large food producing, peasant-cultivator dominated subsistence subsector and a smaller cash crop producing commercialized subsector. For another, it fails to recognize the existence of an often substantial volume of nonagricultural rural activity (including rural industry and services) as well as of informal urban activities (including small scale industry and services), which usually dwarf in size the organized nonagricultural activity: finally, since it is essentially a closed-economy framework, it fails to take into account the relationship between the foreign sector and the domestic employment/output nexus via the possibilities of trade, technology transfer, and capital movements.

---

*"General equilibrium" here is used not in its precise textbook sense but to capture the need for a "wholistic" view of the economy.

The process of labor absorption in a labor surplus economy and the extent to which output and employment objectives are competitive or complementary can, in our view, be analysed, and prescribed for, only in the context of such a fuller "sectoring" of economic activity. Only the training of the interactions among these four or five domestic sectors, with each other and with the rest of the world, provides an adequate analysis of the employment/output problem.

Let us be more specific. Given the unskilled labor characteristics of these societies, a solution of the employment problem, or at least a determination of the nature and extent of trade-offs between output and employment, must be related to the potential range of choices of output mix and the potential range of choices of technology. The possibilities for changing output mixes in a more employment-intensive direction will differ substantially by sector, depending on whether the activity is directed mainly towards the domestic market (indicating more limited flexibility) or the foreign market (indicating substantial flexibility). The possibilities for technological change again will differ by sector, partly due to differential exposure to imported (usually capital-intensive) technology and partly due to differential capacity to innovate adaptively "on top of" imported technology (usually in a labor using direction) or to innovate indigenously de novo (also, we would expect, in a labor-using direction). And, finally, the potential for both output mix and technology change will differ depending on the extent of interaction among and the changing relative role of each of the various major heterogeneous sectors over time.

The task is thus a fairly formidable one. We must understand the sectoral structure of the LDC before us, as well as the nature of the interaction among the sectors and with the rest of the world, in order to assess the nature of the employment problem at a particular point in time. We must also be able to develop a growth-theoretic view of how that interaction may potentially change—and can be helped to change—and how such change will affect the employment problem, via technology changes and output mix changes. Finally, our analysis, and thus our policy advice, will, of course, differ depending on the type of LDC we are concerned with (the sectoral composition and potential for change, including via trade, being quite different for India and Ceylon), as well as the historical stage of development it has already reached (the sectoral composition and potential for change being again quite different in Brazil and Afghanistan). Typological differences among LDCs, in size, human versus natural resources endowment, as well as (possible) colonial heritage, will profoundly affect the diagnosis of the extent of potential complementarity between output and employment objectives.

EMPLOYMENT AND OUTPUT IN TAIWAN AND THE PHILIPPINES

Fortunately we can take advantage of the transferability of knowledge as between typologically similar LDCs both historically and cross-sectionally. To render the problem somewhat more concrete, let us now briefly examine the employment and output performance of two Asian economies, Taiwan and the Philippines, which differ from each other both typologically and in the phase of development in which they are currently engaged.

Both Taiwan and the Philippines may be classified as small-to medium-sized labor surplus economies, that is, economies that at the time of independence had an employment problem and were small enough so that trade and other forms of contact with the rest of the world really mattered. Both their structures showed a preponderant food (mainly rice)-producing agricultural sector, a somewhat smaller, export-oriented cash crop agricultural sector (sugar in Taiwan, sugar, copra, timber, and so forth in the Philippines), and a relatively small nonagricultural sector composed of services and industrial activities.

After independence both governments attempted to break away from their previous colonial resources flow pattern by diverting the proceeds of their cash-crop export sector away from fueling the further expansion of these same activities and into industrialization and supporting overheads and services. This was accomplished in both countries through the institution of an import substitution regime, including exchange controls cum import licensing, budget deficits cum inflation, low (sometimes negative) real rates of interest, favorable tax treatment for industry, and other ways to shift resources from agriculture and into industry. The consequence in both countries was a substantial spurt in the growth of the organized industrial sector and its appended services, directed mainly to the replacement of previously imported industrial consumer goods, and the relative discouragement of domestically oriented agriculture, rural and urban small-scale industry and nonagricultural exports. The basic fuel of development continued to be exploitation of the natural resources base via traditional exports to obtain the capital goods and raw materials required for the expansion of the import substituting industrial sector.

The distortion of relative factor and output prices created in order to provide artificially high industrial investment incentives, however, also biases the industrial sector technology and output mix in a capital- and import-intensive direction. With windfall profits provided to the new industrial class, technology choice is dominated by straight borrowing from abroad and the output mix by previously defined import markets. The seeming inevitability of a conflict between aggregate output, growing quite satisfactorily, and employment, lagging behind population growth, is, in fact, based on the consequences of this regime. Import substitution, while it may well be necessary for a time, in order to encourage entrepreneurial maturation and infrastructure creation, is also difficult to shed, as is evidenced by the fact that most of the developing world is still deeply immersed in it. Yet, at the end of primary (or consumer goods) import substitution, once the market for previously imported commodities has been more or less exhausted, a difficult choice usually faces a given LDC—either to move towards a more open export-oriented regime or to continue import substitution, but now in the area of replacing capital goods imports and processing. Taiwan took the first path, the Philippines the second. The differential consequences for the solution of the employment problem are marked and, we believe, generally instructive.

Taiwan

Taiwan reduced the temperature of its import substitution hothouse around 1960, through the realignment of a number of crucial, previously distorted, relative factor and commodity prices, including the exchange rate, the interest rate, and the internal terms of trade. As a consequence of the replacement of quantitative restrictions on scarce imports and credit by tariffs and higher interest rates, medium and small-scale entrepreneurs gained broader access to resources for the first time. And also the pattern of development, which had previously been natural resource or land intensive, that is, based on the interaction between traditional agricultural exports and large-scale domestically oriented industry, via trade, was radically altered. Specifically, the removal of substantial windfall profits in industry, accompanied by more realistic relative prices throughout the economy, had predictable results: the combination of mature entrepreneurs with ample supplies of unskilled labor led to a rapid expansion of labor-intensive industrial output and exports; food-producing agriculture, no longer fettered by unfavorable terms of trade, expanded rapidly, generating surpluses that provided substantial additional saving, both domestically and via exports. These savings, in turn, fueled additional output-and employment-generating activities, both in the rural and urban sectors.

Most interesting from our perspective here is the importance of the growth of labor-intensive secondary and multiple cropping patterns, on the one hand, and that of a medium- and small-scale industrial sector, tied into large-scale export-oriented industry, as well as the processing of agricultural commodities, on the other.

The resulting changes in intra-and inter-sectoral output mix, with output and employment growing rapidly in a complementary fashion, can only be called dramatic. Taiwan's multiple cropping index rose to 182.2 by 1970. Rural by-employment as a source of total farm family income—a good indicator of rural industry—was as high as 75 percent by the mid-60s. Exports, which constituted 11 percent of GDP in 1952-54, constituted 28 percent of GDP (itself growing at about 10 percent annually) by the end of the 60s; even more impressive evidence of the radical shift in output mix is the fact that labor-intensive industrial exports, which made up 37 percent of total exports during the import substituting 50s, rose to 90 percent of a rapidly growing total in the export substituting 60s.

The technological changes accompanying these changes in output mix, both domestically and via trade, were equally dramatic. In the food-producing agricultural sector, technology change was of the labor-using and land-saving variety associated with the new seed/fertilizer revolution. Thus, while there was a substantial relative decline in the labor force engaged in food production, the double cropping and heavier application of intermediate inputs accompanying the new higher yielding varieties were, in an absolute sense, employment creating rather than displacing.* Not until the end of the 60s when the surplus labor condition had given way to labor shortage did the absolute size of the labor force engaged in agriculture decline, mainly as a consequence of demand pressures shifting towards non-food commodities in a multisectored balanced growth context.

Equally instructive is the explosive growth of labor-intensive secondary crops and rural industries, often in extensions of the family household, for instance, in mushrooms, asparagus production, textiles, fishing, and food processing. Secondary rural activities moving "out" from agriculture and "in" from larger-scale industry via sub-contracting became an increasingly important source of complementary employment and output generation. The close interaction between both the food-producing domestically oriented and the cash crop export-oriented agricultural sectors, on the one hand, and medium- and small-scale industry, on the other, permitted considerable scope for plant-saving innovation as well as for indigenous labor-using technological change.

In the larger-scale industrial sector, marked labor-using technology change was also recorded, especially in the textiles and

---

*One important ingredient of this experience, not duplicated in other countries experiencing the impact of the "Green Revolution," is that Taiwan avoided large scale tractorization and other forms of mechanization by not providing such equipment with favored tariff or interest rate treatment.

electronics industries.* Industrial employment, which grew at annual rates of 3 percent in the 50s, accelerated to more than 8 percent in the 60s. Oshima found the rate of labor absorption in Kuznets' M sector rising from 4.6 percent annually in the 50s to 7.5 percent in the 60s, and from 3.2 percent to 6.5 percent in the S sector, with acceleration to annual rates of 8.7 and 7.2 percent respectively, by the end of the decade.

Examination of a situation like Taiwan's is especially helpful in putting to rest the still stubborn belief that the scope for technology choice, especially in nonagricultural activities, remains limited. There is similar evidence from South Korea, Pakistan, and Brazil. But there also exists substantial cross-sectional evidence to the same effect for countries still substantially in their import substitution phase of development.

The impact of such policy regimes falls unevenly on large and small firms in the same industry; for example, small firms usually face higher costs of capital, higher costs of imports, and lower costs of labor than do large firms. The consequences are most instructive. For example, medium-and small-scale units invariably choose a more "efficient" technology in terms of the more intensive use of scarce capital (or land) as well as in terms of the greater volume of effort expended in devising labor-using adaptations and innovations. Medium-and small-scale firms and landowners face a more competitive environment and are forced to make more careful technology choices from the existing shelf, as well as to adapt and innovate indigenously in the same direction. Large-scale units, favored by a policy environment that bestows substantial windfall profits, are much more likely to permit prestige considerations to dominate and be relaxed about the search for technological alternatives. The difference between a 10 and a 15 percent rate of profit is much more telling than that between 35 and 40 percent.

Technological flexibility and accompanying subtle changes in output mix do not, of course, show up everywhere. They are unlikely to be important in continuous process industries, for example. But their importance has been well established in Taiwan's food-producing agriculture and its services sector, as well as in the metal-working, wood, textiles, electronics, leather, and rubber industries, among others. Repair and light engineering seem to play a special role

---

*Taiwanese subsidiaries of television assembly plants, for example, used 50 percent more labor than parent company plants. The largest electronics factory in Taiwan experienced a 9-fold increase in capital stock and a 16-fold increase in employment between 1965 and 1969.

since this is not only itself a potentially very labor-intensive industry but also capable of providing embodied labor-intensive adaptive technology to other activities, both agricultural and nonagricultural. In these medium-and small-scale industrial activities, both urban and rural, a good deal of latent innovative capacity usually exists, ready to be activated by changes in the economic environment given the appropriate broader science and technology infrastructure.*

The Phillippines

By way of contrast, the Philippine economy is best divided into six main sectors. In the urban sectors, where approximately 40 percent of the people are located, we have the large-scale industrial sector, heavily concentrated in the Greater Manila area, a medium- and small-scale industrial sector, and a substantial services sector. In the rural sectors, with some 60 percent of the population we have the export-oriented cash crop sector, the food (mainly rice and corn)-producing agricultural sector, and a rural and cottage industry sector.

The large scale industrial sector is more capital intensive than the medium-and small-scale sector, while the cash crop agricultural sector is more capital intensive than the food-producing agricultural sector. Until recently, policy seems to have favored the two aforementioned capital-intensive sectors, with the food-producing agricultural sector receiving increasing attention in recent years; however increasing productivity in rice seems to be handicapped by a lack of sufficient irrigation and appropriate credit facilities.

The operation of this system, in terms of intersectoral relationships over time, seems to have followed the same typical import substitution pattern as in Taiwan. The dominant flow has been the utilization of the proceeds of the cash crop agricultural exports to build up the large-scale industrial sector. These flows have been augmented by the reinvestment of the profits of that large-scale industrial sector plus foreign capital inflows (both private and public). Subsidiary resource flows have been between food (rice and corn) agriculture, on the one hand, and the cottage plus small-and medium-

---

*Changes in relative prices and the establishment of a generally more competitive environment are necessary but not sufficient. Public policy must extend beyond into such questions as the support of R and D, adaptive engineering capacities, the breaking of information, patent, and other bottlenecks, that is, science and technology policy generally.

scale industry subsectors, on the other. Other relatively weak subsidiary resources flows have been between urban services and the food-producing agricultural sector and between the food and cash crop export sectors. Modest surpluses from food-producing agriculture have been mainly reinvested in agriculture, and those from distribution and services in the expansion of the distributive trades and, to some extent, in small-scale industry.

The Philippines thus have a rather compartmentalized economic structure, with the large-scale commercialized subsector in agriculture and the large-scale commercialized subsector in industry, connected via foreign trade, the main beneficiaries. The rest of the economy, that is, the four subsectors that contain perhaps 70-80 percent of the population, has been pretty much left out of a generally vigorous (and by international standards, quite satisfactory) growth performance. This compartmentalization seems to hold as well for financial markets and labor markets.

The import substitution policies followed since the early 1950s have led to an import dependent industrial structure with extensive investment in consumer goods industries, a good deal of excess capacity, and a quite capital intensive technology in the large scale industrial sector. Sufficient industrial jobs have not been generated to absorb the growing urban labor supply. In general, the distortion of relative prices has produced an industrial sector not sufficiently responsive to the favorable resource endowment of the country and biased against the production of intermediate and capital goods, as well as of new manufacturing exports.

This pattern of manufacturing growth, the relative lag of the food-producing agricultural sector (including the expansion of secondary crops), the even more pronounced lag of medium-and small-scale nonagricultural activities, and the increasing compartmentalization of the credit and labor markets have probably all had substantial negative effects on output, as well as employment. Inadequate access to the country's substantial entrepreneurial resources was the result.

The pattern of Philippine development to date can thus be characterized as the utilization of land-based resources to finance the expansion of a capital-intensive, import-substituting industrial sector. In contrast to Taiwan, at the end of primary import substitution the Philippines chose to move into the more expensive secondary areas of capital goods and raw materials processing. This was possible because the process could continue to be fueled by the economy's relatively favorable natural resources.

As a consequence, however, the employment problem has worsened though aggregate growth rates have been quite acceptable. A shift to a more labor-intensive, export-oriented industrial pattern may thus be viewed a natural and necessary transition. Although a continued expansion of primary product exports seems possible, likely, and desirable (the recent boom in bananas taking up the slack in other traditional export items), a continuation of past growth patterns, even at higher than historical growth rates, would not be sufficient to solve the current problems of development.

What is required is a move toward export substitution involving a substantial interaction between the large- and the medium- plus small-scale industrial sectors via complementary (instead of competitive) relationships. This will, moreover, require much more interaction of the kind seen in Taiwan between the food-producing agricultural sector and the domestically oriented medium-and small-scale industry. In other words, a fuller utilization of the economy's abundant unskilled labor supply can be achieved partly through the expansion of export-oriented industries and partly through the expansion of labor-intensive consumer goods serving the domestic (largely rural) market. Both the acceleration of labor-intensive industrial exports and accelerated domestically balanced growth as between the hitherto neglected major urban and rural sectors are necessary. Whichever element is emphasized, a sustained productivity increase in the food-producing agricultural sector will be required to provide not only labor and wage goods but also a market for the higher levels of domestic labor-intensive industrial output.

CONCLUSIONS

The understanding and exploitation of complementarities between output growth and employment generation means shifting from a situation in which the agricultural cash crop export sector fuels capital-intensive, large-scale industry to one in which the economy's domestic agricultural sector generates food surpluses and saving, releasing workers and providing markets, and in which the nonagricultural sectors combine an abundant labor supply with entrepreneurial capacity to produce large increments in domestically and export oriented industrial consumer goods and services.

In Taiwan, by the end of the 60s, continuous movement along such a path, with a substantial accent on trade, had brought the economy—largely by dint of its own efforts* to a solution of the unemployment problem and into a situation of labor shortage and substantially rising real wages.

---

*Especially noteworthy is that, contrary to popular belief, something like 94 percent of this effort, in the total investment sense, was financed by domestic saving (foreign aid and foreign capital contributing less than 6 percent).

The Philippines, on the other hand, moved into backward linkage at the end of primary import substitution. By the early 70s growth was satisfactory but a serious problem of unemployment and underemployment remained, and seems to be growing.

No two countries are ever so alike that the lessons learned in one can be unthinkingly applied to the other. We are aware of the argument that Taiwan is exceptional by virtue of its strong entrepreneurial base and the large volume of foreign capital, especially U.S., expended on its development during the period between 1955 and 1970. Nonetheless, the performance of such an economy indicates that many of the so-called insuperable obstacles to development and many of the so-called inevitable rigidities and trade-offs turn out to be man-made rather than nature-made. Other less "special" countries, for example Pakistan (in the early 60s) and Colombia (in the late 60s) experienced similar, if less dramatic, improvements in their development performance once the decision was made to move from import to export substitution.

There is little evidence that the Filipino entrepreneurial capacity is deficient. It has been concentrated in certain narrow areas, that is, the cash crop export and the large scale industrial sectors, but the talent elsewhere exists. Therefore, the situation is not comparable with that of countries like Indonesia, still at a somewhat earlier stage of development. Moreover, it is hard to accept the notion that the addition of substantial natural resources— when contrasted with Taiwan — should be viewed as a handicap rather than as a potential assist to modern growth.

The switch from import substitution to export substitution policies is particularly difficult to effect. Not only are powerful vested interests, which will resist a change in these policies, likely to grow up in the protected large-scale industrial sector but state officials who benefit from the control-oriented policy package and the labor elite, which has a claim on the existing relatively well-paying jobs, will resist changes in policy in the direction indicated. Here the role of a fairly good natural resources base may admittedly turn out, paradoxically, to be something of a disadvantage after all, for it will permit countries to continue on an import substitution path long after it is no longer necessary for entrepreneurial maturation, or likely to guide these industries into anything remotely reflecting comparative advantage in the long run. In other words, international experience to date seems to indicate that only countries somewhat "up against it" in terms of an actual or expected exhaustion of their major fuel for continued import substitution—or countries with a fairly strong government that can overcome the resistance of vested interests—have been able to make the substantial changes in the overall environment required.

Taiwan, for example, in spite of its excellent performance on the agricultural side, is basically a poor country and ultimately had to shift its energies from a land-based to a labor-based, and now after commercialization point, to a skill-and technology-intensive, direction. On the other extreme, countries rich in oil may never have to make such a change. But where, as in the Philippines, the demand conditions facing even the rich and relatively diversified raw material export sector are not dependable and where, more importantly, there exists this large and growing unskilled labor supply, which is both a wasted resource and a substantial human problem, the natural tendency to put off the day of reckoning will have to be resisted. Instead, the availability of resources additional to the savings out of domestic agriculture and to the savings that, in future, can be expected to flow from new industrial exports should be viewed as welcome to assist in the difficult restructuring of the economy.

It is clear that more of the same will no longer do in most of the developing world. The pressure for employment generation by a reallocation of labor from the soft to the hard sectors is going to become increasingly severe. Legislation against the (changing) factor endowment is likely to be costly in both output and employment foregone, regardless of the mix between the roles of the private and public sectors a society determines for itself. The potential for mutual reinforcement of these two central development goals, via output and technology adjustment, is much larger than had once been assumed. The bad record of the 50s and 60s was largely man-made, and appropriate policies in the context of a "more ideal" multisectoral functioning of a LDC system, with proper regard to historical and typological differences, can materially affect the outcome in the future.

DISCUSSION

HANOCH SMITH (Israel): The major reasons for success in Taiwan lie in the conditions that led this country to choose the better alternatives and make the political decisions necessary. Favorite groups or classes in the modern sector, inflexibly structured rural societies that are hard to move, and poor economic policies must share the blame for relative failures in some other countries.

Expanding education and vocational training was thought to be the answer to some manpower problems, but the Ethiopian experience suggests that education in less developed countries can be overstressed at the expense of basic economic development. However, education will continue to be expanded in these states and receive high priority, for political reasons, and in the long run this may not prove a bad thing.

We must seek better mixes of resources, development in the labor-intensive sectors, and policies in which growth, output, employment, and income distribution complement each other. Each state must operate within the framework of its own resources, institutions, and political realities.

School education may even sharpen differences between groups. The fundamental educational conditions are determined before the child enters school, by its society, its family, and its values. Similarly, to formulate effective development policies one must begin by understanding the institutions, the leverages of politicians, and the expectations of the people concerned.

GERT ROSENTHAL (Guatemala): Changes in output mix and technology may increase labor absorption and improve income distribution. However, the problems of export promotion in states committed to industrialization through import substitution were understated by Professor Ranis.

Economic integration schemes in Latin America provided a certain industrial base resting on import substitution, which allowed some economies of scale and created an industrial infrastructure facilitating transition. I believe that during a transitional period import substitution and export promotion can coexist, with the aid of selective tariff, credit, and fiscal policies, the countries later slowly moving from the former to the latter.

DAVID KOCHAV (Israel): The development setup is biased against labor-intensive activities. The financial setup favors larger and more capital-intensive industries and agricultural activities. Most domestic and international financing is at more or less subsidized interest rates, encouraging the use of capital-intensive techniques. No country I know has an effective system of financial incentives for labor-intensive activities.

Most technologies are imported from the developed states, based on capital-intensive techniques, and not really suitable to the conditions in developing countries.

The more active groups in industry and agricultural development are also the politically stronger. They too tend to concentrate on capital-intensive techniques. And the present price mechanism is biased against labor-intensive industries. If we really care about income distribution, measures must be taken to remedy this situation.

Import substitution is a necessary phase of economic development. The transition from it to export orientation is not easy. Israel has been mentioned as an example where it was successfully performed. This is only partly true. Our official exchange rate is $1.00 = IL.4.20. The effective rate for exports is $1.00 = IL.6. The average effective protection rate for imports is $1.00 = IL.8$. Sometimes, the latter is as high as IL. 10.

The transition difficulties are both economic and political. When you establish some heavily protected industries, a change means a waste of physical resources. Politically, various vested interests are opposed to any change reducing their profits or incomes.

My conclusion is that one should be careful not to overprotect during the import substitution period and also that incentives for export promotion and import substitution should be roughly equal. When they differ widely, a change cannot be made without economic harm and political difficulties.

BRUCE F. JOHNSTON (United States): I think Professor Ranis gave a misleading impression on two points: Regarding Taiwan, he related the change in the agricultural sector to the new seed-fertilizer revolution. But in Taiwan this revolution dates back to the early 1920s, under Japanese rule. Professor Ranis also said that land reform in Taiwan took the form of ceilings on rent rather than a redistribution of land. This was true of its first three years, but land redistribution followed almost immediately. And I believe that attempts to regulate landowners' rents through legislated rent ceilings are counterproductive, making the tenants' situation even worse. On the other hand, redistribution of land means redistribution of wealth, affecting in a developing country both income distribution and economic efficiency favorably. This is what really happened in Taiwan since the early 1950s.

Taiwan was able to redistribute land effectively due to some special circumstances. Its regime had been kicked out of the mainland of China and had learnt by bitter experience that if you alienate the rural population you are dead. So in Taiwan they took care. Besides, the politicians who executed the land reform were mostly mainland Chinese, while the landlords who had to give up the land were Taiwanese. The latter had much less political power than, say Indian landlords vis-a-vis Indian policy makers.

Land redistribution is desirable but not indispensable for efficient agricultural development, and can be politically difficult. The really indispensable condition is the size distribution of operational units, not of ownership units.

GUSTAV PAPANEK (United States): There is a danger of overemphasizing labor-intensive export industries, especially in large countries. Korea employed over 500,000 people in labor-intensive industrial exports during the last seven years. For a country of the size of Indonesia, the comparable figure would be 3 million people. Assuming added value at $400 per head, this would mean for Indonesia exports of about $12,000 million, for India exports of over $40,000 million. Imagine the reaction of the developed world (to which Taiwan and Korea have been exporting) if India, Indonesia, and others exported electronics, garments, or textiles on this scale! Over a longer period, such states may be able to shift to manufactured exports not competing directly with politically powerful industries in developed states. In the short run, industrial exports of this size are probably not feasible.

We should not forget that there are labor-intensive import-substituting industries. The bias against import substitution of a labor-intensive kind exists but need not exist. It can be corrected by an undervalued exchange rate, which makes capital goods imports expensive and local labor cheap.

Large countries with big internal markets have an advantage from the view point of labor-intensive import substitution, while their size makes it difficult for them to export manufactures on a large scale.

Labor-intensive construction programs could help to build up the infrastructure and provide jobs in the off-season to agricultural unemployed.

It would be as dangerous to rely wholly on exports of manufactures to absorb unemployed or underemployed labor as it was to rely wholly on import substitution as a means of rapid industrialization and economic growth.

GUSTAV RANIS (United States): I agree that we should think in terms of a gradual shift, even in the small and medium countries, which I discussed in my paper. A balanced rural growth, in terms of traditional and nontraditional rural activity, without regard to what is happening on the trade side, is essential to solve problems of growth and employment simultaneously in medium or large developing states. As you move gradually from import substitution to export promotion, you may require an undervalued exchange rate and low tariffs, as Papanek said. But he seems too pessimistic about the prospects of many countries accepting an outward-looking strategy. Countries like Taiwan and Hong Kong, which expanded their exports dramatically, were able to shift from one item to another when faced with quotas in their foreign markets and still solve their employment problem. Besides, there are possibilities of expanding trade among the poorer countries themselves, as their production capacity, and thus their wealth, increase.

I agree with Mr. Kochav on the subject of interest. No country has a floating interest rate at the moment. In establishing a reasonable exchange rate, some states, like Korea, have done much better than others, like India.

In answer to Johnston, I believe changes in the rent were the major feature. If the use of cultivation did not change much from Japanese days in Taiwan, how did the large resettlement that he mentioned occur? Most of the productivity rise in the 1960s was a function of changes in environment, though this process may have been favored by the infrastructure provided under the Japanese colonial system.

**LABOR ABSORPTION IN
DEVELOPING COUNTRIES**
Jorge Mendez

The subject of employment has gained importance in recent years as many developing countries have observed that a considerable section of their active population does not find minimally well remunerated working opportunities. The problem is of such a magnitude that it has become a central topic for international agencies, governments, and academic centers. A major part of the Second Decade Development Strategy prepared by the United Nations is based on the concept that the problem of employment is very serious in poor countries. The International Labor Organization (ILO) has developed a special employment program of a world scope. The World Bank, the Food Agricultural Organization, UNESCO, have all given greater attention to the subject.

Large foreign financial assistance efforts, technical assistance, international trade cooperation, and national planning efforts carried out during the sixties did not achieve their social goals. Although a certain degree of success was achieved in increasing national product, problems related to employment, a low income level, and the living conditions of major sections of the population of more than 100 countries, remained almost unchanged.

Hence a revision of employment theories has become necessary. To a certain degree, academic, political, and international circles have been taken by surprise when carrying out this revision. They are learning that their technical knowledge is not sufficient to deal with a problem larger and more complex than the one the rich countries faced during their previous development stages, or when cyclical depression and unemployment occurred. Normally the employment problem has been stated in relation to the need for maintaining an adequate investment rate in developed countries. The particular problems of poor countries, where it was not easily understood that investment opportunities would be scarce, were not seriously taken into account.

INSUFFICIENCIES OF PRESENT ANALYSES

A solid body of theory on the subject of employment and growth in underdeveloped countries does not really exist. The immediate important task of economic science seems to be that of gathering dispersed factors, refining them, and developing an integral analysis within this vast field of economic policy.

Three years ago the ILO began its World Employment Program; before then it was possible to identify, especially in Latin America, four "models" or positions.

The first followed the classical school, which states that full employment would simply be a by-product of free competition; under free competition productive resources would be permanently well allocated, with an adequate distribution of national product among different factors of production, and with a rate of economic growth consistent with the capacity of the economic process to accumulate capital, thus increasing productivity. Within this model, which was supported by almost all our countries a relatively short while ago, the elimination of poverty among great masses of population was considered only a matter of time, of adherence to international trade laws. Even if its more or less strict application brought about an acceptable standard of living for Argentina and Uruguay, other countries that did not enjoy such favorable trade possibilities as these two states were never able to extract themselves from a situation of general poverty, although they generally followed those sacred principles. By 1940, after a century of applying the classical postulates by independent countries, average income per capita in Latin America did not reach 180 dollars per annum, excluding Argentina and Uruguay. The dual character of national economies has been strengthened, with a relatively prosperous minority in the cities and a great rural and urban mass among which unemployment, underemployment, and a very low income level predominate.

The second model utilized to deal with problems such as unemployment and a low income level in poor countries is based on the need for stimulating aggregate demand for goods. To some extent, this model is based on Lord Keynes' theory. According to the conclusions of Lauchlin Currie, the problem of poor countries does not rest so much in scarcity of capital, or in constraints deriving from the deficit in the balance of payments, as in insufficiencies of effective demand. If effective demand is stimulated, mainly through the implementation of significant investment plans in housing, a sector where demand is greatly restrained, a series of impulses will be generated in other economic sectors, which will then grow more rapidly, creating a great number of employment opportunities. This position, which presently constitutes the basis of the National

Development Plan of Colombia, is interesting and daring, but it does not seem to go further than the achievement of results in the short term. Moreover, there is a risk of aggravating the inflationary process, because it is doubtful whether the various productive sectors will be able to respond with sufficient flexibility, in additional supply of goods, to the demand stimulus.

In contrast to these two concepts, both possibly incomplete since they do not take into account structural problems of developing societies, Fei and Ranis in their "Development of an Economy with a Labour Surplus" propose a model based on the existence of a natural process of labor absorption from the traditional sector (with a labor surplus because of unemployment and underemployment) to the modern capitalist sector, (where the continuous process of investment creates the possibility of additional jobs). The labor surplus would vanish if the investment process could be performed without interference. The main task of economic policy would be to insure the existence of a "favourable institutional framework," in order for the absorption process to work with maximum flexibility. A necessary condition for this is, for example, that wages in the modern sector do not go beyond subsistence level: thus enterprises will be able to reach a maximum level of profits to be reinvested.

Another condition for optimal absorption is that enterprises adopt production processes characterized by labor-intensive technology. Within this process, the agricultural sector has a twofold role: on the one hand, to provide a labor supply with a low wage level and, on the other hand, to increase agricultural productivity, thus creating an additional labor surplus, which will be transferred to the industrial sector to strengthen its ability to reinvest profits.

Paul Prebisch presents in his "Transformation and Development" (1970) another, global policy of which a higher level of employment is the central goal. His book marks the culmination of a long process that he personally headed from 1950, in the Economic Commission for Latin America. He describes the urgency to promote a greater level of employment by planned and deliberate action. This action must be able to overcome the traditional constraints on steady and accelerated growth. His final point is the existence of a "dynamic insufficiency" in the economics of the region, because of which it is necessary to increase dynamism by higher rates of growth of the national product. He points out the necessity of providing for the immediate necessities and expectations of the great masses of population and not waiting for solutions based on the passage of time or on the mere process of capital accumulation in the modern sectors. Prebisch speaks of "correcting the dynamic insufficiency of the economy with a great social orientation." This means not only dealing with the basic needs of the poorest groups of the population but also searching for a type of growth that will supply the maximum quantity of new job opportunities, both in industry and in agriculture. Agrarian reform turns out to be of significant importance to Prebisch, as does his preoccupation with revindicating the role of the rural sector, in the light of the impressive growth of cities.

Prebisch says that the employment problem in developing countries cannot be solved by a simple process of accumulation in the capitalist sectors. But he concludes that the solution essentially depends on a "critical rate" of investment and an increase in productivity. In essence, the solution continues to depend on the acceleration of growth in the modern sector where a major share of savings has been available. This sector, however, has occupied a relatively unimportant place within the global context.

Research work such as that of Fei's and Ranis', and Dr. Prebisch's, helps to clarify the labor absorption process in the modern dynamic sector. But it is possible that both of them fail to appreciate the degree of absorption that can be achieved in practice. They also fail because of their tendency to consider the development process as depending almost exclusively on the capacity of the modern sector for growth, the other sectors having to remain passive, depending on the opportunities that originate in the privileged sector.

It is relevant that in Latin America despite economies with relatively high rates of growth (between 6 percent and 7 percent annually), relatively important financial resources available, the modern sector enjoying a great degree of preference, and the traditional agricultural sector supplying unlimited quantities of cheap labor, the employment problem is far from being solved and, moreover, tends to be aggravated. In Colombia, for example, while the annual rate of GNP growth has been above 6 percent during recent years, the modern sector has not been able to create more than between 60,000 to 70,000 additional jobs, while the labor force has been growing annually by more than 220,000 workers.

These figures show, first, that the basic conditions of the Fei-Ranis model are not generally met in developing countries. The difference in the wage level between capitalist and traditional sectors is much greater than that which the model assumes to be permissible, due to such factors as labor union pressure. Industrial wages rise continually. Capital formation tends to incorporate capital-intensive technologies; thus labor absorption is of a reduced magnitude. It is difficult for the industrial sector to grow with sufficient intensity, mainly because of market limitations. The great increase in population creates a more than proportional increase in the labor force, thus exceeding the absorption capacity of the dynamic sector. Rural population emigrates to the cities, mainly because the rural sector provides no possibilities for its residents to improve their living standards rather than because the urban sector provides them with really attractive jobs.

These facts indicate that the modern sector is not capable of responding to the challenge represented by the demand for jobs and greater welfare originating in the large traditional and poor sector surrounding the modern sector. The process of profit accumulation and, consequently, of new and bigger investments, is restricted in its capacity to create a large number of jobs, because of a high wage level. But it is equally true that with the wage level effectively maintained at subsistence level, problems of selling industrial goods produced would be accentuated.

Therefore, the process envisioned by Fei and Ranis would only work imperfectly, without solving the problem of unemployment, underemployment, and a low income level in developing countries.

Thus the subject becomes a matter of ratios and time. The ratios are quite unfavorable when the dynamic sector, enterprising and modern, covers only 10 percent of the population and accounts for 80 to 90 percent of national savings. On the other hand, time is a decisive factor. The sluggishness with which the group representing 10 percent of the population can incorporate the great poor majority (which is increasing in absolute number) into its privileged sector may be exasperating.

HOW TO SPREAD EMPLOYMENT AND INCOME IMPROVEMENT OPPORTUNITIES?

Is it possible and desirable to shift part of the emphasis given to the growth of the dynamic and modern business sector towards the depressed traditional sectors, without harming national growth prospects? The possibility of a contradiction between growth and goals such as employment and wealth redistribution is now expressed in new terms. The dilemma does not lie so much in the choice between greater employment and more equipment, or between greater employment and higher productivity from the same productive unit, as in the choice between the continuation of an accelerated development process within a limited area with a high level of technology able to efficiently perform essential economic functions, and the extension of this process to sectors that have not displayed this ability up till now but that may acquire it if given a real opportunity.

The problem is not an easy one. The transfer of resources and a reduction in the concentration of financial power in the privileged modern sector may bring about stagnation affecting the overall process of growth if the objective to stimulate and maintain an efficient dynamism in the traditional sector is not achieved. But since the modern sector does not demonstrate an ability to solve problems affecting great masses of population with sufficient speed, the spreading of opportunities by extending the application of the development model to poor sectors seems to be inevitable.

Until now in no country has the problem of unemployment and a low income level of great national majorities been solved solely through capital accumulation by a small dynamic business class. Brazil is probably the most promising example in Latin America, but authentic social improvements have not yet been evident in that country. In capitalist countries, today industrialized and prosperous, relationships existing between social classes at the time the larger capitalist accumulation process was begun were completely different from those presently predominating in countries such as Colombia, or even Mexico. For example, conditions for the education of the population or the rate of population growth were different. Although it seems that a proletarian mass existed in England that facilitated the growth and high earnings of the Industrial Revolution by accepting very low wages, at the same time the remaining farm population had the possibility of creating a solid base for prosperity. England also benefited in that period from high profits originating from the exploitation of colonies. We can observe that Japan, which is used as an example of what can be achieved through austerity and low incomes, began its rapid process of growth from an agricultural base of high productivity. Already at the beginning of the Meiji Age Japanese agricultural productivity per each 10,000 square meters was four times greater than the productivity of other Asian countries: thus it was able to supply financial resources from the agricultural sector for the growing industry. In none of these countries existed the profound dualism, such as that presently observed in developing countries.

Deliberate support for the growth of backward sectors of the economy may be successful not only in social but also in economic terms. In countries characterized by labor and, usually, land abundance, efforts and resources aimed at increasing labor-intensive production will have to produce more beneficial results, especially in the rural sector, in social costs and benefits, than efforts and resources devoted to capital-intensive projects.

Frequently, a great improvement in the life and working conditions of the poorer groups helps to uncover hidden potential such as ambition for progress and dynamic capacity. Education, health, extension of services, credit, and greater access to land ownership and communications may change the future prospects of millions of people. The rate of return from elementary education is much higher than the rate of return from higher education. It is also known that productivity per 10,000 square meters can be higher in small farms rather than in large farms with mechanized productive equipment and that the expansion capacity of small industries may be very significant for additional employment.

Therefore, a great potential seems to exist for an increase in production if those sectors are provided with special assistance. These are precisely the sectors that have lagged behind achievements of the modern capitalist sectors, becoming great islands of poverty and despair.

A great change in the structure of development is needed and, consequently, a wise choice of the ways of redistributing resources must be made. The modern sector must maintain a leading role. Its force is a decisive factor in maintaining the earning of profits from the large investments carried out, serving as a base for the development of the whole economy, and, at the same time, continuing the process of the absorption of human resources freed by the traditional sector. But an accurate examination of the resources available to the modern sector, of the way in which sometimes excessively capital-intensive investments are made, and of the high consumption expenditures of the wealthy class must make available great financial resources for projects in the poor sectors. It is also necessary to plan a new direction for resources and public activities, leading to a solution of the needs of poor sectors and the creating of employment opportunities. There should be a development model with a wider dynamic base, which will contribute to the optimal utilization of scarce resources, such as capital, and which will reduce the number of limitations on the continuation of the process of intensive industrialization, in the framework of future development.

In a recent study, Professor Harry Hoshima concluded that in a country with such abundant financial resources as Iran there would be serious difficulties in maintaining accelerated industrial growth during a sufficiently long period of time if an adequate redistribution of opportunities was not achieved between the cities and rural regions and between the various social strata.

A redistribution of this kind would increase the possibility of achieving equilibrium in the foreign sector. At least, part of the imports for consumption purposes derived from the demand of the wealthy class would be eliminated by the transfer of resources to the poor class. Industries producing for mass consumption, which have the best competitive capacity in foreign markets, would receive a strong impulse from the increase in internal demand originating from the greater prosperity of traditional sectors.

ELEMENTS OF AN EMPLOYMENT POLICY

An integral employment policy, prepared within the framework of the World Employment Program of the ILO, is based on the factors mentioned above. These ideas have been incorporated into the Reports of High Level Missions that the ILO has sent to Colombia (1969), Ceylon (1970), Iran (1971), and Kenya (1972). They have also been applied by Human Resources Planning Groups and regional employment teams, which have constituted the central activities of this program.

These high-level delegations are autonomous technical teams, and the conclusions they reach depend mostly on their leaders' points of view. Therefore, it is not possible to state with certainty that other missions, for example those completing their tasks in the Philippines and the Dominican Republic at the time of writing, will reach the same conclusions as those of the four previous missions. However, a number of essential subjects should appear in the context of every policy effectively trying to improve the employment situation with a certain degree of urgency.

These subjects include:

- How to increase the emphasis given to employment and income distribution, in the context of national planning and economic policy, instead of framing goals solely in terms of the growth of production. This generally implies the development of models with sectoral employment goals.
- How to indicate or strengthen special programs of action in sectors of the economy that are disconnected from the central process of capital modernization and accumulation. These programs are particularly important for the traditional rural sector and for small industry.
- What is the magnitude of financial, technical, and administrative resources that can and must be transformed in relation to these programs.
- How to introduce and execute a technological policy and a policy of relative prices for factors of production that will enable the best utilization of both scarce capital resources and abundant labor resources.
- How to adapt educational programs to the needs of development directed towards employment. This task requires the establishment of a comprehensive system of human resource planning including every level of education and training, formal and informal.
- How to integrate in the best possible way the modern sector, which has a dynamic of its own, and the traditional sectors, which are to be the subject of constant and special assistance for their improvement.

- What kind of population policy must be followed in order to avoid excessive pressure on available resources.

These factors have been analyzed with different degrees of intensity in the four reports mentioned above. There are doubts about the precision of the adopted recommendations and their feasibility. The technical work required to clarify all the subjects involved in this type of restructuring of development must be continued, because this is only the beginning. But the important conclusion derived from the reports is the failure of traditional policies in the solution of a great social and human problem, and the urgency of undertaking intense efforts in order to rectify the goals.

**AGRICULTURAL STRATEGY
AND INDUSTRIAL GROWTH**
Bruce F. Johnston

This discussion of interrelations between agricultural and industrial growth focuses on the distinctive problems of "late developing countries" in which 60 percent or more of the working population still obtains its livelihood in agriculture. For such countries the modernization of agriculture necessarily involves a transition from a traditional, semisubsistence rural economy to a commercially oriented agricultural sector that is heavily dependent upon the nonfarm economy for inputs and markets. The consequences of policies based on the false dichotomy of agricultural versus industrial growth are especially unfortunate for countries with the structural and demographic features that characterize the contemporary late developing countries.

It is sometimes forgotten that transformation of the predominantly agrarian structure of a late developing economy is a necessary condition for modern economic growth. Moreover, the highly protectionist strategies of import substitution, so often pursued to foster industrialization, have usually led to the establishment of an inefficient industrial enclave and not to the kind of structural change required for sustained growth. Policies of import substitution, and the underpricing of capital and foreign exchange and overpricing of labor with which they have been associated, have aggravated problems of unemployment and underemployment and have accentuated the inequality of income distribution.

The special problems confronting late developing countries are related above all to the fact that they are surrounded by a world economy dominated by economically advanced countries. These industrialized nations use highly productive, science-based technologies adapted to a situation in which capital is relatively abundant and labor is scarce and costly. The problems associated with uncritical transfer of technologies are especially acute because of the exceedingly rapid growth of population and labor force virtually universal in the developing countries.

INTERRELATIONS BETWEEN AGRICULTURAL DEVELOPMENT AND ECONOMIC GROWTH

The decline in the percentage share of agriculture in national product and labor force, which is one of the defining characteristics of the process of structural transformation, is a consequence of increasing specialization in productive activities, accompanied by progressive differentiation in the roles of workers and of institutions. The effects on farm employment of rising productivity within agriculture and the transfer of processing and other functions from the farm household to specialist firms outside agriculture is accentuated by the fact that the coefficient of income elasticity of demand for agricultural products is less than one and falls with rises in per capita income. The resulting changes in the composition of output and in the occupational distribution of the labor force imply increasing interdependence between agriculture and other sectors and, in consequence, expansion of marketing and other branches of service sector.

Growth in the size and in the technical and entrepreneurial competence of the manufacturing sector is a critical aspect of structural transformation. In addition to enhancing the capacity of the economy to satisfy new patterns of demand for final goods, increased diversity and technical competence in the manufacturing sector enhances the flexibility of the economy and its capacity to produce capital goods and intermediate products adapted to a country's resource endowment and relative factor prices.

The development of manufacturing also makes possible increases in farm productivity by satisfying requirements for purchased inputs. Local manufacture of farm equipment can have a highly significant influence in fostering the development of domestic metalworking industries. However, domestic manufacture of products such as chemical fertilizers is likely to be inefficient because the manufacturing processes are so capital intensive and economies of scale are so important. For such items, the principal concern is to ensure their availability to farmers at a low price; and the contribution of the domestic manufacturing sector lies in earning an increasing fraction of the foreign exchange required to finance these and other imports.

One of the most important consequences of the progressive differentiation in the roles of individuals and of institutions is in making possible the application of science and science-based technologies to productive activity. In agriculture, as in other sectors, technological progress leads to improved input-output ratios and to large gains in total factor productivity, that is, increases in output per unit of total input. Increased use of conventional inputs explains only about one-quarter of the growth of per capita output of economically advanced countries. The balance can be attributed to technological change. The potential contribution to technological progress is especially significant in agriculture because of the possibilities of raising the productivity of the large amounts of labor and land that are committed to the agricultural sector.

The great significance of the Green Revolution derives from the fact that some of the cumulative advances in agricultural science and the innovations that have reduced the cost of chemical fertilizers are now beginning to have an impact on many developing countries in the tropical and subtropical regions of the world. Prior to these recent scientific breakthroughs, most of the biological-chemical innovations were only applicable to the temperate regions where they had been developed.

The "architecture" of the semidwarf varieties of rice and wheat and other genetic characteristics of these crops, and of maize as well, mean that production potentials have been sharply raised because the yield response per pound of fertilizer has been increased substantially and favorable response ratios apply to levels of fertilizer application three or four times as high as the levels at which traditional varieties begin to show a decrease in yield because of lodging. (The tall, weak-stemmed plants tend to topple over when they carry a heavy head of grain.) Many problems remain to be resolved before these and other improved seed-fertilizer combinations can have a widespread impact on production in developing countries, but the potential is great. And because of the divisibility of these new inputs, this type of innovation can provide the basis for an efficient agricultural strategy aimed at the progressive modernization of the entire rural population.

The decline in the dominant position of agriculture and the rise in the relative importance of manufacturing and other sectors is bound to be a slow process in late developing countries because the economically active population is growing so rapidly and the weight of the nonfarm sectors in the total labor force is currently so small that even a rapid rate of expansion of employment in those sectors will absorb only a fraction of the annual additions to the labor force. Consequently the farm population will continue to increase in absolute size for several decades at least, and the decline in the percentage share of agriculture will be slow. In India, for example, 70 percent of the labor force was in agriculture in both 1950 and 1960, and it seems likely that the 1970 census will not show any appreciable reduction in the share of agriculture.

STRUCTURAL TRANSFORMATION AND THE CHOICE OR STRATEGY FOR AGRICULTURE

As a result of the structural characteristics of late developing countries, the initial level of farm cash income is small in relation to the number of farm households. Likewise, the expansion of cash receipts and enlarged use of off-farm inputs depend to a large extent on the rate of structural transformation, and the increase in commercial demand relative to the size of the farm work force will be fairly slow because of the initial structure and the rapid rate of growth of the total labor force. For countries that have experienced little structural transformation proceeds from export crops often account for a large fraction of farm cash receipts. And the expansion of agricultural exports is viewed as a particularly attractive means of enlarging farm cash incomes as well as foreign exchange proceeds.*

As structural change proceeds, the domestic commercial market becomes an increasingly important source of farm cash income because of the growth in the size and per capita income of the nonfarm population dependent on purchased food. The transformation process also facilitates the rise in cash receipts per member of the agricultural work force, initially by slowing its rate of growth and eventually by making possible a decline in the absolute size of the farm labor force.

Until considerable structural transformation has occurred, however, the average farm household is subject to a severe purchasing power constraint on the use of off-farm inputs. Widespread involvement of the farm population in the process of agricultural modernization therefore requires a sequence of innovations that permits a gradually expanding use of external inputs.

In general, a rise in agricultural prices does not represent a tenable solution to the problem of restricted farm cash income. Food expenditures typically account for 50 percent or more of total consumption in low-income households, and the price elasticity of demand for food is low. In consequence, the failure of food supplies to expand as rapidly as the effective demand for food means a steep rise in food prices with serious effects on consumer welfare and often political unrest as well.

Because of the low price elasticity of demand for food, however, preoccupation with a "food problem" can quickly change to preoccupation with the low prices and incomes received by the farm population.

---

*This almost universal attractiveness of export crops is a major factor underlying the tendency for exports to expand more rapidly than import demand, often resulting in sharp price declines for primary commodities.

A country that is in a position to expand agricultural exports rapidly (usually by enlarging its share of total exports) does not face that effective demand constraint. Moreover, a country that has considerable scope for replacing food imports by expanding domestic commercial sales will not face a demand constraint until the scope for import substitution has been exhausted. But, in general, the scope for significantly enlarging the ability of the agricultural sector to utilize off-farm inputs depends on structural transformation that increases commercial demand for agricultural products.

Because of this purchasing power constraint, a late developing country faces a difficult choice: If it pursues an agricultural strategy aimed at the progressive modernization of the entire agricultural sector, it must rely on a sequence of divisible innovations. These technological changes can be widely adopted by small farm units with limited cash income, which can only gradually expand their use of purchased inputs. Alternatively, a country can opt for an agricultural strategy in which resources are concentrated in a subsector of large farm units. If these large farms account for the bulk of the country's commercial production, they will not be subject to a severe purchasing power constraint. These farms will be able to expand their use of tractors and other types of mechanical innovations at the same time that they are stepping up their use of fertilizers and other divisible inputs. With such a dual-size structure, there will obviously be a sharp difference between the technologies adopted by the subsector of large units and those used by the remainder of the agricultural sector. Moreover, to the extent the modern enclave dominates commercial sales, the possibility of promoting the progressive modernization of the bulk of the rural population will be severely restricted because the potential for increasing farm productivity without some increase in the use of fertilizer and other off-farm inputs is usually very slight.

This choice between progressive modernization of the entire agricultural sector and a concentration of resources in a subsector of large units is often described as a choice between equity and efficiency. There is no doubt that widespread participation by the rural population in improved opportunities to raise their productivity and incomes is more consistent with the social goals of reducing the inequality of income distribution and expanding opportunities for productive employment. But the converse does not follow. Concentration of resources in large, modern farm enterprises is not necessarily more efficient. The gains in efficiency appear to be impressive when one considers only firms within the modern subsector. The relevant comparison, however, is between the efficiency of the sector-wide expansion paths associated with the two types of strategies. And because of the structural and demographic characteristics of a late developing country, it seems clear that from society's point of view a progressive modernization strategy is to be preferred for reasons of economic efficiency as well as for its greater contribution to social goals.

The historical experience of Japan and Taiwan provides the clearest evidence concerning the advantages and feasibility of agricultural strategies aimed at the progressive modernization of small-scale, labor-intensive farm units. Given effective research and extension programs oriented toward generating and diffusing divisible innovations, it is possible to expand agricultural output by more efficient utilization of the internal resources of the agricultural sector coupled with gradual increases in the use of complementary purchased inputs. Introduction of improved seed-fertilizer combinations, as epitomized by the Green Revolution, is the prime example of a divisible, yield-increasing innovation that permits large increases in factor productivity. These new seed-fertilizer technologies often require substantial investments in irrigation to enlarge the areas suited to the introduction of high-yielding varieties. For many areas more promising and less costly opportunities are related to increasing the productivity of growing rainfed crops. But, with the exception of maize, relatively little research has been carried out to develop the varieties and to determine the agronomic practices needed to exploit that potential. Even in the areas provided with controlled irrigation, where the Green Revolution has had its greatest impact, much more research and farmer training are needed in order to realize the genetic potential of the new varieties. In Pakistan, for example, the new varieties of wheat and rice are essentially being grown by traditional methods. This fact should not be too surprising; learning is always a time-consuming process.

Progressive modernization of the rural economy can also be expected to lead to increased demand for a range of inexpensive but improved farm implements to break seasonal labor bottlenecks and to facilitate better execution of various cultural practices. For example, the dwarf varieties of wheat are sensitive to the depth of planting, and to obtain high yields it is also essential to achieve an optimum plant population per acre. The use of a bullock-drawn seed drill can help in accomplishing both objects. Generating demand for this type of farm equipment can also be expected to stimulate expansion of output and employment in domestic industries dominated by widely dispersed and relatively small firms. Inasmuch as firms of this nature use labor-intensive, capital-saving techniques and rely as much as possible on domestic raw materials, expansion does not depend as heavily on scarce supplies of capital and foreign exchange as increased output by firms that make up the modern industrial sector.

A widespread development of technical and entrepreneurial skills in metalworking firms can also be expected to have significant feedback effects. The relatively simple machine tools used in the manufacture of such items as metal plows, disc harrows, stationary threshers, pumps, and diesel engines give rise to additional backward linkages that are within the technical competence of a fledgling manufacturing sector. These feedback effects and the associated learning experience are vital because of the need to develop an indigenous capacity to produce machine tools. This not only reduces a country's dependence on imported capital equipment, which is biased to the labor-saving requirements of developed countries, but also enhances the country's ability to adapt equipment to meet its own needs. The pattern of rural demand for consumer goods associated with widespread increases in farm cash income will have a stronger impact on the growth of domestic manufacturing than will result if the distribution of farm income is highly skewed. The large incomes that can be earned by farmers within a modern enclave give rise to a demand for sophisticated consumer goods and farm equipment. And whether the comparison is between automobiles and bicycles or between tractors and bullock-drawn equipment, it is apparent that the more sophisticated pattern of demand will be associated with greater reliance on imports or imported components and thus with a more restricted stimulus to domestic manufacturing capacity.

CONCLUDING COMMENTS

This brief review of the interrelations between agricultural and industrial development has emphasized mainly the complementarities between the two sectors. In the long run the reciprocal interactions between agriculture and industry, involving increases in the productivity and output of each, permit rapid growth in national income and in opportunities for productive employment throughout the economy. An appropriate agricultural strategy can stimulate healthy development of a domestic manufacturing sector. Rapid expansion of employment and of per capita income in the nonfarm sectors implies a larger commercial demand for agricultural products, which in turn permits more rapid growth of farm cash income.

This stress on sectoral interdependence does not alter the fact that at any point in time the farm and nonfarm sectors are competing for scarce resources, notably loan funds and foreign exchange. Indeed it has been argued that a significant advantage of a strategy of progressive modernization is that it relies mainly on expanded use of off-farm inputs that are complementary to the farm-supplied resources of labor and land. By achieving large increases in factor productivity, agriculture's claims on scarce resources are minimized. This type of approach permits a sizable net outflow of capital from agriculture to meet a part of the investment requirements for industrial expansion and infrastructure without stifling the growth of agricultural output.

Before bringing this paper to a close, an awkward question should be faced. If a strategy aimed at progressive modernization of the agricultural sector has important economic as well as social advantages, how do we account for the fact that most developing countries appear to be pursuing strategies that lead to a dual-size structure of agriculture with increases in output concentrated in a subsector of large and relatively capital-intensive farms? This important question deserves much more attention than it has received. Six reasons appear to account for the neglect of the progressive modernization alternative:

- Perhaps most basic is the neglect until recently of the measures required to generate an appropriate research base for a strategy aimed at promoting widespread agricultural progress. Even now, the Green Revolution is merely a beginning. In addition to the requirements for adaptive research mentioned earlier, there is a need to develop varieties of rice and wheat that will perform well under a wide variety of local conditions and without controlled water supplies.

- In many countries there has been inadequate investment in infrastructure, especially facilities for water control and roads. As a result, the areas able to benefit from the new varieties now available are much too limited.

- There is a great deal of skepticism concerning the feasibility of significantly increasing the productivity of millions of small and medium farms. This feeling is reinforced by a gross exaggeration of the significance of economies of scale in agriculture and a tendency to pursue modernity as an independent goal.

- Particular groups that wield a great deal of political power recognize that they have much to gain from policies that concentrate resources within a favoured subsector of large farms.

- Various external influences strengthen the position of local groups that have a vested interest in agricultural development based on a dual-size structure. Specifically, the transfer of inappropriate technologies is often encouraged by foreign aid programs. Aid programs have a tendency to emphasize large, identifiable projects; finance foreign exchange but not local costs; tie aid to equipment purchased in the aid-giving country; and use technical experts whose judgment is influenced by an implicit model of efficient agriculture represented by the American Midwest, southern England, or northern France. Those tendencies are reinforced by large international corporations that desire to promote sales in less developed countries.

(This desire is perhaps especially strong for manufacturers of tractors who have excess capacity now that demand in Europe and North America is largely confined to replacement demand.)

- Finally, much too little attention has been given to the formidable administrative and organizational problems involved in the successful implementation of a strategy of progressive modernization. For example, there appears to be a need for more imaginative techniques of training, capable of reaching large numbers of illiterate farmers at a cost that does not overstrain government budget resources. In many areas there appears to be a particular need to develop effective ways to achieve more efficient management of water supplies at the farm level and better coordination between the managers of public irrigation systems and individual users. This points to the need to establish or strengthen organizations that bring farmers together. But many attempts to promote cooperatives proved disappointing and suggest a need to develop additional techniques of organizing activities that require cooperative action.

Given those formidable obstacles, it is difficult to be sanguine about the prospect that many developing countries will pursue strategies of progressive modernization. One would hope that greater recognitions of its advantages, buttressed by a certain amount of enlightened self-interest and growing concern about the explosive consequences of rapid displacement of rural workers, will eventually result in policies that promote wider participation in agricultural progress and more rapid expansion of nonfarm employment opportunities.

DISCUSSION

SOLON BARRACLOUGH (FAO): During the 1950s there were three kinds of agricultural units in Mexico—large, heavily capitalized estates, medium estates of about 5 hectares, and small farms. With the Green Revolution, productivity in these sectors rose 7 percent, 2 percent, and 1 percent per annum respectively over a 10-year period. This shows that in Mexico, which in this respect is similar to many other developing states, the new practices were adopted largely by those with good access to power, land, and labor, that is, by the relatively better off. The mass of the agricultural labor force either did not benefit from the Green Revolution, or was even worse off than before.

EPHRAIM KLEIMAN (Israel): One of the reasons that more states do not encourage agricultural development is that such development causes more people to become underemployed and eventually unemployed. These then flood the urban sectors, and if no capital for investment in nonagricultural sectors is available on a scale permitting their employment, the result is failure even if the agricultural development itself succeeds.

LE VAN PHUC (Vietnam): About half a million hectares of land suitable for rice and other crops were left idle for some years in Vietnam, owing to the war. Would it be wise to expand the money supply to provide farmers with credit for the reclamation of this land? And is it wiser to give credit to agriculture-based industries or to agriculture itself?

ROBERT MUSCAT (AID): I don't think one can draw a firm conclusion that the only way to get lots of farmers involved in a Green Revolution is by carefully administered programs of person-to-person relationships between government administrators and villagers. I will give two examples refuting the theory of the backward farmer afraid of risks who has to be seduced into the modern farming world.

In Thailand during the 1960s experts thought it would be useful if a corn marketing cooperative was established, it being believed that farmers were at the mercy of Chinese traders. But the Thai farmers refused to join this cooperative, realizing that, because the Chinese traders were competing with each other, they were charging very fair prices. Corn production expanded rapidly without the cooperative, and within three years corn became Thailand's fourth largest export.

In India an intensive agricultural program was executed in some districts, and a new seed-fertilizer technology was made available. Yet often output increased fastest in districts where the intensive program was not applied. What mattered was the availability of the technology not the administered instruction.

SHIMON AMIR (Israel): In Venezuela, we introduced a three-pronged supervised project: Credit to agriculture was given in the form of inputs (not money) under supervision of a bank and a committee of farmers. After five years some 20,000 farmers in 250 villages were involved. An institute was formed to train agricultural planners. Credits were granted when the farmer completed his planned tasks. This could be one way of modernizing agriculture.

ELIEZER BRUTZKUS (Israel): Priority must be given to raising the level of subsistence agriculture through modernization and commercialization. This interconnects with urbanization policy. The Green Revolution requires infrastructure for transportation and marketing, technicians, and better educated elements not far from the rural districts. The urbanization policy of most LDCs concentrates on a few points, denuding the countryside of its savings, skills, and technicians. A policy of multiplying urban centers is essential for modernizing and commercializing agriculture.

KASSOUM CONGO (Upper Volta): In Upper Volta, we tried to modernize agriculture but are handicapped by rain. For several years rainfall has been insufficient, and 95 percent of our population works in agriculture. So what should we do?

BRUCE JOHNSTON (United States): Let me emphasize my major conclusion: The strategy of progressive modernization commends itself not only for social reasons but also because it expands employment rapidly. This helps to make for a less unequal income distribution.

Increases in output are not directly linked with increases in major agricultural inputs, such as land, labor, and capital, which account for about 75 percent of total input. The very rapid expansion of agricultural output in Israel, which was accompanied by relatively modest increases in factor inputs, was due to a rise in productivity. Taiwan and Japan also show that factor productivity rises steeply when agricultural strategy is designed to complement abundant resources and does not neglect a large part of the agricultural sector.

In Upper Volta irrigation potential is small because there is not enough rainfall to conserve. The economic future of Upper Volta may perhaps lie in a very extensive cattle-raising type of economy, with less reliance on crop production.

But the Ivory Coast is an interesting example of a country that used imaginative techniques to obtain widespread adoption of more efficient agricultural methods.

The question whether or not inflationary financing makes sense should not be considered in terms of a specific project. If the project described by Mr. Le Van Phuc is worth doing, funds can and should be found for it elsewhere in the Vietnamese budget.

I agree with Mr. Brutzkus' remarks on urbanization.

Progressive modernization of agriculture creates a pattern of demand for agricultural inputs and for consumer goods (by raising most farm incomes) and encourages a healthy, rapid growth of industry more than the alternative policy of crash modernization in a subsector of large units. It is also likely to be more favorable to the rapid spread of family planning. The experience of Taiwan shows that, when farm households are widely involved in processes of technical and economic change, they are much more likely to have the knowledge and motivation to practice family planning. When agricultural improvement is confined to a minority, only a minority will experience the rising aspirations that played so major a role in the acceptance of family planning in the rural areas of Taiwan. When the majority of farmers has no experience of progress, they have no reasons to raise their sights and are unlikely to demand modern consumer goods and services. And unless the birth rate falls in rural areas as well as in the towns, the possibility of successful economic growth in late developing countries is approximately zero.

I do not agree with the criticism of Mr. Amir. The cumbersome apparatus he described might do in oil-rich Venezuela, but most developing states have neither the money nor the staff to reach most of the agricultural population in the way he described. I oppose credit supervision. Interest rates should be realistic and unsubsidized.

Dr. Muscat's criticism is valid, but I must emphasize the importance of finding cheap but effective training techniques, because agricultural modernization is a learning process.

THE ROLES OF INDUSTRY AND AGRICULTURE IN THE DEVELOPMENT OF DEVELOPING COUNTRIES

William Brian Reddaway

"Industry versus Agriculture" implies that there is a conflict between these two sectors of the economy, and to some extent this is true when it is a question of allocating resources that are scarce in a developing country. Nevertheless, the growth of industry and of agriculture are largely complementary in the development process. This comes about in at least two different ways:

1. The growth of output in one of the two sectors increases the size of the market for the other one: this is particularly important where agricultural growth provides a better market for industrial products, since the size of the market is particularly apt to prevent some industries from even getting started in a developing country.

2. Often, agriculture provides industry with an essential raw material (say, raw cotton or sugar cane) without which it would have difficulty in expanding (although sometimes imports can meet the requirements). Similarly, industry can supply agriculture with essential tools, fertilizers, fuels, and the like, which again might be supplied from abroad but which may be more suitable to the particular needs of the agriculturalist in the developing country if they are produced at home; deliveries, repair services, and so on may also be more satisfactory in that case.

The impact of these two points varies a great deal between different developing countries, just as most other generalizations have to be interpreted in the light of local circumstances if one is to know how important they are in a particular case. But complementarity is nearly always of considerable importance.

Very frequently, where industry and agriculture are competing for some particular scarce resource (for example, capital), industry may benefit more from an additional allocation to agriculture (so as to ensure a better supply of raw materials) than it would from a further allocation to itself: if it received an additional allocation of capital in order to increase its own machinery, this might be idle for part of the time through lack of materials, and the industrialist would regret his investment.

The same principle applies if one considers other sectors besides industry and agriculture. It is all too common to discuss development programs as if these two sectors were the only ones in existence, but at the very least one must recognize a third sector, that is, services, including transport. Moreover, industry is frequently interpreted rather narrowly to exclude public utilities such as electricity, although the growth of industrial production may be being held up by the inadequacy of the electricity supplies. With services and public utilities there is usually little scope for making good an inadequate level of local output by bringing in imports, so it is all the more essential to ensure that their development keeps in balance with the production of goods, whether by industry or agriculture.

Many types of service (for instance, petty roadside trading) are overdeveloped in many developing countries and have quite unnecessary numbers of people attached to them because so many people find it difficult to secure better-paid work elsewhere. There is no need for a development program to include active steps for the development of this type of service, which can usually be relied upon to expand (or overexpand) in response to the needs of other sectors. The mutual interdependence of different sectors does not prescribe one particular allocation of resources and one particular distribution of outputs as essential. But the principle of complementarity is nevertheless at least as important as the idea of rivalry.

So far as the supply of workers is concerned, there is very seldom a real conflict between industry and agriculture, unless one is considering quite unrealistic rates of growth: Apart from any surplus of labor that may already exist—whether it is visibly unemployed, or underemployed on small agricultural holdings or in petty trading—the population growth in the country is normally quite fast enough to enable both industry and agriculture to obtain all the additional labor they really want; the only real conflict, on the human side, is likely to be for skilled organizers of one kind or another.

It is even less likely that there will be any difficulty about the output of industry and agriculture expanding simultaneously. The labor force in each can increase, and there is also likely to be an increase in output per worker.

INTERNATIONAL TRADE AND THE PATTERNS OF DEMAND AND PRODUCTION

If international trade were impossible, each country's pattern of production would have to be the same as its pattern of consumption: "what you don't produce you can't have." The growth of production per head would make people better off and raise their real demand for all sorts of things: the relative growth of industry, agriculture, and services would largely reflect the way in which some people wanted to use their bigger real incomes, although it would not necessarily follow that the government had no part to play in influencing the relative growth of industry and agriculture. Thus it could influence the outcome by imposing differential excise duties, changing the relative prices with which consumers would be faced (over and above price changes caused by the varying ease or difficulty of expanding output), and it might be deliberate government policy either to allow market shortages of particular items, or to influence consumer demand by propaganda (say, against alcohol or tobacco, or in favor of contraceptives). The government also plays an important role by its decisions about the size and pattern of its own purchases—for instance, for schools, roads, infrastructure, or the armed forces.

While there would, therefore, be some scope for a deliberate government development policy even in a closed system, the scope for choosing between different policies is enormously increased by international trade. This means that, to a large extent, the pattern of a country's production can be different from its pattern of consumption and investment. Moreover, in practice the government is almost inevitably much more involved in determining policy than it would be in a closed system: the existence of international trade compels it to take many decisions, even if these be of a negative kind. Thus it can give selective protection to different branches of production (whether in industry or in agriculture), it can tax or subsidize selected exports, and it can attract or repel foreign capital and expertise, either generally or selectively. When one also considers the measures that would be available in a closed system (such as government agricultural research stations, or direct government investment in industry) there seems to be a vast range of possibilities for the government of a developing country to influence the pattern of development. And the existence of an international market should ensure that, provided the policies are reasonably wise, there will still be a great deal of **freedom** of choice for consumers.

LIMITATIONS ON CHOICE OF DEVELOPMENT STRATEGY

Nevertheless, there are restraints that limit the freedom of a developing country to choose any particular pattern of development. Some of the main ones are as follows:

1. The principle of balance discussed above must be respected when one is concerned with things that cannot be traded internationally (such as electricity) or that would involve such heavy costs that it would be absurd to import or export them except in freak circumstances

(such as fresh bread). This means, in particular, that there will be serious problems if adequate action is not taken, in good time, to expand the output of electricity or of transport facilities in places where a big increase in requirements will be arising out of (say) the development of an iron-ore field; and it also means that expanding the output of things not easily exported is likely to be wasteful, even though the country seems well equipped to produce them.

2. Developing countries commonly wish to introduce new industries, and superficially this seems attractive where the goods in question were previously imported. It also seems administratively simple to effect, since a tariff or import control can be imposed. However, a formidable collection of difficulties limits the scale and speed of this operation. I will mention three:

- Typically, the new products cannot at first be produced as cheaply as imports, because of learning problems. The new industry therefore requires a subsidy, either from the government or (more commonly) from the purchasers, to whom a high price is charged behind the protection of a tariff wall. The operation may benefit the country in the long run; but it is costly to subsidize a large number of infant industries simultaneously, and it is difficult to know which will grow up successfully.
- There is normally only a small supply of good potential entrepreneurs, managers, and reliable factory workers on which all new (and existing) industries must draw, so that an attempt to do too much too quickly prejudices the chances of success for all.
- Because most developing countries have small populations and even smaller national incomes, the market that they can offer for many industrial products is too small to justify even a single factory of an efficient size—and the market will remain small for as many years as it is reasonable to consider. Hence costs will always remain high, unless export markets can be secured; and in most cases the difficulty of doing that (even through regional groups) is obvious.

It is important to emphasize in this connection that one is not concerned with the size of the market for everything that is classified as (say) steel, but rather with the adequacy of the market for those types of steel that it is efficient to make in a single plant. If this plant finds the market for its merchant bars is inadequate, it is no help to point out that the total market for steel is ten times that size, because the plant cannot product tinplate, girders, and so on.

These arguments do not mean that no new industries should be introduced, nor even that they should only be introduced if they can manage without a subsidy or protection from the outset. But it does mean that a developing country should approach this policy with great circumspection, and with modest expectations as to the number of deserving cases that they should support: if and when these are successfully launched, it may be wise to start on others, which will benefit from the resultant growth of the market and of the industrial base and experience.

3. Many development schemes may seem superficially promising, but require expert appraisal before they are accepted and then skillful negotiations and administration by government officials before all the details are finalized—for example, on concessions for minerals, extension of roads, railways or electricity supplies, site allocations, tariff changes, tax concessions. A developing country may get very valuable help on much of this from outside organizations, such as the World Bank, but ultimate decisions and much of the administrative work must be done by its own officials, and the supply of competent men for these important tasks is normally inadequate, even with a modest program. The most important constraint on the size and speed of the program may be the limited power of government to organize a bigger one. One must not forget that a bigger program will commonly call for more taxation and more borrowing, and this need to collect more money puts a further strain on the limited supply of suitable manpower.

4. A government will frequently decide that the development policy should bring some benefits to a large number of people, and therefore make them willing to accept the various burdens (for example, higher taxes) which may be required. This calls for the inclusion in the program not only of things like better water-supplies for agriculture, but also of schemes for helping small-scale producers, especially in rural areas. If well executed, these may help with the problems of income distribution but there is a real danger of a conflict between this objective and that of increasing agricultural output: once again, the shortage of skilled and impartial administrators is often a great constraint.

5. A developing country will normally seek to secure a high rate of growth in its total output. In some cases this may be produced by a buoyant external demand for oil or minerals, the output of which can be expanded. In most cases, however, the growth is stimulated by internal action and may produce balance of payments problems because:

(a) The development process may require large purchases of imported machinery for capital development.

(b) The higher level of incomes increases the level of consumers' demand in the country and so the demand for consumer goods or materials for their production.

(c) There may be difficulties over increasing the output or sale of goods traditionally exported.

This means that the development policy has to be concentrated on parts of the economy that will ease the balance of payments problem. This problem varies enormously from country to country. However, there will normally be a need to combine many varying elements in order to tackle it on an adequate scale. India, for example, cannot hope to preserve any kind of balance in her international payments unless her output of basic foodstuffs is progressively increased. The amounts of money involved would be impossibly large if it were suggested that she should meet her growing food needs by developing export of manufactures. But, at the same time, a satisfactory long-term solution is impossible unless exports of manufactures are developed.

Though there are elements of choice, in this particular case important contributions from each of a number of possible developments seem essential. In terms of our present topic, India needs to make substantial use of both the Green Revolution and industrial development.

6. Finally, a crucial constraint on a developing country's choice of development strategies is the growth of its population. I certainly do not mean that this constraint is immutable: on the contrary, I would personally regard it as being of the very highest priority that more and more of the people of the country can have the size of family they really want and understand what is involved. But as long as the population grows at more than (say) 1 percent a year, development efforts will have to be concentrated largely on providing for increasing numbers rather than raising standards. This applies not only in agriculture and industry but also in services, such as the provision of education, which again have feed-back effects on production.

One should talk of capital-saving rather than labor-intensive industries in LDCs. A technique will be better if it uses less capital and other scarce resources per unit of output. Not only capital, but skilled managerial staff, electricity, imported raw materials, and so forth may be scarce.

In India a method of hand-spinning cotton was devised, which was very labor-intensive, but people earned little even if they were given the equipment free.

Electricity should be expensive in LDCs, as its production requires an enormous amount of capital.

Techniques, especially complicated modern ones, should not be chosen on the assumption that they will work without breakdowns and produce the maximum theoretically feasible output. It is an advantage to introduce an industry one can learn to operate fairly quickly. LDCs should not pioneer but stick to established methods where problems have already been solved.

Finally, techniques should suit the size of the market one is likely to have—domestic or foreign. Small versions of a modern kind of plant are often unsuitable. Product choice should also take the available market into consideration. One should also ask whether the product will be usable if it is not perfect. Clothes or furniture may be, machines probably will not be. Again, is it reasonable to produce something, even if a market exists in the country, when this product can be imported for half the price?

To sum up, I would say that industries one should not have include oil refining, which has a high capital-output ratio, requires very large units to be efficient, is difficult to run with local staff, and, if you have to import the crude oil and pay expatriates, will cost rather than save foreign exchange. In Ghana, it does not pay to do the last stages of gold refining. In Israel, it does not pay to cut diamonds, since this wastes a lot of valuable imported material.

The kind of industries suitable for LDCs must have a big enough local demand and not be technically difficult. They include cement, beer, furniture made from local materials, shoes, and textiles. These kinds of items give most scope, though not all of them will be suitable for every LDC.

DISCUSSION

FANNY GINOR (Israel): Once agriculture supplied manpower and capital for other sectors. Now, mainly due to the population explosion, industry and other sectors do not have to wait for labor released by agriculture. On the contrary, there is unemployment and underemployment everywhere. So higher productivity in agriculture may make the employment problem more acute, because it liberates more manpower than other sectors can absorb. Higher farm incomes could provide a market for industrial products. On the other hand, if 70 percent or 80 percent of population is in agriculture and we want to transfer domestic capital from agriculture to industry, we must tax agriculture, especially if it exports.

Thus there is still much conflict between industry and agriculture. You can perhaps earn more by allocating more resources to industrial development, but if agriculture is not attended to income distribution will worsen.

PAUL STREETEN (Great Britain): There are three basic strategies: The first is to go ahead with the modern sector—with more modern equipment and more modern products. This has not worked. The second strategy reduces output per capita in the modern sector, increases incentives to foreign trade, and improves the capital and labor markets, allowing the modern sector to absorb more labor in an efficient manner. The third strategy is to increase productivity in the nonorganized services sector, through price policies, research and perhaps institutional improvements.

Policies concerning prices and institutions in the modern industrial sector should take into consideration the effects in the nonorganized services sector, where the majority of the urban population is to be found and where most of the people coming into towns from the countryside are absorbed.

Haircutting may be labor-intensive and making nylon shirts capital-intensive. But you cannot ask all Indians to have their hair cut for this reason. It may be more expensive to produce a shirt requiring ironing using local labor in a developing state than to import drip-dry shirts. And in Kenya a fruit drink made from black currants grown in Britain is imported, instead of using local fruit to make drinks on the spot. However, the objective should be to evolve efficiently produced products appropriate for domestic manufacture by a low-income population.

A Participant: The food industries and industries making technical products from agricultural raw materials are the only hope of raising rural living standards in states where the rural sector accounts for some 80 percent or 90 percent of the population. But if such industrialization is done by foreigners or persons not belonging to the rural sector, it can do more harm than good. There are farmers for example, in Afghanistan, who will produce for themselves but not for factories owned by strangers. Besides, food industries must be established on the basis of what can be sold and what raw materials are available. Disregard of this has turned many of them into stores of rusting equipment. They should be started small and learn from their own experience.

W. REDDAWAY (Great Britain): Neither agriculture nor industry has a God-given right to first priority. Nor can one decide in the abstract whether to build a railway to serve rural areas and carry food, or to develop an iron ore mine. It all depends on the specific circumstances.

Whether to use factory methods or handloom methods of producing cloth is another question to which various answers are possible. Building factories costs capital, while using existing looms saves capital; but there is no real case for building new handlooms unless there are some special designs for which they are good. One could impose an excise tax on the factory product, which would make handloom weaving sufficiently attractive for people to go on doing it but give little encouragement to its expansion, if one thinks future development should be through factories. The two products would then sell at about the same price. Another way of achieving this is to let the factories make a big profit.

We should be able to get products made that require few scarce inputs. But I would rather concentrate on avoiding undesirable product types that occur when interest is low or electricity is cheap or imports cost too little.

The point about farmers refusing to sell raw materials to factories is valid. It happened in Ghana with sugar cane and pineapples. It might be possible to have devices for offering to buy sugar cane before even establishing a sugar factory and finding something to do with it, so as to encourage the production of cane ready for the factory.

The manufacture of artificial fertilizer is unsuitable for most LDCs. This item should be imported. It is better to increase such imports and thus produce more food than to import fancy foodstuffs or books instead.

LATIN AMERICAN AGRARIAN REFORM IN ACTION
Solon Barraclough

In Latin America agrarian problems have been growing more and more critical. For the past several decades agricultural production has been increasing only at about the same rate as population. Incomes of the vast majority of the rural population are low, and in many areas, such as the Andean highlands and northeast Brazil, they are close to bare subsistence levels. Housing, health, and nutritional levels are frequently abominable. Social conflict has been persistent and increasing.

The campesinos, the small farmers and agricultural laborers, who comprise over two-thirds of the rural inhabitants of the region and one-third of the total population have little or no participation in political, social, and economic institutions in most countries. Over three-fourths of the agricultural land is held in large estates (latifundia). Unemployment, both rural and urban, is growing. Rural credit, marketing, and educational and political institutions have been at the almost exclusive service of the larger landowners and commercial producers. The agrarian reform and development programs initiated in many countries have fallen far short of hopes and expectations.

Almost every Latin American government has programs called rural development and agrarian reform. Obviously they are not all talking about the same thing as even a superficial glance at the agrarian reforms in Brazil, Mexico, Peru, and Chile or Cuba would show. Their development goals and strategies differ markedly from one another.

One can distinguish three types of rural development and reform strategies: those emphasizing rapid technological modernization; those chiefly stressing a limited redistribution of land and income; and those contemplating rapid and revolutionary changes in the entire social structure.

In Latin America both modernization and reformist strategies have proved inadequate to reach the region's declared rural development goals of greater national independence, more rapid economic growth, and greater social justice with the elimination of poverty and the democratic participation of all social groups in economic and political decision making.* Strategies of revolutionary structural changes have been adopted in Cuba and announced for Chile, but it is still too early to determine how successful these countries will be in achieving sustained rapid progress towards their goals of economic growth, wider income distribution, and full campesino participation. In any event, all rural development strategies will remain inadequate until the hard political decisions are taken to move directly towards development goals in spite of the powerful interest groups opposed to sharing their power and privileges with the campesinos and other hitherto powerless groups.

POLITICAL CONSTRAINTS ON DEVELOPMENT POLICIES

The Chilean experience with agrarian reform and rural development policies during the past 15 years illustrates the difficulties encountered in attempting to implement these alternative development strategies. It also indicates that economic and political objectives and policies are so closely interrelated that it is highly misleading to analyze them separately. Political leaders are sharply constrained in policy making by economic realities, but that the reverse is at least equally true is not always appreciated by economists and planners.

In fact, the choice among alternative economic policies is so closely circumscribed by political constraints that there are frequently no short-run alternatives to the ones actually chosen. The design of realistic policy alternatives requires an intimate knowledge of the political and economic situation and an infinite finesse in taking both into account. The prerequisite "that national authorities desire development, understand its importance, and are prepared to meet all requirements needed to attain it" seems utopian. This prerequisite may have existed in Israel, but I suspect that this was a unique situation that cannot be repeated in most undeveloped countries.

Understanding of development will always be closely conditioned by the inevitable social conflicts within the society and by the aspirations of the particular social groups and classes upon which the national authorities of the moment depend. Moreover, to be prepared to meet all the requirements to attain development assumes a national

---

*These basic concepts of rural development were unanimously accepted by the official representatives of Latin American governments to the eleventh Regional FAO Conference, Caracas, Venezuela, 5-9 October 1970.

consensus about goals and strategy practically unimaginable in any poor society beginning to industrialize. Another possibility would be a high degree of authoritarian control by an elite group "genuinely desiring development." This seldom happens, however, since the dominant classes upon whom such an elite must depend are usually much more interested in maintaining their own status and privileges than in real development benefiting the low-income rural and urban majorities. In any event, if development implies democratic participation, authoritarian direction of the process by a small elite would appear to be a contradiction of terms.

Alternative development strategies concerning primary specialization, balanced growth, and early industrialization are irrelevant if they are not part of a realistic political strategy. Such a strategy would have to indicate the role of each major social group during the development process, its reponsibilities, its incentives, its sacrifices, and how to obtain and maintain each group's support.

DEVELOPMENT POLICY IN CHILE

The Alessandri Administration— Technological Modernization

The liberal-conservative coalition dominating the Chilean Alessandri administration during 1958-64 pursued a rural development strategy of technological modernization. The idea was to create favorable conditions for private producers to adopt modern technology and to encourage both domestic and foreign investments. The government attempted to make modernization profitable by keeping costs down, substituting some domestically produced goods for imports, and encouraging exports. In agriculture this implied the extension of cheap credits for farm modernization and agro-industrial infrastructure, liberal tax concessions, substantial subsidies for imported farm machinery and inputs, and keeping farm labor relatively cheap. This strategy included limited agrarian reform to permit purchase and expropriation of a few poorly managed large estates for redistribution among small peasant producers. This was to serve both as a stimulus to modernization by the majority of estate owners and as a token concession to those campesino groups pressing for land, better working conditions, and higher wages. It was hoped that general economic growth would enable urban activities to absorb the surplus rural labor supply more rapidly than in the past and also result in more profitable markets for agricultural products.

Followed consistently, this modernization strategy could have resulted in significantly increased agricultural growth, although rural development in the sense of wider income distribution, increased employment and greater campesino participation would have been delayed for a very long time. In reality, however, it was never feasible to implement a consistent rural modernization strategy because of political constraints. While prices of manufactured goods were protected by high tariffs, agricultural prices were kept relatively low by importing nearly one-fifth of domestic food requirements, mostly U.S. surpluses. The political power of nonagricultural employer groups, supported by organized urban laborers on the issue of cheap foodstuffs, precluded agricultural price policies favoring farm producers. At the same time, foreign and allied national interests prevented any vigorous policies to rationalize industrial production patterns and cost structures or to reform government fiscal policies. As a consequence, inflation could not be controlled while strikes and labor unrest, both rural and urban, increased. Agricultural production barely kept pace with population growth while rural living levels deteriorated. Even more serious for the government was the growing alienation of many middle class groups that were being squeezed on all sides.

The rural modernization strategy failed even if judged only by its own criteria of increasing agricultural growth significantly and creating a dynamic capitalist farmer class that together with urban entrepreneurs and property owners be capable of maintaining political power and guiding the economy in the future. The reasons for the failure were an unrealistic appraisal of political forces.

Christian Democrat Administration—
Reformist Development

The Christian Democratic administration from 1964 to 1970 initiated a reformist rural development strategy. This rested primarily on a massive agrarian reform originally projected to expropriate all but the most modern and efficient large estates and to benefit directly some 100,000 campesino families—about one-fourth of the rural population. In addition, the strategy included substantial wage increases for rural and urban workers, an ambitious program for credit and technical assistance for small producers, and the unionization of farm laborers. Agricultural prices were to be increased sharply in relation to those of industrial products, while the previous government's subsidies and other aids to technological modernization were to be continued. The tax structure was to be reformed: a progressive tax on land and other fixed capital was to be introduced, while the heavy social security tax on payrolls was to be greatly reduced. Similar measures in other sectors of the economy were expected to stimulate investment, output, and employment.

Again the strategy was much better thought out in strictly economic terms than in political ones. Property owning groups, powerful not only in the liberal-conservative opposition but also within the governing party, prevented an effective rationalization of taxes and other fiscal reforms. At the same time pressures from labor unions and lower middle class groups in the communist-socialist opposition parties, and within the Christian Democratic party itself, made it imperative to implement some of the proposed redistributive policies even without adequate compensatory fiscal measures. The natural result was continued inflation, which soon attained levels of over 30 percent annually.

The resistance of both foreign and domestic propertied interests plus the financial restraints imposed by inadequate new tax revenues and competing social welfare programs forced a reduction in the original goal of 100,000 families to receive land from the agrarian reform to about 20,000 families. On the other hand, farm worker unions grew rapidly while small producers were organized in cooperatives and precooperative committees. Both the capability to exert political pressure and the level of expectations of the rural poor increased rapidly. The government's inability to meet these aspirations resulted in growing frustration. Rural unemployment increased sharply as higher farm wages, relatively cheap subsidized labor-saving technology, and the fear of labor unrest stimulated commercial farmers to reduce their work force and to speed mechanization. While agricultural prices were increased somewhat in relation to those of manufactured products, higher labor costs and higher prices of some other farm inputs resulted in an actual worsening of the financial position of most large commercial farmers in relation to the previous period.

Effective demand grew rapidly and food imports rose above the already high levels of the early 1960s in spite of a modest increase in agricultural production. The planned increases in savings and investments could not be approached, since no politically feasible mechanisms had been devised to realize them. Favorable copper prices and a continued high level of foreign aid resulted in an actual surplus of foreign exchange even though most of the increases in wages and social services were being indirectly financed from aid and other income from abroad. Nevertheless, political constraints were such that it was simply impossible to implement the reformist strategy in the manner its designers had envisioned.

In spite of the Christian Democratic administration's substantial reforms benefiting some farm laborers and small producers, campesino support for the more radical programs promised by left-wing parties continued to grow. Moreover, the Christian Democrats failed to pick up any substantial new following among urban workers. In the 1970 presidential elections the Popular Unity coalition of leftist parties obtained a plurality. It had maintained the electoral base it had held when the Frei administration assumed the presidency six years earlier with the support of the traditional conservative and center parties. These parties had put up their own candidate in 1970 obtaining the second largest popular vote while the reformist Christian Democrats obtained only third place.

The reformist strategy had been only partly successful in achieving economic and social objectives. In large measure this was because of an inadequate appraisal of political factors. The government had failed to increase its popular electoral support significantly in either rural or urban areas while it had alienated its more conservative allies.

Agrarian reform was a major plank in the campaign platform of Chilean President Salvador Allende's Popular Unity coalition. By July 1972, only 20 months after assuming office, the Allende government had incorporated into its agrarian reform program practically all the private estates larger than an equivalent value of about 200 acres of first class irrigated land that could be legally expropriated under the reform law passed during the Frei administration. It had taken over some 3,282 properties, more than 13 million acres, of which nearly one million were irrigated lands. An additional 45,000 farm workers and small peasants were the direct beneficiaries of the new expropriations. This was nearly twice as many as had benefited during the previous administration; the number of expropriations had doubled and the area in the reform program had increased by 150 percent. The "reformed sector," including areas expropriated by both the Allende and the previous administration, included about 35 percent of the productive farm land of the country. It was controlled and worked by some 75,000 direct beneficiaries (about 12 percent of the country's total agricultural force) together with the responsible state agencies. The situation regarding the distribution of land, labor, and production in mid-1972 is summarized in Table 9.

Farm workers' strikes and illegal land occupations increased precipitously upon the new government's election. There had been nearly 2,000 land occupations since the Allende government took office until July 1972, as compared with some 400 during the last 20 months of the Frei administration. Most of these, however, were of short duration with little or no violence or property damage. Some were by Mapuche Indians who reoccupied ancestral communal lands to which they possessed legal titles. Others were made by the farm workers of estates about to be expropriated in order to prevent

TABLE 9

Distribution of Land, Labor, and Production—
Chile, 1972
(in percent)

Rural sector	Land (HRB)	Full-time and Temporary labor[b]	Value of total production	Value of total market production	Proportion of production of sector that is marketed
Reformed	36	18	29	29	80
Small farms of less than 20 HRB	22	60	28	15	45
Medium and large farms of 20 to 80 HRB[a]	42	22	43	56	95
Total	100	100	100	100	76

[a]Including reservas plus about three percent of the total HRB in remaining properties larger than 80 HRB.
[b]Including unemployed.

the owners from selling off livestock and machinery and leaving only the bare ground for the reform beneficiaries. Still other farms were occupied to hasten expropriation or to protest nonpayment of wages or in support of neighboring peasants who were pressing for what appeared to be legitimate demands. Almost all these farms were soon expropriated under the law or else returned to their former owners. Most of these conflicts were incited by progovernment political parties and some by parties in opposition such as the Christian Democrats, although, of course, their political aims were different. All things considered, the disorder and violence associated with the reform were minimal compared with what usually accompanies agrarian changes of this scope.

The expropriation of the legally defined latifundios was virtually finished in mid-1972. The most pressing agrarian problem now is to increase production. Santiago and may other cities are plagued by recurrent shortages of beef, poultry, milk, butter, and many other foodstuffs. Queuing in front of shops with limited stocks of these items is commonplace and there is a flourishing blackmarket, especially in high income districts. The opposition is capitalizing on the resulting irritations among the populace, and there is a widespread but mistaken impression that the food scarcities are primarily a result of the agrarian reform.

In reality the overall production of crops and livestock officially increased by about 5 percent in the agricultural year ending May 1971, surpassing for the first time the predrought production high of 1968. During the agricultural year ending April 1973, production declined as compared to 1971-72 by about 10 percent. In large measure this was because of heavy rains, problems with the transport of fertilizers and seeds, growing uncertainties, disorganization accentuated by sabotage, and the distortion of traditional economic incentives.

Much of the recovery in 1971 was represented by wine production while in 1972 a 4 percent drop in crop production was more than offset by a sharp increase in output of broiler-chickens and pork. Wheat production declined in 1972 and again in 1973, which was serious for a country that has been importing about one-third of its consumption for a decade; the problem was worsened by the diversion of some wheat to poultry and pigs because of a shortage of maize and high meat prices. Nonetheless, food production had apparently increased during 1971 and 1972, the period the Allende government began its massive and rapid agrarian reform. Even on the expropriated estates, which accounted for about 30 percent of gross output, the area planted was in general maintained, although there were some declines in yields of industrial crops and a shift from large scale production.

During the two-year period 1971-72 food imports doubled in volume. As agricultural prices rose by some 50 percent in world markets, the cost of food imports tripled in value reaching an estimated $400 million in 1972. Total availability of food per capita in 1972 in comparison with 1970 rose by 16.6 percent for wheat, 23.8 percent for sugar, 53.8 percent for milk, 25.6 percent for meat, and 13.5 percent for eggs. In general, this high level of agricultural imports was being maintained in 1973 in spite of foreign exchange difficulties.

How does one explain the paradox of an approximate 25 percent increase of total food supplies (imports plus production) in 1972 over 1970 accompanied by growing food scarcities? Population only increased by about 4 percent and national income per capita by a little more than 6 percent, so at most only about seven percent of the increase in consumption could be explained by these two variables. Part of the explanation is obviously income redistribution. Unemployment dropped from eight percent of the work force to about three percent from 1970 to 1972 while salaries of low-income workers were increased more rapidly than those in higher income brackets. At the same time nearly everyone's money incomes rose rapidly. Inflation was over 40 percent in 1971, and in 1972 it exceeded 150 percent; it will be more than 200 percent in 1973.

To the extent that controls successfully held down food prices to less than the increase in monetary incomes, food consumption climbed rapidly, especially among low-income groups whose nutritional levels had long been far below acceptable standards. To this must be added the government's free distribution of a pint of milk daily to young children and nursing mothers and the highly subsidized distribution of fish (hake) caught and frozen by Soviet trawlers. In addition, there has been widespread speculative hoarding of some products, such as canned goods, rice, sugar, and dried milk, by producers, wholesalers, retailers, and consumers. Finally, the unrealistic foreign exchange rates maintained to curb international inflation made the smuggling of Chilean products into neighboring Argentina, Bolivia, and Peru a lucrative business.

The government must now take drastic measures in order to avoid a sharp decline in the real incomes of the low-income two-thirds of the population that benefited by its redistribution policies after 1970. The foreign exchange situation became increasingly critical with the fall in copper prices after 1970 and the practical embargo on credits from the United States in order to apply pressure for higher indemnization for the expropriated copper mines and other foreign-owned industries. In 1972 food imports alone amounted to 30 percent of the Chilean export earnings, and if imports of agricultural raw materials such as wool, cotton, and tobacco are included they were 45 percent. Unless large-scale foreign aid in foodstuffs can be obtained promptly, food imports must be reduced in the very near future. The government has practically stopped imports of beef and butter. The immediate food supply situation was, of course, seriously worsened by the month-long truck-owners' and merchants' strike in October-November of 1972 that tied up international transport and commerce.

For obvious political reasons, the government would prefer to avoid food rationing. In theory, its objectives of further increasing food consumption by low income groups could be attained by drastic income redistribution, more efficient marketing, and greater monetary stability. But without a majority in Congress its hands are tied. In the absence of new legislation, the inflation cannot be brought under control without sacrificing the government's objectives of expanding the socialized area of the economy, maintaining full employment, and increasing workers' wages at least as fast as the cost of living rises.

Rationing of basic foods is not a satisfactory long-term solution to the imbalance between supply and demand. The possibilities of maintaining the real income and consumption gains already achieved by the low-income groups, upon whose support the Allende administration depends, and of increasing these gains in the future, depend largely upon more agricultural production. A continuation of past trends, with food production increasing about the same as population growth, as it has been doing for the last three decades, will not do. Land resources abound within existing farm units, but long use must become more intense. The problem remains basically one of organization, planning, and incentives, as it was before the reform. Now, with the dramatic rise in consumption, it is more urgent. But with over a third of the productive land expropriated and nearly all agricultural credit and farm inputs under government control, effective planning to raise production should be more feasible than it was in the past if minimal political stability and agreement could be achieved.

The government hopes to combine the use of price, marketing, credit, and tax policies to create a more rational set of production incentives. Privately owned medium-size farms still account for over half of the food production that actually enters the market while the reformed units account for only about 30 percent. An increasing proportion of production originates on small individually worked plots within the agrarian reform units (precooperatives that differ little from each other except in name, and a few state farms). Moreover, much of the production from both the medium-sized farms and the reform units enters the black market as does that of the small independent family size producers and minifundistas. These small independent producers account for nearly 30 percent of the gross agricultural production, but only half of this is marketed; they include over half the farm population, much of it still living at sub-poverty levels.

The greatest opportunities for rapid production expansion lie in the reformed units. They control the vast underutilized land resources of the expropriated latifundios but are very short on capital and trained management. The government's aim is for most of these units to become self-managed cooperatives. Opposition tactics plus interparty disputes within the U.P., however, have delayed a clear definition of the form and operating structures of these land reform units. Meanwhile, the individual family units within the land reform cooperatives have proliferated while production on the cooperatively worked lands has stagnated. The government will have to move rapidly to rationalize the management of these expropriated estates if it is to have any chance of improving production rapidly within the next two or three years.

Whether the Allende administration's strategy will be more successful in meeting the goals of independence, economic growth, social justice, and worker and peasant participation than were the modernization and the reformist strategies of previous administrations, depends primarily on how the country's major urban social and political conflicts are resolved. With less than one-fourth of the work force and one-tenth of GNP originating in agriculture one can hardly expect what happens in the rural sector to be decisive. In the 1973 congressional elections the government increased its popular electoral support considerably, especially in rural districts, but it still lacked the necessary majority in Congress to enact essential new legislation. Results in respect of agricultural production have been disappointing, but it would have been highly unrealistic to expect substantial production increases while massive expropriations were taking place and when a lack of internal unity in the administration itself, a traditional civil service, and an opposition-dominated Congress made coherent agrarian policies impossible.

Clearly, as was the case during the previous two governments, the principal obstacles to implementing the Allende administration's strategy have been political. There has been no possibility of a coordinated set of realistic and consistent economic policies designed to direct decisions at all levels of the agricultural sector in support of government goals. Political constraints have caused agrarian policies to be adopted without taking into account programs and resource limitations in other sectors of the economy. At the same time, agricultural policies frequently contradicted each other.

Lessons from the Chilean Experience

The Chilean experience with agrarian reform and rural development forces one to question what role economists and "development planners" can play in such processes. At best their influence is marginal. Planning implies foresight and control. But control is impossible when the most important variables are constantly changing in political responses to social conflicts. The planner has influence on actual policy only to the extent that he is himself a skillful administrator-politician or is able to present politically attractive solutions to the national authorities. In either case, a keen appreciation of social trends and political forces is of paramount importance.

The same political uncertainties that make national economic planning a virtual impossibility in most underdeveloped countries also limit the effectiveness of planning for particular industries, farms, regions, and economic subsectors. Plans at these subnational levels are closely conditioned by relative prices, income distribution and demand, credit, import, export policies, taxes, and institutional organization, all of which are likely to change capriciously in response to the zigs and zags of national politics. Nonetheless, economic planning at these lower levels becomes progressively more feasible because the number of variables that can be controlled or the behavior of which can be foreseen by the planners is proportionally greater than at the level of national government. A really sound plan for the development of forest industries or of a particular irrigation district or farm, for example, can usually be much more readily adapted to changing political and institutional parameters than a national development plan.

But there should be no illusions about the contribution subnational, sectoral, regional, and project planning can make to rural development in the absence of a coherent national development strategy. Unfortunately, the sum of several well planned and successful individual projects may not be rural development at all. Instead, it may merely improve incomes and productivities of a few direct beneficiaries at the expense of greater unemployment and misery of the majority of the rural population. How individual projects affect development depends upon the social structure in which they occur.

Most technical assistance in economic planning of national policy extended by international and bilateral aid agencies to countries with social structures such as that of Chile has been largely irrelevant for development. In fact, it may frequently have had negative results. Aid tends to reinforce traditional conflicts that would have been resolved much sooner but for the additional support obtained from outside by traditional governing groups whose dominance is being challenged by popular movements. This is not to say that effective technical assistance and financial aid to the underdeveloped countries is inherently impossible or bad. Obviously it often contributes to economic growth by providing new skills, technology, and capital. It may also increase pressures for greater social justice and participation by intensifying social contradictions, raising aspirations, and sharpening perceptions. But it is naive to believe that real development can be planned with the help of outsiders in situations where planning at the level of national economic policies is practically impossible because of the social structure.

The experience of Chile during the last two decades has not been atypical. Political bargaining and social conflicts have been extremely transparent in Chile because they took place in a context of formal political democracy and exceptional liberty of expression and communications. The same social conflicts and underlying political instability, however, exist in most of the so-called underdeveloped countries. As one high bureaucrat remarked to me in a nearby Latin American nation that had recently changed from an obviously unstable formal congressional democracy to an apparently stable military government: "The biggest difference is that now all the bargaining goes on behind the scenes. Before, senators used to call me for favor and influence. Now it is the colonels. But national planning is as difficult as ever."

DISCUSSION

YITZHAK ABT (Israel): The 1960s were not favorable to agrarian reform, especially in the price structure of agricultural goods. In 1973 the market prices of such goods give a much better chance for countries trying partial or complete reforms.

Industry should not be viewed as a separate sector from agriculture in the framework of agricultural development programs. In Chile agrarian reform maintained added value in various areas of the country, creating a new industrial and marketing base. Only when dealing with agriculture and industry together, can one achieve medium-term successes. Short-term successes are not really possible.

I disagree with the idea that the technician has little influence. He sets the trend and wheels in motion. And he has given too little attention to the problem of a supporting system for an agrarian reform program.

THOMAS CARROLL (IDB Washington, D.C.): How should one deal with land reform? I disagree with Dr. Barraclough's thesis that unless there are large structural changes, work on a limited micro-scale may be useless or counterproductive. Much work on the micro-level has been successful, even in terms of the political game. Micro-planning and experimentation have a very profound effect on setting up the next stage of reform.

BRUCE JOHNSTON (United States): I object to the presentation of a typology of agrarian reform on the basis of either modernization through technology or reformist policies or structural change. No approach to agricultural development can succeed without very significant structural changes. Improved technologies can and should contribute importantly to structural change in agriculture—whether accompanied by land reform or not.

In Latin America, tractorization was regarded as improved technology. In Chile some 40 percent of agricultural land (by value) is in the agrarian reform sector yet only 12-15 percent of the rural labor force. This means that inappropriate technologies were probably emphasized there.

SOLON BARRACLOUGH (FAO): I agree with Mr. Abt that technicians have something to offer. When I said I had nothing to offer as a social scientist, or as a highly trained economist, I didn't mean I had nothing to offer as a land reform technician. When a country really decides to have agrarian reform, of any type mentioned, we can be useful. But we technicians do not usually set the wheels in motion. These are set in motion by social forces.

Prices are a double-edged sword. It is easier to plan successful agrarian reform projects when the international price structure is favorable, but in such periods the big landowners can consolidate themselves and agrarian reform becomes politically much more difficult.

My typology is not analytical. Land reform accompanied by many other changes, permitting cooperation of low-income small producers, subsistence farmers, and landless laborers within the labour force in a big way, would come into my category of revolutionary structural changes.

I agree with Professor Johnston about inappropriate technologies. They are caused not by stupidity but by political and economic conditions. Chile, for instance, could only get a big foreign credit from Romania. Romania had surplus tractors. So Chile got tractors. Another example: those who benefited from land reform in Chile are not at all anxious to bring the 250,000 landless or almost landless rural workers into the land reform area. The same problem exists even in the Israeli kibbutz, which is not usually anxious to permit hired workers, mostly later immigrants from North Africa and Asia, to become members or even to increase its hired labour force. As a technician one has to think about these things.

**RAPPORTEUR'S REPORT—
GROUP A**
John Adler

It was not the purpose of the conference to arrive at a majority view of development problems. The participants have in common only their interest in development and their experience of some aspect of it.

Working Group A discussed resources, technology, and income distribution, but participants extended its scope to include population policies, employment, the distribution of property (especially agricultural land), the economic and social costs of development, as well as the expansion of agricultural output and the role of cooperatives in it.

Several papers and much of the discussion ventured into the tricky field of political institutions and the impact of political power on economic progress. Some specific topics were related to broader issues of economic development and social change.

Our debate reflected the present state of development economics. Gone are the days when growth of GNP or of GNP per capita of population was all that mattered and higher savings rates or larger imports of foreign capital were considered a panacea. Gone is the preoccupation with the conditions necessary for "take-off" into social growth. We have moved away from the simple mechanistic question: "What makes an economy grow?" and the equally simple answers.

Policy objectives have become more complex, including such things as income distribution, employment, welfare, and the quality of life. We are still far from the answers but have at least started to ask the right questions. The papers and their discussions conveyed the impression that specific answers to specific questions exist and that these answers vary in accordance with institutional arrangements, social structures, and cultural values rather than according to the stage of development. We dealt here mainly with practical matters of policy not with problems of analysis. Development economists, like development planners, are no longer unready to offer policy advice to civil servants, and political leaders are ready to listen to them. They have therefore exposed themselves to the risks of misjudging the political, social, and cultural feasibility of their advice.

This has had at least two beneficial consequences: It brought home to the economists the uniqueness of the problems that exist at any particular time in any country; and it has taught them the difficulty of applying general propositions to specific conditions. The need is for a mix of policies making up a strategy consistent in economic terms, feasible in political terms, and acceptable in the sociocultural context. Reasoning and experience gained elsewhere help, but it takes more than self-righteousness and logic to make policies work. It takes detailed knowledge of the specific situation that the economist, civil servants, and political leaders face to devise the right diagnosis and the correct policy.

Development economists no longer mind becoming involved in institutional arrangements. They have become aware of the practical problems of public administration, legislation, and economic management. The distinction between inevitably good policy prescription and inevitably bad policy execution has disappeared. There is growing awareness that the practical rules of development must be simple, though much complex thought must go into their formulation.

We witnessed here a remarkable optimism regarding the manageability of development problems. As recently as 15 years ago development economics was little more than a catalogue of impediments to economic progress and of preconditions to be fulfilled before one could even think of economic growth. It is no accident that our papers and discussions abound with references to states that achieved very rapid growth, and there is a strong implication that other states could have done equally well had they tried harder or followed good advice. Nobody referred to the absence of natural resources as a permanent constraint on economic progress. Imported resources, technical aid, education, training, and human ingenuity can overcome the handicaps of resource limitations.

The optimism extended even to the new objectives of employment generation, greater equality, population control, and prevention of a deterioration in the quality of life. It may be exaggerated but on balance is a good thing, stimulating thought and committing the experts and policy makers to find answers to the problems in hand.

The active participation of government officials from developing countries in the discussion made it clear that their interest in development is practical and real. They were eager to relate the propositions in the papers to their problems. This shows that experts can help policy makers to find solutions to problems and encourage them to rely on expert guidance. And also the experts benefit, because they see that the issues that interest them also interest policy makers.

Hence, the usefulness of the Rehovot Conference and similar conferences has been firmly established. Opportunities for presenting ideas in a forum of peers and men of responsibility are only too rare.

The organizers of the conference brought together academic economists, civil servants, staff or international organizations, and elected officials—not to confront theories with practical men but for a friendly and fruitful exchange of ideas. All participants have benefited from this.

PART III
EXTERNAL CONSTRAINTS ON DEVELOPMENT

**THE USE AND ABUSE
OF CAPITAL IN
DEVELOPING COUNTRIES
I. M. D. Little**

Foreign capital inflow in a narrow sense is now a small part of LDC investment. If we included the acquisition of skills and knowledge from abroad, it might be much more important. But either way it is impossible to discuss sensibly the use of foreign capital without first discussing the use of capital in general.

Making good use of savings is as important as saving. It is as good for growth to raise the effectiveness of investment by fifty percent, as it is to raise the rate of savings from, say, 10 percent of income to 15 percent. But in many models the efficiency of investment is taken for granted, while the importance of raising the savings rate has been stressed.

LOW CAPACITY WORKING

There is now widespread evidence of low use of capacity in developing countries. Indeed, this is one of the most valid generalizations that can be made about them. In many countries of Latin America and Southern Asia use of capacity is considerably lower even than in the United States. Yet the opposite should be expected if either the price mechanism or physical planning works properly. Capital is supposed to be scarce and should be expensive, and the opposite should be true of labor. In fact in many countries capital goods are cheap and also are underused—often much more so than labor.

Cheap capital goods and low interest rates for some sectors lead to planned underutilization of capacity. There will tend to be too much building ahead of demand, and investors will plan to use factories for fewer hours in the year than is socially justifiable. Another reason for planned underutilization is monopolistic competition, often reinforced by governments that license too many producers in a protected market.

Unplanned underutilization is caused by many factors: First, demand may be lower than expected. An example of chronic lack of demand is the heavy machinery plants in India, where the investment demand anticipated by planners in the late 1950s could not be sustained. In some countries (including India) there are periodic recessions.

But demand failure is not usually the reason for chronic underutilization: all too often increases in demand result in increased capacity and not increased utilization. Second, materials and components may not be available; this could be avoided by greater reliance on the price mechanism to keep imports in check. And, perhaps less frequently, nontradeable inputs (now, for example, power in India) may be insufficient. Third, bad management and bad labor relations are among the most important causes in come countries. The causes are probably related to inappropriate labor legislation, which puts the employed in an excessively strong position relative to the unemployed. Last, technical failure occurs more often than in developed countries and takes longer to put right. This must be expected to some extent, since techniques are imported from far away and operated in strange climates by strange hands.

Too little is known as yet about the relative importance of the various causes of underutilization. However, many of them seem to relate to the policy of industrialization by import substitution and to labor legislation.

Underutilization is not confined to industry; it also occurs in services and in agriculture. Excessively extensive use of land, largely as a result of unequal ownership, is a misuse of capital.

LOW SOCIAL YIELDS FOR OTHER REASONS

Inefficient use of capital is by no means confined to underutilization. Many plants in LDCs are operating more or less as planned but add little or nothing to national income (and very little to employment), and may even be reducing the national income and worsening the balance of payments. The primary cause is that the plants have been planned, privately or publicly, in the light of a price mechanism that gives a distorted reflection of both social costs and benefits. Alternatively, they have been set up according to some inappropriate theory or strategy of development, and the price mechanism has been distorted to suit them. Things are produced that should not be produced at all. Other things are made on too small a scale, since exports should have been planned but were not.

INVESTMENT PLANNING

Some of the poor use of capital is unavoidable and should be expected. It is inevitable that some technical problems will arise with the transfer of technology to strange climates and inexperienced hands. Management is inexperienced in commerce and labor management as well as in technical matters. One also cannot expect the infrastructure of nontraded inputs to be as reliable as in developed countries. There is less skill and experience available for the sectoral planning of these services, and more new problems have to be faced. On the other hand, much is avoidable; and one might have hoped that the shortage of new capital and the relative abundance of labor would have led to offsetting effects, such as more instead of less multi-shift working than in developed countries. In most LDCs investment is generally planned by private people for profit or pleasure, with expected prices as their guides. The government may affect these plans by influencing prices and profitability directly (through taxes and subsidies) and indirectly (by restricting competition, or by legislation—for example, labor laws), or through manipulating quantities (by its own demands and the general macroeconomic management of the economy). It may also kill plans, in embryo or at any later stage, by controls. In the public sector the central planners, where they exist, do not plan investments. This is done by public industries, other government agencies, and sometimes by ministries (often the down-to-earth planning is still done by private firms employed by these authorities). In general, these agencies are expected to plan, just like private industry, in the light of market prices.

The most important measure of good central planning in a mixed economy is the extent to which the government, by its influence over prices, demand, and so on, improves the social yield of investments. Unfortunately this is not the way that planning has been looked at. The social evaluation of investments has been virtually nonexistent. Planning commissions pay little attention to, or have little influence over, the policy levers that really govern most of the investment undertaken. The emphasis has been on producing paper plans.

In my opinion the emphasis has been topsy-turvy. The primary question should be: "how do we get good investment projects?" The first requirement is, of course, people who can plan well—good entrepreneurs and planning staffs in both the public and private sectors. The second requirement, with which I am more concerned, is that these planners plan in the public interest. This latter implies (a) getting taxes, subsidies, and the price mechanism right, with the right incentives for economizing capital, using labor, producing what saves or earns the country most, and so forth; (b) using (negative) controls or their threat only where the price mechanism fails or can be improved on—examples might be preventing too many car assembly lines or bargaining with a foreign firm.

Projects can be evaluated in isolation. In fact, the vast majority of projects are planned in isolation. Moreover, it is in the social interest that they should be. The exceptions are where externalities are significant. Here the procedure is to delimit a system within which most of the important pecuniary externalities are internalized, such as the electricity system, railway system, or land use in a particular town. Thus a requirement for some sectoral plans is generated. In an open economy trade largely breaks the links, so it is the non-traded good sectors with lumpy investments that most urgently require sectoral investment plans.

Finally, what can be done to avoid excess capacity and investments that, for other reasons, have low or negative social rates of return? The single most important thing is probably to keep the economy advancing at as steady a rate as possible and to avoid the need for quantitative controls over producer goods (whether imported or domestic). This implies all the usual problems of balance of payments management, with adequate reserves of foreign currency. These goals, long recognized as important for rich countries, have been strangely neglected in developing countries.

The priorities I am suggesting are a far cry from those apparent in at least some LDC planning. Aside from general macroeconomic management, I feel that the project planning level is the most important and then the sectoral planning level. There are well-developed planning techniques at these levels. Planning can be a reality at the project level—that is, the plan may be implemented. This can also occur at the sectoral level in some cases, where there is an implementing authority. Planning further ahead has a different meaning. Plans then become no more than forward looks, in the light of long-run objectives. Such perspective plans are of very limited use since the economist's techniques for looking forward for more than a year are highly unreliable.

PLANNING THE USE OF FOREIGN CAPITAL

If a country is handling its own investment well, then it will also get the best out of foreign capital. That is why my discussion of the use or abuse of foreign capital has been prefaced by a discussion of capital in general.

Foreign capital takes three main forms: (a) commercial borrowing, (b) aid, and (c) foreign private direct investment.

Commercial borrowing is the easiest to deal with. If domestic prices correctly measure costs and benefits, then it pays the country to borrow provided the use of the money gives a higher social yield than the rate of interest on the loan. The "if" looks after the balance of payments. There is no difference between a cost-benefit analysis of a project financed by a foreign loan and one financed by the country's own reserve, apart from the difference between a borrowing and a lending rate. If a country uses its own money well, it will use foreign capital well provided all investments are well planned and appraised. In practice, a number of inexperienced, misguided, or corrupt administrations have been seduced by equipment salesmen and have used contractor finance or other borrowing for socially low-yielding or negative-yielding investments. But this is less likely to happen if there is a sound domestic system for evaluating investments and if the price mechanism is in good working order. Low social yields are the primary reason that countries run into trouble by borrowing.

Aid should by definition be cheaper than commercial credit. Of course, aid-tying can substantially raise the real terms above the apparent. In project aid all this comes out in any proper evaluation of the project. It is sometimes argued that not all aid is additional capital because it discourages domestic saving. It is largely in the hands of the host government to see this does not happen. But if it cannot be helped, it is quite easy to allow for (one needs only a shadow price for savings in terms of consumption, or vice versa). It is often claimed of project aid that donors' preferences distort the investment programmes of LDCs, that there is a conflict of ends. If a country invests well, the accepted aid project will still be beneficial, though not as beneficial as it might be if it accorded better with the recipient's aims. This circumstance is of nothing like the importance supposed by some. More often the disagreement is about means. For this reason, if the host government is not very good at investing, project aid (where the donor evaluates) can do a lot of good. Many persons in LDCs accept this.

It is harder for the host to handle direct foreign investments to maximum advantage than other capital inflows. In theory the general incentives and disincentives that apply for private domestic entrepreneurs should not be applied to foreigners. For instance, if the supply of foreign entrepreneurship is less elastic than that of domestic entrepreneurship, the country can in principle benefit from restricting foreign investment by offering it less good conditions than apply domestically. There can also be differences so far as reinvestment is concerned, while externalities may favor better incentives for foreigners, although general political considerations tell in the opposite direction.

I have no doubt that some foreign investment has damaged the host country. But this has usually been because the encouragement given to industrialization was of the wrong kind. The most obvious example is excessive protection. Excessive protection taxes the domestic consumer in order to make production of something profitable (sometimes too profitable), and quite often that something should never have been produced at all. It is bound to seem worse if the profit earner is foreign, although the damage may be almost as great if he is domestic (because the social value to the country of profits accruing to a local millionaire may be only a little greater than of those accruing to foreigners).

The forms of encouragement given have been wrong. Counting tax remissions as subsidies, one can say that almost everything has been subsidized in some countries, except employment. Companies have been allowed to import duty free, have obtained export subsidies, have been supplied with power, and even land, below their social cost and have received long "holidays" from direct tax. At the same time high wages are encouraged and employment is taxed (in the form of social security payments, and even, in at least one country, of a specific employment tax). This makes no sense. What the host gains from foreign investment is mainly taxes and employment. So why try to see that it pays little tax and gives little employment?

A good social cost-benefit analysis of the project will tell how far it is worth going in making concessions and which particular concessions demanded by the foreigner will reduce the social value least. One cannot bargain well without being able to assess the value of what one may be getting and giving away.

If the host thinks he has struck as good a bargain on taxes and subsidies as he can without driving the foreigner away, and that the social PV is positive, there is still another possibility. The post-tax yield to the foreigner should be calculated. If it is higher than the government thinks it can get from its own marginal investments, then it should try to participate in the equity (and even consider whether to take all the equity, hiring foreign management if necessary).

A lot depends on the host government's not being bamboozled. It is most important for it to acquire a good knowledge of the industry in question. This is easier said than done. Yet more effort to acquire this knowledge would have been a very good investment for some countries.

A sound calculating approach to private foreign investment would take much of the heat out of the subject. It would prevent LDCs from exploiting themselves by having the wrong rules. It could go some way to prevent foreign exploitation in the shape of excessively good bargains (though, overall, the return from private foreign investment to the capital-supplying countries does not appear to be extremely high). This would be beneficial. Of course, some heat would remain. There are the ITTs of the world, and there is also plenty of sheer xenophobia.

DISCUSSION

NADAV HALEVY (Israel): I agree that the efficient use of investment capital is more important than the scale of the investment and also that the proper use of capital can best be obtained by setting up the right price mechanism. However, a basic problem for any developing state is to make sure that most of the foreign capital mobilized ostensibly to expand investment does in fact end up as new investment—not as a substitute for consumption or a fat bank account in Switzerland.

In the late 1960s only about 2 percent on average of total resources in developing states came from foreign sources, though there were big differences between individual states. In Israel 25 percent to 33 percent of investment is financed from abroad.

I have two questions: The first is whether it is better to have a detailed overall plan and work on many things at once or to have individual project planning. The second is this, whether if you have the right price system you need no planning. If you don't, how can you evaluate individual projects, let alone make an overall plan?

ASHER HALPERIN (Israel): The difference between the use of external capital and that of internal capital is that the former has to be repaid in foreign exchange. So the return use of such capital should be defined as producing sufficient foreign exchange to pay the interest on it, as well as eventually the principal. However, many investments are useful without earning foreign exchange or saving it. This may apply to investments in transportation, communications, education, and even housing, depending on whether they only improve welfare or also increase productivity. Foreign investment may also diversify the economy without earning foreign exchange. To my mind, diversification is a target in itself, which should not be ignored.

CARLOS DIAZ ALEJANDRO (Department of Economics, Economic Growth Center, Yale University, United States): Why do rich states restrict immigration? For economics, it would obviously be good if many people moved to England or West Germany. But the social implications of this are out of the question. Much the same applies to restrictions imposed by some developing states on direct foreign investment. Here too, there are social and political implications. There have been scandals of the ITT kind, when a foreign investor tried to overthrow a government and then get paid for it. Canada has recently tried to buy back its foreign investments in natural resources.

So the general presumption against foreign capital may be quite sensible as a way of avoiding risks or getting entangled in troubles with foreign governments. Companies are instruments of national policy. A country with a lot of foreign investments will not have many institutions responding to its national purpose.

YOSEF YORAN (Israel): Underutilization of capacity in LDCs may be a manifestation of the poorer economic performance in these states, or alternatively of a scarcity of skilled and managerial personnel. It may be due to shortages of materials reflecting balance of payments difficulties caused by poor high-level management. Or it may reflect a price system containing gross distortions due to government actions, leading to the planning in advance of the operation of capacity at low level.

Inefficiency can also result from a price system distorting the true picture of social costs and benefits.

Misuse of capital is thus often due to a distorted price system. Inefficiency due to scarcity of certain resources in LDCs may often be caused by their having to use capital equipment adapted to a different economic context and different prices.

The main conclusions should be greater reliance on an efficient price mechanism, more liberalization, and detailed analysis of situations where government planning is called for. Many governments are too anxious to intervene and often do so in the wrong manner, channelling scarce entrepreneurship in the wrong directions.

HELEN HUGHES (Chief, Industrialization Division, Economic Department, International Bank for Reconstruction and Development): While labor was treated as homogeneous, there were many inexplicable uses of capital rather than labor because the shortage of skilled labor was not recognized as an important production factor. Similarly, not all types of capital can be substituted for each other. Capital available for manufacturing may not be available for agriculture.

I. LITTLE (Oxford University): A country using domestic capital will also use foreign capital, and they may be mixed up. Project analysis of foreign investments should take into account how much they will borrow locally and whether inflow of foreign capital will expand consumption within the country.

I disagree strongly with Professor Halperin. If domestic prices correctly measure costs and benefits, borrowing abroad is worthwhile if use of the money gives a higher social yield than the interest on the loan. But where we employ a low shadow price of labor, that is, the project is already giving away part of the social benefit in the form of consumption, the social profit of the investment will not add up to a balance of payments saving. Only if the shadow wage rate equals the actual wage rate, will your project evaluation show a profit equal to the balance of payments saving. A good investment will pay itself back if you have the rate of growth of consumption under control. Only bad investments cause balance of payments struggles with a debt problem. Diversification can be viewed as an additional benefit to be quantified, but does not affect my conclusions.

If a state feels that it does not want too much foreign investment, it can simply demand in its project appraisals that a foreign investment must have a social yield of at least 20-25 percent, whereas a domestic investment can have one of only 10 percent. It is always simple to turn a project down.

In some LDCs entrepreneurship is used to obtain licenses and permits from ministers, and once one has got them one can virtually print money. This certainly exaggerates the price of entrepreneurship. One should perhaps make industry more profitable than under free trade, but without introducing big distortions. In Pakistan someone got a cheap loan from the government and then imported machinery without any tariff on it with a tariff rebate. This kind of thing can make capital very cheap indeed.

One of the hardest problems in investment analysis is deciding what was the real opportunity cost of the particular capital used for the particular project proposed. Some of it may be new savings, some may come from consumption, some, and occasionally all, of it may be diverted from another private investment. Or perhaps some of the money might have been lent to the government. Certainly capital is not homogeneous, and I would put a high priority on government intervention to improve the capital market.

**PROS AND CONS OF
PROTECTION AND
IMPORT SUBSTITUTION**
Helen Hughes

The dangers of import substitution and protection in developing countries have received considerable attention in recent years. The evidence, however, is rather one-sided. Japan, the outstanding example of rapid and successful development, has been largely ignored, although a barrage of protectionist instruments that culminated in an almost total prohibition of competing imports (and of foreign investment) was an integral part of the policy mix of the 1950s and 1960s rapid growth period. Studies of protection, moreover, have tended to regard trade policy as the dominant policy factor in development and to neglect issues of policy implementation. The economic costs of export subsidies are only now beginning to receive attention.

Despite the reaction against the extreme import substitution ideology of the 1950s and early 1960s, protectionist views persist. Developing countries are keenly interested in the Japanese development model, and some have successfully begun to adapt it to their needs. The infant industry argument for some measure of protection is still strong in least developed countries, although those that have made some progress in industrialization are moving from protection for import substitution to subsidies for exports. The emphasis on the social objectives of development, and particularly on employment, is strengthening the employment argument for protection.

THE CASE FOR PROTECTION

The "infant industry" argument has remained the core of the protectionist case. The economic justification of providing public subsidies to offset an entrepreneur's costs on account of future social gains remains basically unchanged. A direct subsidy for this purpose is in practice so costly to administer that a tariff may turn out to be the solution. Typically then, the infant industry case leads to tariff protection.

Further arguments for the infant industry case include the "terms of trade" case for diversification and the protection of the balance of payments, which has been stated principally in import substitution terms. Countries dependent on one or two agricultural exports with an elastic supply and inelastic demand experienced declining terms of trade in the 1920s and 1930s. Their imports of industrial goods were interrupted during World War II, and they feared a repetition of the 1930s experience after the wartime boom. Balance of payments considerations and the need for industrialization were thus linked in theory; they became more closely linked in practice through quantitative trade controls as balance of payments problems reasserted themselves in the late 1940s.

Diversification through industrial development seemed also to be relevant to the solution of growing unemployment and low-income problems in developing countries. Whereas earnings in agriculture and agricultural countries were low, earnings in industry and in industrialized countries were high, promising rapid wage increases.

The "trade retaliation" argument for protection began to gain momentum in the 1950s and 1960s. During the LDCs' main move towards industrialization, after World War II, monetary and trade restrictions were widespread. There has been much monetary liberalization since the 1950s; but many primary product markets are still restricted, and trade liberalization in industrial goods was largely confined to goods traded among industrial countries. Developed country tariff protection against key products in which developing countries might be expected to have a comparative advantage, processed raw materials and labor-intensive goods such as textiles and footwear, has been retained; and in many instances tariffs have been bolstered by quantitative restrictions. Recently even subcontracted labor-intensive exports such as electronic components and assemblies have come under threat of protection in the United States. The much vaunted generalized preference schemes do not include sensitive products. During most of their industrialization process the developing countries were thus faced with an international economy far removed from free trade.

Moreover, imperfect competition and product differentiation are characteristic of many manufactured product markets. Strong oligopoly groups were beginning to take a commanding role in the world economy before World War II, and in the 1950s and 1960s they considerably extended their power. The developing countries noted Japan's emergence as a major industrial power with its own multinational corporations.

Discriminatory pricing followed imperfect competition. Developing countries have long been familiar with variations in f.o.b. prices by country of destination, according to what the market will bear. Such practices made the evaluation of comparative advantage difficult and led to price instabilities that magnified the difficulties of planning. Some LDCs were able to benefit by buying marginally priced goods, in times of excess capacity, both for their own consumption and as inputs for exports. However, in recent times of boom and scarcity, their input costs rose disproportionately, and sometimes inputs were simply not available. Domestic consumers and the volume of exports suffered. There have also been clear cases of dumping, the temporary lowering of prices to prevent import substitution and establish dominance in a market so as to raise prices later.

There are two principal obstacles when developing countries try to enter manufacturing. Multinational corporations were frequently able to establish a consumer market for their branded differentiated product before a country's industrialization was begun. Internationally advertised products continue to enjoy an advantage in most national markets, and LDCs are no exception. Local manufacturers of soap, toothpaste, and food products usually have great difficulty in penetrating such a market. Second, the oligopolistic nature of industry is particularly marked in the market for sophisticated technology. Often such technology can only be obtained as part of a package deal with capital and market participation by a multnational corporation; thus independent entry by local producers is difficult unless a government takes very strong protective measures.

Internal communications, shipping, and insurance services are no more competitive than manufacturing. Shipping freight rates are notoriously set by regional cartels. The building up of LDC shipping fleets, however costly and inefficient in its early stages, is a protectionist reaction against cartelization. Japan had a long struggle before it was accepted by the shipping conferences.

Since the 1930s developed countries have built up complex export subsidy systems that further distort international trading. Nationalist neomercantilism and marginal pricing for export markets gained respectability when GATT was persuaded to make drawbacks of indirect taxes a legitimate form of export subsidy. This introduced some extremely dubious concepts into international trade practice.* Substantial credit subsidies to exporters by leading industrialized countries further diversified international prices.

The strongest argument for protection is that some self-sufficiency is desirable for its own sake, as a symbol of newly acquired independence.

The case for subsidizing exports, particularly of manufactures, is essentially an extension of the infant industry, diversification and balance of payments, and employment and trade retaliation arguments.

---

*The implication suggests that consumers will be better off if they always buy imported rather than locally produced goods.

The dichotomy between inward and outward orientation is not one of import substitution versus exports, but rather of the difference between maintaining international standards of efficiency in production and ignoring such standards. The administrative difficulties of paying direct cash subsidies to exporters have been overcome in many instances, but it has not yet been possible to evolve a practical direct subsidy to producers of import substituting products, though there are many instances of cash or near cash payments to exports of manufactured products. Often, at least part of the subsidy may be passed on to consumers of other countries. The mercantilist strains underlying nationalist thinking are very strong indeed.

THE CASE AGAINST IMPORT SUBSTITUTION AND PROTECTION

Protection creates distortions in the exploitation of comparative advantage, and hence in the allocation of resources. The greater the distortions, the higher the social costs of protection. As the measurement of distortions is in terms of market prices, the reference firm is the marginal firm, which determines domestic prices. Thus reducing protection, even substantially, would not normally mean eliminating an industry, though the marginal firm, or firms, could be forced out of business. A high rate of protection does not necessarily imply that an industry is inefficient per se but rather that it is using resources inefficiently. An industry that would under more optimal conditions enjoy a comparative advantage, might thus require a very high rate of protection.

Protection, and particularly high protection, leads to inefficiency in the conduct of business. In the absence of foreign competition, domestic competition may be too weak to ensure competent entrepreneurial and managerial performance. Low levels of production typical of early industrialization are frequently characterized by monopoly or oligopoly, and by weak competition, because all competitors are infant firms.

Protection has other costs. Contrary to expectations, import substitution with high protection has tended to worsen the balance of payments. The high costs and prices of highly protected manufactures discriminated against nonindustrial exports, hindering their expansion. High prices have tended to limit the domestic market, restraining import substitution by raising the costs of producing intermediates and capital goods. Balance of payments problems grew, as imports of intermediates could not be reduced or cut off in lean times (as imports of nonessential final products had been in pre-import-substitution days) because urban employment was dependent on imported inputs. High costs made the export of manufactures very difficult, limiting opportunities for export earnings, particularly in labor-intensive products in which LDCs may have a comparative advantage.

The case against import substitution at all costs was recognized in the 1950s and early 1960s when Israel, Taiwan, and Korea began to subsidize manufactured exports to offset high domestic production costs and the high profits under protection, encouraging manufacturers to produce only for the domestic market. Singapore followed but, having had little protection, was able to use a low-cost export-incentive package. Pakistan was the most spectacular, if not the most successful, convert to export subsidies. By the early 1970s export subsidies were commonplace amongst countries which had previously followed high protection principally for import substitution.

Protection also has social costs. High costs reduce the potential for industrial growth, and hence for employment in industry. Employment creation was in any case limited because protectionist policies, such as import duty rebates on capital goods, stimulated capital-intensive production methods. Import licensing and foreign exchange control tended to favor large, capital-intensive producers. Foreign and local funds have been often available to privileged, generally large-scale borrowers at low, sometimes negative, interest rates, through development banks. Other forms of incentives associated with protection—income tax holidays, subsidized land, and public utilities—have also tended to favor large-scale and capital-intensive producers. Multinational corporations benefited particularly. Small producers, who would have tended to use more labor-intensive production methods, were placed at a disadvantage.

Attracted by the possibilities of tariffs and import licensing, many countries have created unwieldly administrative systems. Not satisfied with the trade protection afforded manufacturing industries by trade policy measures, they subsidize manufacturers further by giving them income tax holidays of varying duration, and by subsidizing credit, land, and public utilities. The high costs of these policies have now been well established. They include a stimulus to capital intensiveness and, in foreign investment, frequently transfers of revenues to the government of the lending country. The benefits are small. Yet developing countries throughout the world continue to compete with each other in the extent and duration of such giveaways.

The manufacturers' opportunities for profits through the manipulation of the "rules of the game" often exceed those that may be earned in the course of business. Access to government offices has thus become an important locational factor, reinforcing the tendency towards geographical concentration in large urban centers. It pays entrepreneurs to spend more time in ministers' waiting rooms than on the shop floor. The multinational corporation with its superior resources, which may include political pressure through its own government, usually benefits.

Subsidies for exports have similar effects. They are sometimes financed through high domestic prices; taxpayers contribute to cash subsidies; or public services and investment are reduced by revenues foregone. In East Asia the subsidies have been concentrated on low-skill, low-capital, cheap labor industries, and this has tended to stimulate employment, albeit in low-productivity, low-wage occupations. Singapore followed more enlightened policies, seeking to build skill industries, as soon as a stopgap low-wage industry program gave it breathing space to do so. Korea is now planning on these lines. In Latin America, however, export subsidies have tended to go to relatively capital-intensive industries. Multinational corporations have frequently been best able to exploit export subsidies directly by taking advantage of incentives, and by transfer pricing that maximizes tax benefits.

In some countries strong trade unions have been able to share in the economic "rents" of protection through relatively high wages and fringe benefits. To the extent that such a share came out of profits, and was distributed fairly widely, this was probably a more efficient form of profit redistribution than company income taxes might have been. High wages, however, also contributed to capital intensiveness; where they were additional to high profits, they raised prices and reduced international competitiveness and hence employment opportunities.

The case against import-substitution-oriented protection stated, many tiresome problems remain. Japan's experience is the most obvious. Protection became important in the 1930s and only began to be dismantled in the late 1960s. Much still remains. Consciously following the Japanese model, Iran showed steady and rapid growth with high protection from the early 1960s. The contribution of manufacturing to growth was more important than petroleum until 1970, domestic prices of mass consumption goods were close to international prices by 1971, and with the first import substitution phase well established, manufactured exports were by then growing at 40 percent per annum.

The Japanese experience needs to be compared in detail with other cases of protection to sift out elements leading to success from those spelling disaster. It is clearly possible to combine protectionist policies with internal competitiveness and significant levels of exports, and to administer even complex protective measures effectively so that a highly protected economy can remain very sensitive to international economic trends. Thus it seems that the crucial factors determining the outcome of a protectionist development strategy are not protection as such, its level or the variations in protection among industries, but rather the way in which various protectionist and other development policies are combined and administered.

PROS AND CONS OF PROTECTION AND IMPORT SUBSTITUTION
In Sang Song

Infant industries of less developed nations are the buds of industries to enjoy comparative advantages in the future. Some of the industries that a nation is protecting may survive for long with comparative advantage. Other industries may show strong competitiveness and assure the nation foreign exchange earnings needed to introduce advanced equipment and technologies for further industrialization.

One should protect selected industries only. No one will protect hopeless industries if they know they are hopeless.

Selection is hard, especially if one industry is advantageous at a certain stage and another industry at another stage of development. Besides, almost all developing nations experience balance of payment difficulties. So foreign trade restrictions are made to protect infant industries, with the effect of reducing imports.

OLD INDUSTRY—ITS MERITS FOR THE PAST

All industries that have existed in advanced nations have in the past rendered help to national development. But if any industry turns out to be no longer competitive at any stage, it will become a burden for the nation, as well as for the competing nations, if protected, thus hurting the world's consumers.

Old industries, here, refers to those that were fully competitive at one stage of development but later became uncompetitive. A country ought to shift from such industries to other competitive industries. For example, a grand old nation might have done better to have admitted earlier the uncompetitiveness of, say, her textile industry, and concentrated her efforts on stimulating, say, electronic industries. The same may be said of some industries of nations now prospering.

In Sang Song is President of the Korean Development Association, Korea.

IMPORT SUBSTITUTION AND NATIONAL INTERESTS

If part of the world sticks to national interests, others also cannot help but do so. In this manner the world can never be unified.

Let us remember a saying, "The boughs that bear more hang lower." Mature economies should be more generous and get out of the way in order to allow the less mature more sun. The rich have some income to spare, but the poor have nothing to spare. Concessions ought to be sought from those who can give, not from those who cannot.

Though protection ought to be lifted in the richer countries, it should not be in the poorer ones, since it helps not merely to improve their balance of payments but also to secure means of payments for their investment requirements and to increase their future purchasing power. If they are forbidden to protect, their buying will increase for some years only, since sooner or later they will have nothing to pay with.

CONTRIBUTION OF PROTECTION AND IMPORT SUBSTITUTION IN TRANSFORMING THE KOREAN ECONOMY

The Korean economy, prior to the rapid growth in the 1960s, was characterized by scarcity of natural resources, surplus labor, an agricultural sector dominating the economic structure, and a chronic balance of payment deficit. Under such circumstances there was no alternative but to adopt the policy of import substitution as a first step towards rapid industrialization.

Considerable progress was made in the fifties and the early sixties in developing import-substitute industries of consumer goods. The policy of protection and import substitution not only contributed to balance of payments improvement but also restructured a stagnant agrarian economy into a dynamic, growth-oriented one.

Since Korea is a relatively small country in size of domestic market, a limit to import substitution of consumer goods came much faster than in some other developing countries. At this point it was realized that a single measure alone cannot do much to remedy the difficulties of the national economy. Deliberate control of imports, without accompanying supplementary measures, cannot ease the balance of payments position. Devaluation in 1964, the interest rate reform in 1965, and successive tax reforms signified a turning point in the Korean economy—reorientation of trade and related policies towards manufactured exports.

The rapid industrialization of the Korean economy in the 1960s was generated by the sharp increase of demand stemming from the expansion of exports and import substitutes. Exports of manufactured goods increased at 52 percent per annum during 1962-69, almost four times faster than the growth rate of value added in manufacturing. As a result, the proportion of exports in total domestic industrial production rose from 1 percent in 1962 to about 15 percent in 1969. The share of manufactured goods in total commodity exports rose from 27 percent in 1962 to 83 percent in 1970.

During the later 1960s, growth of consumer goods industries was much slower than in earlier years, reflecting the cumulative effects of past growth which reduced further possibilities of import substitution. On the other hand, both the capital and intermediate goods industries started to expand rapidly owing to the sharp increase in investment and development of import-substitute industries in these groups. Within each group, the export-oriented commodities and import substitutes recorded the most growth.

The differential growth rates among the manufactured goods in the 1960s showed substantial changes. The share of consumer goods industries in total value added declined from over 80 percent in 1960 to 55 percent in 1970. The structural changes reflected the government's emphasis on the development of heavy industries such as chemical products, petroleum products, iron and steel, and machinery industries (including electronics and transport equipments). Nevertheless, the manufacturing sector was still dominated by the labor-intensive, consumer-goods-oriented industries.

The recent government emphasis on the development of heavy industries was prompted by the major weakness of the industrial structure in Korea. This may be seen in connection with the major trends in imports.

During the second half of the 1960s total imports increased at the rate of about 40 percent per annum. Their composition underwent a drastic change in the 1960s, the share of consumer goods declining from 23 percent to 13 percent with a parallel increase in imports of raw materials and capital goods. This reflects the increasing dependence of the manufacturing sector on imports of raw materials and capital goods. Thus in order to improve the industrial structure and to ease the balance of payment position the development of heavy industries was required.

Here again, the first step toward the development of heavy industries was to promote import substitution by backward integration, through domestic production of inputs for the metal, petrochemical, mechanical, and electronic industries.

LESSONS FROM THE KOREAN EXPERIENCE

During the 1960s the policy of the Korean government was to promote rapid industrialization through various incentive schemes. The policy of protection was initially adopted to induce the development of import-substituting industries. Thus, protection and import substitution together were an essential part of industrial strategy in Korea. However, given the limited size of domestic market and balance of payments difficulties, it was essential to develop next the labor-intensive, export-oriented industries, for which additional incentive schemes were initially required. This led to heavy dependence on imports of raw materials and capital goods. In order to improve the industrial structure, protection and import substitution of intermediate goods and capital goods were required.

Import substitution ought to be exercised step by step; in this process impatience is the enemy of national development. Suppose a country imports plastic bowls: domestic production at the initial stage of import substitution should be of the molding process, importing resin; after that, if further import substitution is required, the polymerization process could follow, and then monomer production and lastly naphtha cracking. The optimal extent of import substitution of different processes of a commodity may differ from country to country.

Korea has been successful in the recent past in transforming its stagnant agrarian economy into a dynamic industrial one. Given the poor natural resources endowment, this was the only development strategy open to us. The policy of protection and import substitution was an indispensable part in the package of government policies that successfully accomplished the economic transformation in the sixties. And the task of completing the transformation of the economy into a mature industrial state is still going on, with protection and import substitution playing an important role.

Protection is one of the measures needed to develop import substitution. Other measures to increase the rate of saving, to give incentives to invest, or to reform institutional or material shortcomings must follow.

Among the critical problems confronting less developed countries is attaining structural transformations corresponding to the different levels of income growth. Here real bottlenecks prevail, stemming from market imperfection, factor proportion problems, institutional rigidities, and so on. To overcome these difficulties, thereby achieving the restructuring of the economy necessary for growth, the policy of protection and import substitution accompanied by other relevant and appropriate measures has proved to be very effective. The crux of the issue, however, is the duration of the protection policy. The Korean experience seems to indicate that switching policies from import substitution (during the early phase of restructuring the economy) to export promotion (based on the new structure thus created) is essential if the developing countries are to avoid the economic waste and misallocation of resources arising from the misuse of import-substituting industrialization.

PROTECTION AND EXPORT—THE EXPERIENCE OF KOREA

If protection contributes to import substitution, it affects exports unfavorably. But Korean experience shows that, by selective duty exemption, the effect of protection on exports was neutralized.

The Korean industries with rates of tariff and special customs duty together above 100 percent were in the later sixties 12 percent of total output. Many of those affected products the use of which was generally felt to be a luxury and not a necessity. The group with the same rates below 100 percent and above 50 percent accounted for 18 percent of total output. Many of these were the final or semifinal products that the government wanted to develop for domestic supply and if possible to export. The remaining 70 percent of total output were protected at rates of below 50 percent or zero. These were mostly agricultural or mining products, increase of their domestic production being limited by nature.

This was the natural outcome of a tariff structure aimed at regulating consumption of imported goods. And although some changes in tariff rates have taken place, the basic structure is still more or less the same. The antiluxury type of tariff structure was kept throughout the years of export-first policy. As shown in Table 10,

TABLE 10

Export of Selected Korean Products
(in thousand dollars)

	1967	1968	1969	1970	1971
Electric machinery, apparatus, and appliances	7,000	19,000	37,000	44,000	68,486
Textile fiber, yarn, and fabrics	49,000	61,000	66,000	85,000	137,834
Clothing	59,000	112,000	161,000	214,000	304,265
Wood products	37,000	66,000	80,000	93,000	128,923

Source: Statistical Yearbook, 1971. Office of Customs Administration.

TABLE 11

Nominal and Effective Tariff Rates for
Industries of Selected Nations
(percentages)

	Wood Products (including furniture)	Clothing	Textile Fabrics	Electrical Machinery
United States				
nominal	12.8	25.1	24.1	12.2
effective	26.4	35.9	50.6	18.1
United Kingdom				
nominal	14.8	25.5	20.7	19.7
effective	25.5	40.5	42.2	30.0
Sweden				
nominal	6.8	14.0	12.7	10.7
effective	14.5	21.1	33.4	17.7
Japan				
nominal	19.5	25.2	19.7	18.1
effective	33.9	42.2	48.8	25.3
Korea				
nominal	55.6	110.1	77.4	42.1
effective	25.6	74.0	61.0	22.5
Common Market				
nominal	15.1	18.5	17.6	14.5
effective	28.6	25.1	44.4	21.2

Source: Bela Balassa, "Tariff Protection in Industrial Countries," *Journal of Political Economy*, December, 1965. Figures for

exports of several selected items grew rapidly during recent years. But nominal as well as effective rates of protection of the corresponding items, as shown in Table 11, were neither too high nor too low. Nominal tax rates on those items ranged from the high of 110 percent (on clothing) to the low of 42 percent (on electric machines). The effective rates of the same items were 74 percent and 22 percent. Export of electric machines increased just as rapidly as of clothing, and of wood products (nominal rate, 55 percent effective rate; 25 percent no less than of textile fibre and fabrics (nominal, 77 percent; effective, 61 percent).

Thus exports were not influenced by protection. In fact, export was facilitated by exempting imported inputs from tariffs and other duties. Hence protection relates to home market only and acts as a means to reduce the balance of payment deficit.

Protection rates in industrialized countries are also shown in Table 11. They are in most cases much lower than in Korea. The Korean rates will be lowered as Korean industries grow. In fact, the special customs duty was completely repealed by the beginning of this year.

**TURNING FROM IMPORT
SUBSTITUTION TO EXPORT
PROMOTION IN COLOMBIA**
Carlos F. Diaz-Alejandro

Recent literature emphasizes the negative consequences of domestic policies in less developed countries (LDCs) that encourage import substitution much beyond the level stimulated by market forces. It suggests giving additional incentives to exports, particularly non-traditional exports, as a way to accelerate growth and achieve other development goals.

Colombia is an interesting case study of the switch from import substitution to export promotion. Within the Latin American picture Colombia is a typical country. Its population (about 22 million in 1970) is neither too big nor too small. Its per capita income (roughly U.S. $350) is near the Latin American average. Its foreign trade has been traditionally dependent on one crop, coffee, the international price of which has been unstable.

The switch from import substitution to export promotion should not be overdramatized. It took place mainly in Colombia in 1967, though special incentives for minor exports existed before that date and several economically debatable import substitution projects were launched after it. Nevertheless, during 1967 a comprehensive set of measures was enacted increasing the incentives to exports.

THE RECORD BEFORE AND AFTER 1967

Between 1967 and 1972, the dollar value of Colombian merchandise exports, excluding coffee, crude petroleum, and smuggled goods, rose from $127 million to about $390 million. During the previous five years, 1962-67, the rise had been from $71 million to $127 million. These exports accounted for 15 percent of all exports in 1962, 25 percent in 1967, and about 46 percent in 1972. Their average annual growth rate doubled from 12.5 percent during 1962-67 to 25.0 percent during 1967-72. Both higher prices and larger quantities played important roles in this statistical expansion.

Real gross domestic product, which was growing at 4.5 percent per year during 1962-67, grew at an estimated 6.4 percent per year during 1967-72. The acceleration of industrial growth from 5.1 to 7.8 percent per year paralleled that in agriculture from 2.9 to 4.4

percent per year. The dollar values of merchandise imports during 1972 were about 60 percent above the depressed levels of 1967. Though there has been an acceleration in the overall growth rate, the precise profile of this growth still remains obscure. It is not obvious that the post-1967 growth is significantly more labor-intensive than that before 1967.

THE NEW EXPORTS

It is often assumed that recent export expansion in many LDCs is based on labor-intensive manufactured goods. In Colombia the breakdown of the net increase in exports other than coffee and oil between 1957 and 1970 was as follows:

Exports	Percentage Increase
Bananas, sugar, cotton, and tobacco	27.6
Manufactures	40.4
Miscellaneous	32.0

Thus less than half the increase can be attributed to manufactured goods. The importance of the miscellaneous category is particularly encouraging and emphasizes growing diversification. The extent of export diversification is reflected by the following table, giving the number of SITC three digit categories showing the indicated export values:

	In 1966	In 1970
More than one million U.S. dollars	20	33
Between half and one million U.S. dollars	9	12
More than $100,000 but less than $500,000	31	47

Import substituting industrialization was hardly a necessary precondition for the development of Colombian exports under SITC chapters 0, 1, 2, and 9. Other exports may be divided into two categories: those going to countries within the Latin American Free Trade Association (LAFTA) and those going to the rest of the world. Exports to LAFTA tend to originate in newer industries that are probably more capital intensive and import intensive than the activities generating exports to the rest of the world (see Table 12).

Many manufactures exported primarily to non-LAFTA countries have been established in Colombia for a long time, and it would be

TABLE 12

Exports to LAFTA as Percentage of Total Exports

SITC		LAFTA Share	1970 Value of All Exports (million U.S. dollars)
512	Organic chemicals	43.2	0.35
513	Inorganic chemicals, type I	61.4	2.43
514	Inorganic chemicals, type II	93.8	0.60
541	Medical and pharmaceutical products	75.8	2.68
581	Plastics	69.4	1.02
612	Leather and manufactures	0.6	0.88
629	Rubber products (tires)	82.7	1.19
631	Plywood and semi-processed wood	0.5	1.61
651	Threads and spun fibers	8.3	4.18
652	Cotton textiles	8.6	7.51
841	Clothing	11.2	1.10
851	Shoes	0.3	0.74

difficult to argue that the import-substituting policies of the 1950s and 1960s were a necessary precondition for their export expansion in recent years. Textiles, for example, were the leading sector of industrialization during the 1930s, as in Argentina. Furthermore, already during the Second World War Colombia, as well as Argentina, exported cotton cloth. These exports dried up after the war and were not renewed in substantial amounts until fairly recently, though some other LDCs expanded their textile exports substantially between 1945 and 1965.

Most exports to LAFTA owe their existence to the import substitution policies of the 1950s and 1960s. But all economic consequences of such an evolution are not necessarily positive. They will only be positive to the extent that the new intra-LAFTA trade represents regional import substitution justified by regional economies of scale, or a rationalization of existing industries in each LAFTA country. But some of these new exports could be a symptom that the excesses of national import substituting policies are being repeated at the regional level.

There is another disturbing characteristic of intra-LAFTA manufacturing exports: in 1969, more than 40 percent of them were handled by 175 big companies owned 90 percent or more by foreigners. The percentage is likely to be somewhat less for Colombia. Colombia is also a member of a subgroup within LAFTA, the Andean Common Market, that has wisely imposed strict rules on direct foreign investments in exchange for allowing access to the protected Andean market.

POLICY CHANGES INDUCING EXPORT EXPANSION

During 1965-66 Colombia experimented with simultaneous import liberalization and export promotion. This proved a traumatic experience, import growth far exceeding the growth of exports. Import liberalization was therefore abandoned towards the end of 1966.

In April 1967, the Colombians decided, quite sensibly, to launch export promotion measures, making import liberalization depend on the success of these measures. The new policy consolidated and coordinated previous export incentives. A flat subsidy (CAT) was given to all exports except coffee and oil, which were also aided by special credit and insurance facilities as well as by a powerful government export promotion agency.

Perhaps the most important part of the package was the adoption of a "crawling peg" exchange rate with small changes several times a month. Between 1966 and 1972 the net real exchange rate rose by 26 percent. However, the rise between the averages for 1961-62-63 and for 1970-71-72 was only 11 percent. This reflects the dramatic contrast between the effects of pre- and post-1966 policies on the stability of the net real exchange rate. Gone are the wild swings that characterized the years before the establishment of the crawling peg.

After the unhappy 1965-66 experience Colombian authorities tightened quantitative import controls. Towards the middle of 1966 import quotas had been almost eliminated, the exchange rate and tariffs remaining as the major import-repressing mechanisms. But during 1967 import licensing became very strict, and only about 4 percent of registered imports remained on the free list. The corresponding percentage in October 1966 had been 80 percent. As the foreign exchange situation improved after 1967, as a result of higher coffee prices, the expansion of other exports, and larger capital inflows, quantitative import controls were loosened. But the licensing mechanism has been retained and is still administered with a frankly protectionist intent.

How was export expansion possible though the mechanisms from the import substitution days were retained? The basic answer is that economies such as that of Colombia do not consist solely of an import-competing and an export sector. The resources channeled into recent export expansion appear to have come not so much from existing or potential import-substituting activities but from a sector producing "nontradeable" or "home" goods. The 1967 policies tilted relative incentives towards exports and away from import substitution. But, more importantly, they strengthened incentives for both selected import substituting and exports relative to the nontradeable sector.

Since 1967 regimes allowing the duty-free importation of inputs for exports have been consolidated and extended, and subsidized credit has been increasingly channeled to exporters. On the whole, exporters are not a new breed of entrepreneurs. Frequently firms engaged in import substitution turn marginally towards exports, partly in response to new incentives and partly due to direct pressures from public authorities, whose goodwill is very important to them.

Few Colombian firms export 100 percent of their output. The expansion of manufactured exports was largely due to major companies' increasing the share of exports in their total sales from negligible proportions to some 10 percent. Not surprisingly, foreign sales are frequently priced at marginal cost, while the domestic market, suitably protected with import restrictions, covers fixed costs. These powerful economic corporations are better able to take advantage of new incentives offered by the public sector than small entrepreneurs and typically have higher capital-labor ratios than smaller firms.

While traditional tools, such as the exchange rate, were part of the post-1966 policies stimulating the switch from import substitution to export promotion, these policies also included "moral suasion" and pressure by import control or credit authorities on companies that have to get their subsidized import licenses and loans approved. Credit for export expansion also helped the fast growth of minor exports.

Given the complexity and variety of export promotion tools, it would not be surprising to find some exports whose net economic payoff to Colombia may be lower than that of some import substituting activities. The following example may resemble some actual situations, although I would not regard it as typical. An item with an import component (exempted from customs duties) of 40 percent receives a flat subsidy on export values amounting to about 19 percent of gross sales. Its effective protection would then be:

Assumed world sale	$100
Price to exporter including subsidy (CAT)	$119
Value added at domestic prices	$ 79
Value added at world prices	$ 60
"Effective protection"	32 percent

Exports to a LAFTA country may fetch higher prices than those ruling in world markets. This would be fine for Colombia if she were not expected to buy commodities from LAFTA partners at prices that are also higher than world prices. In such a case, the de facto effective protection could be even higher.

However, the misallocations that haphazard export promotion policies can generate are likely to be less damaging to growth and efficiency than import-substitution policies. It is generally easier to correct the consequences of this type of mistake at higher than at lower levels of foreign trade. In particular, for small- and medium-sized countries the consequences for capital formation of too much export promotion are likely to be far less damaging than those of too much import substitution.

EXPORT EXPANSION, GROWTH, AND DEVELOPMENT

Colombian growth has accelerated since 1967; and, although terms-of-trade improvements partly account for this trend, the new domestic policies were probably responsible for a good part of the high expansion rate. It seems that better short-run management of fiscal, monetary, and exchange rate policy since 1967 deserves much of the credit. These policies, particularly the crawling peg, have succeeded in avoiding the stop-go cycles related to governmental efforts to maintain pegged exchange rates, which were devalued only in crisis situations but then were devalued massively. Since 1967 the smoother expansion pattern has allowed fuller use of capacity and steadier entrepreneurial expectations.

In short, in semi-industrialized economies, such as Colombia, Keynesian-type short-run economic problems and their management can have important medium-run consequences for the growth rate. Trade and development theorists focusing on long-run effects of resource reallocation between the import-competing and export sectors, in full employment or full capacity models, seriously neglect this important aspect of reality.

As export expansion is accompanied by growing links with foreign capital markets, the need for coordinating fiscal, credit, and exchange rate policy becomes even greater as the new foreign trade measures begin to pay off. The Colombia of 1972-73, for example, faces assignment problems in its struggle to hold down inflationary pressures, to a much greater extent than before 1967. And the available policy tools in the fiscal and monetary field still leave much to be desired.

The new policies have accelerated growth, but what can they do for other Colombian development goals? As in most Latin American countries, in Colombia, income and wealth distribution is unjust; and nearly all policy makers pay lip service to improving it. Disguised and open unemployment are related to the unjust income distribution, and their decrease is also a much advertised policy goal. Will export expansion help to move Colombia closer to fuller employment and a better income distribution and, if so, by how much?

Contrary to the optimism of some export promotion enthusiasts, the answer is not at all obvious. Faster overall expansion could be expected to generate, ceteris paribus, a higher employment level. But there may be some negative side effects on employment. Greater foreign exchange earnings could lead to a larger inflow of labor-displacing equipment for existing industries and rural activities. As noted earlier, many of the new exports are land intensive, and their expansion and modernization could create serious disturbances in the countryside, with a negative net effect on employment. Given the social tensions existing in the Colombian rural sector, it is very tempting for private entrepreneurs, say, in sugar or cotton, to adopt capital-intensive techniques of production.

Even if overall employment expands as a result of higher exports and faster GNP growth, it is doubtful that this will improve income distribution. Most of the output gains are likely to accrue to those controlling factors of production in short supply, such as land, capital, and skilled labor. Even if all minor exports were intensive users of unskilled labour, which they are not, such exports amounted to only about 7 percent of the Colombian GNP in 1972.

Another important Colombian development goal is the achievement of a greater degree of national autonomy in economic decisions. For all LDCs it will be increasingly difficult to reconcile growing openness of the economy to world markets with the desire for greater national control over the domestic economy. As already noted, Colombia and her Andean partners exert tight controls over direct foreign investors, particularly in import-competing and export activities. This seems a necessary precondition for a stable balance among different development policy goals. An export expansion heavily dependent on foreign investors would sooner or later produce a nationalist reaction jeopardizing the continuation of export-promotion policies.

CONCLUSION

The new export promotion policies can be expected to achieve faster GNP growth but not a drastic improvement in income distribution in the near future. Tinkering with the exchange rate is important but will not have a significant impact on the lives of the poorest segments of Colombian society for a long, long time.

DISCUSSION

JOAN FLANDERS (Israel): Not every attempt to protect import substitution is bad, and not every attempt to promote exports is good. But effective import substitution can protect the local producers' right or ability to make poor-quality goods. This has happened in some instances in Israel. It is much easier to get away with selling poor products in the home market than in foreign markets.

Protecting import substitution does not necessarily mean protecting capital-intensive production techniques. On the other hand, export promotion may well encourage strongly capital-intensive processes. This can be done by lending on very easy terms to exporters.

A way must be found to promote exports or import substitutes without raising the capital-labor ratio. Realistic exchange rates can help. Some states, like Israel, prefer complicated and constantly changing import surcharges and export subsidies to straightforward devaluation, which could do much for better allocation of resources.

Import substitution, paradoxically, can make a country very dependent on imports if it concentrates on nonessential goods and the final stages of manufacture. This necessitates large imports of raw materials and heavy capital goods, and when one has to cut imports for any reason there is a serious crisis. In some Latin American states this has actually happened.

Export promotion may perhaps be safer than import substitution because it is easier to stop when you go wrong and because of the quality aspect I have mentioned. But there is a political bias against export subsidies. In Israel, when a subsidized exporter does well, they start to ask why he is allowed to make such lovely profits and there seems to be an incentive to take the subsidy away. This applies much less to import substitution.

STEPHEN ENKE (United States): Protectionism takes the form of tariffs and brings revenue. Many LDCs have difficulty with income tax collection, and therefore are dependent on customs duties.

One kind of import substitution is to make a deal with a foreign company to set up a factory in the country in return for excluding imports from its competitors. There are often opportunities for this, as in the tire industry; and it is a legitimate form.

Politics in developed states play a part. If any LDC is really successful in exporting goods to the United States, a special protection will be slapped on almost immediately. It is easier to give aid to foreign states in the form of helping U.S. exporters.

I. LITTLE (Great Britain): Import substitution and export promotion should vanish as economic discussion topics. You either produce for the home market only, or both for the home market and for export.

One has got to produce before one can export, so one must start with import substitution. But this has nothing to do with protection. One has import controls without protection. And it is nonsense to say that economic growth depends either on import substitution or on export promotion. Protection means protection of the home market, and promotion means encouraging industry in a way that is indifferent between the home market and exports.

Industry should be promoted, but not too heavily and not only in the home market. And why does everybody insist on promoting it by subsidizing capital when we are all worrying about labor? Why promote it by controls leading to distortions and not by the price mechanism? These are the important questions.

Who the hell wants to promote exports? What we are really talking about is removing biases against exports. If small producers do not know international markets and the government steps in and helps, well and good. But the same can be done for the home market if the price mechanism does not look after the problem.

Most economists regard export subsidies as second best to a realistic exchange rate. But there is an alternative, when the price mechanism is not functioning properly—to subsidize labor instead.

I am not ruling out 10 percent or 15 percent import tariffs. But if you want to promote industry, you can do it by subsidizing it, not just its exports, by subsidizing its labor. This is just as legitimate as subsidizing its capital by tax holidays, cheap machinery, and low interest rates, as is now done.

Changing LDC policies for the better by realistic exchange rates and cutting protection of the home market is difficult because of political backlash. India will never get anywhere until she abandons her present economic regime, but it is hard to see how she will. How can one get production going there on a sufficient scale, when one is thwarted on every turn by controls?

ALFREDO NOYOLA (El Salvador): I should like Professor Diaz Alejandro to comment on two points: First, does he regard the protection of the home market against competition from imports an essential preliminary stage on the way to export promotion?

In Salvador and Central America generally, the market reached a saturation point during the 1960s, and industrial expansion decelerated as a result. One problem with import substitution is that high protection tariffs caused producers to charge high prices and incur high costs, leading to inefficiency and reducing the purchasing power of the consumers. When a saturation point in the domestic market is reached, producers tend to ask for export incentives.

The question arises: Should export incentives cover the same items as those protected by tariffs in the home market? Or should they be much more selective?

I think that in El Salvador we have had overprotection. There are no incentives for producers to export outside the Central American market. Are there any practical criteria for the degree of protection required to yield optimum results?

HELEN HUGHES (I.B.R.D.): Most economists say we must minimize protection. But most policy makers say that, if anything is to get going in their countries, one has to give producers a 50 percent protective tariff, plus a loan and a tax incentive.

Import substitution and export promotion are basically one process, attempting to diversify the economy and increase the productivity of capital and labor. The criterion of progress is that output should be as competitive internationally as possible. It does not matter whether production is for the home market or for export if it is competitive. If it is not, something must be done about the incentive system in the state concerned.

The amount of protection should be as little as is necessary. The tendencies in the developed world indicate that LDCs wanting to grow rapidly must do something about trade between themselves by cutting tariffs obstructing it and putting it on a competitive basis. There is nothing wrong with exporting capital-intensive products to LAFTA. But what is the resource cost of such exports?

Very small states cannot practice import substitution on a big scale. For a state like Liberia, after it has some 15 plants, further import substitution becomes costly. And there is a danger of a few small states combining into a common market and then permitting themselves excesses in import substitution they would have avoided on their own. This applies to Central America, East Central Africa, the Caribbean Free Trade Association (CARIFTA), and so forth.

As regards labor subsidies: In some states the number of workers has been added to the amount of capital as a basis for tax incentives or credit qualifications. But it is difficult to introduce direct labor subsidies. It is difficult to devise a corruption-proof system that will not be exploited by workers, employers, or both. People always return to the protection tariff, because it provides revenue when moderate.

When an LDC has wrong incentives, it encourages motor cars to clutter up its roads instead of providing urban transportation and bicycles for the masses. Then come tires. The Michelins and Goodyears pressure the government to put up plants, citing production costs that are often wrong. Then you may get three or four tire firms, each uneconomic because it produces less than the economic minimum of 70,000 tires a year. And the government is helpless, because if it threatens to import tires they claim that they have to dismiss workers—and this developing states don't like.

In Southeast Asia there is an exchange agreement on car parts, which means in practice that instead of stopping at assembly the manufacturers and the authorities in the Philippines, Malaysia, and Indonesia are pushing each other into more and more lunatic ventures. Yet even this is better than having 22 firms assembling cars, as in Indonesia, or even more, as in Thailand.

The multinational corporations have their eye on the long-term market. Many Latin American states have illustrated how expensive it is to go along with their policies. One can keep them—and their excesses—out if one concentrates on the right products, such as low-cost textiles, pots and pans, hose, roofing iron, which don't need high protection because production costs are low. However, removing already existing incentives can be difficult, especially for politicians who have to take pressure groups into account.

NADAV HALEVY (Israel): I do not see why one has to choose between development towards exports or towards import substitution. The best solution is to get an ideal price list and then develop what can best develop under such circumstances.

Since many of the additional Colombian exports were to LAFTA states, are we dealing here with exports in a real sense or with import substitution in a wider framework? And what industries should be promoted in Colombia instead of those actually promoted in order to stimulate employment?

JURGEN DONGES (Federal Republic of Germany): In six or seven states besides Colombia, the data confirm that expansion of industrial exports had little impact on employment. Is this because the share of such exports in total output is still low? If we look at West Germany and make the same calculations that Professor Alejandro made for Colombia, we find that the industrial export sector not only creates employment in the country but also absorbs employment from other countries.

So the question is whether in another 10 or 20 years, when export expansion in Colombia has generated more output relatively to other uses, the effect on employment will still be the same there.

I believe most of their exports are labor intensive, but this is not a panacea solving all their problems.

LE BA NHON (South Vietnam): A developing state must face the problem of cutting imports and trying to increase exports, so as not to have to borrow from other states, quite regardless of the economic effects. Does anyone have an alternative to import substitution and export promotion that would cut the LDCs foreign exchange expenditure on the things that must be bought abroad?

I. LITTLE (Great Britain): A protective tariff does not raise money. It reduces revenue. If it is really protective home output rises, and since it is untaxed revenue declines. If you want revenue, you can and should tax domestic output as well as imports.

Do pots and pans and textiles really need protection? Many states started producing them without protection. If they need it now it is because of inefficiency, or overvalued exchange rates. The Indian textile industry was thriving before it was protected.

CARLOS DIAZ ALEJANDRO: Import substitution means only a change in the ratio of imports to domestic output. It can occur, as in Latin America during the 1930s, owing to changes in terms of trade, or because the currency is devalued, or because tariffs are imposed.

In Colombia, certain sectors may be getting more help than under a neutral classical system, though some of the new policies are simply offsetting discrimination against exports under old import-substituting policies. I was taking the starting point for granted.

Comparing a very capital-intensive import substitution project, like petrochemicals, with a very labor-intensive export industry, like clothing, exaggerates the employment effect of different policies. I feel that both import substitution and export promotion tend to be capital intensive. The firms operating in both these spheres tend to be large, and large firms in developing countries tend to be very capital intensive. In Colombia a large exporting textile factory and a large import-substituting machine tool industry will have very similar capital-labor ratios.

Until about 1953 import substitution in Argentina generated a lot of employment, because small- and medium-sized industries were favored. Foreign trade policies should not be used to achieve employment objectives.

A dollar received by Colombia for exports to Ecuador is different from the dollar received for exports to the United States, since it presumably cannot be used for general purchases in the world market.

Colombia could have been exporting cotton and textiles about 15 years ago with the right kind of policy. It was not necessary to go through what the country went through to achieve its present exports.

One has to rely on project evaluation to decide which individual exports are good for a country. It is harder to give an excessive subsidy to exports than to import substitution, because the government officials are much more conscious of what the export subsidy costs in the political sense.

If there is a severe foreign exchange constraint, foreign exchange savings from import substitution tend to be overestimated, so export promotion is more promising under these circumstances. In Colombia exports came before import substitution, and its experience, especially since 1967, proves that much can be done in the export field without dismantling the import substitution machinery. Besides, import liberalization becomes politically easier when exports begin to grow and foreign exchange begins to come in.

S. ENKE (United States): Suppose a state does not produce cement and imports it, levying high tariffs for revenue purposes. The tax may suffice to start a local cement industry that would supply half or all the domestic demand. Now you would not want to tax the local cement, by sack, but you may have an income tax on the industry profit.

OBSTACLES TO EXPANSION OF MANUFACTURED EXPORTS IN LDCs
Juergen Donges

A BRIEF REVIEW OF THE FACTS

The past two decades have been a period of exceptionally great expansion in world trade. The value of world exports increased from U.S. $93.8 billion in 1955 to U.S. $312.3 billion in 1970, or by 8.4 percent per annum at current prices. Trade in primary commodities increased much less than trade in manufactures (which in 1970 accounted for 64.6 percent of world trade compared with 48.9 percent in 1955). There was also a shift away from vertical trade between developing and developed countries towards horizontal trade in manufactures among industrialized economies.

Exports of manufactures from LDCs rose relatively fast, and their share in LDCs' total exports increased (Table 13). However, one should be careful in interpreting these facts since:

- LDC exports of manufactures started from a relatively low base (U.S. $3.1 billion, equivalent to 6.7 percent of world trade, in 1955).
- The experience of major developing regions varies substantially. This holds for the expansion of total manufactured goods as well as for changes in the structure of these exports (Tables 14 and 15).
- About 60 percent of LDC manufactured exports come from 13 countries, which diversified the structure of these exports (Table 14). Among them manufactures weigh heavily (over 50 percent) only in the exports of Hong Kong, Taiwan, South Korea, Pakistan, and India. But even in these countries exports are small in relation to industrial output, except for Hong Kong, which exported about 85 percent of its output by the end of the sixties. In contrast, the export-output ratios were approximately 26 percent in South Korea, 4 percent in Pakistan, and 5 percent in India.

I am grateful to Herbert Giersch and James Riedel for many valuable comments.

TABLE 13

Growth Rates and Commodity Structure of LDCs' Exports
(percentages)

Commodity Groups	Annual Compound Growth Rate		Commodity Structure			Share in World Exports		
	1955-60	1960-70	1955	1960	1970	1955	1960	1970
Primary goods	2.5	5.8	87.1	85.7	76.4	44.8	41.6	39.9
Food, beverages, and tobacco	1.0	5.0	32.5	29.7	24.5	42.0	36.4	31.9
Raw materials, oils, and fats	1.9	2.6	29.4	28.0	18.4	39.9	35.8	30.0
Mineral fuels	5.0	9.0	25.2	28.0	33.5	58.3	60.5	62.9
Manufactured goods	4.9	12.6	12.9	14.3	23.6	6.7	5.5	6.3
Chemicals	4.6	10.3	1.0	1.1	1.5	5.1	4.0	3.7
Machinery and transport equipment	8.7	21.4	0.5	0.7	2.5	0.7	0.7	1.5
Other manufactures	4.7	12.0	11.4	12.5	19.6	11.2	9.8	11.7
Total	2.8	7.2	100.0	100.0	100.0	25.4	21.4	17.6

TABLE 14

Manufactured Exports[a] of Selected LDCs

Country	Exports Total (millions U.S. dollars)	Value 1969 per capita (U.S. dollars)	Annual Compound Growth Rate (percentages)			Share of Manufactures in Total Exports	
			1955-62	1962-69	1955-69	1955	1969
Argentina[a]	220.1	9.17	-5.3[b]	28.0	9.9[b]	6.3[b]	13.7
Brazil[c]	306.9	3.30	11.8	32.1	22.8	1.7	11.3
Hong Kong[c]	1,953.9	493.40	2.8	21.5	12.4	75.4	95.8
India	1,038.3	1.98	-0.1[b]	8.0	4.6[b]	49.4[b]	55.3
Iran	62.2	2.23	5.8	11.8	10.3	5.1	3.2
Israel	298.1	102.43	6.6[d]	15.5	12.4	33.6[e]	38.4
Korea (South)	469.8	15.10	21.0	70.0	44.0	5.9	76.2
Malaysia	104.7	9.87	n.a.	12.5	n.a.	5.4[e]	7.9
Mexico	341.0	6.97	9.7	16.4	13.1	9.4	23.9
Pakistan	382.1	3.01	n.a.	22.0	n.a.	24.5[e]	56.1
Philippines	66.6	1.86	18.5[f]	14.6	16.4	2.0[f]	8.1
Singapore[c,g]	431.4	208.40	n.a.	4.5	n.a.	27.2[e]	27.8
Taiwan[c]	1,092.2	77.79	n.a.	34.5	n.a.	46.2[e]	76.5

[a]Excluding unwrought nonferrous metals, pearls, and precious stones; [b]1957-62(60); [c]1970; [d]1958-62(70); [e]1962; [f]1956-62(69); [g]Including re-exports.

TABLE 15

Manufactured Exports and Economic Policy Indicators
in Selected LDCs[a]

Country	Percentage Share of Manufactures[b] in Total Exports (average 1968-69)	Index of Industrial Policy-orientation	Annual Compound Rate Increase (percentages)	
			Consumer Prices	Real Exchange Rate
Africa				
Egypt	21.5	11	1.9	1.6
Kenya	11.3	7	1.7	0.1
Nigeria	1.3	2	3.1	-1.4
Tunisia	21.0	6	2.3	2.1
Uganda	0.6	0	2.7	-1.0
Zambia	0.1	0	3.8	-1.9
Asia				
Burma	0.7	2	0.9	0.9
Ceylon	0.8	2	1.2	2.1
Cyprus	10.5	29	0.9	1.8
Hong Kong	91.7	118	1.6	0.5
India	50.9	13	4.8	0.2
Iran	3.2	7	3.6	4.4
Israel	38.6	52	5.7	4.7
Jordan	15.1	32	0.4	1.3
Korea (South)	70.8	38	17.1	4.4
Malaysia	8.0	51	- 0.1	1.9
Pakistan	48.4	30	3.6	-1.5
Philippines	10.3	12	3.0	3.3
Singapore	25.1	57	0.7	0.3
Syria	13.0	9	1.8	3.8
Taiwan	60.9	56	6.0	0.9
Thailand	2.1	5	2.3	4.6
Latin America				
Argentina	10.3	4	26.7	-0.1
Brazil	9.0	3	37.0	-1.8
Chile	5.7	4	30.2	-5.1
Colombia	9.3	7	9.3	5.8
Costa Rica	18.3	27	2.0	0.9
Honduras	8.4	18	1.7	0.2
Mexico	18.3	6	4.5	0.2
Peru	1.0	1	7.9	-1.4
Venezuela	1.3	1	1.3	2.5

[a]The data cover the period 1953-68, except for Egypt and Iran (1953-67), Hong Kong (1951-68), Singapore (1960-68), and Chile and Mexico (1950-68).

[b]Without unwrought nonferrous metals, pearls, precious stones, and nonindustrial diamonds.

[c]Calculated as incremental ratio of exports to output in manufacturing. The higher the index the more outward looking the industrial policy is.

[d]Nominal exchange rate divided by the rate of internal inflation and multiplied by the rate of United States inflation.

DEMAND VERSUS SUPPLY FACTORS

Professional economists tended to attribute the fall in the LDC share of world exports to unfavorable external demand conditions. Their arguments cited the low and declining income and price elasticities of import demand for many primary commodities, raw-material-saving technological progress, increased competition from synthetic substitutes, and discriminatory trade policies of the industrialized countries. There is some truth in these arguments insofar as primary commodities form a much larger part in the exports of LDCs than in the exports of developed countries. However, exports of primary products could have expanded much more if individual producers in the LDCs had been encouraged more by government economic policies. Since many LDCs, particularly in Africa and Latin America, have a surplus productive capacity in the agricultural sector, there should have been scope for additional export growth by exploiting underutilized resources.

Many LDCs promoted economic development by industrialization based on import substitution. In many countries, the overemphasis placed on industrialization has, deliberately or incidentally, turned the internal terms of trade between agriculture and industry against peasant producers and thus held back the development of the agricultural sector, where these countries might have had comparative advantages and produced for the export market. Argentina, Chile, and the Philippines are cases in point.* Although world demand for many primary products exported by LDCs has not increased as much as the world demand for manufactured products, developing countries failed in many cases (including live animals, dairy products, corn, sugar, coffee, hides, oilseeds, crude rubber, wool) to keep pace even with this weak demand development. If governments desisted from introducing market distortions, they would establish an important precondition for improved export performance in the future.

As regards manufactured exports, there is too much emphasis on unfavorable external demand conditions and too little consideration of supply-oriented factors that influence the growth and level of these exports. The expansion of manufactured exports requires that domestic producers first gain experience in supplying the domestic market. There seems to be a systematic association between changes in the export structure (from primary towards manufactured products) and supply-oriented factors such as growth in per capita income, degree

---

*There are only a few exceptions to this rule. The most outstanding are Peru and Thailand.

of industrialization, size and density of population, and availability of skills.

Economic planning, which was practiced by most LDCs (although not to the same degree in all of them), did not lead to an optimal allocation of resources between import-substituting and export activities. It led, instead, to a great number of inefficiencies in production and instabilities in the flow of supplies. It caused defective cost structures in certain branches as well as throughout the manufacturing sector. It increased the attractiveness of the domestic market. And it favored private foreign investors.

The key to understanding why most LDCs failed to expand manufactured exports, although they expanded their domestic industrial production, is provided by the industrialization strategy they pursued. Countries that followed an outward-looking path of industrial development proved their ability to specialize according to comparative advantages, to make effective use of trade opportunities, and to surmount import obstacles imposed by industrialized countries. Hong Kong and Singapore (from the very beginning of their industrialization, as well as Israel, Malaysia, South Korea, and Taiwan (from a more advanced stage of industrial development) provide the outstanding success stories.

But in most countries the industrialization strategy was inward looking. States following this type of industrialization policy generally found it very difficult to develop competitive exports of manufactured products.

Policies determining the level of effective protection have been the principal tool of industrial promotion in most LDCs. They discouraged manufactured exports by raising production costs of exporters as they made inputs more expensive, and by keeping the exchange rate (units of domestic currency per dollar) lower than it would be under free-trade conditions (or in a situation with only optimum import tariffs and exports subsidies). To form an idea of the extent to which exporters are discriminated against, one can compare the value added of production sold domestically with that exported. One will find that bias against manufactured exports caused by the import tariff system is substantial (Table 16). Entrepreneurs in LDCs, being generally inexperienced in exporting, will therefore assess their export possibilities too pessimistically. Hence even products that would appear internationally competitive under a free-trade exchange rate are not exported because they are too expensive, given the actual, protection-determined overvalued currency. An unjustified illusion of inefficiency and an inferiority complex emerge, which are the most powerful obstacle to manufactured export expansion in LDCs.

TABLE 16

Rates of Effective Protection* and Degree of Antiexport
Bias in Manufacturing Industry in Brazil and the
Philippines
(percentages)

Industrial Branch	Brazil (1967)		Philippines (1965)	
	Effective Protection	Bias against Exporting	Effective Protection	Bias against Exporting
Food manufactures	40	52	-24	327
Beverages	137	632	39	40
Tobacco	124	151	74	75
Textiles	162	427	-932	100
Clothing	142	195	-124	infinite
Footwear	n.a.	n.a.	21	22
Wood products	25	29	400	283
Furniture	124	211	23	24
Leather manufactures	85	133	-461	infinite
Paper products	59	84	72	127
Printed matter	67	94	n.a.	n.a.
Rubber products	116	145	35	135
Industrial and agricultural chemicals	42	51	32	63
Pharmaceutical products	35	51	22	56
Perfumes, soaps, and other chemicals	3,670	infinite	121	146
Plastic materials	58	103	485	infinite
Petroleum, coal, and gas products	n.a.	n.a.	34	99
Nonmetallic mineral products	39	57	65	92
Iron and steel	36	48	48	140
Nonferrous metals			n.a.	n.a.
Finished metal products	n.a.	n.a.	230	676
Nonelectrical machinery	32	40	110	409
Electrical machinery	97	176	147	infinite
Transport equipment	75	118	209	infinite
Miscellaneous manufactures	72	104	-381	904

*According to the Corden method.

How much weight should be attributed to external demand and domestic supply factors as determinants of LDC export performance? An answer to this question may be found by comparing actual exports with exports that would have taken place if the LDC share in the world market had remained unchanged over time. Four effects can be distinguished: First, there is an average change effect of export growth, which results from the constant share norm. Second, there is a commodity composition effect, which arises when LDCs' exports are concentrated on products with different rates of world import demand. Third, there is a market structure effect, which points to different rates of import demand of individual markets to which LDCs' exports are directed. And fourth, there is a competitiveness effect, which can be ascribed to factors tending to increase or reduce the export capacity of the domestic industry (such as changes in productivity levels, in selling prices, in the quality of the products exported, in the efficiency of export marketing, and in the terms of payment and delivery, vis-a-vis foreign competitors). Some empirical evidence about the interaction of these factors during the period 1960-70 is given in Table 17. Demand-related factors had, with the exception of Africa, no substantial negative impact on the growth of LDCs' manufactured exports. Latin America's industry made the greatest progress in improving its international competitiveness, which may be ascribed to the remarkable shift in policy orientation made in a number of countries during the sixties.

POLICY REQUIREMENTS FOR EXPORT PROMOTION

LDCs could expand export of manufactures if industrialization policies discriminating against such exports were replaced by a program designed to promote them. This does not mean that further import substituting industrialization should be stopped but only that export industries must be given an equal chance to develop. There is no reason that a developing country's industrialization policy should discriminate against exports. If it makes sense to promote production of refrigerators, motorcycles, or cars for the domestic market, then it can make just as much sense to promote the export of these products, provided that the domestic resource costs in earning the foreign exchange justify such an effort.

What are the policies that would enable LDCs to benefit more than in the past from international trade in manufactures?

Countries still at the beginning of industrialization should promote industrial development selectively rather than across the board. They should select products most likely to reflect the country's

TABLE 17

Sources of Manufactured Export Growth in Developing Regions, 1960-70

Commodity	Africa	Asia	Latin America	All developing regions
Chemicals				
Change in exports	77	133	317	527
Percentage contribution of:				
increased world trade	141.2	149.4	68.0	99.3
commodity composition	2.4	2.5	1.2	1.7
market structure	-6.3	-15.4	-4.7	7.6
competitiveness	-37.3	-36.5	35.5	6.6
Machinery and transport equipment				
Change in exports	40	769	320	1,129
Percentage contribution of:				
increased world trade	129.4	34.2	11.7	31.2
commodity composition	15.8	6.4	2.2	5.5
market structure	2.4	50.3	25.7	41.6
competitiveness	-47.6	9.1	60.4	21.7
Other manufactures				
Change in exports	1,476	3,925	1,713	7,114
Percentage contribution of:				
increased world trade	113.6	84.8	74.4	88.3
commodity composition	-17.3	-12.9	-11.3	-13.4
market structure	-0.3	7.1	-5.1	2.6
competitiveness	4.0	21.0	42.0	22.5
All manufactures				
Change in exports	1,593	4,827	2,350	8,770
Percentage contribution of:				
increased world trade	115.3	78.5	65.0	81.6
commodity composition	-15.5	-9.4	-7.8	-10.1
market structure	-0.5	13.3	-0.9	7.0
competitiveness	0.7	17.6	43.7	21.5

Note: Change in exports is given in millions of U.S. dollars.

Sources: UNCTAD, Handbook of International Trade and Development Statistics, 1972; UN, Monthly Bulletin of Statistics, April and July 1972.

(long-term) comparative advantage. Industries based upon the processing of natural resources or producing with labor intensive techniques, which at the same time face a fairly high income elasticity of demand, are obviously good candidates. Infant industries with a promising development potential should be assisted by tariff protection (or production subsidies), but at moderate rates and only on a temporary basis.

Countries that have pursued a policy of import substitution for a long period should take the following steps:

- Effective import protection rates should be reduced gradually (or at least not increased) and roughly harmonized. Given moderate protection of, say 20-30 percent, the bias against export industries can be easily eliminated. The effective protection offered to domestic producers has to be matched by equal subsidies to export value added and by simple drawback regulations for imported raw materials, spare parts, and capital equipment used in export production.
- A sensible tariff-cum-subsidy policy requires appropriate fiscal and monetary policies to control domestic inflation and correct any existing overvaluation of the local currency. Should LDCs continue to be more susceptible to inflation than the countries to which they want to export, an exchange-rate policy becomes essential to avoid a deterioration of the earnings-to-cost ratio in export enterprises. Gradual adjustments of the exchange rate, as in Brazil, Colombia, or the Philippines, are to be preferred to major devaluations from time to time, since they give entrepreneurs the certainty that their competitive position will not be artificially distorted. Such a policy, to be successful, must bring about an exchange rate that is in line with unit costs differentials in manufacturing between the home country and the world. Hence, developing countries that mainly export primary products with a high income elasticity of demand (such as oil, copper, tin, timber) may have a problem: gradual exchange-rate adjustments, while maintaining the dollar price of the domestic currency in equilibrium, may still overvalue this currency as far as manufactures are concerned. To avoid a discouragement of manufactured exports there are two alternative policies. The country in question can either undervalue the (single) dollar rate of its currency (combined with an export tax on primary products, if required to remove "windfall profits") or introduce multiple exchange rates and keep the export rate devalued in comparison with the equilibrium rate.
- Even where tariff reform takes place and currency overvaluation is corrected, it will often be necessary to move toward a more rational pricing policy for labor and capital. This means keeping interest rates, import duties on investment goods, and income

taxes high enough to reflect the scarcity value of capital in the economy. On the other hand, wage levels and social welfare programs should not be allowed to overstate the opportunity costs of labor.

- Strong comparative advantages arising from their abundance of cheap and trainable labor should induce LDCs to attract private foreign investments to firms ready to export a major proportion of their output. With the persistent rise of labor costs in industrialized countries, an increasing number of firms (particularly multinational corporations) are trying to transfer labor-intensive segments of their production program to low-wage developing states and to export from there. Perhaps the most promising means of attracting such investors would be the establishment of export free-trade zones provided with general facilities, technical services, and public utilities. The experience of Taiwan, South Korea, Singapore, Malaysia, and Mexico impressively reveal the possibilities involved.

LDCs need not wait for action by developed countries. The export performances of a number of developing countries (other than Hong Kong and Singapore) show that export promotion measures, if properly conceived and implemented, do work. The use of idle productive capacities, typically created by excessive import substitution, contributes to rapid export expansion. It enables firms to lower prices thus permitting them to penetrate markets abroad. A developing country willing to export need not confine its efforts to breaking into the highly industrialized markets, but can benefit from trade among LDCs.

COMPLEMENTARY CHANGES IN THE TRADE AND STRUCTURAL POLICIES OF INDUSTRIALIZED COUNTRIES

Industrialized countries have adopted—largely for domestic reasons—protectionist policies that may inhibit the possible expansion of manufactured exports from the developing world: Manufactures are subject to higher rates of effective tariff protection than raw materials, and many imports of labor-intensive products are subject to import quotas. The extent to which these protectionist policies actually restrict manufactured exports of LDCs may not be very great for as long as supply elasticities of manufacturing industries in LDCs are low. But the real danger of protectionist policies is a psychological one: In an "infant-export" economy, where entrepreneurs are used to considering exporting as a marginal activity, protectionism in industrialized countries will become a source of unjustified export pessimism; exports will be considered impossible, steps to stimulate them will be regarded as useless, and therefore exports will be less than they would be otherewise.

LDCs would greatly benefit if the industrialized countries could be persuaded to support rather than hinder the improvement of the international division of labor. True, the Kennedy Round has brought about some substantial tariff reductions. Moreover, most rich countries with the exception of the United States and Canada, have recently implemented schemes of nonreciprocal tariff preferences favoring LDCs' exports of manufacutred goods. However, the regulations agreed upon are, broadly speaking, more generous the less competitive the LDCs' export commodities are or the more inelastic the export supply is. Many manufactures of special export interest to LDCs (particularly textiles, leather goods, footwear, and petroleum products) are still restricted to the import market of one or more donor countries. Two major schemes, that of the EEC and that of Japan, embody restrictive ceilings for preferential imports either from all beneficiary countries or from a single beneficiary supplier. The enlargement of the EEC is likely to result in important intra-Western-European trade creation and may erode the present value of EEC preferences. Increasing pressure towards protectionism is exerted by domestic producers and labor unions in these countries.

Three lines of action by industrialized countries seem to be advisable: First, import tariffs should be reduced further and nontariff barriers should be phased out. The forthcoming sixth GATT round of negotiations to reduce trade restrictions offers the opportunity to approach this problem on a multilateral basis. Second, structural changes caused by the process of integrating LDCs into international trade in manufactures (and thus bringing the least efficient domestic producers under increasing competition) should be encouraged by appropriate measures. And third, the international monetary negotiations now under way should increase exchange-rate flexibility so as to reduce the undervaluation of the currencies of the industrialized countries in comparison with those of the LDCs. Those policy actions, while beneficial to LDCs, would also add to economic growth and welfare in the industrialized countries.

PRICE AND SCALE OBSTACLES TO EXPORT EXPANSION IN LESS DEVELOPED COUNTRIES
Daniel Schydlowsky

THE CONTEXT

Industrial exports are a central concern of development policy in semi-industrialized LDCs. Typically, these states chose industrial growth a decade ago as the path to a higher per capita income, more employment, and better distribution of income and wealth. Policies involving protection and tax exemptions were designed to stimulate industrial expansion and often succeeded in making industry the leading sector, with a growth rate above that of GNP. And since industry requires some imported inputs for producing, the import bill grew as industrial growth proceeded.

The primary sectors had to provide foreign exchange, and their growth was usually slower than that of industry. Thus the bigger demand for foreign exchange caused by rapid industrial growth put pressure on the slower-growing foreign currency supplies for primary activities. The industrial growth rate would have had to decelerate, had it not been possible to free foreign exchange from existing uses through industrial import substitution, which—behind ever increasing protective barriers—temporarily brought into balance the disparate rates of growth for production and for foreign exchange utilization.

In the early 1970s the possibilities of import substitution are virtually exhausted in large semi-industrialized LDCs. The same will soon apply to the medium and small ones. Now, industry can continue to expand rapidly only if either more foreign exchange is forthcoming from the primary industries, new methods of import substituting are devised, or industry becomes a foreign exchange generator, and not only a foreign exchange user.

Foreign aid may delay the slowing of the industrial growth rate, but its eventual repayment would require a sharp contraction of industrial activity to free the foreign exchange needed. Repayment can hardly be postponed forever. Foreign private investment in new industrial products may use foreign exchange even more than most previously existing industries. Only if such investment directs itself to export-oriented industries, will it help to alleviate the situation.

Industrial exports are thus one of the main policy options open to LDCs desiring to industrialize quickly. Yet such exporting requires, among other things, competitive prices and a sufficient volume to justify developing foreign markets. These conditions are hard to meet. LDCs are typically high-cost producers of industrial goods, and their domestic markets and production volumes are usually small relatively to their potential markets in developed states.

THE UNCOMPETITIVENESS OF INDUSTRIAL EXPORTS

The uncompetitiveness of industrial exports is very often due to policies followed in the past. The growth of industry was fostered by import restrictions, which accumulated and eventually led to a biased exchange rate structure making industrial exports unprofitable. The number of local currency units needed to obtain one dollar for financial transitions is best called the financial exchange rate. This exchange rate must be analyzed together with trade taxation and other trade restrictions. A large number of commodity exchange rates are the multiple exchange rate equivalents of taxes and trade restrictions. Each commodity rate equals the financial rate plus all the trade taxation and restriction assessed on the import or export of that particular commodity. Often a single commodity may have more than one rate.

In Latin America, most states apply import restrictions raising the commodity exchange rate for imports far above the financial rate, while some countries imposed export taxes on traditional export commodities, pushing the commodity rate for such exports below the financial exchange rate. Argentina was operating in 1966 with approximately the following exchange rate system:

Rate	Composition	Pesos per Dollar
Agricultural exports	Financial less 10 percent tax	200
Financial	Financial	220
Nontraditional exports	Financial + 18 percent tax rebate	260
Raw material imports	Financial + 50 percent duties	330
Semimanufactured imports	Financial + 120 percent duties	460

Rate	Composition	Pesos per Dollar
Components imports	Financial + 175 percent duties	600
Finished products imports	Financial + 220 percent duties	700

This rate structure shows why industry fails to generate foreign exchange. Industry buys its raw materials at 330 pesos per dollar, its imported semimanufactures at 460, and its components at 600. The average exchange rate for imported inputs is about 400 pesos per dollar. Implicit rates for domestic material inputs are only slightly lower, since most local producers sell at prices not much below those of similar imports. And the wages industry pays reflect an exchange rate of some 600 pesos per dollar. Hence, total industrial costs are based on an exchange rate averaging 450 to 500 pesos per dollar. And exports yield only 260 pesos per dollar! The would-be industrial exporter thus faces an implicit tax of nearly 50 percent levied through the exchange rate system. The consequences for the profit rate on exports are dramatic.

The Argentinian exchange rate structure is not untypical for semi-industrialized states, such as Brazil, Chile, and Pakistan. This kind of rate structure causes the "inefficiency illusion" of LDC industry. Most LDC industry is regarded as inefficient and uncompetitive. This is "demonstrated" by translating domestic industrial costs into dollars. The costs turn out to be far above the price of comparative imports, according to the financial exchange rate. But since domestic costs are based on commodity exchange rates, which are usually much higher than the financial rate, these costs must normally be higher than international prices when converted at an exchange rate lower than the one on which they are based.

The inefficiency illusion effect has given LDCs the impression that they have hopelessly inefficient industrial structures. However, much of the "inefficiency" is due to an improper comparison. When domestic costs are deflated by the difference between the financial exchange rate and the appropriate commodity exchange rates, it turns out that LDC industry is much more efficient than generally believed.

Table 18 indicates the size of the inefficiency illusion in Argentina by converting domestic production costs into dollars with an exchange rate reflecting the cost exchange rates for the industries concerned.

The inefficiency illusion and the antiexport bias in the exchange rate system interact. The inefficiency illusion reinforces the belief of policy makers that industry is not efficient enough to export; the antiexport bias in the exchange rate structure makes exports

TABLE 18

The Inefficiency Illusion in Argentina

	Excess of cost over import price	
Branch	At current exchange rate	At industrial cost exchange rate
Agriculture	-10	-1
Metallic mineral mining	51	4
Nonmetallic mineral mining	28	4
Food products	5	5
Beverages	50	25
Textiles	65	17
Wood and cork	48	15
Paper and paper products	62	15
Leather and leather products	6	0
Rubber products	110	38
Chemicals	68	23
Nonmetallic mineral products	35	8
Basic metal industries	60	19
Metal products	75	24
Nonelectric machinery	86	14
Transport equipment	109	28

impossible. This causes lack of foreign exchange, and necessitates additional import substitution. So still higher import restrictions are imposed, increasing the inefficiency illusion and the antiexport bias alike, and convincing policy makers even more that industry is inefficient and unable to export.

THE LIMITED POTENTIAL SUPPLY OF EXPORTS

In the phase of transition into an industrial export economy the supply of exports is the residual after domestic demand has been satisfied. The export supply depends chiefly on two factors: domestic demand and maximum profitable output. The former depends in turn on the income level of the state and the respective income and price elasticities; the latter depends on factor availabilities and on rates of factor utilization.

Insufficient attention has been paid to the existence of unemployment, with the attendant excess of wage rates over the social cost of labor. This implies the existence of a potential output not reflected by the market supply. Besides, evidence is accumulating that capital is underutilized as well, working only one or one and one-half shifts on the average. Were supply based on a three-shift use of capital, it might well be two or three times larger! The single shift use of capital in LDCs, where capital is scarce and labor plentiful, presents a paradox. Private profit maximizers tend to operate three plants at one shift, while national interests require one plant working three shifts—thus economizing on the scarcer resource, capital, and using labor extensively. This happens because the private sector makes its decisions at market prices, while the public sector evaluates them at very different social or shadow prices. The causes of distortions between private and shadow prices in most semi-industrialized economies are:

- The entrepreneur is concerned with marginal revenue in the home market. In many commodity markets, the seller perceives a low demand elasticity for his sales and a marginal return well below the going price. Society holds his potential output to be worth the foreign exchange it would earn if exported, multiplied by the shadow price of foreign exchange. Yet the value of output is a multiple of the privately perceived marginal revenue. Hence, output tends to be too low.
- Most LDC tariff structures and industrial promotion laws provide for the duty-free import of capital goods. This implies charging the private buyer of capital goods too little for the scarce foreign exchange and the scarce investment funds he is using, thus encouraging overly capital-intensive operations.
- In most LDCs the wage rate in the industrial sector is set by government and unions. In all cases, the result is far above what a free labor market would produce. Hence the market wage exceeds the social marginal cost of labor (labor's shadow price), and private decisions tend to underutilize labor. Social security legislation, fringe benefits,* severance pay, and dismissal regulations raise the cost of employing labor beyond its take-home pay and further widen the gap between its market cost and its social cost.
- In most LDCs credit for installing fixed assets is available on much easier terms and in larger quantities than credit for working capital. The latter is essential for multiple-shift-working plants, since the weight of goods in process within total capital investment

---

*Fringe benefits in Latin America are large. Ferrero (1957) found them to be 45 percent of wages in Peru, while Gregory (1967) found them to be about 100 percent of on-the-job earnings in Chile.

is much greater in such plants. This biases entrepreneurs' decisions towards excess fixed capital intensity.

- In most LDCs depreciation deductible from profits for income tax purposes is based on the years of life of the equipment, with no allowance for intensity of use. As a result, second and third shift profits are taxed at a higher rate than first shift profits. This is a disincentive for private business to install capital-intensive multiple-shifting operations.
- The total unavailability of skilled and supervisory staff could prevent production altogether. In family firms, management is fully concentrated in the owner, who cannot work 24 hours a day. In larger firms with hired management, availability becomes a cost problem. As this type of labor is very scarce, its price is high—especially at night. But the price of night-time labor is partly the function of the lack of night-time amenities, such as transportation. If three shifts were introduced throughout the economy, night-time services would be available on the day-time scale, and the price of night-time supervisory labor would fall.

The causes of underutilization of capital fall into three categories:

1. Nonprice constraints. These prevent multiple shift work, no matter what the desires of the employer. Into this group fall:

a) The lack of foreign exchange allocation or raw material allocations enabling more than a single shift operation of the plant;
b) Government regulations prohibiting night work for women or shift work;
c) Lack of balance of production line equipment (for example, one section's capital stock produces in one shift enough to keep a downstream section working three shifts);
d) The inability of owner-managers to work continuously for 16 or 24 hours.

2) Profitability modifiers. The elements making the profits from second or third shifts different from the profitability of the first shift or of the additional shift at shadow prices. These include:

(i) Wages and wage premia for shift work.
(ii) Taxes, tax depreciation rules, and investment incentives.
(iii) Import duties and duty exemptions on capital goods.
(iv) Interest rates and credit rationing for both working capital and fixed assets.
(v) Prices and the demand situation.

3) Maximization characteristics determining entrepreneur behavior. These include:

(i) Profits, retention of property or control, labor peace, flexibility, and other aims.
(ii) The character of the private owner, union, worker organization, and so on.
(iii) The environment, that is, stability or lack of it, including the economic "rules of the game."

Some variants of the above elements may lead to multiple shifting and other not. Often, the second shift will not be allowed because (1,ii) it is unprofitable; (1,iv) it is managerially unfeasible; (3,iii) it is opposed by the workers. Each cause alone would be sufficient. This dramatizes the overcausation producing idleness of capital in the midst of capital scarcity and limiting the potential output available for export.

POLICY ALTERNATIVES FOR PRICE COMPETITIVENESS

Competitiveness requires a modification of the exchange rate system. Two techniques are available for this: compensated devaluation and export subsidies.

In a compensated devaluation adjustments are made both in the financial exchange rate and in trade restrictions, so that all commodity exchange rates for imports and traditional exports remain unaltered, the only changes being in the financial rate and the nontraditional export rate. The results of a compensated devaluation by 50 percent of the Argentinian exchange rate structure shown earlier would be as follows: The financial rate would rise from 220 to 330 pesos per dollar. The tax on agricultural exports would be raised from 10 percent to 40 percent, leaving the rate at 200 pesos per dollar. The duty on raw material imports, semimanufactured imports, imports of components, and finished product imports would be cut to leave their effective rates at 330, 460, 600, and 700 pesos to the dollar respectively. Only nontraditional exports would be taxed as before, so the exchange rate for them would rise from 220 to 390 pesos per dollar, much closer to the industrial cost rates than before and exceeding the raw material imports rate.

An export subsidy achieves the same result by raising the commodity exchange rate concerned, thus eliminating the existing bias. If the subsidy is given as a fixed percentage of the f.o.b. value of exports, its administration is simple. Export subsidies generate their own partial or total financing. In semi-industrialized LDCs expenditure of public funds on the creation of exports generates a higher level of economic activity and therefore an increase in revenue. A simple model allows the calculation of a full utilization budget and the maximal subsidy payable without net fiscal costs to the exchequer. In Argentina a subsidy of up to 130 percent of the f.o.b. value of exports will not worsen the fiscal balance. Other states may have lower cutoff points but still room for substantial export subsidies without fiscal damage.

In chosing between the two alternative policies, the following should be considered:

- Compensated devaluation causes losses to holders of foreign liabilities and gains to holders of foreign assets. It reduces the capital outlay of foreign investors on labor and local costs but also the repatriation value of their profits.
- Compensated devaluation reduces the inefficiency illusion proportionately to the change in the exchange rate. Export subsidies do not.
- GATT rules frown on subsidies but permit devaluation. The IMF finds devaluation acceptable.
- Compensated devaluation discriminates against traditional as against new exports. However, selective export subsidies do the same.

Both economic policies enhance efficiency in semi-industrial economies. By changing the nature of industry from foreign exchange using to foreign exchange generating the major cause of balance of payments crises is removed, together with the foreign exchange restraint on growth. And a basis is also laid for using idle domestic labor and capital. More shifts are possible only if the foreign exchange needed to pay for extra imported input can be earned. Thus export promotion raises efficiency through more intensive use of existing production factors.

AN EXPORT SUPPLY POLICY

Rapid growth of potential export supply depends on the use of plant capacity. Imported inputs necessary for product must be available. As exports earn more than enough foreign exchange to pay for their import content, the problem is financing.

Another condition for capacity utilization is profitability and the elimination of nonprice restrictions on multiple shifting.

An adequate compensated devaluation or export subsidy may suffice in the short run, if marginal revenue from sales is high enough. But in the long run it is also essential to raise the relative profitability of multiple shifts as against multiple plant operation. This can be done in the following four ways:

Wage Policy. The gap between second and third shift wages and the marginal social cost of labor must be narrowed. This means ending shift premia, fringe benefits on second and third shifts, social security exemptions, and tenure rules—that is, abolishing many social welfare gains labor obtained by law over the years. Because this is very difficult, the same result must be obtained without the wholesale abolition of acquired privileges. This can be done by shifting some fringe benefit costs from firms to the government or by a law exempting firms from normal labor legislation on second and third shift labor for a limited but fairly long period.

Pricing Policy. Capital goods prices can be affected by raising import tariffs on them. This would raise the profitability of multiple shifting as against multiple plant operation. Higher tariffs on capital goods may reduce real private fixed investment if the government uses part of this revenue for consumption but not if such revenue is lent back to the private sector for investment purposes.

Tax Policy. Tax laws should be changed to allow deductible depreciation. A machine operating three shifts should be depreciated three times as fast as a machine operating one shift only. This would eliminate the progressive taxation of profits from second and third shifts now in force. Tax incentives now paid for investment or reinvestment require proof of purchase of fixed assets. Multiple shifting should be regarded as expansion and receive the same tax benefits, investment in capacity utilization being equivalent to investment in capacity expansion.

Credit Policy. Loans for working capital should be at the same preferential rates as loans for capital asset purchases. Increasing capacity utilization in this way would lead to a big increase in the potential supply of exports.

CONCLUSIONS

To sell abroad LDCs must be competitive in price and able to supply quantities sufficient to justify marketing costs. These conditions are rarely met today.

High production costs are basically due to the import origin of LDC industrial output. The use of tariffs favored industries producing for the home market. The higher commodity exchange rates so created were gradually incorporated in the domestic cost structure. Exporters are now taxed by an implicit devaluation, which raised their input prices without a corresponding exchange rate adjustment on their output. Hence their costs translated into dollars seem high. This is largely an inefficiency illusion.

A sound export policy must bring the export exchange rate into line with the industrial cost exchange rate by a compensated devaluation or by export subsidies.

The home market normally absorbs over 80 percent of the industrial output of an LDC. But full capacity is a price-determined variable. LDCs typically operate on a low shift definition of full capacity, consistent with their price distortions, taxes, and credit systems favoring capital-intensive production techniques. At shadow prices the definition of full capacity changes upwards, and a much larger volume of potential exports becomes available.

A sound utilization policy would move concurrently on factor costs, output price, tax structure, and credit availability to increase the incentives for multiple shifting. Exports and capacity utilization are closely connected. Utilization provides an export supply but requires imported inputs (and exports to pay for them). The export price depends on production costs for newly activated capacity. An effective utilization and export policy must comprise higher export exchange rates, cuts in the cost of second and third shift labor, a rise in the cost of capital goods, a direct tie of tax depreciation rates to the number of shifts worked, and the provision of working capital on favorable terms.

DISCUSSION

MORRIS TOUVAL (Israel): There are constraints on exports from the perspective of comparative advantage and from the perspective of growth. If the actual export level is lower than that allowing full utilization of the state's comparative advantages, this is caused by a constraint. Most constraints are institutional or derived from government legislation.

From the perspective of growth, there are constraints such as import barriers in the export markets of the LDCs. Over these the LDCs have no control. Other such constraints include the limited capital resources of the economy or of the export industries, the limited output capacity of these industries, and an inadequate supply of skills or of information.

Infrastructure constraints—for example, lack of dams and roads,—must be dealt with by providing goods and services within the country. Liberating the skill constraint of an economy may require educational activities that must be supplied en bloc. Information for potential exporters, like education, yields increasing returns, since everyone can use it once it is available.

Where the scale factor is an important constraint, the government should financially aid the export industries concerned in their early stages of development. This would apply to marketing abroad, which is subject to increasing returns. Professor Schydlowsky dealt mainly with constraints caused by legislation. I wish to stress chiefly the importance of the infrastructure constraints and the need to provide the skills, the education, the information about foreign markets, as well as the roads, dams, and irrigation projects necessary to permit export expansion.

MOSHE MANDELBAUM (Israel): In some states the exchange rate for imports for re-export is different from that for the local market. If so, the export sector should be isolated so that exports for each import pay a lower exchange rate. This would give a rebate only to imports for re-export.

The main obstacle to exports are those of the newcomer to the field, especially in semifinished and finished products. Large amounts are invested in promotion, and a new country faces high costs when trying to penetrate export market.

The need is for incentives to long-term export growth. If devaluation and export rebates are used, the policy should be set for a longer period.

Importers make sample orders, then trial orders. Only if these are satisfactory do they order larger quantities. Once the supplier is established, the buyer does not easily shift to a competitor, even if offered better terms.

I would suggest manufacturers should be helped with funds for export promotion, catalogues, and so on.

The problem of export capacity is often connected with the problem of monopoly. Exports being more risky, a monopoly will adjust capacity to local needs. One can increase exports by breaking the monopoly—introducing new investors to create an oligopoly, or even even free competition. In Israel the growth rate of oligopolies has been faster than that of monopolies. In some cases mergers, ostensibly for increased efficiency, resulted in the contraction of exports, partly because the exchange rate here does not make export expansion profitable.

The government should supply short-term loans for exporters, since long-term financing only can result in unutilized investments.

HARVEY LEIBENSTEIN (United States): Two questions: The first is whether free trade and free exchange would produce the same results. The second is whether changing from one to three shifts will make a difference when the exporting country is small and the importing market large.

One can find in the world all kinds of interferences with free trade and flexible exchange rates. One can point to states where these interferences exist and where the growth rate or exports have suffered. But it is also possible to point to states where, despite the same interferences, economic development has succeeded. Japan might be an example.

There are many situations where constraints exist and desirable things don't happen. This has to do with incentives. We should consider whether "liberating constraints" is necessary, or whether it would not be better to concentrate on incentives.

PETER DAVIES (Economist, Ministry of Finance, Swaziland): The speakers mentioned that the main problem of export expansion was on the supply side. This means LDC governments can tackle it. Then they said that most of the constraints are institutional. This is also encouraging, because it means the governments can do something about them.

But in Swaziland and some other African states the real problems are different. There is no manufacturing industry. And the natural resources available do not lend themselves to processing that could produce manufactured exports. Swaziland's main export is sugar. It is refined to a certain extent and exported as polarized sugar. We produce sawn timber and wood pulp, but have insufficient water to produce paper.

Besides, our manpower is untrained and has few skills; so we have no comparative advantages. Most African states have small populations and cannot start by catering to a local market. Are we therefore doomed to remain exporters of primary products?

JOSE MARIA DAGNINO PASTORE (Argentina): Should we keep the export subsidy geared to the level of effective protection, or should it be uniform? There is a natural ceiling to export subsidies.

As Professor Schydlowsky said, costs will exceed import prices by different margins in different sectors, depending on the exchange rate system. However, it seems that the industrial cost exchange rate does not generate an equilibrium in the balance of payments.

HELEN HUGHES (IBRD): One cannot lump all developing states together. Some Asian countries have problems of low capacity utilization without distortions in capital and labor markets and without foreign exchange constraints.

Supply factors are important, but demand factors should not be underestimated. There are problems of inelastic demand in areas where LDCs have the greatest comparative advantage. Comparing a state's quota with its performance can indicate clearly whether supply or demand factors are checking exports. For instance, in textiles Taiwan, Hong Kong, and Korea have high quota fulfillment, while India's performance is bad, which suggests that India's problems are on the supply side.

As regards capacity exploitation, in some industries it may be economic to increase the number of shifts, and in others not.

Increasing employment may reduce poverty. But a combined devaluation plus liberalization policy could have very adverse effects on incomes, as international financial insitutions found out in the fifties and the sixties.

Countries with very high effective protection and few exports probably have a wrong balance between agriculture and industry.

ZEHAVIT WEISER (Israel): In time one forgets which part of the export subsidy compensates for the higher exchange rate of imports and which part is really to encourage exports. The first part is positive and necessary, and the attitude of GATT towards it should be changed. But the part of the subsidy designed to encourage exports is not really sound in the long run. For in the long run it encourages inflation, which works against exports. It would be better to encourage exports by information about marketing or credits, rather than through such subsidies.

The main problem with exports is on the supply side, like that of the shoemakers who produce at low cost but know nothing about selling abroad. It is the problem of how to get small manufacturers to export, when they don't know how to deal with exports. If you leave marketing to the government or to big marketing organizations, you eliminate the incentives for the producers.

CARLOS DIAZ ALEJANDRO (Yale University): Exports of manufactures from LDCs were suggested when economists were saying that there was no future in primary products, owing to low demand elasticities, and so forth. Yet recent trends show that primary products, new and traditional, have a future.

So perhaps we should not worry about new manufactured exports from LDCs. The primary exports may prove enough. Promoting exports does not necessarily mean getting better income distribution. Figures show that only 60 percent of output capacity has been used in the early sixties, but putting this capacity to work by strong incentives may not be the ideal answer.

It is too easy to argue for putting unemployed to work on excess capacity and producing exports. ILO studies show that most of the openly unemployed are middle-class teenagers and women—not the poorest part of the labor force. Nor are these necessarily suitable for working night shifts.

The question of export quality is related to what are tradeable goods. You may have excess capacity in dairy produce plants in Colombia, but will this help if they make a kind of cheese which only has a market in Bogota.

JUERGEN DONGES (Federal Republic of Germany): Concerning the points raised by Doctor Mandelbaum: Giving drawbacks for imports to promote manufactured exports is not enough. Export subsidies also will be needed, because the exporting industries are using domestic as well as imported input. If domestic industries are protected by tariffs, one needs an export subsidy protecting added value of exports to the same extent that tariffs protect added value for the domestic market.

The export promotion measures I suggested are long-term as well as short-term, though policies should be adjusted to changing conditions when necessary. This applies especially to the exchange rate. Germany and Japan had undervalued currencies for 10 to 15 years, yet this worked well. Some LDCs might do the same.

As regards Professor Leibenstein's points: LDCs should follow industrialization and trade policies avoiding distortions. States successful despite interferences with free trade include Brazil, Mexico, and perhaps Spain, but their success was in growth, not in employment creation or income distribution. The case for industrial export expansion is mainly that one cannot expect industries to produce efficiently for a long time if they don't also produce for the world market.

If Swaziland and most other African countries want to industrialize, they have to take the decision and then start producing for the domestic market, but without discriminating against potential production for export.

I agree with Dr. Dagnino Pastore that manufactured exports can be oversubsidized. South Korea and Brazil are doing this. Export subsidies of up to 30 percent of added value should avoid this danger.

The demand elasticity of electronics, components, and some types of simple machinery is high. Some semi-industrialized states are producing such items, and their problems are more on the supply side. Demand elasticities for textiles, clothing, shoes, and leather are lower, and quota fulfillment is a good indicator of what the problems are.

I was discussing only states which want to industrialize. In this case efficient economic development is very difficult to achieve with an inward-looking industrialization pattern. The trade-off between expanding primary exports and industrial exports is another problem.

DANIEL SCHYDLOWSKY (Peru): There are many constraints to growth—some due to foreign exchange policy and some to capitalization policy. Removing these constraints will not solve all growth problems, but leaving them is worse. Straightening out exchange rate systems is a necessary condition of progress.

You only pay subsidies if people export. If they don't, you don't pay. So there are few bad effects if the policy fails. The same applies to utilization. If you have idle capital and idle labor, you should try to use them. If you succeed, you will be much better off. If not, at worst you will be where you started.

The policy package suggested may not solve all economic problems or apply to all states. It certainly does not apply to Swaziland. However, it is not true to say it is a Latin American package not applying to Asia. India has a crazy exchange rate system and a problem similar in nature to that of Latin America. So have the Philippines, and Ceylon is not very different. Even Indonesia is very similar in this respect to Peru in the fifties or to Costa Rica now. In Africa, Ghana and the Ivory Coast show similarities.

Free trade for states having a big competitive advantage in raw materials, like Kuwait, results in huge exports of one commodity with everyone not living off this commodity unemployed. This is undesirable on social grounds. Hence many states need a multiple exchange rate structure to generate employment and equity. This is preferable to free trade.

We are now calculating what moving to three shifts will mean for supplying likely export markets for Venezuela, Colombia, and Peru.

A good example of the bad effects of devaluation and liberalization, is Argentina, where recession often resulted. But the liberalization there consisted of the replacing of exchange controls and quotas by new exchange rates and higher tariffs, with a tight monetary policy. This is a very different package from the one I suggested. I discussed a situation where there are import duties, not quotas, and where liberalization means devaluing and lowering import duties—not one where import duties are raised and quotas removed. In the policy I suggested, since lower import duties are precisely offset by the change in the exchange rate, domestic prices remain unchanged. Only prices of nontraditional exports and the financial exchange rate change. And there is no reason for a tight monetary policy.

A policy of massive devaluation, removal of trade controls, higher tariffs, and tight money is guaranteed to cause depressions.

I was not trying to compute an equilibrium exchange rate for Argentina, but only to calculate industrial costs at the exchange rates that each industry pays for its inputs. It is not a set of exchange rates that ought to be implemented on the market.

I cannot believe that the price increases in primary products will last. Their causes have to do with weather, poor crops, and some strange U.S. policies. The United States will increase its output of primary products for domestic political reasons, and this should lower prices. It has been restricting output for years; now it will expand and dump this output on the world markets. Within two years prices should drop. And the time for the primary producers to introduce reforms is now, when they have the necessary foreign exchange, not in two years' time when they will again be short of it.

Underutilization of capital is due to distortions causing conflicts of interest between private profit and social benefit. Specific policies should be applied to bring these two factors into balance.

THE ENLARGED COMMUNITY AND DEVELOPING COUNTRIES

Hans Broder Krohn

INTRODUCTION

The enlargement of the EEC from six to nine members will have a profound impact on the Community's relations with developing countries. The enlarged Community is not only the most important outlet for LDCs; it also contributes to the LDCs' economic and social development by aid.

Taken together, the Community's nine member states absorb some 40 percent of the developing countries' exports (1971). They supply some 40 percent of official and private financial resources put at the LDCs' disposal by OECD countries, as much as the United States, which was the most important donor during the sixties. More than 70,000 experts and teachers from the Community are working in developing countries under various technical assistance programs. At the same time, 57,000 students from these countries receive their training in the Community. In both fields the enlarged Community traditionally plays a much more important role than the United States.

The Community is equally dependent on developing countries, since these supply an important part of its demand for energy, agricultural goods, and industrial raw materials. In this respect, Europe's situation has always been more vulnerable than that of the United States and the Soviet Union.

In addition, LDCs constitute an important outlet for Community industry. Taken together, they absorb about one third of EEC exports, more than any other group of countries.

There is thus a very high degree of economic interdependence between the Community and the LDCs. It is probably higher than that existing between the LDCs and any other industrialized country with the possible exception of Japan.

The Community as such has only limited responsibilities, as compared with those of its individual member states, for cooperation with developing countries. This must be kept in mind if one wants to understand the relations between the enlarged Community and the LDCs.

While fully admitting the Community's responsibility towards all LDCs, the EEC states stressed the need for concentrating on certain groups of countries mostly situated in Africa and in the Mediterranean, to which the enlarged Community is specially committed by links of history or by juridical obligations. Most of these states happen to be among the 25 countries identified as the least developed However, the policies presently defined in a more narrow geographic scope may be considered a first step towards a world-wide cooperati policy with all LDCs.

COOPERATION POLICY IN THE FRAMEWORK OF ASSOCIATION AGREEMENTS BETWEEN THE COMMUNITY AND CERTAIN DEVELOPING COUNTRIES

Immediately after its enlargement the EEC finds itself embark upon a series of negotiations with more than 40 LDCs. The purpose of these negotiations is the establishment of contractual relations, fo: a specified period (five years), between the Community and certain developing countries or groups of them, covering essentially trade and financial and technical cooperation.

The Community's partners in these negotiations are on the one hand the three Maghreb countries (Morocco, Algeria, Tunisia), on the other hand the so-called "Yaounde" and "Protocol no.22" countries.

Negotiations with the three Maghreb states were already starte before the enlargement of the Community. This effort was dictated by the awareness of the extremely close economic interdependence between the various Mediterranean countries and the Community. The problem of establishing suitable relationships, however, is complicated by the fact that some Mediterranean countries, the European ones, are juridically entitled to membership* and therefore to a most favorable treatment, especially in access to the Community market, while others are not. In addition, only some Mediterranean countries those on the south and east, are still considered developing countries. The Community, therefore, has to negotiate a series of individual agreements, striking a balance between the competing interests of its partners (as suppliers of identical or similar products) and the legitimate desire of producers within the Community not to be unduly exposed to competition from outside.

---

*Association agreements with Greece and Turkey were conclude in the early sixties. Agreements with Spain and Malta are being nego tiated. Portugal has been dealt with in the context of the EFTA agree ments.

All Mediterranean agreements provide for preferential access of exports from the partner countries to the Community market. In the case of the "developed" northern Mediterranean countries, these are part of a customs union (Greece, Turkey) or of a free trade area (Spain) to be gradually established with the Community. In the case of the "developing" Mediterranean countries, the precise juridical form of the future trade arrangements is yet to be defined. The concept of a free trade area between the Community and developing countries is repudiated by all concerned because of the reciprocity it involves on the part of the developing countries. For the Community the offer of preferential access to its market means a considerable strain both economically and politically: economically because some of its own agricultural production (fruits and vegetables) is likely to be replaced by the competition from Mediterranean countries; politically because the burden of any trade liberalization in favor of Mediterranean countries' agricultural exports is essentially supported by only two member states, Italy and France.

In addition to the trade provisions, the future association agreements may contain stipulations concerning economic cooperation, which will generally be related to trade. Financial and technical cooperation will be provided only in exceptional cases. The Community has admitted the principle of such cooperation, the terms of which will have to be defined during the negotiations, in the case of the Maghreb countries.

Negotiations with some 40 LDCs situated in Africa, in the Caribbean Sea, and in the Pacific Ocean were formally opened on July 25/26, 1973. The following LDCs are concerned:

- 19 presently associated African countries, Madagascar and Mauritius (Yaounde Convention)
- 3 presently associated East-African countries (Arusha Agreement)
- 9 African Commonwealth countries (Botswana, Gambia, Ghana, Lesotho, Malawi, Nigeria, Sierra Leone, Swaziland, Zambia)
- 4 Caribbean Commonwealth countries (Barbados, Guyana, Jamaica, Trinidad-Tobago)
- 3 Pacific Commonwealth countries (Fiji, Tonga, Samoa)
- 3 African countries of economic structure similar to the already associated countries (Ethiopia, Liberia, Sudan)

All these states expressed interest in negotiating a global agreement with the enlarged Community covering cooperation in the fields of trade and financial flows.

Negotiations with these 40 countries do not start from zero. The Yaounde Convention, first concluded in 1964 and renewed in 1971, provides for cooperation with 19 of the countries concerned* in the fields of trade and financial and technical assistance. Through joint institutions the partners decide on the practical application of the agreement. Trade provisions guarantee them virtually free entry to the Community market, while the Community enjoys free access to their markets.

Financial and technical assistance is provided by the Communi through the European Development Fund and the European Investmen Bank on very advantageous terms as regards volume per capita and conditions (80 percent being supplied in form of grants, partial untyi financing of foreign exchange and local currency expenditures).

In contrast to the Yaounde Convention, the Arusha Agreement, concluded in 1971 with Kenya, Tanzania, and Uganda, is less comprehensive in scope and does not contain any provisions for financial an technical cooperation.

Both the Yaounde Convention and the Arusha Agreement expire on January 31, 1975. Their renegotiation has been fundamentally affected by the enlargement of the Community. According to Protoco no. 22 of the Acts of Accession, the enlarged Community has agreed to extend the advantages of its present cooperation with the associate states to 20 LDCs,† all members of the Commonwealth and enjoying trading advantages in the British market. They are given the choice of becoming partners either to the future agreement to be negotiated with the Yaounde countries, to association agreements sui generis, or to trade agreements with the Community.

In addition, the Community included in its offer African LDCs with economic structures similar to those of the associated countries so practically all tropical Africa will be involved in the negotiations with the Community.‡

Future relations between Africa and Europe have become a political issue for the Organization of African Unity (OAU). At their summit conference in May 1973, the African Heads of State and

---

*Except for Mauritius, which acceded only in 1973, these Africa associated countries were colonies of France, Belgium, or Italy, whe the Community was founded in 1958. They include Madagascar, Mauritania, Senegal, Mali, Upper Volta, Niger, Chad, Ivory Coast, Togo, Dahomey, Cameroon, Central African Republic, Gabon, Congo, Zaire, Rwanda, Burundi, and Somalia.

†Mauritius, Kenya, Uganda, Tanzania, Botswana, Lesotho, Swaziland, Gambia, Ghana, Malawi, Nigeria, Sierra Leone, Zambia, Barbados, Jamaica, Guyana, Trinidad, Fiji, Tonga and Samoa.

‡Only Guinea refused to enter into negotiations with the Community.

Government agreed on eight principles, which they accepted as basic guidelines for their negotiations with the Community.

The fundamental objective of the negotiations is the conclusion of a comprehensive agreement containing provisions for access to the Community market, stabilization of the export earnings of primary products, financial and technical assistance, and certain joint institutions.

The Community's partners appear resolved to enter negotiations as a "united front," composed of three subgroups: the African, the Caribbean, and the Pacific countries. This is of considerable political importance, substantially enhancing their negotiating power.*

The main issues of the negotiations are likely to be access to the Community market, reciprocity, measures for the stabilization of primary exports, sugar, and financial cooperation.

On the question of access, the Community's partners demand free and unrestricted entry to the EEC for all their exports, agricultural and industrial. Industrial exports do not present formidable difficulties, since these are anyhow admitted duty free under the Community's general system of preferences (GSP),† and since most of the countries concerned do not yet have a developed export industry.

The situation is different for a small number of fruits, vegetables, and grains that compete with Community production. In the past the EEC usually conceded limited tariff reductions for these exports, considered as sensitive despite the small volume of trade involved. It remains to be seen whether a more liberal attitude will now be adopted.

After successful conclusion of the negotiations, about half of the LDCs, mainly the poorest, will enjoy completely free access for almost all their exports to the world's biggest import market.

The issue of reciprocity is more of political than of economic importance to the Community's partners. In conformity with GATT rules, the Community may depart from the most favored nation clause in only two cases: free trade area or customs union, according to article 24, GATT; waiver, according to article 25, GATT. In the past the Community and its associated partners have opted for the establishment of free trade areas, the associated countries being authorized to maintain or introduce duties against the Community whenever this

---

*The African group includes two categories whose interests may be divergent: the present associated countries, mainly Francophonic Africa, and the potential future associates, mainly English speaking. The Caribbean group comprises four independent and eight dependent countries.

†Sensitive products are, however, subject to quantitative limits.

is deemed necessary for the sake of economic development (protection of infant industries) or of public finance (duties as main source of government revenue).

Nevertheless, the principle of reciprocity has now been openly attacked by the Community's partners. They claim that reciprocity between developed and developing countries is unfair to the latter and contrary to the fundamental rule of unilateral preferential treatment, which the developed countries ought to apply in their relations with developing countries, in conformity with UNCTAD resolutions and Part IV of GATT. So far the Community has no answer to this new problem.

The third main issue of the negotiations will be the stabilization of export revenues from primary products. For years the present associated countries, whose economies are largely dependent on two or three major primary export crops (such as groundnuts, coffee, cocoa, bananas, and cotton) have asked for stable and remunerative prices for their primary products, without any adequate response from the EEC.

In its memorandum on the future association agreement published in April 1973, the EEC Commission made an original proposal for primary products. This is based on the principle that for the associated countries it is not so much price stability that matters but stability of export receipts.

For eight main export products* of its future partners characterized by instability of export receipts, it is suggested that the Community automatically intervene with compensatory payments, whenever exports to the Community fall below an agreed reference value to be determined on the basis of past records (for example, five-year variable averages). Basically these payments (which are to be reimbursed when export prices rise beyond the reference level) are to compensate the income gaps in the national economy, which result from a drop in export earnings.

This scheme of compensatory payments would not interfere with the market mechanism. It remains, however, to be seen to what extent it will be considered as a satisfactory solution by the Community's partners. The African countries would prefer some type of regional market organization that would guarantee "stable, equitable and remunerative prices in EEC markets for their main products." If some compromise is finally agreed upon by the Community and its partners, this would be the first systematic attempt undertaken in common by a group of developed and developing countries to mitigate the harmful effects of market instability of primary products.

---

*Sugar, cotton, bananas, groundnuts inclusive of oil, coffee, cocoa, copper.

Sugar may become a significant test case of the Community's political determination to take into due account the interests of developing countries, when formulating domestic policies.

Under the Commonwealth Sugar Agreement, Great Britain is importing some 1.4 million tons of sugar at agreed stable prices, generally above world market level, from Commonwealth developing countries. When Britain joined the EEC the latter specifically agreed to take into consideration the interests of the sugar exporting Commonwealth LDCs.

The EEC Commission recently submitted a set of proposals that, if adopted by the Community, would offer the developing countries concerned guaranteed access to the Community for 1.4 million tons of sugar, at stable remunerative prices. This proposal is remarkable because the absorption of 1.4 million tons of sugar from developing countries will imply considerable sacrifices for sugar producers within the Community. It would thus constitute an important step towards a better division of labor between developed and developing countries.

Financial and technical cooperation will also be an important issue in the negotiations. For the Community, doubling the number of associated countries will imply a heavy financial burden, since it has agreed not to reduce the real volume of its aid to the presently associated countries, while treating any newcomers on an equal footing. It may also have to maintain the present favorable terms of its aid, characterized by the predominance of grants.

In addition to claims on the Community's generosity, the African and Caribbean countries have asked to participate in the administration of the aid funds put at their disposal. Under the present association agreement, the associated states already participate in basic policy decisions concerning aid administration (for example, guidelines for the sectoral priorities of the aid efforts and questions concerning the financing of maintenance and repair works). However, effective co-responsibility for individual financing decisions would require fundamental changes in the present aid mechanism of the EEC under which its Commission assumes the final responsibility before the European taxpayer for the economic and efficient use of the funds made available to associated states.

RELATIONS BETWEEN THE ENLARGED COMMUNITY AND NON-ASSOCIATED COUNTRIES

Apart from sizeable amounts of food aid granted by the EEC under the International Food Aid Convention,* developing countries in Asia and Latin America have not received any financial or technical assistance from the Community. So far the Community's "constitution" has been interpreted restrictively, allowing for financial and technical assistance only to countries that had been dependencies of certain member states when the Rome Treaty was signed. (Since 1973, Mauritius has been the first exception to this rule.)

However, in determining trade policy the Community has been taking into account the interests of all developing countries. Both the substantial tariff reductions on major tropical products (coffee, tea, cocoa, spices) decided upon in 1964 and 1971, on the occasions of the conclusion and the renewal of the Yaounde Convention, and the introduction of general tariff preferences (GSP) for manufactured exports from all LDCs were intended to be political and economic gestures towards the nonassociated LDCs. Indeed, Latin American and Asian countries were the main beneficiaries of these measures.

In October 1972, the heads of government of the nine member states decided that the enlarged Community will further improve its general system of preferences. This† may constitute an additional stimulus to industrial development in LDCs, especially in processed agricultural products and consumer goods, where LDCs seem to enjoy the greatest competitive advantages.

After the successful conclusion of the forthcoming multilateral trade negotiations, the enlarged Community will have arrived at the point of optimum trade liberalization towards LDCs, where duties or levies will either have been abolished or reduced to the lowest level compatible with the Community's political or economic obligations towards certain industries and agriculture within the Community or the associated states.

Some changes in financial and technical assistance to nonassociated LDCs may also reasonably be expected. Some EEC states are pressing to make the Community's aid funds available to all developing

---

*Since 1968 the Community and the member states annually have given away more than one million tons of grains (roughly 60-70 million dollars per year) the counterpart funds of which served to finance development projects.

†In particular inclusion of more processed agricultural products in the system, increases in the quantitative ceilings applied to sensitive manufactured products like textiles.

countries. Considering the commitments that the enlarged Community has made towards its future associates in Africa, the Caribbean, and the Pacific, any extension of the Community's aid activity beyond this scope would require additional resources that would then no longer be available for intra-Community purposes (agricultural, regional, and social funds). Any such decision would therefore underline the fact that the enlarged Community considers the improvement of living conditions in developing countries one of its political priorities.

DISCUSSION

ITZHAK MINERBI (Israel): How much did the European Development Fund actually help the 18 associated countries? It seems industrialization of the associates was not sufficiently taken into account. It is generally assumed that processed agricultural goods and consumer goods should eventually be produced in these states.

Fund aid was mainly given to the better-off coastal states, while landlocked states like Upper Volta, Niger, and Chad were neglected. Something should be done about this.

Preferences are of much smaller value to developing states than rises in primary product prices. Recently prices of cocoa, coffee, rubber, and copper have risen steeply, but nobody knows if the rise will be maintained. Stabilization measures are important. There is also a question of taxes on coffee in some EEC states.

As regards reciprocity, it could be calculated what the associated states received through the European Development Fund and what the Community received back in the form of reverse preferences.

The enlargement of the EEC affected Israel considerably. It is strange that a free trade area for most industrial products should be established already by 1977, when for such states as Greece 12 years were necessary. The agricultural products problem remains unsolved.

PAUL MORAWETZ (Australia): If the EEC is not asking for preferences for goods it exports to LDCs, what kind of reciprocal preferences can be provided? Also, how can the shortfall in quantity and price be established? And are the 2 or 3 billion dollars the EEC is going to give to its members to be deducted from its contributions to UN development projects?

J. ENNIFUL (Ghana): Has the EEC tried to appraise why reciprocity is now objectionable to the associated states and was not before?

JUERGEN DONGES (Federal Republic of Germany): Sensitive products are subject to quotas in the EEC states. These products include textiles, footwear, and leather goods, which are of particular export interest to LDCs. Is an improvement likely in this sphere, and how will the resistance of EEC states likely to be affected by imports from LDCs be overcome?

How is the value of the general preferences scheme assessed within the framework of the enlarged Community? Britain and Denmark have schemes more liberal than that of the EEC but may adopt the latter from the beginning of 1974.

HANS BRODER KROHN (EEC, Brussels): The activity of the first, second, and third European Development Funds was concentrated on hospitals, schools, roads, harbors, railways, agriculture, and industry. The first fund, from 1958 to 1963, emphasized school and hospital construction. The second fund, created under the first Yaounde Convention put more emphasis on roads, harbors, and railways. Note that in the Yaounde states, road construction is of political as well as economic importance, helping to create internal stability. The third fund, since 1969, has mainly emphasized agriculture. The Ivory Coast, Senegal, Gabon, and Zaire are interested in industrialization. But in Chad, Upper Volta, and Niger, agricultural development is the main priority.

Producer prices of primary products must be stabilized, but loans should also be given to help diversify the economy.

All EEC states reckon their contribution to the European Development Fund as part of their aid to LDCs.

When the Fund was established in 1958, there were difficulties in getting projects from the landlocked states in Africa. The resulting discrimination against these states was made good in the second and third funds.

Reciprocity and reversed preferences are not the same thing. The first and second Yaounde Convention gave preferential treatment to EEC goods in the associates' market, but tariffs could be maintained to protect young industries or for fiscal reasons without requiring EEC consent.

The EEC Commission has suggested that the EEC should not ask for reversed preferences in the associates' market. But this view has not yet been accepted.

The United States objects to reversed preferences because they discriminate in favor of European as against American goods in the market of the associated countries.

The money given to associated states comes not only from the E.D. Fund, but also from bilateral aid. Indeed, 90 percent of French, 86 percent of British, and 76 percent of German aid is bilateral.

The EEC Commission opposes taxes on coffee and other tropical products in Europe. But many economists claim that the higher price of coffee or cocoa does not influence consumption, and thus export quantities of the LDCs remain unaffected.

Tariff preferences are losing importance for associated countries. The stabilization of their exports is more important. I am sorry that the general system of EEC preferences for LDCs was not adopted by the United States. We are now likely to improve this system further on the lines of the more liberal British and Danish systems, smoothing the quotas for sensitive goods like textiles.

It is illogical to give money to develop industries in LDCs, and, when these countries start to produce, say the goods are not for us. This is certainly true for the textile and rubber industries.

**EFFECTS OF THE EXPANDING
EUROPEAN COMMON MARKET
ON DEVELOPING COUNTRIES**
Pius Okigbo

The Third or Developing World is a varied assortment of countries at different stages of development. Most of them have very primitive agriculture that provides the main occupation of the population. Some, like Libya and Nigeria, have within one decade dramatically emerged from very low income from agriculture to very high income from oil. Usually, however, not only is agriculture hardly developed, but the country depends on a single crop—Ghana on cocoa, Sudan on cotton—for its wealth. Attempts, as in Ghana, to diversify by installing manufactures have fared badly and piled up foreign obligations. But countries such as India, Argentina, and Mexico are fast becoming industrialized and are nearly as close to the poorer nations of the First and Second as to those of the Third World.

The EEC attitude towards Africa and the developing world has been paternalistic. France felt an obligation towards the Francophone countries of Africa, arranging an association agreement for them in 1958 when the Treaty of Rome came into force. That Britain did not join the Community in 1958 introduced into Euro-African cooperation a bifurcation that has plagued not only European relations with Africa but also intra-African relations, which became polarized between the Francophone and the Anglophone countries.

The EEC saw future prospects of enlarging the trade of its members yet wanted the immediate safeguard of protectionist policies particularly in trade relations with the Third World. A certain ambiguity remained. France had closed privileges in her colonies; these were retained but opened to the Six in Yaoundé 1. Even ten years later the EEC has not quite come to accept that opinion in Africa and in the Third World generally opposes the maintenance of these pockets of privilege in Africa and elsewhere.

The Community took its duty to the associated states very seriously. France has been outstanding in the extent of aid offered to her former dependencies. Much of this aid, however, was technical

---

Pius Okigbo is a Business and Economic Consultant, Lagos, Nigeria, Head, Skoup & Company, Limited.

assistance—the provision of experts and technicians at all levels for states still desperately short of skills of all descriptions. The recipients of the aid often lacked the ability to define their priorities for aid and development assistance. Consequently, their selection of priorities seemed to many observers incorrect.

Politically, the African countries paid lip service to African economic integration but proceeded to establish small and large economic groups exclusive to each other and pursuing policies more favorable to the metropolitan countries than to themselves. The idea of an African Common Market, under study since 1958, always recedes when some African states want to give it concrete reality. But ten years of slogans, lip service and shibboleths more than sated the younger generations who now demand more action. Therefore this decade may see more concrete steps towards African economic integration aided by the need to come to terms with an enlarged EEC.

THE ENLARGED COMMUNITY

The accession of the United Kingdom, Norway, Denmark, and Ireland on 22 January 1972 is bound to alter fundamentally not only the way the EEC looks at the world but also the way the world looks at the EEC. The changes will affect the politics, the trade patterns, and the development of Europe and of the Third World. Table 19 presents the facts about the enlarged EEC in summary form.

Although much smaller in area than the United States or Russia, the new Ten have a larger population than either. GNP per capita has dropped slightly to $2,500 compared to some $2,600 for the Six. The Ten now outdistance the United States in steel output and have a merchant fleet three times larger than the former Six. Indeed, the Ten have emerged as potentially the most powerful economic bloc in the world surpassing the United States in several important indicators. Once their political unity approaches their economic strength, the rest of the world may again gravitate toward Europe, seeking accomodation and looking for aid. No country, except perhaps China, can afford to ignore the development of this economic constellation.

The Association Convention in the Treaty of Rome (1958) represented a solution to the problems arising from France's special relationship with her then dependent territories, although it did not meet the needs of these territories. Five years later, Yaoundé 1 (1963) marked an improvement but only by recognizing the new status of the newly independent states. In 1969, Yaoundé 11 was signed, representing a logical extension of the process that began in 1963.

TABLE 19

The Six and The Ten (1970)

	The Six	The Ten	United States	Japan	Russia
Area ('000 km^2)	1,168	1,847	9,363	370	22,402
Population (millions)	189.8	257.2	205.4	103.5	244
GNP ('000 millions of dollars)	485.2	637.4	993.3	196.2	288
Steel (Crude) (mill. metric tons)	109.2	138.9	122.1	93.3	116.0
External Trade					
Imports (millions of dollars)	39,988	60,054	39.963	18,881	11,739
Exports (millions of dollars)	39,052	55,362	43,226	19,318	12,800
Intra EEC Trade					
Imports (millions of dollars)	48,035	59,743	—	—	—
Exports (millions of dollars)	49,446	59,304	—	—	—
Merchant Fleet (mill. gross tons)	28.66	77.32	18.46	27.0	14.83
Motor Vehicle Output ('000)		11,000	8,300	4,800	1,000
Computers in Use ('000)		30	80	9	7
Reserves (millions of dollars)	36,697	40,097	10,450	14,063	—

    Africa remained, however, polarized into two main blocks: the eighteen states with a predominantly Franco-African connection, and the East and West African English-speaking countries with a predominantly Anglo-Saxon historical connection. This polarization continued even after the independence movement of the 1960s despite the efforts of the Organisation of African Unity to heal the breach.

    For so long as Britain was not in the EEC the attempt by the English-speaking African states to come to terms with the EEC of the Six was received in cool silence by the associated African States. Britain's entry offered the EEC a ready bridge to tighten its economic relations with Africa, parts of Asia, and the Caribbean through the special terms offered by the EEC to Commonwealth countries.

The Yaoundé 1 association rested on three main planks: a system of preferences, tariff quotas, and development aid. The preferential system offered duty-free entry (or reduced duty) to the raw materials of the associated states in return for free entry of products originating in EEC states. With industrial products the position was more difficult: while EEC members enjoyed duty-free movement of goods within the Community, the associated states under Yaoundé 1 faced duties on their manufactures and processed goods, although these were lower than for nonassociated states. By 1963 the value of preferences granted by the EEC had been reduced by EEC agreements with Britain and GATT to lower the common external tariff on certain agricultural products.

Britain and the Commonwealth, on the other hand, operated a system of preferences the value of which was eroding because of the tendency among the major industrial countries to reduce the duties on raw materials for their industries.

Hence, between 1963 and 1971:

- The preferential system of the EEC had lost much of its lustre because it had been extended to the Arusha countries, Tunisia, Morocco, Greece and Turkey. Simultaneously, the agreements between the EEC and Britain in the GATT and the Kennedy Round had reduced the value of the EEC's preferential margin.
- The Commonwealth preferential system had similarly been eroded by these agreements.
- UNCTAD II had urged the liberalization of trade concessions to the Third World generally, rather than to enclaves of special privilege.
- In 1971, generalized preferences came into force in favor of 77 developing states, further eroding any advantages the special groups might have retained. Significantly, the EEC was the first major trading block to apply these generalized preferences.
- International commodity agreements had been signed in respect of certain commodities of special interest to the developing world: sugar, tea, cocoa and coffee.

TRADE PATTERNS

Yaoundé System

The Yaoundé agreements culminating in Yaoundé II of 29 July, 1969, set up a system of preferences in favor of the Associated African and Malagasy States (A.A.M.A.). However, the preferences obtained by Yaoundé associates in the EEC market were subject to the export restrictions covered by the EEC's common agricultural policy, under which the EEC instituted a regime of levies without fixed rebates for basic commodities or processed products from the associated states. Thus the preferences under the Yaoundé system do not amount to much and have not led to any significant improvement in the trade of African associated states, nor significantly decreased the competition from nonassociated states. The main commodities covered by the preferences—coffee, cocoa, groundnuts, palm oil, and bananas—constitute some 84 percent of the preferential trade of the African States (1970).

Commonwealth System

The Commonwealth system also has been so weakened by special clauses and concessions that its value has become nominal. When in 1963 the duties on tea and timber were reduced and the duties on groundnuts abolished, the value of the Community preferences declined further. The attraction of the EEC as an export market for African states has not caused any great upsurge in the trade between the Community and the associated states. On the other hand, the EEC has become increasingly attractive to nonassociated states.

General Preferences

The main features of this system are as follows:
- Very low (or zero) tariff is imposed on manufactures imported from the less developed countries except for such products as textiles or leather goods.
- Selected agricultural commodities of interest to less developed countries are eligible for special preferences.
- The less developed countries will apply the principle of self selection to determine who is eligible for which preferences.
- Developed countries will have an escape clause, for example, a tariff quota.

The EEC prides itself on being the first major block to adopt the system of generalized preferences on July 1971 for manufactures and semimanufactures from 91 developing countries. The EEC was followed by Norway, Japan, Britain, Sweden, Denmark, Finland, New Zealand, Hungary, Czechoslovakia, Switzerland, and Austria. The United States has yet to apply the system.

Reverse Preferences

The system of generalized preferences does not involve the principle of reciprocity as the EEC (and, in some cases, the Commonwealth) system does. In the EEC system developing states grant preferences in their market to developed states to the disadvantage of neighboring or other developing countries. This is one of the most objectionable features of the Yaoundé agreements. In the Commonwealth system, neither Nigeria nor Ghana grants reciprocal preferences to the United Kingdom, and in cases where they exist there is no accompanying tariff quota. The adoption of the system of generalized preferences is a vindication of the stand taken by the developing world against the principle of reciprocity in trade negotiations between developed and developing nations. The negotiations for the renewal of Yaoundé in the framework of the enlarged EEC may eliminate the reciprocal element.

IMPACT OF ENLARGEMENT ON AFRICAN TRADE

The two most important countries for the export trade of Africa are Britain and France, the former for the English-speaking African countries and the latter for the Yaounde associates. France accounted for 13.9 percent of total African exports in 1970 while Britain accounted for 16.3 percent; but France took 26 percent and Britain 25 percent of all exports from the Yaoundé and Commonwealth African countries respectively. The EEC as a whole took 44 percent of all African exports and 66.7 percent of all Yaoundé associates' exports.

As inter-African trade is of the order of less than 6 percent, African countries are more dependent on trade with Europe than are the Latin American or Asian countries. Thus the enlargement of the EEC should link African countries more closely with the Community.

African states have few manufactures to trade in. Britain imported in 1970 $65.0 million of manufactures from developing African countries out of a total $1,972 million worth of imports of all categories from that zone. Textile import from Africa accounted for $6.7 million. Out of the $65 million of imports, African Commonwealth countries accounted for $24.2 million and Yaoundé associates for some $4.1 million.

With France the picture is reversed. Imports from developing Africa amounted to $2,307.0 million, with manufactures accounting for $50.5 million, of which textiles represented $18.5 million. Imports of manufactures from the Yaoundé associates accounted for $12.6 million, while African Commonwealth countries accounted for $0.8 million.

In effect, therefore, African countries have no manufactures to speak of. A more interesting question relates to the future: Will the common external tariff of the enlarged EEC be subordinated to the generalized preferences of the Community?

Africa's trade with Europe is predominantly agricultural and mineral. In 1970 of the $7,318 million worth of trade $965.0 million was in tropical products, $1,407.6 million in agricultural raw materials and $2,966.1 million in oil. Minerals and oil constitute a category deserving of special treatment. But agricultural products, such as coffee, bananas, cocoa, and oil seeds, still dominate the economic future of most of the associated states. Mineral and oil products enter duty free or under special agreements concluded by the large multinational petroleum companies. Other commodities, like timber and cotton, enter the EEC duty free. Hence the enlargement of the EEC is not likely to affect the trade of these African countries beyond the four major commodities.

TRADE IN COMMODITIES

Coffee

In the Yaoundé group coffee is significant in the trade of the Ivory Coast, Cameroon, Central African Republic, Madagascar and Rwanda. In Commonwealth Africa, Uganda, Tanzania and Kenya are coffee growers.

The EEC is a much more important coffee market than Britain, whose margin at 1.5 percent is not as favorable as that of the EEC at zero duty. The growth in demand for robusta coffee, due to the spread of the taste for instant and freeze dried coffee, will benefit Africa more than Latin America, which grows arabica coffee. Since, however, all the African coffee growing countries are already associated under either Yaoundé or Arusha, the enlargement of the EEC will not affect the African coffee trade.

Cocoa

The major Yaoundé producers are Ivory Coast, Cameroon, and Togo, but these are small (except for Ivory Coast) compared to Nigeria and Ghana. The duty on cocoa beans is small, but it is high for cocoa paste and butter. Britain's accession could affect Nigeria and Ghana, but since Britain's cocoa trade is mostly in African cocoa there is little risk of supplies being switched.

Oil Seeds—Groundnut, Palm Oil

The preference margin for oils is high—10 percent in the Commonwealth and 9 to 15 percent in the EEC. Few problems are posed by the enlargement of the Community. The Yaoundé group and the Commonwealth nonassociated states (notably Nigeria) have the same level of preference in their respective markets. Nigeria will simply have to face keener competition.

Britain buys palm oil mostly from Malaysia and Singapore, two Asian states not eligible for association; African nonassociated states— Nigeria and Ghana—will have a small advantage if they associate. If they do not, the level of competition will remain just as it is after Britain's entry. Thus Britain's accession will not create problems for the nonassociated African countries. Finally, Commonwealth Africa does not trade much in products like bananas, so here the entry of Britain will not have a serious impact.

AID

Britain and other European countries were to join the EEC without prejudice to the advantages accruing to associated states from their association agreements. Under Yaoundé II the EEC was to make available to the associated states 828 million units of account through the Third European Development Fund. In real terms, the increase in aid funds between the second and the third European Development Fund (E.D.F.) just about made up for the inflation rate of about 4 percent per annum, or 25 percent between 1965 and 1971. Aid was expanded by 24 percent between these two dates. If the "real" aid was to be maintained, the minimum requirement was about 1,035 million units of account. But the most important feature of development aid during this period is that 90.4 percent was in the form of grants, the rest being soft loans. The enlargement of the EEC should thus extend the scope of untied aid.

The pattern of aid between 1969 and 1972 was as follows: In the old Community of Six, the main aid giver was France, which gave roughly 0.68 percent of her GNP for the years 1969-71 totaling $1,021.4 million. Germany followed with 0.35 percent of her GNP ($637.5 million). Of the new members only Britain is significant as an aid giver at 0.39 percent of her GNP ($479.6 million). Some 90 percent of French aid, 86 percent of British, and 76 percent of German aid is bilateral. While France gave 34 percent of all her bilateral aid to the associated African and Malagasy States (A.A.M.S.), only 0.5 percent of British bilateral aid has gone to these states.

Thus the major part of the bilateral aid from the EEC has gone to nonassociated countries. This being so, the accession of Britain to the EEC will not harm the interests of the nonassociated. Since bilateral aid is still the main channel for EEC aid to Africa, the aid received by the associated states from the Development Fund will not suffer as a result of the accession of Britain and other States or the association of other African countries. On the average, the Six gave 0.52 percent of their combined GNP in aid, but what passed through the Development Fund in 1971 represented only 0.27 percent.

The European Development Fund, set up in 1958, has now introduced practical innovations in procedure: forward commitment of funds, joint undertakings, integration of aid with economic and technical cooperation and assistance, coverage of total costs of a project rather than simply the foreign exchange costs. However, the assistance from the Fund remains project rather than program oriented.

The EEC is aware of the gap between the associated and the nonassociated states. Consequently, at the signature of the Yaoundé I, the Council of Ministers issued a declaration of intent offering the following procedures to the then nonassociated states: accession to the Yaoundé Convention in accordance with Article 58 thereof; or association agreements with mutual rights and obligations particularly in the field of trade; or commercial agreements to facilitate and expand trade between the EEC and these countries. A country taking up any of these options had to possess an economic and production structure compatible with those of the associated states.

The provisions of Yaoundé II are similar, the alternatives offered to the associables being basically the same in 1970 as in 1963. Experience since 1963, however, has been instructive: Nigeria concluded but did not implement an agreement in July 1966; the East African Community concluded and implemented an agreement in September 1969. Each of these was an association agreement distinct and different from Yaoundé II, but, like Yaoundé II, founded on the principle of reciprocity.

Britain's accession was bound to affect the trade flows between the EEC and the Third World—it channeled 68 percent of all exports from developing Africa into the enlarged Community. Table 20 illustrates this.

Evidently, nearly 70 percent of the trade of developing Africa is tied up with the enlarged EEC: Consequently the African states must determine their pattern of diversification for the next decade and work out their relations with the EEC accordingly.

Moreover, developing Africa is polarized into several exclusive camps: associated and nonassociated; Francophone and Anglophone; franc area and sterling area. This is creating ambiguities: the Arusha States are associated but are also in the British Commonwealth; those

TABLE 20

Trade Flow from Developing Africa
(in millions of dollars)

	Total	EEC	Percentages	U.K.	Percentages
A.A.M.S.[a]	1,833	970	53	66	4
Commonwealth Africa[b]	3,340	891	27	918	28
Unassociated[c]	5,338	3,034	57	504	10
Total	9,511	4,895		1,488	
Percent	100		52		16

[a] For Yaoundé associates data not available beyond 1969.
[b] For Commonwealth Africa, including Arusha States, 1970.
[c] Guinea (1966) Tunisia, U.A.R., Liberia, Sudan, Morocco, Libya, Ethiopia, Algeria, 1969-70.

promoting an African Common Market are already in OCAM (Organisation Commune Africaine et Malagache), which was recently weakened by the withdrawals of Mauritania, Zaire, Congo (Brazzaville), Cameroon, and Chad.

For the twenty states affected by British accession the options are similar to those open since 1963: participation in the Convention of Association that governs relations between the EEC and the Associated African and Malagasy States; conclusion of one or more special Conventions of Association on the basis of Article 238 of the EEC Treaty comprising reciprocal rights and obligations, particularly in the field of trade; conclusion of trade agreements with a view to developing trade with the EEC.

How open are these options in fact? The economic structure of the African countries is by no means identical. Each will have to determine where its real interest lies and reconcile this interest with those of the other members of the group. Of the three possibilities ostensibly open, one seems remote—the conclusion of a purely commercial agreement such as those Iran and India concluded in the 1960s. Such agreements require that changes in tariffs have to be applied to all with whom the parties have a most-favored-nation agreement. Left with either accession to Yaoundé or an agreement sui generis such as the Lagos or the Arusha agreements, the African states have very little to choose from, since both types involve reciprocal rights and obligations.

The EEC has established that the associables from Africa and the Caribbean would begin negotiations on August 1973, the associated states (Yaoundé) would start on 24 July, while the Arusha associates would start on 27 July. Thus three parallel negotiations are in progress simultaneously. Commonwealth countries that chose the Yaoundé option may sit together with the Yaoundé associates.

This procedure has made it all the more necessary for African countries to evolve a common platform demanding at least that all members of the Organization of African Unity join in with the Yaoundé states. With the backing of all Africa, the Yaoundé states could refuse to accept the principle of reciprocity and reverse preferences. Faced by such determination, the EEC could hardly demand the terms it obtained in Yaoundé 11. This concession the EEC could give without losing much.

Joint action does not necessarily imply uniform results for each state. The interests of the African states differ. There will be a need for flexibility in finding solutions to the problems of individual states. The sacrifices required from each state must be carefully evaluated. Nigeria and Libya, for example, have little to sacrifice since they earn their wealth more from oil than from agricultural exports. Ivory Coast and Ghana have more to lose, though not as much as Senegal. Therefore, the options open offer unequal advantages to the different states. What state obtains which advantage from either option should be carefully weighed in any joint approach.

Finally, the outcome of the negotiations will be decided and evaluated by reference to arrangements for technical and financial cooperation. For most of Africa, the trade problems of the 1970s cannot be worsened by the enlargement of the EEC. But the countries of Africa and the Caribbean will have to secure more financial aid and technical assistance; they will have to slowly diversify their trade portfolios with the United States, Japan, and the Eastern bloc countries; they will have to emulate the EEC in setting up their own institutions to further similar political and economic aims. Most of all, the accession of Britain signifies a closing of ranks in Europe, and African students of geopolitics will see in this a signal for Africa to close its own ranks or else face a new carving up to replace the jealousies and antagonisms of the past two decades.

THE TRANSFER OF MANAGERIAL AND TECHNICAL KNOWLEDGE
Harvey Leibenstein

WHY CARE?

To indicate the nature of the problem, consider an example from a paper by H. W. Singer, comparing Kenya and the United Kingdom. Kenya has a rate of labor force growth of 3.3 percent per annum compared with 0.4 percent in the United Kingdom. Hence, Kenya must find, per million population, eight times as many additional productive jobs as the United Kingdom. But Kenya has available for this purpose only one-fifteenth the resources per million population. If Kenya tried to provide the additional jobs in such a way that the employment opportunities created would be of exactly the same kind as in the United Kingdom, then less than 1 percent of the number of additional jobs needed could be provided. The example shows vividly that unless the technology is very radically different in Kenya than in the United Kingdom there will be increasing unemployment.

Two facts must be kept in mind if we consider the question of technology from a relevant viewpoint: First, labor force growth in developing countries is much more rapid than it was in the developed countries when they were undergoing their modernization. Second, the techniques available at the modern end of the spectrum are much more labor saving or labor displacing than ever before. If during the nineteenth century there were few problems in the transfer of technical knowledge, the changed magnitude of the situation poses serious problems today. But we cannot avoid the essential truth that development necessarily implies the introduction of new technologies.

There are significant "holes" in the continuum of technological options available to developed countries. New approaches to the choice of technology and to the provision and transfer of knowledge in the technique-lending countries are required if such holes are to be filled.

THE SIGNIFICANCE OF HOLES IN THE PRODUCTION FUNCTION

A point on a production function implies a combination of capital and labor. If there is continuity in the production function, this implies that we can always substitute labor for capital. Thus, by substituting labor for capital, we can always get full employment. Continuity in the production function is a necessary but not a sufficient condition to achieve full employment. Prices or other circumstances may be such that there are no incentives for a full employment technique to be chosen. However, we need not worry about the incentives at this point. Suppose there is a hole in the production function; that is, a set of capital and labor ratios commensurate with full employment does not exist. The technical options available may be such that the choice is between a scarcity of labor or unemployment.

These ideas are illustrated in Figure 1. $Q_1, Q_2 \ldots$ represent two out of a set of isoquants. Each point on an isoquant represents a given combination of capital and labor and hence a technique of production. A ray from the origin represents techniques that have the same capital-labor ratio. Three rays are shown—K/L_1, K/L_2, K/L_3. The point x_1 on K/L_2 represents the current resources available in terms of capital and labor. On the x-axis, we show three quantities of labor: U (unemployment), F (full employment), and S (scarcity of labor). Now let us suppose that the portions of the isoquants between K/L_1 and K/L_3 are missing. Technologies on K/L_2

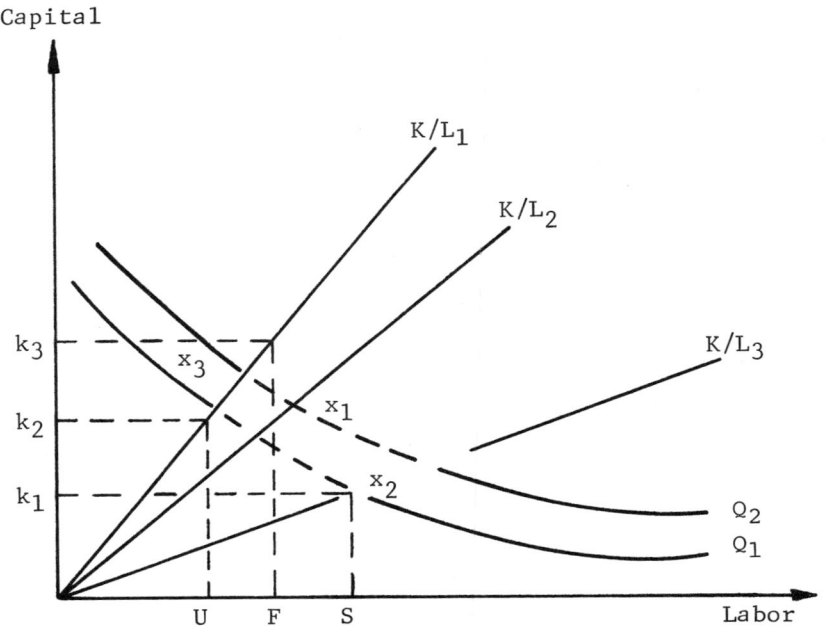

Figure 1

are not available. We show in heavy unbroken lines those portions of Q_1 and Q_2 that represent technologies that are available. At the current level of capital that has been accumulated full employment is not possible. There are no visible techniques that would employ both capital and labor fully. We could use technique x_2 associated with the low capital intensity k_1, but this would involve a scarcity of labor. It would be easy to draw the iso-cost lines in such a way that the scarcity of labor implies a wage rate sufficiently high to be inconsistent with x_2 and one that induces a shift towards the point x_3. Under such circumstances full employment of both capital and labor simultaneously is not achievable.* However, we should not draw the conclusion that capital accumulation, a process that must take time, will lead to full employment. While capital is accumulating, the labor force grows. Even if we were to move along the ray K/L_1, there would be a race between capital accumulation and labor force growth. There is no reason why this race cannot eventually be won by capital accumulation. There is an upper limit to labor force growth.

The significance of holes in the production function can be seen more readily if we look at the process from a dynamic view point. In figure 2, k_0 is the initial amount of capital available. The initial

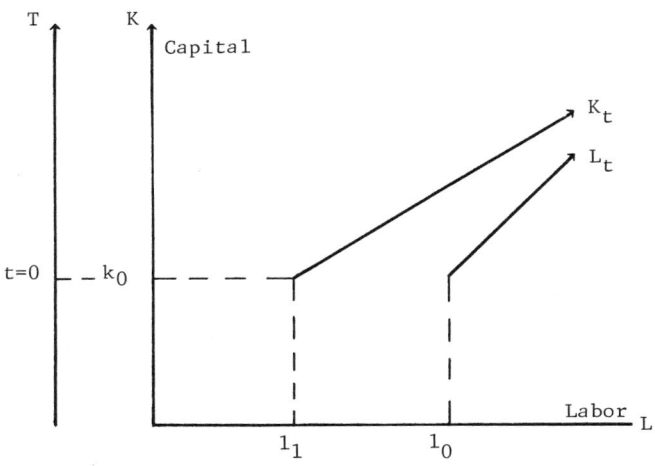

Figure 2

---

*If free market firms have the incentive to use their capital as fully as possible, and capital or labor must be underemployed, it will be labor that will be underemployed.

309

labor supply is l_0. Labor actually employed is designated l_1. The distance l_1-l_0 represents the amount of unemployment. The line L_t indicates labor force growth over time. Similarly the line K_t indicates capital growth and associated labor employed over the same period. The ordinate is also the time axis T, and the initial time is t_0. Equal distances on the ordinate represent equal units of time and form the basis on which the curve L_t is drawn. Now, the slope of K_t depends (a) on the rate of capital accumulation; (b) on the techniques supplied, that is, in part on the extent to which the holes in the production function are filled; and (c) on the techniques demanded, that is, the motivational system that determines the techniques actually chosen.

A technique is a bundle of attributes or specifications involved in some specific way of carrying out a production process. This requires not only differences in inputs but also differences in knowledge. If a technique does not appear to be available owing to inadequate knowledge, it cannot be chosen. Returning to Figure 2, we can visualize a capital accumulation technique supply vector K_t chasing labor force growth L_t, which, if rapid enough, eventually leads to full employment. The rate at which new techniques are supplied will determine how soon full employment can be realized. What is meant by "new" in this context is part of the essence of the problem we have to try to understand.

WHY DO HOLES IN THE PRODUCTION FUNCTION EXIST?

Economic theory presumes that all alternative ways of producing something are known. What is known in some detail is the production process actually in use. We may know in somewhat lesser detail alternative production processes. But such differences in degree of knowledge are vital. The differences in degrees of knowledge are the critical elements in what we claim to be fillable holes in the production function. A little bit of knowledge about a production process is frequently no better than none. There is a critical amount of knowledge less than which cannot reasonably be acted upon.

In every economy markets are imperfect, especially in developing countries. There are, so to speak, holes in the network of input availabilities, where input is defined to include knowledge and motivations. Entrepreneurs are characteristically "input gap-fillers." The entrepreneur, broadly defined, is a significant element in the process of putting knowledge borrowing into effect. For some types of activities, especially those connected with inputs vital to the borrowing of technology, these are frequently rare skills. Besides, the setting in which entrepreneurs operate is subject to different degrees of inertia and "X-inefficiency" on the part of entrepreneurs and firms.* Constraints placed on firms by the environment and governments add to the problem.

Not all aspects of the technological borrowing process are transferable with the same degree of ease. The following are listed in order of probable ease of transfer, from easiest to most difficult: (1) physical goods such as machines and equipment; (2) well-defined services, such as engineering services and insurance; (3) knowledge and ideas, such as engineering knowledge about a specific technique of production; (4) the motivational system, including the managerial system executing a new technique of production. Hence, what a country needs for successful borrowing is likely to be in reverse order of the ease of transferability.

To see what is involved let us look at the technical borrowing process from the borrower's viewpoint, and at the way the production process is used in the lending country given the lender's input scarcities. Suppose the process involved requires equipment of a certain type. The equipment or some aspects of it are likely to be the most readily knowable and visible part of the technique. Next in knowability is likely to be the routine operation of the equipment. The elements that follow and the order in which they follow may be either unknown or underappreciated to a degree making these particular aspects difficult to adapt effectively in the borrowing country. The likely elements in this category are: (1) procedures for maintenance and repairs, including the handling of breakdowns and the stocking of spare parts, (2) management procedures, especially the coordination and integration of the manpower within the firm and aspects involving informal knowledge about the requisite dovetailing of the skills and personality characteristics of various individuals involved in the production process, (3) the sociopsychological relationships taken for granted in most normal systems of authority and communication within organizations, which are essential parts of production processes that involve specialization, and (4) the adaptation of the equipment and routines of operation to different circumstances and factor scarcities.

Suppose that the requisite hardware from the lending country can be shipped to the borrowing country and some of the operational routines described in manuals and other necessary information can

---

*My X-inefficiency theory argues that human inputs rarely if ever work in such a way as to maximize output. In this context, if maximum output is taken as the norm, then the degree of X-inefficiency is the difference between actual and maximum output.

be learned in some way, then usually what will be transmitted is the process as it is carried out in the lending country. But this process involves a high capital-labor ratio likely to be unsuitable to the factor scarcities of the borrowing developing country. The essence of the problem is whether the same equipment, or similar equipment modified in some way, could be used, maintained, repaired, and managed so that very different quantities of labor could be used with the capital involved. It is possible, in principle, to visualize much of this equipment being adapted in a variety of ways, so that it uses the relatively inexpensive inputs of borrowing countries. But this is precisely what will not be manufactured by the developed lending country for its own use where the major market for the equipment will normally exist. Nor will the engineers in the lending country, or other technicians, be attuned to the needs of the borrowing country. In general, the borrowing country will have available its own traditional techniques. The lending country will offer so-called modern techniques that are highly capital intensive. In between there may be significant gaps that are not filled.

WHY THE HOLES IN THE PRODUCTION FUNCTION ARE NOT FILLED

The latest technologies, which may be most efficient in purely technical terms, have mostly been designed to meet the quite different circumstances prevailing in the advanced economies. More and more investment decisions are being made or influenced by government planners who lack the technical know-how and experience to make the best choices. Techniques were biased in a capital-intensive direction by many policies that make capital cheap compared with labor, especially by overvalued exchange rates. The Pearson Report states that there has been a tendency for aid-giving agencies and foreign contractors to transfer most modern technology without modification. Another contributing factor may be the nature of the firm in the modern sector.

Labor contracts are incomplete. What is purchased is labor time. What enters into production is labor effort. Time and effort are not the same. For a given amount of contracted time considerable variations in effort are possible. Effort can be decomposed into (1) the activities chosen by the employee, denoted by A, (2) the pace at which activities are carried out, P, (3) the quality aspect of each activity, Q, and (4) the time sequence, T, of activities and hence the way in which these dovetail with other persons' activities. Thus each person in a firm may be said to interpret his job by chosing an APQT bundle within externally imposed constraints so as to maximize his personal utility. There is no reason that APQT bundles chosen in such a way should minimize costs. If the incentives for coordinating one person's activities with another's are strong enough, this should lead to more effective production activities, providing there are clear indications of the types of activities that advance the firm's objectives. If such incentives are not strong, then we should expect that the effort levels (that is the APQT bundles) chosen freely would be sufficiently low to cause low levels of production. Even under considerable supervision, employees can perform at a wide variety of effort levels along each dimension.

Hence the firm should provide incentives to keep effort levels high or to prevent them from falling to unusually low levels. Now relatively high wages compared to the transfer wage from agriculture may provide such an incentive. Thus we can visualize a wage-effort bargain, and a wage-effort relation that in part influences the wage rate actually paid. Such a relation is illustrated in Figure 3. The curve WE represents the wage-effort relation. Up to some point the higher the wage the greater the effort produced, but above some wage no additional effort is forthcoming. Rays drawn from the origin marked $w_1, w_2, w_3 \ldots$ represent constant wage-effort ratios. Clearly

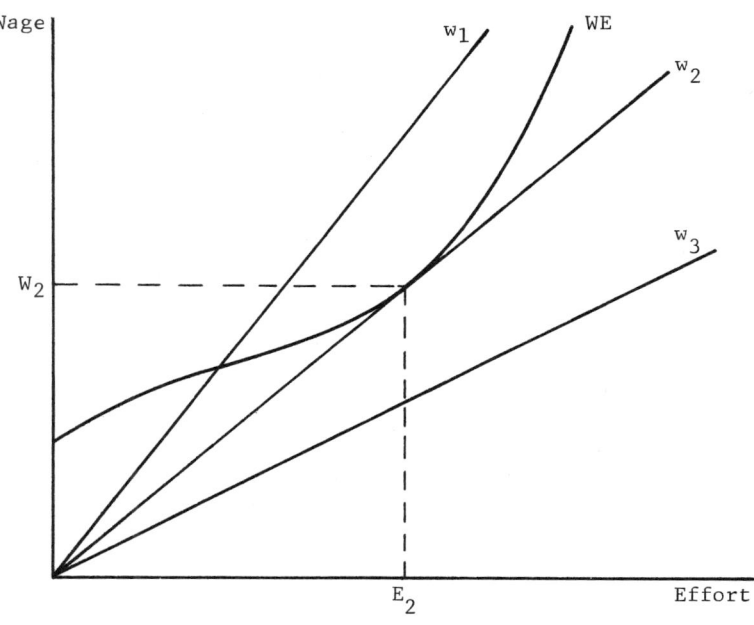

Figure 3

the firm wants to be on as low a wage ray as possible. Hence the point of tangency between WE and w_2 represents a wage rate associated with the lowest cost per unit of effort. W_2 is an efficiency wage, sets a floor to the wage rate. If such efficiency wages are fairly universal in the modern sector, then free market wage flexibility cannot lead to full employment.

There is an important and elusive psychological aspect involved: the assessment of risk and the firm's attitude towards risk. If things are going reasonably well when each firm adopts the relatively capital-intensive technique borrowed from abroad, one successful in the lending country, there is no need for any specific firm to take the risk of initiating a more labor intensive technique. In general, innovators feel that they face greater risks than followers. The followers have the advantage of being able to obtain some knowledge of what works as against what does not work for the innovator. Thus a conservative policy for a borrowing country innovator is to copy a process that works well in the lending country. An exact copy may appear to offer a lower risk than experimenting with possible variants of the lending country's technology that are consistent with higher labor intensity but for which there is no previous experience. Once the innovating firm copies the lending country's procedure, it would seem natural for follower firms in the borrowing country to copy the same procedure in the hope of minimizing risk. Hence the potential risk elements in the situation create incentives against developing technological adaptations more suitable to the borrowing country. If the government tries to encourage investments by subsidizing the importation of equipment from abroad without regard to its adaptation to local conditions, this increases any existing tendency to avoid labor-using adaptations, since it lowers the relative price of capital.

The above analysis suggests that the policy a country should follow in the interest of reducing unemployment is to tax "unadapted" imported equipment and to subsidize imports of equipment adapted so that it is labor absorbing. In Figure 4 below such a tax and subsidy scheme is illustrated. The initial point x_0 represents the capital-labor ratio of the equipment as used in the lending country. The line TS represents capital costs inclusive of taxes or subsidies as the number of workers changes. L_1 represents an estimate of the proportionate share of workers that this particular piece of equipment would have to absorb so that full employment would result if all planned additions to capital absorbed their share. The amount $s_0 s_1$ represents the subsidy necessary per \$1000 worth of capital (K_0 is assumed to be \$1000) to induce the adaptation of capital to absorb labor to the degree indicated. Needless to say, this is not intended as a theory of optimal subsidies for developing countries. Many other considerations would have to be taken into account to work out an optimal

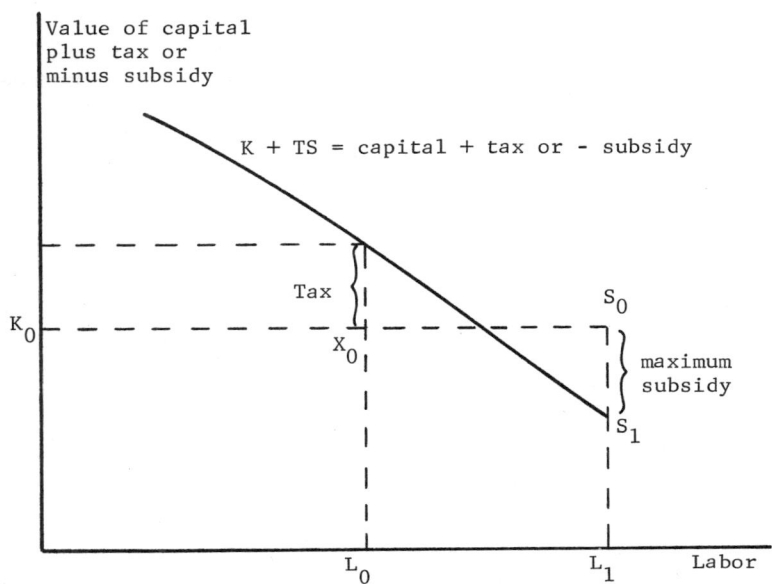

K_0 = value of capital without tax or subsidy

Figure 4

program. But there probably is a need in many countries to subsidize the adaptation of imported hardware and managerial knowledge so as to provide the incentives for the borrowing country to insist on equipment that contributes to development and at the same time is labor absorbing.

CONCLUSION

There are holes in the production function precisely for those points that imply borrowed technologies appropriate to the developing countries' factor endowments. The most visible aspect of production procedures is inappropriate to the borrowing country's factor endowments. A given production procedure is likely to be characterized by two highly visible elements: a critical or focal apparatus or piece of equipment, and an effective routine mode of operation. But the basic and applied knowledge surrounding these two basic elements usually implies the possible development of many potential variants of the hardware and the mode of operation, as well as various other aspects that form the nonroutine parts of the production process. Thus, implicit in the highly visible aspects of the production process, there may exist a relatively large set of variants much more appropriate to the factor availabilities in the developing country—if only very strong incentives existed in the developing country to search for such variants.

DISCUSSION

SHIMON AMIR (Israel): My comments relate to the 25 least developed countries. Transfer of technology should be regarded as complementary to training. Transfers are imported. Training is usually done in one's own country.

In the least developed states the main problem is to increase output capacity. Israel has engaged mainly in technical assistance in agriculture. But sometimes we have been asked to help with industrialization. Someone comes and asks us to establish a school for entrepreneurs. How can one explain that there is no such thing.

The major is the quantity of knowledge available. This can be supplemented; but there is also a shortage of managerial capacity—the capacity to organize, direct, and manage—or of material resources. Finally, there is a shortage of entrepreneurial capacity—the ability to manage finance or marketing, and to forecast and to take risks.

We tried to tackle the problem by establishing joint enterprises, such as the Black Star Line in Ghana. This worked until the local partner said that he was ready to take over. Then the joint venture was transformed into a management contract, the Israeli company (ZIM Navigation) becoming simply a manager. At the third stage ZIM was only providing consultant services. Finally, ZIM remained just an agent for the Black Star Line.

Mixed companies were established in building and construction in several states of Africa and Asia. In the Ivory Coast, an Israeli company has a management contract to direct and maintain a large quantity of agricultural machinery. The local corporation now insists that the Israelis should become partners and participate in the risks.

The concept of rural centers is important. A rural center for 80 or 100 villages can provide services that each individual village cannot provide because it is too small. These can include social and economic services, a small cooperative shop, a school, a clinic, and an agricultural machinery center.

Another idea we have tried out in Israel are industrial estates, aimed at modernizing the small business with less than 20 employees.

The estate provides modern buildings and facilities, water, power, and—at a later stage—joint accounting or joint marketing for those interested.

PAUL P. STREETEN (Great Britain): How can one transfer the simple technology of a spade to a society where people don't wear shoes ? One cannot use a spade barefoot. One would have to find a very ingenious adaptation.

The problem of filling the holes in the production function is difficult because we are trying to fill two types of gaps, which may demand contradictory actions. One problem is to collect information about technologies available, to have catalogues, to have incentives to use capital-saving technologies or low-tax technologies. This may be called the communications gap. The more we improve information and incentives, possibly provide subsidies and taxes, the more incentive there is to make the appropriate technologies available to the state concerned.

But there is also what may be called the suitability gap. Even if all the information were available, certain types of technologies would still be inappropriate and inefficient for certain countries. The crucial point is that the incentive to fill this suitability gap is reduced by a very open type of economy, by training abroad, and by catalogues of foreign technologies. The need to partly close off some economies is comprehensible only in terms of creating incentives and the capacity to evolve appropriate indigenous technologies. This conflicts with narrowing the communications gap. Communist China and Tanzania succeeded in this sphere by keeping their economies largely closed.

Companies producing for high-income markets have no incentives to evolve simple technologies that are easily initiated. So to provide incentives for sound local technologies, it may be better to reduce communications and the transfer of technologies from developed states. Instead, an indigenous research capacity should be created.

SOLON BARRACLOUGH (Food & Agriculture Organization, Santiago): There is a modern technological system that will impose itself in most situations, unless action is taken to close the economy, as in China.

In the Mississippi Delta, where there is a labor surplus, I put in a sawmill with a labor-intensive logging technology, using newels, handsaws, and labor. This was most profitable at the going wage rates. But since the TVA had a power line in the area, I plugged the newels into it with electric motors and suddenly had excess capacity. So I had to speed up logging — and put in some chain saws. Then I needed a derrick to load logs and also a bulldozer. And I found they now only make big bulldozers. So my whole system had excess capacity, and I had to enlarge my mill again. The same sort of thing happens in LDCs.

We wanted to put in labor-intensive equipment for logging in southern Chile, but such equipment is not available because it is not being made any more. The Chilean planners are aware of employment problems but don't want to put in second-best equipment.

Professor Streeten has suggested a possible approach, but except for China few states are likely to take it.

GUSTAV PAPANEK (United States): Taxing advanced technology and subsidizing labor-intensive technology may provide more employment. In Indonesia they adopted differential taxes on different methods of making cigarettes and bottling soft drinks. One can tell easily by inspection if cigarettes are rolled by hand or produced by an automated machine, or whether bottles are being put into cases by hand or by a machine. Other suitable industries for such a policy were not found.

But subsidizing labor-intensive technologies is unfeasible in most countries, for administrative reasons. The next best solution may be to subsidize unskilled labor. This, too, is difficult. The third-best solution would be to raise the price of capital or lower the real wage indirectly. The easiest way to lower the real wage is to undervalue your own exchange rate. In practice, most states overvalue their currency.

Undervaluation of currency means - unless wages adjust very quickly - a raising of the prices of traded goods and a lowering of the real wage rate. This is not undesirable on equity grounds, as those who receive a regular wage are usually not the poorest. One could also raise the price of imported capital goods by tariffs. Again, most states lower the price of such goods artificially, which is the opposite of what is needed.

HELEN HUGHES (IBRD): In many countries there is a wide range of adaptive technology. You can find it in the back streets of Taipei, Hong Kong, Singapore, or Bangkok and also in Brazil.

Labor-intensive technologies are very tied to certain types of products. There is a range of products for which there is a real choice of capital-labor techniques, and there is a range of products for which there isn't. If you have much oil refining, or produce sophisticated products such as motor cars, there are hardly any adaptive technologies. The real policy choice is therefore in the choice of products.

Production can be restricted to products lending themselves to labor-intensive technologies. One can put high taxes on air conditioners and make water coolers (which lend themselves to labor-intensive technologies) instead. But this means, for instance, that people like us would have to go to work by bicycle or bus instead of by car. In most LDCs this is a political problem. The people who rule do not want to live in the kind of world implied by more labor-intensive production.

Anyway, manufacturing employs only a very small proportion of the labor force in LDCs—even in Taiwan and Korea only 10 percent to 15 percent. Now governments can influence the nonmanufacturing sector much more easily. In public works, they can use more labor-intensive factor proportions than they do. We should therefore be concentrating on agriculture, construction, public works, and the modern service sectors to solve the employment problem in LDCs.

WILFRED BECKERMAN (Great Britain): How far do the holes in the production function exist simply because some prices are not right? Would they disappear if prices were right? The reasons cited by the ILO study are, in fact, price distortions: cheap capital, low interest rates, an overvalued exchange rate, high wages in modern sectors.

If I am right, we don't have to look for new tax or subsidy policies to correct the situation. We have simply to get rid of some of the existing taxes, subsidies, and wrong exchange rates. Information is also a product, and it probably is not correctly priced. I would thus like to question the basic position that the holes are independent of the price structure.

THOMAS CARROLL (Inter-American Development Bank): The labor-managed or cooperative economy might be a good way for better technological adaptation, especially in agriculture. In this system labor has a share in the ownership of assets and a share of the profits. The behaviour of such firms tends to be more in line with the public interest in favoring labor-intensive technologies. Since labor is not only a cost here but also a participant in the profits, its minimization is not a major objective.

Where large-scale machinery use is unavoidable, the labor-managed system is more likely to succeed in combining a highly capital-intensive technology with a more labor-intensive one. A cooperative in Honduras managed to combine a highly computerized banana packing plant with nontractorized banana production on 7-acre family units. The units were kept small to increase the number of members.

Today there are few strong incentives in LDCs to search for labor-intensive technology variants, except in states like China where there is a social commitment to this sort of thing. Research and development are crucial, and their cost should be borne largely by the public sector. Tinkering with the price system and taxation will not solve our basic problem.

RICHARD ABLIN (Israel): If efficiency is positively linked to capital intensity, as I think it may be, reducing capital intensity of certain production forms may actually reduce efficiency. This makes me worry about raising interest rates or taxing capital goods, since the result may be a deceleration of economic growth and less efficiency.

It seems to me that excessively high wage rates in the modern sector (inclusive of fringe benefits) are a serious cause of unemployment and of the apparent holes in the production function discussed by Professor Leibenstein.

ASHER HALPERIN (Israel): It was recommended that transfer of capital-intensive technology should be discouraged, and labor-intensive technology should be encouraged. This suits LDCs with a surplus of labor, disguised unemployment, or underemployment. But in some LDCs there are labor shortages, anyway in certain sectors. Would this policy recommendation be applicable to these states?

HARVEY LEIBENSTEIN (United States): The answer to Professor Halperin's question is negative. My recommendation was intended for countries with a relatively high degree of unemployment or underemployment.

I recommend an incentives system under which an entrepreneur, engineer, or anyone else who has an idea should have an incentive to labor-stretch whatever the equipment happens to be or whatever service is involved.

Professor Beckerman suggests that the existence of the holes I mentioned in the production function is due to wrong prices. Wrong prices are frequently good reasons. They are partially real reasons but not the only real reasons. Let us take knowledge or information. I cannot convince you to buy an idea before I indicate to you what it is. So I have to give it away before I have an opportunity to charge you for it. Here you have one gap that exists.

There is a feeling among economists that the burden of proof always rests on someone who makes an assertion that is new. I do not accept this. I cannot answer whether no holes would exist if all prices were right, because some prices are always wrong owing to government interventions. No price will create an incentive to get all prices right.

What you have to do is to change institutions. If you have a monopoly, you must make it into a competitive industry, for example. Frequently prices do not create incentives to break up monopolies but work the other way.

Some of Mr. Amir's ideas seem very good. I agree with Mrs. Hughes that we should not emphasize manufacturing. I did not mean to. But even services and construction use equipment of various kinds. In fact, construction is a good example of a sector in which there are many alternative possibilities, and in which perhaps the wrong ones are used.

I do not agree that the policy choice is only the choice of products. I am not sure that it is necessary to eliminate motor cars and force everyone to use a bicycle. There may be some optimal combination of the two. But bicycles need safe paths just as much as cars need safe roads.

Professor Streeten has a good point. It is not good to give every user of information the same catalogue. He may choose something not appropriate for him. Firms in developed countries selling equipment or knowledge should prepare different catalogues for different countries.

Some states have a comparative advantage in manufacturing, others in agricultural produce. It is possible to have highly capital-intensive commodities in manufacturing and highly labor-intensive methods in agriculture, with very different wage rates in the two sectors and everyone employed. However, this does not strike me as desirable. An income distribution with a well-to-do urban population and a poor agricultural population is not to be recommended.

My three main recommendations are as follows:

- Countries should review their tax subsidies and control procedures, so as to remove incentives to borrowing inappropriate technologies.
- Countries should prepare tax or subsidy schemes and other types of incentives to induce their entrepreneurs to search for less visible adaptations of borrowable technology appropriate to local conditions.
- States should attempt to arrange research and development cooperation with manufacturers and engineers in advanced countries, so that the latter attempt to design equipment appropriate to the conditions and factor prices of the borrowing state.

**A POLICY FOR THE
PURCHASE OF TECHNOLOGY
BY LATIN AMERICAN COUNTRIES**
José Maria Dagnino Pastore

Here the concept of technology transfer is limited to elements of technical knowledge necessary to build and operate new productive facilities.

So defined, technology transfers may adopt the following forms: equipment (and parts); inputs (raw materials, intermediate products, components); advice by foreign technicians; training for local technicians; disembodied items, such as industrial patents, designs and trademarks, details engineering, blue prints, diagrams, models, instructions, formulations, specifications, studies and reports.

A national technology policy covers four areas: imports of new knowledge, adaptation and application of new knowledge, production of new knowledge, and exports of new knowledge. They are related: If the production of technology is promoted, neglecting imports completely, the effort may well be fruitless. It is also impossible to restrict imports without supporting the local productive structure. To develop an autonomous capacity for managing the technological flow, a simultaneous capacity to create technology and to control its imports must be developed.

The technology trade excludes unilateral technology transfers.

The technology trade relevant for Latin America and Argentina is that in which developed countries (DCs) sell and LDCs buy. Exchanges between DCs and LDCs are excluded, as are the insignificant technology exports from LDC to DC.

In the last years Latin America has witnessed an important movement of opinion and serious research efforts resulting in new legislation on technology transfer and industrial property, as well as increasing activity of regional and international organizations on these subjects.

THE TECHNOLOGY TRADE

LDCs can supply their domestic markets with goods not produced internally so far by: imports from abroad, foreign investment for their local production by a foreign firm, or foreign licencing for their local production by a national enterprise. There are, of course, intermediate ways of doing it. The forms of technology transfer corresponding to the procurement alternatives are: final goods (insignificant productive effect); equipment inputs, persons, and disembodied items; or the latter, with a higher proportion of disembodied items and local experts.

For the infant industry argument to hold, not only must the protected industry eventually become competitive with foreign suppliers but it must yield an acceptable social rate of return on the investment during the initial protection period.

The appraisal of the technology transfer situation performed by the United Nations Conference on Trade and Development (UNCTAD) in April 1972 points out that foreign payments by LDCs for technology transfers reached U.S. $1,500 million in 1970. The forecast is that they will reach U.S. $9,000 million, or some 15 percent of the estimated value of LDC exports, in 1980.

The tendency to substitute technology purchases for imports of final products is also clear in LDCs.

What factors cause these trends? One explanation is that the demand for technology has grown and keeps growing fast. This is reflected by new products and processes as well as by new forms of old products and processes with a higher technology content.

On the other hand, the supply of technology has been geographically concentrated in DCs. Exports of equipment, inputs, technicians, and disembodied items from DCs to LDCs have shown a rapid increase.

From the LDCs' viewpoint, they needed more technology for their exports, for their domestic markets, and for import substitution. Their internal technology output lagged as compared with requirements. The result has been a sharp rise in the need for technology imports. This has caused rapid increases in payments abroad for technology, balance of payments problems, or failure to meet the requirements with a consequent reduction in the rate of growth. The mix and intensity of these effects vary according to the LDC considered.

What is at stake is not only the cost of technology in foreign exchange and control, but also the choice and adaptation of technology and, in the final instance, the development of a local capability for technological innovation.

In the international technology market there are built-in tendencies towards insufficient quantities of transference and towards excessively high costs for LDCs.

Some of the reasons supporting the first statement are: the payments situation of some LDCs, which prevents the satisfaction of their technology needs; the notorious imperfection of the technology market in reference to buyers, sellers, and information; and the artificially high costs of transfers.

The excessively high costs for the LDCs are caused by monopolistic elements inherent in the supply, inadequate purchasing policies of LDCs, the weak bargaining position of local licencees, and the excessive risk and cost of development resulting from a given form of transfer.

The following indicate the qualitative importance of the subject:
- Foreign payments for technology by LDCs will reach US $9.000 million by 1980.
- Such payments increase by 20 percent annually, exclusive of payments for technology disguised as other forms of foreign transfers

The high cost of technology especially affects LDCs with balance of payments problems but also those without them. Where the actual restriction derives from the trade gap, any exchange saving frees funds for other uses permitting an acceleration of the growth rate.

In LDCs without balance of payments problems the high cost of technology reduces welfare, since it lowers their participation in the gains from international trade and affects their income levels negatively

Finally, the excessively high costs of technology limit the quantities transferred leading to an inefficient resource allocation.

From the LDCs' viewpoint, the cost of technology imports is composed of foreign payments, explicit or otherwise. Explicit foreign payments include those for:

(a) the right to use patents, licenses, know-how, and trade marks; (b) technical knowledge and know-how required in preinvestment, investment, and operating stages.

Nonexplicit foreign payments include those for:

(a) overpricing of equipment and input imports; (b) profits on the capitalization of know-how; (c) part of the remittance of benefits by branches or joint ventures that do not make specific provisions for payment of technology transfers; (d) imports of capital and other technical equipment, the prices of which usually include the cost of technology to the exporter.

Other components of the cost to LDCs of technology imports result from restrictive practices of transnational enterprises or from restrictive clauses in technology transfer contracts with local firms. They include: tied equipment and input supplies, export limitations, mandatory purchase of service from captive firms (for example, advertising), selling price determination, restriction of output volume and structure, exclusive technology and prohibition of change, mandatory transfer of inventions or improvements, and royalty payments on unused patents or trade marks.

In several LDCs, nonexplicit foreign payments are several times larger than the explicit. In Colombia the overpricing of inputs varied for the pharmaceutical industry between 19 and 55 percent; for the rubber industry between 0 and 40 percent; for the chemical industry between 20 and 25 percent; and for the electronic industry between 6 and 70 percent. This means that overpricing was in many cases the largest remittance to the licensing firms, well above those for profits and royalties.

As to equipment overpricing, there are reasons to overstate values both in investment and in licensing: capital recovery clauses, profit remittances, rules of access to local credit, and so on.

THE PURCHASE OF TECHNOLOGY BY LATIN AMERICAN COUNTRIES

Here I consider the alternative open to LDCs for the acquisition of technology with domestic market destination. The discussion applies especially to LDCs with relatively large internal markets and processes of industrialization already launched. The purchase of technology for exports is left aside.

The discussion is geared towards policies and instruments available to LDCs to pursue specific import substitution objectives at the least possible cost. Generally LDCs have followed during the last decades an industrialization policy based upon high tariffs on imports of consumption goods. The results of this policy can be summarized as follows:

In national enterprises high levels of internal prices, caused by protection levels that originate and maintain degopolistic structures, mean a transfer of income from domestic consumers to national producers. Income so transferred will have secondary effects inside the country. As regards international enterprises, a protectionist policy leads, through high internal prices, to the transfer of income from local consumers to foreign consumers or producers.

Consequently we pass on to discuss import substitution through foreign investment and through national investment with foreign technology.

Import Substitution Through Foreign Investment

In import substitution through foreign investment the LDC's objectives are to attract foreign investment and to get it at the lowest total cost (including foreign payments and other components) and at the lowest foreign exchange cost.

If conditions prevailing previously have not attracted foreign investment to manufacture locally a given product, the most effective method is to raise the level of effective protection for the local manufacture of the product (taxes, credits, and so on affecting costs are also part of effective protection). This level is the main determinant of the rate of return on investment for the foreign firm and of the cost of substitution for the LDC. Its determination is the most important policy decision regarding foreign investment for import substitution.

Potential foreign investors are willing to produce locally a given good if the expected rate of return exceeds the rate of return on alternative investments. If they are exporters, they will include in their calculations the loss of their market share if they do not invest. They will also perceive that, if they do not produce locally, the market will be closed to them for future investments. The opportunity cost of funds sets a floor to the levels of effective protection that make foreign investment feasible.

On the other hand, the LDC may raise the level of effective protection to that needed to generate the same product level in other sectors.

If the LDC suffers from a trade gap, it will raise the level of effective protection to that needed to generate the same foreign exchange level in other sectors. These are ceilings to the level of effective protection that make foreign investment possible in a given activity.

If the floor is higher than the ceiling, there is no level of effective protection that makes foreign investment possible in the given activity. If the floor is lower than the ceiling, there is a range of effective protection levels that makes such investment possible. Where the level of protection, and the consequent rates of return for the foreign firm and substitution costs for LDCs, settle within the range depends on the international capital market situation.

The LDC needs additional instruments to avoid the transfer of funds abroad in excess of the terms agreed. The control of the behavior agreed upon by the foreign firm in the transfer of funds abroad requires exchange control with the unavoidable black market problems. Without exchange control the system falls apart.

Generally, under an exchange control system, there are a commercial exchange market and a financial one. Foreign exchange is cheaper in the first. Imports are subject to tariffs. Operations not permitted in either market are illegally carried on in the black market, where foreign exchange is more expensive than in the financial market.

Under these circumstances the foreign enterprise can transfer funds abroad, in excess of the terms agreed upon, by overpricing imports, or through the black markets. In general, overinvoicing imports is not illegal. The transfer of funds through the illegal black market can generate additional costs.

Under those conditions, if the foreign enterprise transfers funds abroad in excess of the terms agreed, it does so by paying the commercial foreign exchange rate plus the ad valorem tariff on the overpriced goods or by buying illegal foreign exchange in the black market with funds previously extracted from the firm. In the latter case—the illegal character of the operation aside—the foreign exchange cost is composed of the black foreign exchange rate plus an eventual additional cost of extracting the funds from the firm.

Under the free exchange market system there is only one exchange market and one exchange rate. Imports are subject to tariffs of different heights.

Under these circumstances, the foreign enterprise can transfer funds abroad in excess of the terms agreed by overpricing imports, or through the free market. The transfer of funds through the free market is legal but requires the previous extraction of funds from the firm. According to the tax system of the countries involved, this can generate additional costs. In general, overinvoicing of imports is not illegal.

Overpricing of imports is more convenient for the foreign enterprise than the transfer of funds through the free market if the ad valorem tariff on overinvoiced goods is lower than the eventual additional cost of extracting funds from the firm.

Import Substitution Through National Investment with Foreign Technology

In import substitution with national investment and foreign technology, the LDC's objectives are to get the project done and to get it at the lowest total cost (including foreign payments and other components) and at the lowest foreign exchange cost. In this case the LDCs substitution cost is not so strongly correlated with the rate of return on investment, because part of the benefits go to the local producer and part to the supplier of foreign technology.

If conditions previously prevailing have not attracted national investment to manufacture locally a given product, the LDC should create some attractive conditions by raising the level of effective protection for the local manufacture of this product (nontariff incentives, including tax concessions, credits, and supplies, affecting costs are also part of effective protection).

But such measures attract not only national but also foreign investment. If the first is wanted, a differential advantage should be offered to national firms. Potential national investors are willing to produce locally a given good if the expected rate of return exceeds the expected rate of return on alternative investments. An important factor in the computation of profitability is the cost to the national firm of getting foreign technology. The opportunity cost of funds sets a floor to the levels of effective protection that make national investment possible.

On the other hand, the LDC will raise the level of effective protection insofar as it does not exceed the level needed to generate the same product level in other sectors. This sets a ceiling on levels of effective protection that make national investment in a given activity possible.

If the floor is higher than the ceiling there is no level of effective protection that makes national investment possible in the given activity. If the floor is lower than the ceiling there is a range of effective protection levels making such investment feasible. Where the level of protection settles within the range depends on the internal capital market situation but also on the bargaining position of national firms vis-a-vis the suppliers of foreign technology.

State approval of the technology contracts with firms abroad is based on the need to strengthen the bargaining power of national firms to get a more equitable partition of benefits and avoid the raising of the floor up to the ceiling of effective protection, which would increase the substitution cost for the LDC.

The state can strengthen the local firms' bargaining position by refusing to approve some contracts and providing information.

A POLICY FOR THE PURCHASE OF TECHNOLOGY BY LATIN AMERICAN COUNTRIES

The level of effective protection is the key element in the determination of the cost of import substitution in foreign investment. It also determines the volume of national investment with foreign technology.

A careful policy of foreign technology purchases should be complemented by a policy of internal technological development. This policy should include the following elements: (a) a general design of effective protection sectorial levels, both current and desired. The concept of effective protection should include nontariff components that affect costs (such as taxes, credits, and supplies); (b) knowledge of input and product prices in LDCs and abroad; and (c) a system of import substitution that induces competition.

There should be a public bidding system, national or international, for installation and operation of productive facilities. In many cases this method stimulates the interest of investors and induces them to approach with their offers their rentability floor. Besides, a proper design of the bidding system makes it possible to collect from each offer the information necessary to determine effective protection. This facilitates comparisons of different offers.

State selection of international or national investment offers should include the following elements: (a) tax advantages assuring that in some sectors import substitution is reserved for national firms, or (b) establishment of differential incentives in favor of national firms; (c) prerequisite of government approval of foreign investments, and (d) prerequisite of government approval of national investments with foreign technology.

The first two elements complement each other as components of an import substitution policy. The first instrument applies when extraeconomic considerations are dominant. The second instrument, more flexible, may constitute an indicator of the relative advantages of foreign over national firms in different sectors.

The third element happens naturally, since the foreign investor requests a state guarantee for capital recovery and the transfer of benefits. But it is not enough for the state to set conditions and to grant guarantees to foreign enterprises willing to invest. Frequently the size of the market requires, to avoid waste of resources, a limited number of plants. Besides, if the number of offers exceeds the reasonable number of plants (often just one), selection is needed. Then it becomes a state function to set the number of plants and to select the more convenient offers. These conditions apply also to the fourth element.

Foreign payments should not exceed the amounts stipulated after consideration of welfare and balance of payments.

This aspect of policy implementation should include the following elements: (a) detailed determination of the concepts and conditions ruling foreign payments at the time of approval of the investment or contract; (b) a system that limits overpricing of equipment and inputs; (c) a system that limits the extraction of funds from the firms.

The first element leads to the sums to be transferred for each of the approved concepts. The second element admits many alternative instruments directed to penalize overpricing. Such instruments have a common prerequisite—information on input and product prices abroad.

The third element may be accomplished in two alternative ways: initial agreement as to reinvestment levels or establishment of the system of nominative shares for corporations.

The first instrument partially avoids the extraction of funds from the firm with unknown destination. The second traces the destination of funds and consequently, through fiscal control, makes more difficult their transfer abroad.

It must be mentioned that the system of nominative shares has many other effects, probably more far reaching, which must be considered before deciding upon it.

The enhancement of the bargaining power of national firms vis-a-vis the suppliers of foreign technology is aimed at reaching a more equitable distribution of the benefits of projects and at avoiding the increase in the cost of import substitution, via the level of effective protection, to the LDC resulting from the bargaining power of the said suppliers.

This aspect of policy implementation should include the following elements: (a) prerequisite of government approval of technology contracts with foreign firms; (b) provision of technological information and of data on inputs and products prices abroad to national firms; and (c) the adoption of an intellectual property system adjusted to the interests of the LDC.

The first element is another face of the prerequisite of government approval of national investments with foreign technology. The chance of a LDC's not approving a contract opens up the possibility of its replacing the national firms at the negotiation table, thus turning the structure of the demand for technology from competitive into monopolistic.

The diffusion of technological information is one of the central subjects of any national technological policy. Not as frequent, however, is the preoccupation with information of inputs and product prices abroad. Nevertheless such information is necessary for the LDCs to execute the policy designed for the purchase of technology.

The last element refers to the fact that under very different technological conditions a legal system of equal or reciprocal treatment leads to inequitable results for some states. This justifies the existence of different laws for LDCs.

National legislation in LDCs should (a) grant rights for the use and exploitation of patents and similar instruments for relatively short periods, which should help to reduce the duration of royalty payments; (b) include clauses of compulsory licensing or working after brief periods, which should help to reduce the duration of export monopolies in LDCs markets; (c) grant rights for the use and exploitations of trademarks only when they bring some innovation or technical progress; (d) provide wide publicity for patents, designs, and models.

International action should aim at (a) strengthening the World Intellectual Property Organization as an instrument for the collection and distribution of technological information protected by property rights, and (b) creating regional centers to support the action of national patents offices with technological information.

APPENDIX

The Purchase of Technology in Argentina

1. Imports of Services (millions of dollars)

Year	Royalties	Com-missions	Fees, Expenses, and Salaries	Benefits and Dividends	Total
1967	57.6	15.6	5.0	55.8	134.0
1968	64.3	18.7	5.5	97.0	185.5
1969	68.1	24.9	6.4	107.9	207.3
1970	70.5	24.7	6.3	72.5	174.0
1971	79.8	27.7	7.6	47.8	162.9

2. Technological balance of payments (millions of dollars)

Year	Royalties	Com-missions	Fees, Expenses, and Salaries	Benefits and Dividends	Total
1967	−55.9	−6.8	2.7	−54.2	−114.2
1968	−62.6	−9.0	3.0	−92.2	−160.8
1969	−63.8	−12.9	3.5	−104.8	−178.0
1970	−61.2	−11.6	3.3	−69.5	−139.0
1971	−75.1	−14.9	4.0	−46.0	−132.0

3. Data from a sample of 60 license contracts, 1970

Objects of contracts (in decreasing order of frequency)
technical assistance in production
rights of use of trademarks
rights of use of patents
rights of use plans, formulae, processes, and so on.
others

Explicit costs of transfer
| Average | 5 percent over sales |
| Extreme case | 35 percent over sales |

Duration of contracts
| From 2 to 3 years | 20 percent |
| From 7 to 10 years | 30 percent |

Clauses on exports
Prohibition 30 percent

4. Input Overpricing in the Pharmaceutical Industry

Pharmaceutical active principles	Country of Origin	Overpricing Percentages, 1970
Polaramina and its synonymes	Germany	60
	United States	7100
Diphenyl-Hydantoine and its salts	United States	950
	Switzerland	40
	United Kingdom	20
Perfenazina and its synonymes	United States	1600
	Panama	1400
9 alfa fluor	France	700
Predmisolona	Portugal	770
Betametasona	United Kingdom	900
	Switzerland	4250
Librium and its synonymes	Germany	64
	Italy	11
	Switzerland	4800
Chlorotrimeton and its derivatives	United States	900
	Japan	50
	Netherlands	140
	Switzerland	4

DISCUSSION

GINTON SHALEV (Israel): There are problems between governments, and even within the same country, in connection with the transfer of technology. Let us assume we have an optimal pricing policy, the right general principles. What happens next?

Policy is important. I will give you an Israeli example. Some 20 years ago we bought French Chausson buses. You don't see them on the roads any more; they were junk. We also bought all the ancient taxis of New York and an old steel mill that failed, partly because it was a junkyard. Besides, a government policy on the transfer of personal effects to Israel by immigrants favored imports of junk, not new things.

All this was corrected in the last 20 years, but the problem of junk transfers to developing countries remains. Nobody learned from our experience.

Big Israeli companies acquired topflight automation equipment. Israel power stations have the latest technology, so have some of our chemical plants such as the Dead Sea Works. But this has had no effect at all on the rest of Israeli industry. The successful transfer of technologies to some big industries, therefore, does not mean that the whole country has acquired them.

The average size of an Israeli company is 13.5 workers, as against about 50 in England and about 200 in the United States; but some Israeli companies employ more than 10,000. So the large majority are very small. If a big company has computers, this has no bearing on the small one. This problem must be faced.

Economic incentives to use new technologies may not be enough. The most difficult thing is to get management going. Unfortunately, people don't start working on administrative, maintenance, or marketing problems before they have bought equipment. From Germany we bought the most recent machinery for making wooden doors, for which there is a big market. We import them from Taiwan, Yugoslavia, and Spain. Yet the machinery stands idle because nobody knows how to operate it. Apparently other countries do the same sort of thing. We ourselves have done it many times before.

So how do we know when a technology transfer is successful? If we buy technology, modify it to our needs, add to it by our own research, and then interest another developing country in accepting it from us and successfully train them in its use—only then do we know that the first policy decision was correct. Only when a country is successful as a donor of technology does it know that it was successful as its acceptor.

LE VAN PHUC (Vietnam): If foreign investors are permitted to invest only on condition that a certain percentage of their output will be exported, it may be possible to control them through free-market forces, as they are then unlikely to overprice equipment imports and will be more concerned with costs.

In Southeast Asia we have an Export Processing Zone, where foreign investors can bring and sell anything they wish, without interference from the host country. But still the host country benefits through the use of its labor. Besides, if so desired, the foreign investor can be permitted to sell in the domestic market on the same terms that he sells for export.

SHIMON AMIR (Israel): In new assembly industries there was a high motivation to produce on the basis of very little local added value. To encourage the import of improved technology time limits were imposed. First one just assembled. After five years or so, one was supposed to produce locally 10 percent-15 perent of the finished product. At the end of the process, the produced item was sometimes junk.

JOSE MARIA DAGNINO PASTORE (Argentina): I agree that many problems of technological development cannot be solved by policy alone. I would not accept exports as a total indicator of successful technological developments, but they can be a partial indicator. A point should be reached that one produces at competitive prices. But there are nontraded goods and services, which are never exported; so exports cannot be a total indicator. One can be competitive without exporting.

The deepening of local production has an important impact on technology transfers. It is up to the enterprise to select the inputs most convenient to produce locally. Multinational corporations sometimes tend to a comparative advantage division of labor between the different states where they operate.

On 80 percent of the automobile production input, the difference between costs of imports and local output may be small. But if you demand that 95 percent of the input be produced locally, you may be incurring heavy additional costs.

**RAPPORTEUR'S REPORT—
GROUP B**
Meir Heth

Economic growth of individual states cannot take place in isolation from the outside world. Cooperation between developed and less developed countries can accelerate the growth processes of the latter.

This field was dealt with by Working Group B under the heading of "External Constraints on Development." Though much attention was devoted to constraints on growth caused by external factors, it was recognized that international trade, capital imports, and technology transfers can be agents of growth rather than constraints.

To most developing states growth is synonymous with industrialization. Transforming low-income agrarian, nearly self-sufficient economies into diversified industrial ones inevitably involves trade development. The concepts of free trade and comparative advantage appeal to common sense, but the realities of industrialization often conflict with free trade principles. Developing states are faced by trade barriers erected by more developed nations, while internal pressures demand inward-looking policies protected by tariffs, and so forth.

Mrs. Helen Hughes, in her paper on protection and import substitution, argued that in many states high protective tariffs created inefficiencies in the protected industries and distorted the allocation of resources but that there are good grounds to protect industry in the early stages of its development, while a certain level of self-sufficiency and some diversification are regarded by newly independent states as desirable for their own sakes. The choice for most LDCs is not between protection and free trade but between a cumbersome system of high, differentiated tariffs and a simple structure of moderate tariffs that would protect infant industries to some extent without distorting the economic structure.

Japan made good use of protection; so did South Korea. Professor Song of the Sung Kiang Kwang University of Seoul described the protective policy of Korea as the stepping stone to its remarkable industrial expansion in the 1960s, stressing that the success should

---

Meir Heth is from Israel.

be attributed to a shift from protection of import substitutes to the promotion of industrial exports.

The distorting effects of promoting exports by subsidies may be as severe as those of tariff protection for import substitutes. Yet export promotion seems to yield better results than import substitution. This was elaborated by Carlos Diaz Alejandro of Cuba, professor at Yale University, with reference to Colombia. Export promotion policies had positive effects on Colombia's growth rate and the stability of its balance of payments but not on the employment level or on income distribution.

Export promotion has succeeded in stimulating industrial growth in only a few LDCs. The obstacles facing LDCs trying to expand industrial exports were dealt with by Dr. Juergen Donges of Kiel University and by Daniel Schydlowsky of Peru, a professor at Boston University. Misguided industrial development has led to the creation of inefficient industries producing import substitutes, which have not the scale necessary for efficiency and cannot expand exports owing to the poor quality of their products and a price structure distorted by differential tariffs discriminating against exports. Donges and Schydlowsky saw LDC export expansion as chiefly a supply problem, given the pursuing of correct policies. Other participants had their doubts, arguing that LDCs may face trade barriers when their industrial exports become large and competitive.

Thus Dr. Krohn, Director-General for Development and Cooperation in the EEC Commission sketched a policy of cooperation between the EEC and LDCs based on trade preferences, financial aid, and reciprocity. Yet despite the feeling of responsibility towards LDCs in the EEC, he admitted that political pressures may lead to arrangements less satisfactory than the LDCs desire.

Industrial growth in LDCs is linked with the development of their foreign trade and capital imports. The importance of accelerating capital formation in LDCs through imports of foreign capital was apparently taken for granted. But the equally important subject of the efficiency of utilization of the LDCs' scarce capital resources was dealt with by Professor Ian Little of Oxford University, who stressed that making good use of savings is as important as saving. Development plans usually stress the importance of a higher saving rate, but the efficiency of the investment is assumed. His second point was that underutilization of capital is best avoided by sound investment projects with high social yields, it making no difference whether local or foreign capital is invested.

Numerous participants asserted that LDCs often err in reducing the cost of capital to encourage investments, since this policy leads to the creation of capital-intensive industries unsuitable to the factor endowments of most LDCs, which are rich in labor and poor in capital.

Appropriate use of capital calls for proper technologies. Professor Harvey Leibenstein of Harvard University suggested a system of incentives that would encourage labor-intensive technologies in LDCs, while pointing to the existing difficulties in the transfer of managerial and technical knowledge.

Dr. Dagnino Pastore from the Catholic University of Argentina suggested that Latin American states should avoid the purchase of costly, inappropriate technologies, which are often coupled with investment projects initiated by foreign investors.

Another recurring theme in the discussions was the need to judge development plans not only by the growth rates achieved but also by their impact on employment and income distribution. Policies encouraging industrialization appear to have raised growth rates and expanded exports but have not absorbed unemployed and have worsened income distribution.

Planners should take social justice problems into account when deciding on the ends and means of their plans and should possess instruments enabling them to evaluate the ramifications of their policy recommendations. Professor Irma Adelman of the University of Maryland presented an experimental tool of this kind: Her microeconomic planning model of Korea will enable policy makers to evaluate the socioeconomic implications of various measures designed to foster industrialization and economic growth.

The papers presented criticized various aspects of economic policies pursued by LDCs in the past decade and recommended many changes in policy orientation. It was suggested that sound policies can solve many problems, even without foreign aid, though developed countries have a duty to help the LDCs. Trade among the LDCs themselves may also help their industrial growth.

A major benefit of this Rehovot Conference has been the exchange of views between economists and policy makers. The latter should indicate their pressing problems, while the former should demonstrate that economic analysis is relevant to the solution of these problems.

PART IV
PLANNING AND IMPLEMENTATION

DEVELOPMENT PLANNING—
TOOL OR TOY?
John Adler

This paper attempts to bring the story of development planning up to date, to assess its present standing as a tool of economic managements in developing countries, and to evaluate its contribution to economic development.

The data summarized in Table 21 and detailed in the Appendix Table indicate the prevalence of some kind of formal development planning in most developing countries*: 74 out of a total of 93 countries have development plans or programs usually covering three to six years. This reflects the political commitment of the governments and the political leaders of LDCs to pursue the generally recognized objectives of economic development—improvement of living standards, acceleration of economic growth, mitigation of low productivity, underemployment, illiteracy, and so on. A development plan is, of course, no proof of the seriousness of a government's intention and of the vigor of its pursuit of development objectives, just as the absence of a formal development plan (as in Mexico and Brazil), does not mean that a government is not committed to economic advancement. But a plan is prima facie evidence that economic development objectives play a major role in national policies.

It is unavoidable and frequently essential that development plans have some public relations content. The propaganda may enhance general support for the government's development efforts or for specific measures believed to be good for development.

For reasons such as the multiplicity of sources of development assistance, or the difference in time between the commitment of aid funds and their disbursement and appearance in the recipient country's balance of payments, it is not plausible to argue that the preparation of development programs has been instigated from abroad.

It has also been suggested that the authorities of some developing countries have taken the initiative of establishing a resource gap

---

*The countries included in the tables are all active IBRD and IDA borrowers except for Finland, Iceland, Ireland, Israel, and New Zealand, which, because of their per capita GNP and economic structure, cannot properly be considered developing countries.

TABLE 21

Data on Development Plans and Public Sector Management

	Asia	Eastern Africa	Western Africa	Latin America and Caribbean	Europe, Middle East, and North Africa	Total
Total number of countries	16	16	20	20	19	93
Countries with formal development plans	13	13	16	15	17	74
Plan agency in president's or prime minister's office or ministry of finance[a]	13(1)	9(2)	9	8(2)	5	44(5)
Competent Management and control of Public expenditure[b]	12(2)	10(1)	3	7(2)	13	45(5)

[a]Figure in parenthesis shows number of countries with planning agency in the office of the head of state or the ministry of finance, without having adopted a formal plan.
[b]Figure in parenthesis shows number of countries without formal development plan with competent public sector management.

Source: Appendix Tables.

by means of development programs in order to obtain foreign aid.
There is, however, ample evidence that the development programs
that show a creditable resources gap commit the countries claiming
the need for aid to austerity measures or improved economic management, which are likely to be politically burdensome. Therefore, even
when the initiative for engaging in formal development planning stemmed
from the desire to obtain foreign aid, the adoption of a development
program may have helped to improve the formulation and execution
of economic policies. Moreover, if owing to the preparation of a
development program a country obtains more external resources
than it otherwise would, economic progress is helped.

It remains to be shown that the countries with a formal development plan make effective use of it. Conclusive proof of this proposition
is impossible. The figures shown in lines 3 and 4 of Table 21 may,
however, be taken as rough indications of the impact of development
planning on the quality of economic management. Line 3 shows that
in 44 out of 93 countries a planning agency is located in the office of
the head of government or in the ministry of finance, the parts of the
government where the major decisions on economic policy are made
or prepared. This of course does not prove that in 47 percent of all
countries development planning is effective while in the other 53 percent it is not. Some countries included in the list have a planning
agency attached to the office of the head of government that is ineffective or nothing but a tool of political propaganda. Conversely,
a planning agency operating elsewhere in the government machinery,
or even outside it, may have a decisive influence on the formulation
of economic policies. In some states a planning body is operating
in a strategic location though there is no formal development plan.

The objective of development planning in mixed economies is
description and analysis on the one hand and the formulation of a
development strategy on the other. In the past too much development
planning was dedicated to descriptive-analytic efforts and not enough
to helping policy makers decide what to do and how to do it. The
activities of planners gave rise to harsh accusations that they were
wasting their time (and somebody else's money) to analyze the relations
of various parts of the economy with each other, and to record and
study past events, which in times of swift changes had little bearing
on the immediate issues of economic management. Given the limitations on the supply of analytic talent and technical skills, planning
has been accused of absorbing scarce resources that should have
been used more productively elsewhere in government, in the educational system, or in the management of private or public enterprises. To make matters worse, the hard analysis was often based
on very soft data.

The propensity to analyze data beyond the point of diminishing returns is greater if the analysts are not pressed to provide answers to urgent questions. An organizational connection between planning and the making of policy decisions may thus reduce the preoccupation with analytic refinements and force the planners to reach conclusions and offer advice based on incomplete evidence.

There was a time when foreign economic advisers complained that they were unable to prepare development plans because they were too frequently interrupted to advise on short-term problems. "To put out brush fires" was considered an annoyance and an unwelcome distraction from the nobler task of helping to shape the future by means of a Great Blueprint. Today most planning agencies participate in day-to-day decision making, and only part of their time is devoted to models and projections. This participation has led to the recognition that development plans must allow for swiftly changing circumstances —in the external accounts of the economy, the supply of production factors and of final and intermediate goods, in the pattern of demand, in the location of various activities, and, last but not the least, in the political strengths of various sectors. As a result, the relevance of the planners' analytic work to the solution of policy problems has increased.

In many countries the primary task of the planning agency has been changed from the preparation of a multiyear plan, with a macroeconomic projection for the economy as a whole and more detailed recommendations for the public sector, to the formulation of a national (and, where appropriate, regional) development strategy and a framework for a continual process of planning public expenditures and their financing.

The combination of the use of input-output models and the derivation of the most important macroeconomic parameters with the objective of formulating development strategies has enabled development planners to avoid the adoption of internally inconsistent policy objectives. Though the development strategy chosen is not necessarily the best, given internal and external political constraints, the unavoidably uncertain data base, and the limitations of foresight, it provides a basis for better understanding of the workings of the economy, enabling corrective action if economic developments diverge from planned objectives.

Bringing development planning closer to where decisions are made also improved the quality of public investment decisions and the management of public sector finances. IBRD economists have indicated that 61 percent of the countries that prepared a formal development plan (45 out of 74) but only 26 percent of countries without one (5 out of 19) have competent management and control of public expenditures. Of course, competent management does not mean good management, appraised by some absolute standards of public administration, or even by standards prevailing in advanced countries. Yet the comparison with past performance justifies the conclusion that better management of public finances is at least in part the result of improved planning efforts. Since in most countries planning has moved closer to the administration of policies and public investment, the success of a development plan is no longer assessed by its internal consistency and intellectual integrity but by the success of the investments and policies. Planners are now held at least in part responsible for the practical success of their plans. This has enhanced their realism, moderated their expectations, and made their predictions more modest and useful.

The proportion of countries with a development plan is high in all regions except Latin America. Though the Economic Commission for Latin America was for many years very active in promoting development planning and providing technical assistance for it, it seems that there was disappointment with the limited usefulness of the early development plans prepared in a number of Latin American countries with the help of ECLA projections based on heroic assumptions.

The location of the planning effort outside the office of the head of government or the ministry of finance in many Latin American and Middle Eastern states is probably not of special significance. More important is the judgment that in West Africa and Latin America only few countries have competent management and control of public expenditures, even by the relative standards explained before.

Table 22 throws light on the objectives of development as reflected in development plans or in policy statements of 84 countries (74 of them have development plans). The four objectives shown in the table include two major policy objectives (GDP growth and equitable income distribution) and two operational objectives not strictly comparable with the first two.

Many development plans are little more than general statements of intentions to accelerate growth and change the structures of production, based on an analysis of current data and past trends. The implementation of these intentions is frequently left to subsequent legislative or administrative action. Other plans are very specific about some policies or investment projects but vague about others. Moreover, some development plans deal with the economy in aggregate terms, usually through the use of econometric models, while others consider the economy as a framework within which specific plans of public expenditures, especially on investment, are sufficiently detailed to be acted on immediately.

The highest priority objective of most countries (57 percent, or 48 out of 84 countries) is growth of production and income. The priority rating of GDP growth of 3.3 in a scale at which 4.0 is the limit must of course be assessed in conjunction with the ratings

TABLE 22

Major Development Policy Objectives*

	Asia	Eastern Africa	Western Africa	Latin America and Caribbean	Europe, Middle East, and North Africa	Total
Number of countries in sample	14	14	18	19	19	84
Objectives						
GDP Growth	3.6	3.7	3.0	2.7	3.7	3.3
Equitable income distribution or employment	1.9	2.5	2.1	2.8	1.8	2.2
Development of infrastructure	2.6	2.2	3.1	2.6	2.8	2.7
Stimulation of private investment	1.6	1.6	1.7	1.8	1.7	1.7

*Based on Annex Tables; measurement based on ranking of objective. The expressed (or presumed) highest priority objective is ranked 4, the next highest 3, the lowest 1. The average priority is 2.5 ($(4 + 3 + 2 + 1) \div 4$), the lowest 1. If the plans, or "strategy pronouncements," are completely negative, a 0 has been entered.

given to the other three objectives, which, it should be stressed, are not competing but complementary. Emphasis on equitable income distribution and on the alleviation of unemployment and underemployment does not mean that the development plans do not aim at increases in production and income; it only means that the development plans stress the policies through which a larger share of the increased output accrues to the lower income groups, or that in the formulation of policies aiming at increased production special account should be taken of the need to provide employment opportunities for the unemployed and underemployed.

The policy aim in the majority of countries is growth, without special consideration for the incidence of the benefits of growth on income. Only in 20 countries are growth and equity rated as the two highest priority objectives. In many plans the emphasis on equity has the appearance of pious hopes, with little or no indication in the treatment of the economy or of specific investment activities that a deterioration in the pattern of income distribution is to be avoided. Development plans that pay special attention to the growth of agricultural income may be considered exceptions to this general appearance, because per capita and family income in agriculture is generally lower than in the rest of the economy. But one cannot be sure, because in many countries the primary aim is more production for export or for urban consumption, and the increased income resulting from greater output is more likely to accrue to medium-sized and large-scale producers than to farmers in the lowest income group.

Equity considerations play a secondary role in the formulation of development plans owing to the almost universal emphasis on increased investment and savings as the key to successful development. The formulation that the rate of investment divided by the capital-output ratio equals the rate of GNP growth is the core element of macroeconomic development plans. This approach has the effect of neglecting the role of all other factors in the development process.

The preparation of development plan growth models relating growth primarily to investment (either in the aggregate or by sector or by industrial subgroups, depending on the complexity of the model) has two consequences: The first is an emphasis on investment and the relative downgrading of other measures to accelerate development. The second is a heavy reliance on public investment with only a minor role for private investment. The latter may be the psychologically inevitable outcome of the planners' endeavors to assure the implementation of their proposals, but could reflect the political mood prevailing in many countries, where little reliance is placed on private investment and private initiative, though the private sector usually accounts for by far the larger part of GDP, especially in the portion originating in agriculture.

The emphasis on investment as the prime engine of growth, and the consequent playing down of the importance of factors such as improvements in public administration, more education, or educational reform, are perhaps the greatest drawback of development planning as practiced in the majority of LDCs today. This assertion is reinforced by the experience of developed countries. Their growth was largely caused by technical and organizational innovation, improvements in efficiency, the advancement of technical skills, and a host of other factors. However, the long-term growth of their per capita income was slower than in the more successful developing countries today. Moreover, the countries that led the growth of income in Western Europe were not able, like the LDCs of today, to import the technical advances of their forerunners on the road to development. Unlike what was needed 100 or 150 years ago, what is needed now is capital formation, at the fastest possible pace, in order to absorb modern techniques of production. The need for capital may be the greater because, though modern techniques are more capital-intensive than the factor supply in the developing countries would require, the capital-intensive techniques are practically the only ones available.

Despite these arguments justifying a high rate of capital formation, one is left with an uneasy feeling that improving the supply of some other factors would be less costly in consumption foregone. Unfortunately, efficient methods to improve the supply of other production factors are not easy to come by.

The development of strains of food crops especially suitable to the climatic conditions of developing countries, and the efforts to evolve intermediate technologies adapted to supply and institutional conditions in LDCs for industry and construction, may raise the effectiveness of capital formation, but are still only promises. Perhaps the great increase in educational efforts—in absolute volume rather than in relation to estimated needs—now under way in most LDCs will accelerate productivity gains and income growth, or maintain present growth rates with less capital formation. Perhaps improvements in public administration, in the management of private and public enterprises, in the credit structure, in the transport system, and so on will receive greater attention than hitherto and will redress the balance between concern for capital formation and other efforts to stimulate development. But one cannot be sure.

An urgent reason for changing the emphasis in the planning of development strategy is the effects of policies aiming at a high rate of capital formation and growth on the distribution of income. If the marginal savings rate is higher in the upper income groups than in the lower—as it is bound to be in countries where per capita income of the lower income groups is barely sufficient to provide for minimum nutritional needs—any policy aiming at a higher rate of savings must spare the upper classes that save and limit increases in consumption by reducing income through taxation. Moreover, investment is more effective as a means of increasing output in sectors where more capital-intensive methods of production are employed, such as industry, than in sectors such as peasant agriculture, where increased output often depends on greater food consumption and improvement in the nutritional balance. Since in virtually all countries the lowest income groups are engaged in agriculture or service industries, capital expenditures affect their productivity and income only indirectly, by facilitating their transfer to other sectors.

The high priority given in most plans to the development of the infrastructure, or, more generally, to public investment, partly reflects the belief that capital is the prime moving force in the developing process and that the best way to foster development is through public investment. Though a part of public investment is designed to improve the supply and efficiency of production factors other than capital and ultimately benefits the private sector, public investment expenditures are on the economic infrastructure and state enterprises. Planners and decision-making authorities apparently rely on public investment as the vehicle for accelerating development in preference to measures stimulating private investment.

The stimulation of private investment has by far the lowest priority among the objectives shown in Table 22 in all regions, although private investment has been among the major causes of the development success stories of recent years in Brazil, Mexico, Hong Kong, Singapore, and Taiwan. Yet only Chile, Guinea, and Sri Lanka list the conversion of the economy to socialism among their priority objectives.

A noteworthy aspect of the list of other objectives is the incidence of political aims such as economic sovereignty (which presumably means more national control over production), Africanization, racial balance, national unity, internal security, and defense. In states where these noneconomic objectives are specifically mentioned, the references to them in development plans may indicate that these plans are close to the political realities and therefore may be useful instruments in the shaping of policies affecting the pace and direction of economic growth.

This paper concerned itself with the following questions:

1. Has planning been really useful or has it served mostly as a public relations exercise?

2. Has planning improved performance in overall management of national economies?

3. Has planning affected sector and project contents of development?

4. Has planning been flexible enough to take care of unforeseen changes in exogenous sectors?

To question 1 the answer is that it has been useful, including its public relations effect.

To question 2 the answer is yes, though development planning may have contributed significantly to the disregard of income distribution and social justice considerations.

To question 3 my answer is yes, with the important qualification that the effect has often not been beneficial.

The affirmative answer to the second question implies that my answer to question 4 should also be yes, but this is an expression of hope not a reflection of evidence.

DISCUSSION

A Participant: A reason why planners are sceptical about the value of their plans is that planning is a political act. Political leaders tend to concentrate on a single set of objectives and to be optimistic. They rarely discuss alternative patterns of development.

Besides, politicians do not stress that some aims must be sacrificed if others are to be achieved, since this is rarely popular. Nor do they like to commit themselves on budgetary and fiscal matters.

For planning to be of use, there must be some mutual understanding between planners and political leaders, and the former must not be blind to the political aspects of their plans. Otherwise, planning may even be harmful.

ALEJANDRO SUELS (Venezuela): Dr. Adler said that capital formation tends to favor the industrial sector, forgetting agriculture, and that planning has hitherto failed to solve the problem of income distribution. Concerning the first point, many LDCs regard industry as the focus of economic development, as did the European states after the Second World War, which became net importers of agricultural products after having been net exporters of these products. Planning conformed to political targets. Thus the failure to create capital in agriculture was due to political decisions rather than to planning.

The first priority for most states is the growth of the national product; income distribution is a second or third priority. In those states where income redistribution was implemented via radical structural changes it was not difficult to achieve. This depended on political decisions. But where an attempt was made to alter income distribution gradually by fiscal or public expenditure policies,

APPENDIX TABLE 1

Development Planning and Planning Objectives

Country	1970 GNP Per Capita	1960-70 Per Capita Growth Rate	Does Country Have Multi-Year Development Plan?	Does Country Have Competent Management and Control of Public Expenditures	Planning Body in Prime Minister's Office or Ministry of Finance	Development Planning Objectives*					
						GDP Growth	Equitable Income Distribution and Employment	Development of Infrastructure	Stimulation of Private Investment	Ranking	Other Substance
Asia											
Bangladesh	n.a.	n.a.	No	Yes	Yes	4	2	3	1	—	—
Burma	80	0.6	Yes	No	Yes	2	4	3	1	—	—
China (Taiwan)	390	7.1	Yes	Yes	Yes	4	1	2	3	—	—
Fiji	430	2.5	Yes	Yes	Yes	4	0	3	2	—	—
India	110	1.2	Yes	Yes	Yes	4	3	2	1	—	—
Indonesia	80	1.0	Yes	Yes	No	4	1	3	2	—	—
Korea	250	6.8	Yes	Yes	Yes	4	1	3	2	—	—
Malaysia	380	3.1	Yes	Yes	Yes	4	3	1	2	3	racial balance
Nepal	80	0.5	Yes	No	Yes	4	2	3	1	—	—
Pakistan	100	2.4	Yes	Yes	Yes	4	1	3	2	—	—
Papua and New Guinea	300	4.5	No	Yes	No	—	—	—	—	1	regional development
Philippines	210	2.9	Yes	Yes	Yes	4	3	1	2	—	—
Singapore	920	5.2	No	Yes	No	—	—	—	—	1	socialist economy
Sri Lanka	110	1.3	Yes	No	Yes	3	4	2	0	4	—
Thailand	200	4.9	Yes	Yes	Yes	4	1	3	2	3	regional development
Western Samoa	140	-1.1	Yes	No	Yes	3	1	4	2	—	—

(continued)

APPENDIX TABLE 1 (continued)

Country	1970 GNP Per Capita	1960-70 Per Capita Growth Rate	Does Country Have Multi-Year Development Plan?	Does Country Have Competent Management and Control of Public Expenditures	Planning Body in Prime Minister's Office or Ministry of Finance	Development Planning Objectives*					Other	
						GDP Growth	Equitable Income Distribution and Employment	Development of Infrastructure	Stimulation of Private Investment	Ranking	Substance	
Eastern Africa												
Botswana	110	1.4	Yes	Yes	Yes	4	3	1	2	1	public savings	
Burundi	60	0.8	No	No	No	–	–	–	–	–	–	
Ethiopia	80	2.8	Yes	Yes	Yes	4	3	1	2	3	agricultural development	
Kenya	150	3.6	Yes	Yes	Yes	4	2	3	1	–	–	
Lesotho	90	0.0	Yes	Yes	Yes	3	4	1	2	2	public savings	
Madagascar	130	1.2	No	Yes	Yes	–	–	–	–	–	–	
Malawi	80	2.1	Yes	Yes	Yes	4	2	3	1	–	–	
Mauritius	240	-0.7	Yes	Yes	No	4	3	1	2	–	–	
Rwanda	60	1.5	Yes	No	Yes	4	1	3	2	–	–	
Somalia	70	-1.1	Yes	Yes	No	3	4	2	1	–	–	
Sudan	120	1.0	Yes	No	Yes	4	1	3	2	–	–	
Swaziland	180	5.2	Yes	Yes	Yes	4	2	1	3	–	–	
Tanzania	100	3.6	Yes	Yes	No	3	4	2	1	2	Decentralization (of development effort)	
Uganda	130	2.4	Yes	No	No	4	1	3	2	–	–	
Zaire	90	2.7	No	No	Yes	3	2	4	1	3	economic sovereignty	
Zambia	400	7.1	Yes	No	No	4	2	3	1	2	agricultural development	

Western Africa

Cameroon	180	3.8	Yes	No	No	4	3	2	1	—	—
Central African Republic	140	0.2	No	No	No	—	—	—	—	—	—
Chad	80	0.4	Yes	No	Yes	4	3	1	2	—	—
Congo	300	4.8	Yes	No	No	2	4	3	1	—	—
Dahomey	90	0.1	Yes	No	No	4	2	3	1	—	—
Equatorial Guinea	210	3.6	No	No	No	—	—	—	—	—	—
Gabon	630	5.1	Yes	No	Yes	3	1	4	2	—	—
Gambia	120	1.1	Yes	No	Yes	3	1	4	2	—	—
Ghana	310	-0.4	Yes	No	Yes	4	2	3	1	3	diversification
Guinea	120	2.7	Yes	No	Yes	3	2	4	1	2	socialist economy
Ivory Coast	310	4.5	Yes	Yes	No	4	1	3	2	2	Africanization
Liberia	240	0.9	No	No	No	1	4	2	2	4	diversification
Mali	70	4.4	Yes	No	Yes	3	4	2	1	2	diversification
Mauritania	140	4.5	Yes	No	No	2	1	4	3	—	
Niger	90	-2.0	Yes	No	No	4	2	3	0	4	agricultural development
Nigeria	120	0.1	Yes	Yes	Yes	4	1	3	2	3	national unity
Senegal	230	0.0	Yes	No	Yes	1	2	4	3	—	—
Sierra Leone	190	4.7	No	No	No	2	1	4	3	—	—
Togo	140	1.2	Yes	Yes	Yes	4	1	3	2	2	Africanization
Upper Volta	60	-0.6	Yes	No	No	4	2	3	1	—	—

(continued)

APPENDIX TABLE 1 (continued)

Country	1970 GNP Per Capita	1960-70 Per Capita Growth Rate	Does Country Have Multi-Year Development Plan?	Does Country Have Competent Management and Control of Public Expenditures	Planning Body in Prime Minister's Office or Ministry of Finance	Development Planning Objectives*					Other	
						GDP Growth	Equitable Income Distribution and Employment	Development of Infrastructure	Stimulation of Private Investment	Ranking	Substance	
Latin America and The Caribbean												
Argentina	1160	2.5	Yes	No	Yes	3	4	1	2	1	regional development	
Bolivia	180	2.5	Yes	No	No	4	1	2	3	—	—	
Brazil	420	2.4	Yes	Yes	No	4	1	3	2	1	control of inflation	
Chile	720	1.6	Yes	Yes	No	3	4	2	0	3	socialist economy	
Colombia	340	1.7	Yes	No	No	3	4	2	1	2	export promotion	
Costa Rica	560	3.2	No	No	No	—	—	—	—	—	—	
Dominican Republic	350	0.5	No	Yes	Yes	2	1	3	4	—	—	
Ecuador	290	1.7	Yes	No	No	4	2	3	1	—	—	
El Salvador	300	1.7	Yes	No	No	1	4	2	3	—	—	
Guatemala	360	2.0	Yes	No	No	1	4	3	2	—	—	
Guyana	370	1.1	Yes	No	No	2	3	4	1	3	regional development	
Haiti	110	-0.9	Yes	Yes	Yes	3	1	4	2	—	—	
Honduras	280	1.8	No	No	No	—	—	—	—	—	—	
Jamaica	670	3.5	No	No	Yes	1	3	4	2	—	—	
Mexico	670	3.7	No	Yes	No	4	3	2	1	2	economic sovereignty	
Nicaragua	430	2.8	No	No	No	—	—	—	—	—	—	
Panama	730	4.2	No	No	No	2	4	3	1	1	—	
Paraguay	260	1.3	Yes	No	Yes	2	1	3	4	2	fiscal reform	
Peru	450	1.4	Yes	No	Yes	3	4	2	1	2	economic sovereignty	
Trinidad and Tobago	860	1.9	Yes	No	Yes	1	3	4	2	—	—	
Uruguay	820	-0.4	Yes	Yes	Yes	4	3	1	2	2	export promotion	

Europe, Middle East, and North Africa										
Afghanistan	80	0.5	Yes	No	3	2	4	1	—	—
Algeria	300	1.7	Yes	No	4	1	2	3	4	diversification
Cyprus	950	5.3	Yes	Yes	4	1	3	2	—	—
Egypt	210	1.7	Yes	Yes	4	2	3	1	—	—
Greece	1090	6.6	Yes	No	4	1	2	3	—	—
Iran	380	5.4	Yes	No	4	2	3	1	4	defense
Iraq	320	2.5	Yes	No	4	2	3	1	—	—
Jordan	250	2.9	Yes	Yes	3	2	4	1	4	internal security
Lebanon	590	0.5	Yes	No	3	1	2	4	—	—
Malta	810	5.8	Yes	Yes	3	4	1	2	4	economic sovereignty
Morocco	230	1.0	Yes	Yes	4	1	3	2	2	social reform
Oman	350	17.1	No	No	3	2	4	1	4	education and health
Spain	1020	6.1	Yes	No	4	3	2	1	3	regional development
Syria	290	3.4	Yes	No	4	2	3	1	4	defense
Tunisia	250	0.5	Yes	No	4	1	3	2	—	—
Turkey	310	3.9	Yes	Yes	4	1	3	2	4	industrialization
Yemen A.R.	80	2.0	No	No	3	1	4	2	—	—
Yemen PDR	120	-5.0	Yes	No	4	3	2	1	—	—
Yugoslavia	650	4.3	Yes	No	4	3	2	1	3	regional development

*Linked in order of priority. The highest priority objective is marked 4, the second highest 3, the lowest 1. "Other" objectives are marked independently from 4 (highest) to 1 (lowest).

a problem had to be faced: Even when there was improvement at
the conclusion of the planning period, no attempt to describe it quantitatively was made, since some inequalities remained and it was inconvenient for politicians to stress them.

SIMCHA LANDAU (Israel): What is meant by "the project and
sector content of development planning has not been beneficial recently"? I also think there is a contradiction in criticizing the neglect
of the income distribution aspect in planning while simultaneously
claiming that not enough is being done to stimulate private investment.
Third, does not the involvement of planners in implementation on
the government level lead to a kind of "dictatorship" of the planners?

ALFREDO BENJAMIN NOYOLA (El Salvador): One must distinguish between planning and its implementation. Planning is a
technical matter, but its implementation is a political matter.

One requirement of good planning is the provision for continued
comparisons between planned targets and actual achievements. The
preparation of even medium-range plans tend to be inefficient without
a long-term framework.

JULIO CESAR ESTRELLA (Dominican Republic): What is the
role of foreign aid in planning?

RUTH SILBERBERG (Israel): Since developing states suffer
from shortages of economists, sociologists, and so on, I would like
to hear what foreign assistance can do to help these countries with
their planning.

JOHN ADLER (IBRD): I agree that political realities must be
taken into account. I see no difficulty in weighing alternatives and
do not see how any development plan can be formulated without this
being done.

In Nigeria I was asked by planners how to reconcile political
decision making with planning. I answered that the job of a planner
is to present alternative costs clearly. If you build a road from A
to B, the benefits are x and the costs are y. If you extend the road
from A to C via B, the benefits may be smaller or larger relative to
costs. But to decide, as one consultant firm did after analyzing costs,
not to provide any roads in northern Nigeria, the most important
region politically and in population, is political nonsense, since the
political concept of regional equity will not permit such behavior.

I agree with Mr. Suels that not only industrialization leads to
higher incomes and that agricultural development has been neglected
the world over. But I think we have overestimated the difficulties of

industrialization and underestimated the difficulties of raising agricultural productivity.

Strategies should be sought that will avoid the deterioration of income distribution, while aiming at an improvement while growth is proceeding. This implies shifting emphasis from capital formation to institutional changes.

What I meant by saying that planning has not always affected sector and project content in a positive sense is that project selection has often disregarded the qualities of the specific project. Projects have a time dimension. Some plans go all out for, say, more roads and more education, irrespective of the balance, which gets distorted.

I do not deplore the neglect of the private sector. I take the driving force of private development as a fact of life, and despite its great contribution in states with very high growth rates I am not pleading for more consideration for the private sector.

If the government holds a large part of the GNP and wants to focus on investment, it must keep consumption down. It must take away by fiscal means from people who have tried to save. This leads to distortions in income distribution and adverse welfare effects.

I did not mean that planners have to get involved in everything. But I am much more afraid of their doing nothing but planning and letting the economy run away from the plan.

Mr. Noyola is right that planning has been effective as far as the growth rate is concerned, but very ineffective as regards income distribution. I also agree that the purpose of planning is not only to make a plan but also to have a strategy that covers more than the planning period only. A country must have an idea where it is going and by what means it wants to get there.

The role of foreign assistance in planning should be mainly technical. In Nigeria I tried to teach how to measure alternatives by comparison. One should not try to advocate an economically sounder but politically less desirable solution. That is not the foreigner's business. Nor is it his business to advise a state to accept foreign investment. Decisions with political significance should be left to the local politicians.

**PLANNING AND
PERFORMANCE**
Koichi Mera

A distinction must be made between planning and plans. Planning is an act of selecting a future course of action to suit the objectives of the planning body, that is, to improve performance. A plan is a product of planning at a certain point in time when a specific future course of action is selected. Planning usually goes on after a plan is made and leads to another later plan that usually differs from the previous plan. Planning is a continuous process, but plans are sections at time points of the continuous act of planning.

In a number of developing countries planning at the national level has been given an explicit form in five-year plans. To have official, explicit plans at the national level is frequently considered as national planning, although implicit planning is always going on in some form at every organization. Since it is difficult to analyze the relationship between implicit planning and performance, let me first discuss the relationship between official national plans and performance.

CHARACTERISTICS OF NATIONAL PLANS

National plans in countries with market-oriented economies are the medium-term in time perspective, indicative rather than directive, and macroscopic rather than microscopic in approach.

National plans are characteristically medium-term plans, typically for five years. If the major concerns are fiscal and monetary policies, the plan should be for a much shorter time span. Five years roughly corresponds to the time required for investment projects from initial identification or feasibility study to completion. Much longer time spans can be considered, but beyond five years uncertainty would increase very much. Some years being required for producing a plan, the total time span involved corresponds roughly to the entire cycle of investment projects.

Generally there are two types of national plans; directive and indicative. In an authoritarian economy planning leads to a plan that is implemented through allocation of assignments to organizations and then individuals. On the other hand, planning in a market-oriented economy must be a mixture of planning by the private sector and by the government. Let me examine some salient aspects of national planning in such an economy.

First, the authority of the government is limited: its major tools are spending, taxing, and policing. Individuals and firms are allowed to plan and act according to their own preferences and judgment within the limitations of the law. This freedom itself is a major raison d'etre of market-oriented society. Therefore the government plans its program of activities by anticipating what the private sector would do under different government programs. This limits the usefulness of planning as a tool for improving performance of the economy. The performance of the private sector can only be projected, but not directed. If the government holds a view that private savings are desirable, it has to provide financial and other incentives to achieve this objective. But other implications of providing the financial incentives are not necessarily desirable. If the private sector does not respond to incentives sensitively, then incentives must become stronger. If other costs are associated with the incentives, the government will not be able to achieve its objective. Therefore, this method of implementing planned objectives, that is, planning to achieve objectives without altering the behavior of most economic actors, is faced with a serious limitation.

Second, since the authority of the government is limited, it cannot plan drastic improvements in performance. Plans must be based on realistic expectations of the private sector. In other words, plans tend to be projections rather than to depict desirable improvements in performance. It is true that most plans set a growth rate higher than the rate previously observed, but nonetheless the rate is set within a realistic range.

The third characteristic of national plans is their macroscopic nature. Aggregate, sectoral, and regional growth are "planned" in plans, but at the level of investment projects no definite plan is usually available. There are justifications for this. At the time of producing a national plan not enough studies have been made for specific projects to provide enough detail at the microscopic level. Such detailed planning is expected to be undertaken in the course of the planning period. In addition, though specific knowledge about projects is not available, it is considered that macroscopic aggregates can be projected and planned with sufficient accuracy to make the plan meaningful.

To summarize, national plans in a market-oriented economy are usually produced to improve the performance of the economy but are based primarily on the examination of macroscopic aggregates, projections of the private sector, and the selection of alternative courses of action in fields where the government has the power to decide. Among the macroscopic aggregates those in the private sector are at best conditional projections, with conditions corresponding to alternative courses of action by the government. As far as the private sector is concerned, a plan only indicates its probable future. What the government is able to commit in a national plan is a set of government actions during the plan period, particularly the amounts of public investment in different sectors and regions. Even for those actual budgeting has to be made on an annual basis or on a piecemeal basis, because detailed information is not available at the time the plan is drawn up. In other words, national plans are expressions of government intentions, primarily on public investment based on preliminary information on the project level.

LIMITATIONS OF NATIONAL PLANS

The usual justifications for having a national plan despite such limitations are to provide a reasonable development framework that can become a basis for private decisions and to improve the decision making of the government through the process of planning. By showing to the public the probable picture of the economy in the future, it is intended that individual decision makers will be able to plan with less uncertainty and consequently for a longer range. Planning with less uncertainty for longer periods facilitates better utilization of resources. For this reason, indicative planning is useful and should contribute to the improvement of performance.

Nonetheless, such an indicative plan, if it has any effect on planning in the private sector, has an adverse effect on the national economy. Since such plans provide a broad framework that can become a basis for individual planning, a plan tends to become a self-fulfilling prophecy. In other words, since the future stream of consumption provided in the plan is used for projecting future consumption of a commodity and its production schedule is tailored to meet the consumption stream, the production capacity would grow in accordance with the projected consumption stream. If the planned consumption stream or the growth rate of the economy requires reasonable efforts from the private sector, this plan would lead to improvements in performance. However, the plan usually does not set an ambitious target but sets one within easy reach. This, in turn, implies that plans themselves restrict dynamic growth. This conclusion may not be obvious, but observations of some countries in Asia would support this hypothesis: The countries that have shown remarkable growth in the past, such as Japan, Singapore, and Hong Kong, are among the very countries that did not produce official five-year plans.

---

*It is not technically correct to state that the government of Japan has not produced medium-range plans for national development.

They have demonstrated dynamic growth of the economy and have done so without being constrained by official medium-range plans. Korea which has achieved a high rate of growth in spite of five-year plans, is a notable exception. Therefore it can be concluded that medium-term plans do not necessarily depress the growth rate of the economy, but there is no indication that such plans increase the rate of growth.

Thus planning in the form of the usual five-year plans does not materially contribute to improvement in performance. And there are reasons in addition to those I have already presented that it does not. One is psychological. Having a plan that depicts satisfactory improvements in performance may satisfy people's desire for progress. People might feel they are assured of progress through the plan before planned actions are implemented. Such satisfaction before the facts tends to diminish people's devotion for work towards progress. Plans may become disincentives to progress rather than tools for progress.

Another reason is the rigidity inherent in plans. Plans are usually made with macroscopic information and scanty information on the project level. But once a plan is established it binds allocation of resources. In the meantime more detailed information is uncovered and investment projects are carefully examined. Such analysis may indicate that a major reallocation of resources should be made from those indicated in the plan. In fact, in many countries annual revisions are made for five-year plans. But the extent of flexibility allowed for annual revisions must be limited if the five-year plan is to have a more than symbolic value. For this reason, the rigidity inherent in a plan restricts improvements in performance. Plans made with inferior information tend to override plans based on more detailed information.

CONCLUSIONS

The above analysis leads to the following conclusions: (1) Government investment projects must be planned and programed with

---

In fact the government has produced seven national plans from 1955 to 1973, on the average one in two and a half years. Unlike most five-year plans in developing countries, however, these plans do not contain detailed investment programs; nor are they intended to be carried out by the end of the planning period, which is usually five years. Instead the plans consist of development strategies and policies and are expected to be revised within two to three years. Owing to this flexibility consideration of their interdependence and the demands on them from the private sector. (2) However enough flexibility must be preserved in the plan to allow substantial revisions in the public investment program, and (3) plans should encourage dynamic improvement in performance. Among the above three statements, only the first calls for quantitative plans. But, as far as public investment in infrastructure is concerned, quantitative projections of the private sector are not necessarily needed since the input coefficients of infrastructure for production sections can vary a great deal. For a public investment program a wide range of the private sector performance can be allowed to develop. Therefore, if the probable description of the private sector is needed for the purpose of presenting a plan, a range of projections should be presented.

Does planning contribute to the betterment of performance? As manifested in indicative national plans it does not, but it can. The way would be to avoid publishing useless figures but to implement development strategies and policies developed in the process of planning. To develop such strategies and policies a comprehensive examination of the economy as a whole is needed. Planning of such policies and strategies should be the major concern of the planning process. National plans themselves in the traditional sense should not be considered as a major element in planning if planning is aimed at improvement in performance.

DISCUSSION

SIMCHA LANDAU (Israel): In few states with a mixed economy is there a clear-cut boundary between the private and the public sector. In most LDCs there is something in between, and in this sector the government can exercise influence in various forms.

I do not accept the distinction between planning and a plan. No planner can work without trying to quantify, using the best figures available, and reaching conclusions—not just general conclusions, such as, it is good to promote exports, but how fast and by what devices to promote exports. This must be part of what the planner should say to the policy makers. So some figures are essential when suggesting policies, and these figures must not be kept secret.

There is a danger that planners may become emotionally involved with their figures and be reluctant to change them even when change is needed. But most planners are honest enough to agree to

---

of the national plans, I have not included Japan in the group with official five-year plans.

changes when necessary, providing revisions in basic policies are not made too often. On this basis revisions can be a useful tool.

A plan may have ingredients of GNP growth, of social aims, and even of a regional character. Any plan is changeable, and politicians should give the planners opportunities to change it. But one cannot have an efficient planning process without something written that is called a plan.

J. ENNINFUL (Ghana): Most LDCs have the problem of depending on one or two commodities to earn their foreign exchange. Under these conditions how can one produce a specific program of government investment, give the private sector a free hand to plan, and allow the economy to develop rapidly?

IASSU ANDEMICAEL (United Nations Economic Commission for Africa): How can planning have a negative effect on performance? Unless there is empirical evidence that in some states the planning process retarded growth, it is more reasonable to argue that planning is an incentive. At worst, a plan may remain unimplemented.

EPHRAIM KLEIMANN (Israel): In countries with mixed economies there may perhaps be a negative correlation between indicative planning and performance. But one of the reasons may be that the states with a good performance do not need a plan. So planning is not necessarily bad for performance.

DAVID KATZ (Israel): I think it is a simplification to equate preparation of a development plan with planning. Often the preparation of a national development plan becomes a goal in itself, for reasons of prestige, though real planning is not taking place and no plans are reflected by policy decisions. The states that made progress have some characteristics in common. The first is government determination to interfere in economic activity so as to guide the economy along desired lines, side by side with readiness to take unpopular decisions. This readiness may exist in states that have no plan and may be absent in states that have one. The second characteristic is good budgeting. A plan without good budgeting will not get far. You are more likely to make progress with a strong budget department and an effective allocation of public resources. The third characteristic is project identification and preparation, the lack of which has been one of the prime constraints on the implementation of plans in Africa. Countries without effective development institutions tend to make little progress whether they have a planning agency and a plan or not.

ISAAC KERSTENETZKY (Brazil): The political framework of the planning system is important. Should a plan be submitted only to the government or the parliament? Or should intermediate political stages of discussion take place?

Another problem is the quality of available statistics. A sophisticated plan based on poor statistics is no use.

Rapid growth achieved by Brazil during the last four years was not due to its five-year plan but rather to the budget dimension of the plan.

KOICHI MERA (Japan): Figures should not be kept secret, but they should be kept as reference to a basic policy statement, which should be the core of a plan.

Planning should be expressed in plans. Government intentions should be publicly announced. But the usual five-year plans are not a particularly good way of announcing government intentions. More flexibility is needed. Certain programs should be made public at appropriate times, though the rest of the plan is not ready for announcement. There should be regular updating.

The government can affect the private sector in various ways, so the distinction between the private and the public sector is difficult to make.

The growth of GNP should be only one objective of planning. There are also social and regional objectives.

For an economy depending on one or two export commodities, I would suggest that the plan or policies should encourage the maximum participation of the private sector, by providing incentives or by other means.

I have no solid proof for my conjecture that a fixed plan has a negative psychological effect, but I feel that, having dealt with the quantitative aspects, planners may be inclined to devote less effort to improving the performance of the economy.

I agree that good budgeting is important for planning. Budgeting is usually done on a short-term basis. There must also be a long-term perspective for the development of the economy.

**PLANNING AND
THE MARKET IN
ECONOMIC DEVELOPMENT**
Peter Bauer

SCOPE AND TERMINOLOGY

In the current development literature planning refers primarily to actual or attempted state control of economic activity in the exchange sector. Some advocates of planning, however, envisage it as a more comprehensive policy in the sense of attempted remolding of man and society, by force if necessary. Most of my observations deal with the former interpretation, although they apply to the second interpretation also. Indigenous governments, whose personnel is drawn from the local population, are likely to content themselves with close control over economic life to promote centralization of power. But often specific policies of so-called development planning reflect no more than controls introduced under the pressure of sectional interests from the private and the public sector. These escape examination if they can be spuriously justified as components of a supposedly desirable overall plan.

In less developed countries (LDCs), as elsewhere, there is an extensive range of tasks that must be performed largely or wholly by the government. These include the conduct of external affairs, the management of the monetary and fiscal system, the promotion of an institutional framework conducive to material progress, the provision of basic health, educational, and communication services, and also agricultural extension work.

The appropriate scope of these tasks and their execution must depend on the specific conditions of the society. There are wide differences in this respect. One point should be noted. When I mention the promotion of an institutional structure conducive to material progress as one of the tasks of government, I do not mean the expropriation or expulsion of unpopular and politically ineffective groups, such as land owners or economically successful ethnic minorities.

The provision of basic facilities yielding indiscriminate benefits can at times be performed in part by the private sector. In many

---

Peter Bauer is from Great Britain.

LDCs, mining, plantation and trading enterprises have contributed substantially to the construction and maintenance of the infrastructure or to agricultural extension work. But many of these activities must be performed or at least overseen by the government. And the government must also play a large part in the preservation and encouragement of external commercial contacts, which have been of the greatest importance in promoting the material progress of LDCs. To be most effective in promoting development these contacts should be widely dispersed among the population.

STATE PLANNING AS AXIOM

Current development literature claims that comprehensive planning is indispensable for the material progress of less developed countries. I shall illustrate this axiomatic approach with quotations from two writers.

Professor Gunnar Myrdal writes:

"The special advisers to underdeveloped countries who have taken the time and trouble to acquaint themselves with the problem, no matter who they are . . . . all recommend central planning as the first condition of progress."*

Professor H. Kitamura of Tokyo University argues similarly:

"Only planned economic development can hope to achieve a rate of growth that is politically acceptable and capable of commanding popular enthusiasm and support."†

Professor Kitamura's opinion is unexpected because the phenomenal progress of his own country was achieved without the policies he specifies as indispensable.‡

---

*Gunnar Myrdal, An International Economy (London, 1956), p. 201.

†H. Kitamura, "Foreign Trade Problems in Planned Economic Development," in Kenneth Berrill, ed., Economic Development With Special Reference to East Asia (London, 1964), p. 202.

‡A popular argument is that the central planning is necessary to increase saving and investment, which in turn are necessary for material progress. This argument is irrelevant. First, much of planning is not designed with this end in view; indeed, major constituent

In fact, central planning played no part in the development of
Europe, North America, Japan, or Australasia. Indeed, it played no
part in the development of any one of the new highly developed countries. The Soviet experience provides no exception to this statement:
general living standards, the usual yard stick of development, are
vastly lower there than in the advanced economies of the West. Nor
did central planning play any part in the advance of the many less
developed countries that progressed rapidly in the last century. In
short, the axiomatic statements that comprehensive planning is essential for progress from poverty are not merely unsubstantiated
assertions, but are in obvious conflict with simple evidence.

Central planning, that is extensive state control of the exchange
economy, does not augment resources. It only concentrates power.
And by concentrating power such a policy creates power, because
in a decentralized system of decision making there do not normally
exist such positions of power as are created by comprehensive planning.* Centralization and creation of power is a necessary result of
comprehensive planning. The result is rarely noted by its advocates,
who state or clearly imply that it increases the volume of productive
resources without explaining why and how this comes about.

The fundamental issue here is often obscured by regarding
accrual of resources to the government, or the development of a
favored activity, as a net addition to resources or output, without
noting that the resources have been diverted from alternative uses.
The politicians and civil servants who direct policy cannot create
new resources: they dispose only of resources diverted from other
public or private uses. Nor does the overriding of private decisions
promote development.

The flow of goods and services that constitute the standard of
living is not increased by such a policy. Yet higher living standards
are almost always the declared aim of comprehensive planning.
Professor Myrdal writes this explicitly. But later in the same lecture

---

elements of development plans obstruct saving and investment. Second, central planning is not required to promote saving and investment in less developed countries since this can be brought about by
fiscal and financial policies or by various measures designed to encourage private saving and investment.

*Power here means the capacity to restrict the choice open
to other men. There are large corporations and rich men in a market system. But their resources do not confer power on them in this
material sense, at any rate to anything like the extent to which comprehensive planning confers it on politicians and civil servants.

he writes that comprehensive planning implies utmost austerity, without resolving the contradiction.

> "There is no other road to economic development than a forceful rise in the part of the national income which is withheld from consumption and devoted to investments, and this implies a policy of the utmost austerity.... The frugality, which must be applied to the level of living of the masses of the people for the simple reason that they are the many....*

When planning is regarded as necessary for material progress, evidence becomes irrelevant. Whatever the actual course of events, it can always be adduced in support of a policy that is axiomatically deemed desirable: progress as evidence of its success and lack of progress as evidence of the need for its reinforcement.

STATE PLANNING AND MATERIAL PROGRESS

It is clear from the earlier history of developed countries and from recent events in many less developed ones that comprehensive planning is not necessary for material progress. This still leaves open the question whether it is more likely to promote or to retard it. I think it is much more likely to retard it.

Economic development requires modernization of the mind. It requires a revision of attitudes, motivations, and institutions adverse to material progress. State economic control does not promote the required changes. By extending state control over people's lives, central planning reinforces the subjection of the individual to authority. It discourages self-reliance, personal provision for the future, sustained curiosity, and an experimental turn of mind.

The close controls of central planning restrict the movement of people and of physical and financial resources into directions yielding the highest return. They also restrict the movement of people between places and jobs, thereby retarding the erosion of attitudes and customs that inhibit material progress.

---

*<u>Development and Underdevelopment</u>, p. 64. Large-scale increase in investment expenditure through enforced increase in the savings ratio is neither a necessary nor a sufficient condition of economic development. Nor would increased investment necessarily imply utmost austerity though it often serves as a pretext for a scarcity of consumer goods.

Close state control of foreign trade is usually a pivot of comprehensive planning. External economic relations, that is migration, trade, and capital movements, serve not only to channel the movement of people, skills, commodities, and financial transactions, but also of new ideas and attitudes, crops, methods of production, and wants. These contacts often first suggest to the population the idea and possibility of a change in the existing scheme of things, including the idea of economic improvement. External economic contacts make possible such changes by voluntary adjustment to new opportunities, without the hardships and costs of compulsion.

Under central planning much output is unrelated to consumer demand. Thus even if the policy were to increase total output, which is improbable, this increase would be largely unrelated to living standards, the improvement of which is the ostensible objective of the policy. This divorce of output from living standards is in itself likely to retard a rise both in output and in living standards. This is so because the prospect of a higher and more varied level of consumption is usually an important incentive to higher economic performance through additional effort, saving, and enterprise. This is notably so in poor countries.

The argument that close state controls obstruct a rise in living standards is reinforced by the character and operation of most economic controls introduced under central planning. In less developed countries the principal controls include state monopoly of major branches of industry and commerce; extensive licensing of commercial and industrial activity, notably imports, exports, and international financial transactions; the establishment of many state owned and operated enterprises; large scale support to cooperative societies (which are in effect extensions of government departments rather than genuine cooperatives); and restrictions on the external and domestic movement of persons and commodities.

Some of these measures, especially state monopolies of agricultural exports, and extensive commercial and industrial licensing, provide governments with direct control over the livelihood of large sections of the population. For instance, politicians and civil servants in charge of the state monopolies of agricultural exports in West Africa, East Africa, and Burma practically prescribe the living standards of the producers subject to them.

Such controls cause a situation in which the economic opportunities of producers, consumers, workers, and traders in the exchange sector of the economy, depend on the government, that is on the politicians and civil servants who run it.

Many measures introduced in the name of economic planning do not in fact reflect any systematic examination of their likely social, political, and economic results, or even an attempted cost benefit analysis. Instead, they usually reflect the play of political forces, the vagaries of intellectual fashion, short-term administrative convenience, or pressures of sectional interests from the public or private sector. Their principal common feature is that they politicize social and economic life and increase the power and patronage of politicians and civil servants.

SOME POLITICAL RESULTS

Extensive state control largely politicizes social and economic life in the exchange sector. This provokes and exacerbates political tension in many LDCs, because it becomes all-important who has the government. The stakes in the fight for political power increase greatly, and so does the intensity of struggle for it, especially in multiracial societies. The history of Indonesia, Malaysia, Pakistan, East Africa, and Nigeria since about 1960 cannot be understood without this factor.

A further practical result is discontent with government policy, at least until all opposition has been suppressed. When state control over economic life is extensive, people will blame the government for all adverse economic change; and practically all change affects some groups adversely. These grievances may not be justified but are rendered plausible by the existence of controls and by the demands for state action. This further exacerbates political tension.

Material progress is adversely affected when political action is all important, since the energies and activities of ambitious or resourceful men are diverted from economic activity to political life.

In many less developed countries state controls have caused large-scale corruption. The controls have conferred great power on politicians and civil servants. In some instances, the policies have placed very large sums of money at the disposal of persons in charge of state export monopolies. Again, under conditions prevailing in many less developed economies, the allocation of import licenses or foreign exchange is tantamount to a cash gift.

Inevitably, many politicians and civil servants used this situation for political advantage and personal gain. Moreover, in many less developed countries, notably in Africa and Southeast Asia, the primary loyalties and obligations of men in responsible positions are to their families and not to abstract concepts of public good. In many countries corruption is so widespread as to justify their designation as kleptocracies.

Clearly adverse to material progress in LDCs is the preferential treatment of relatives in the allocation of licenses and of responsible posts in the public service. The politicizing of economic life also widens the range of posts and licenses allocated according to the need to balance the claims of different groups and communities. This leads to formal or informal quota systems on a communal basis, superimposed on the quotas implicit in the specific licensing of imports, foreign exchange, and other controlled commodities and services.

The results of central planning noted above reflect the wide discrepancy between the theoretical objectives of a policy and its actual implementation.

WIDER IMPLICATIONS

An untoward and paradoxical result of central planning is a serious neglect of the primary tasks of the government. Governments unable to perform their primary tasks are attempting to exercise close control over their economies. This phenomenon can be observed in many parts of the less developed world. The governments are anxious to plan while being unable to govern.

Comprehensive planning has nowhere benefited general living standards. In the Soviet-type economies comprehensive planning is the essence of economic policy. After decades of operation, general living standards remain extremely low; they are almost certainly much lower than they would have been under different economic systems. The contrast in the development of living standards in East and West Germany makes this point even more tellingly, because the populations of the two Germanys are ethnically identical. On the other hand, the nature and texture of communist societies reflect the pervasive character of sustained comprehensive planning. And these countries have strict frontier controls to prevent people from leaving, which clearly suggests widespread dissatisfaction with the material and nonmaterial conditions of their societies.

DISCUSSION

RICHARD ABLIN (Israel): The antimarket bias in planning is harmful. There is a distinction between loss of product or economic welfare caused by misallocation of resources and a failure to expand output over time, even when resources are efficiently used. Either type of failure is bad for a poor country. However, differences in per capita product between states are usually due to differences in efficiency in the use of production factors.

Most of the rise in real income in an LDC will be caused by improving efficiency. When efficiency rises, additional capital is needed as well.

In Israel inattention to market forces and encouragement of import substitution through high protection have shifted resources away from exports, creating a situation in which a much higher price is attached to dollars' worth of import savings than to dollars' worth of export earnings. Much waste results. Recently the rate of exchange for import substitution (industrial products) was about double that for export earnings. There is a similar tendency in agriculture. Israel may be losing something like 8 percent to 10 percent of potential GNP as a result of these distortions. There is probably a very serious loss of efficiency due to nonexploitation of economies of scale too.

The narrowing of markets caused by such distortions is conducive to monopolies and cartels and thus to loss of competitive pressures. This again decreases efficiency. To the extent that productivity of additional capital per worker depends on larger-scale output (especially of homogeneous products) investment incentives decrease and capital formation becomes slower. Incentives to raise managerial and labor skills also become weaker.

In Israel, borrowing abroad by private firms is restricted, partly because high nominal interest rates at home, caused by inflation, together with a fixed exchange rate and lower interest rates abroad, make foreign capital look cheaper to the individual than it is to the economy. A floating exchange rate, leading to gradual devaluation under inflationary conditions, would raise the apparent cost of foreign loans to their actual social costs.

The Israeli government restricts private capital imports at higher costs than credit obtained by the government abroad but then does not supply its own capital imports to the economy to lower market costs, and instead tries to stimulate local saving by cutting its own participation in marginal investment projects, which would not have been undertaken at the high local cost of capital. The selection of such projects for investment is done less efficiently than it would be done by private firms.

MEIR MERHAV (Israel): Professor Bauer assumes that market forces lead to complete dispersion of power. The individual enterprises neutralize each other, preventing each other from concentrating economic or political power. The political power resides elsewhere and has nothing to do with economics.

Yet some 20 years ago Professor Bauer showed in "Oligopoly in West African Trade" that this oligopoly is not a Machiavellian conspiracy but a necessary phenomenon, because in African conditions only large companies can stand up to adverse effects of market fluctuations and so on.

If so, the market forces would put power not in the hands of civil servants but in the hands of the owners of oligopolies and monopolies in such states. These are not likely to be more benevolent than civil servants or politicians. Besides, politicians are ultimately answerable; owners of oligopolies are answerable to no one. And politicians change faster than property owners.

In Venezuela, the people wielding real power have been in power whoever was in office. Even Stalin lasted only 20 years.

Professor Bauer says that planning reduces the level of output below its potential because it is unrelated to consumer demand. But which consumer demand—that of tomorrow or of five years hence? Shifting investment through planning into activities consumer demand would not stimulate may augment resources. Israeli agriculture is a good example. Consumer demand would not have created it, nor can it create the infrastructure in LDCs.

The LDCs have seen the ugly face of laisser faire through such companies as Unilever, Anaconda Copper, and United Fruit Company.

There are states that have had no comprehensive planning—Greece, Portugal, Spain. Is there real liberty there? Is there a lack of corruption in Haiti? Is there a concern for individuals' future in most African states? Can the poor people in the ranches of Venezuela rely on the evolution of their self-reliance, or must they be helped collectively?

Professor Bauer states that in Soviet-type economies based on comprehensive planning, living standards, after decades of operation, are low—lower than they would have been under a different system. He cites the contrast between West and East Germany to prove his point. But living standards have remained low in all except about a dozen of the states that have been operating under the capitalist system for centuries. And the contrast between the living standards of northern and southern Italy, ethnically identical like the Germanies, is just as striking. The same applies to northern and southern Brazil. The LDCs have suffered from market forces for about 150 years. Human liberty is only enjoyed by fewer than 20 states, in any meaningful sense, though capitalism has been around for some 200 years. Socialism has only existed for some 50 years. It has been subverted in the Soviet Union, and its planning invades areas it should have left alone. But private enterprise does the same when it produces or sells arms or pollutes the air and destroys the countryside in the name of market forces. Perhaps it is not too much to hope that there can be a humanist socialism, with individual liberty, satisfaction of private wants under conditions of public ownership of many means of production, and collective help to meet collective demands that cannot be presented in the market place.

SOLON BARRACLOUGH (FAO): Dr. Bauer starts with wrong concepts, uses fallacious arguments, and avoids the real issues having to do with planning. He identifies planning with control of the market. But planning does not mean that market forces cannot operate. They can operate, even in a labor-managed economy.

Then he compares an idealized capitalist model with the worst features of planning and control to be found anywhere. This is nonsense. Power and corruption need not be identified only with politicians and civil servants. We had the ITT case in the United States. There is plenty of corruption not related to the government in Latin America, the Near East, and elsewhere. In the southern United States and some parts of Latin America plantation owners can put workers in jail if they so wish. It is nonsense to identify power with government only.

Dr. Bauer forgets that the market is a human institution shaped by the present distribution of power and assets in the world. One cannot accept it as the final point of reference, when there are some 200 underdeveloped states.

The British do not accept Pakistanis into their labor force freely, nor do Americans accept Mexicans freely. People may want to leave East Germany because they don't want a redistribution of income that gives the poor more and the rich less. Some richer people began to leave in Chile and Cuba too, when this began to occur. As for the Soviet Union, it raised living standards considerably in 50 years. It might or might not have done better with capitalism.

GEORGIOS V. HADJIANASTASSIOU (Cyprus): Professor Bauer's definition of comprehensive planning encompasses even states with a modest type of comprehensive plan, and this is where the objections to his approach arise. He assumes that conditions in LDCs approach perfect competition and knowledge in the factor and product markets and that therefore planning prevents more efficient resource allocation. But this is not true of many LDCs. National plans attempt to correct imperfections prevalent in the world market. They are also useful when a state is confronted with sudden changes in the world market. Thus the creation of the European Economic Community presented Cyprus and some other open economies with the need for structural and institutional changes, which had to be planned. One has at least to define the economic environment of one's state, identify bottlenecks, suggest measures to deal with market imperfections, and plan structural changes to meet new conditions in the international market.

EPHRAIM KLEIMAN (Israel): The fact that economically successful states had no planning does not prove anything. Economic growth, in the long term, may be independent of economic systems. We may have to choose social systems according to our value judgments and not according to whether or not they succeed economically.

The uncertainties in international trade are great; so up to a point import substitution may be a better policy than export promotion, especially in states that are primary producers. This would justify the diversification programs in such states.

JOSEPH SHATIL (Israel): Government intervention and control are normal today—not only in LDCs—since even in the United States one cannot rely any more on the market to regulate the economy. Does such intervention and control require a comprehensive plan?

Israel is an example of excessive intervention and controls without planning. Planning here has been a pretence. Though it was right to encourage new industries since there was a potential of unutilized labor, when the time came to reduce the high tariffs protecting them the industrialists and private importers combined to keep prices up.

As regards import substitution: Some years ago there was a big argument here whether to grow sugar beet and refine sugar locally or to rely on imports. The world price of sugar was then $80.00 per ton. Now the world price of sugar is $260.00 per ton. The moral is that when planning one should not rely too much on current world prices or on imports.

YAIR MUNDLAK (Israel): The question is whether, at all levels, the growth rate will be the same regardless of government policy. I think here the government has a role and the regime is important.

ERROL HACKER (Israel): In theory, it can be argued that redistributing resources in favor of civil servants, who use them for development, is sound if they make better use of them than market forces. In a dynamic setting such redistribution would produce more resources, since the existing ones would be better utilized. It can also be argued that through frugality one accumulates capital and later this capital is used to produce more consumer goods. But the question is whether civil servants really make better use of resources than anyone else?

When economic power is concentrated in the hands of a few ministers and civil servants, these people should be assumed to have the necessary knowledge and expertise. But have they? In Israel it is difficult to make the right decisions about a single exchange rate. There are states where there are tens of exchange rates, and such decisions become even more difficult.

As regards industrialization, you set up a framework, tell people the rules of the game, and then let them act accordingly to make money. Now setting up an adequate framework is difficult enough. But when in addition you have to make decisions on a centralized planning basis as to how many textile factories should be in the country, what their size should be, and where they should be located, an enormous amount of knowledge is needed that is not always forthcoming.

Planning is wonderful on paper but never really works out in practice. Greece is a much less planned economy than Turkey yet has been doing much better. The same applies to Lebanon as compared with Egypt or Iraq, or to Kenya as compared with Tanzania. The most efficient definition of planning in a positive sense is "an effort to supplement the market process, where it requires supplementation."

RICHARD ABLIN (Israel) answering the discussion in place of Peter Bauer: The answer to Mr. Merhav, who says that oligopolies and monopolies are not usually more socially responsible than civil servants, is that the economic power granted by oligopoly is more restricted than that granted to planners by law.

Neither the choice of planning nor that of the market determines the level of progress in a society alone. The most important other factor is the level of skill, energy, and enthusiasm shown in the particular economy concerned. Skill and energy may be concentrated among civil servants or among private entrepreneurs or be equally balanced between the two groups. But an economy with much skill, energy, and enthusiasm for growth and development will probably succeed more than others.

Nevertheless, other things being equal (such as the technology and skills available), a bias towards substituting central allocative decisions for market processes will reduce the potential efficiency and the potential growth of the economy.

POLITICAL, SOCIAL, AND ADMINISTRATIVE CONSTRAINTS ON PLANNING
Ephraim Kleiman

WHAT SORT OF PLANNING

The word planning lends itself to a number of different interpretations.
- Government planning, as distinguished from planning by enterprises or households.
- Overall macroeconomic or macrosocial planning, rather than that of individual plants or industries.
- Planning for medium- and long-term targets rather than for contingencies.
- Indicative planning, for what are basically market economies, and not planning by directive for centralistic ones.

This limitation of the subject itself reflects a cardinal constraint on planning, for it postulates political factors that constrain planners to the indicative type of planning, as opposed to planning by directive of the Soviet type.

We are still left with an ambiguity in the title: does it refer to constraints on planning or on the implementation of plans? I will refer below to both types of constraints.

A plan constructed along the above-mentioned lines will have as a kernel a set of national accounts for some target year four or five years hence (possibly also for the intervening years).

This is something between a declaration of intentions and a forecast, the policies required for its fulfillment constituting part of the underlying assumptions. The plan may also contain more detailed blueprints for specific sectors or branches, such as agriculture, manufacturing, and transportation. While the responsibility for its fulfillment is governmental, only part of it is to be carried out (investment- and production-wise) by bodies directly controlled by the government. The rest (perhaps the greater part of it) is to be executed by private firms and households, the government's role being limited to the creation of conditions under which they will behave in the manner required by the plan.

To be effective such a plan has to be well publicized. By acquainting the public with the government's intentions, the plan becomes one of the policy measures employed to secure its own fulfillment.

REAL CONFLICTS OF INTERESTS

Politically speaking, the most fundamental constraint on planning is the degree of regimentation that the government may impose on the economy. In other words, a country's political regime rules out certain types of planning. Besides, many constraints may be imposed on the plan by political considerations. Some of them may be major—for example, the effects the plan is allowed to have on income distribution, where this is not one of the plan's explicit objectives. Others may be minor but nevertheless significant: for instance, the plan may be proscribed from affecting the situation of certain industries or of certain geographical areas because of the electoral offense this may give. Beyond their main objectives, such as economic growth, plans have many subsidiary ones. These minor objectives are usually expressed negatively, in the form of constraints that the plan is not allowed to violate.

Theoretical planning models normally postulate the existence of some social welfare function for the community. In real life, however, the plan will reflect values on which a wide consensus may be reached but never an unanimous one. There will always be groups whose welfare may be increased by minimizing the plan's maximands. This is due to the conflict of economic interests that scarcity of resources imposes on society, so that more for one must necessarily mean less for another. The "needs of the economy," the "good of the nation" can be no more than majority statements; to some groups the policies justified by them must be objectionable.

Indicative planning tries to achieve its objectives through the operation of market forces. The government creates such conditions that, in order to maximize their welfare, individuals must behave in a way ensuring the plan's fulfillment. Therefore, groups adversely affected by the plan will not express their objection to it through their economic behavior, for this would reduce their welfare even further. The only venue open to them is that of political action. Constant lobbying by pressure groups may restrict the plan and the policies designed to achieve its targets quite effectively.

THE CONFUSION OF MEANS AND ENDS

Planning is only a means to achieve desired ends. But in politics it has been elevated to the status of an end in itself. Thus social-democratic or labor governments are often committed to a much more comprehensive and detailed plan than can be pursued in the mixed economy that they operate. Similarly, conservative parties may eschew planning (as supposedly associated with totalitarian and expropriatory regimes) to a degree irreconcilable with governing once they are in power. The former may prepare plans for which the means of implementation cannot be provided. The latter may make unplanned or uncoordinated use of policy measures. Thus the meaning with which the term planning came to be charged may result in, respectively, over- or underplanning.

The confusion of means and ends manifests itself also in the policy measures required to implement plans. Thus, politically speaking, currency devaluation is considered a sign of failure, irrespective of its effect on economic activity or on the distribution of incomes. Hence, except at the moment of actual implementation, devaluation is not formally admitted to be one of the policy instruments available to the government. Even long-run plans are not allowed to postulate changes in the exchange rate. Since much national planning is aimed at improving unfavorable balance of payments situations, the straight jacket thus imposed on it becomes apparent.

The false identification of means as ends may not only eliminate some policy instruments but also compel the utilization of others. For example, suppose that under conditions obtaining some time in the past a certain type of tax was more progressive than others. In the eyes of the public, it became identified with progressiveness irrespectively of the prevailing conditions. Depending on the politics of the government of the day, the said tax (rather than its effect on income distribution) may either be proscribed or forced on the plan as an end unto itself. This would limit the choice of means available to achieve real, rather than illusory, ends.

COMPETING ENDS, AND THE TRADE-OFF BETWEEN FUTURE AND PRESENT

Perhaps the most important role of indicative planning is that of outlining the area in which policy decisions are meaningful. Planning underlines the constraints imposed by the data of the economy, such as the size and structure of the labor force and the quantity of capital available. It should reveal the mutual exclusiveness of competing ends and estimate the trade-off rates among them.

Ultimately, however, planning belongs in the realm of politics, which, as the old maxim has it, is the art of compromise not of contradiction. In politics one would like to claim that the usual objectives of plants—growth, equity, accumulation of foreign reserves—can be obtained simultaneously, not one at the expense of the other. Thus planning emphasizes precisely those conflicts the extent, or even the existence, of which the politician is unwilling to admit. Consequently the conflicts revealed by the planning process are toned down, in the best case in presentation only and in the worst case in the underlying analysis as well.

Long-term planning reduces the freedom that governments have in their short-run behavior. It does so by supplying criteria by which such behavior can be judged. One political requirement of the plan may therefore be that it allows the government some latitude in its day-to-day running of the economy. Such a requirement imposes, of course, a further constraint on the plan and its implementation.

The idea that a government committed to a long-run plan will obstruct its implementation seems paradoxical. That this may happen is illustrated by many a government's unwillingness to subordinate its current budgeting to the dictates of long-term planning. Under indicative planning the government budget is the main vehicle of implementation. To become operational it must be translated either into itemized expenditure positions or into overall sums of revenue and expenditure through which macropolicies are expressed. But instead of the plan providing the framework to which short-run budgets have to conform, the two are often expected to coexist peacefully side by side. Since in LDCs government action to implement the plan is practically limited to its budget, such departures from the plan can seriously affect its chances of fulfillment. The excuse usually given is that developments occurred for which no allowance was made in the plan. However, departures from the plan in annual budgets usually reflect considerations of short-term political expediency.

The political undesirability of emphasizing competing ends and the conflict between long-term planning and short-term political expediency stem from a basic characteristic of the sort of planning discussed here: its promise of jam tomorrow at the price of only bread today. As a rule, the prime objectives of such planning have been more rapid economic growth and the reversal of an adverse balance of trade situation. Both objectives usually require a decrease in living standards in the short-run. The constraints this imposes on planning will be stricter the more the public discounts future income.

DISTRUST AND LACK OF CONFIDENCE

Planning is a continuous process, requiring a constant revision in view of changes in circumstances and objectives. It is also a two-way process: basic data are absorbed from various economic and administrative units, to which provisional plan outlines are then circulated for reviews and criticism. The success of the plan depends on the degree of cooperation the planners receive from others in these preparatory stages as well as on their readiness to implement it.

In a mixed economy cooperation is required from government departments and various statutory bodies and agencies. In principle these are supposed to be part of the planning machinery, though this may not be true in practice. The cooperation of privately owned business firms is usually both loudly solicited and, if obtained, even more loudly praised; but a viable plan ought not to depend on it. The cooperation of profit-motivated firms is secured not by exhortations but by the creation of conditions under which the most profitable behavior is also that which serves the plan best. An intermediate position is occupied by the semipublic sector that characterizes mixed economies. This includes publicly owned but autonomously run enterprises, as well as those privately owned but, because of their size or importance, partially government controlled.

Information that government departments should supply to the planner refers to (a) the conditions prevailing in the fields of their respective responsibility (such as power, manufacturing, housing, education); (b) their forecast of developments expected in the absence of planning and, possibly, under a number of planning alternatives; (c) the development of their budgetary requirements in view of the plan's targets. If, as is probably the case, bureaucracy's maximand is the size of its budget allocation, it has a strong incentive to overestimate (c) above by underestimating (a) and (b). No conscious falsification probably takes place, but the judgment used in the choice of underlying assumptions, may deliberately leave wide safety margins. For example, forecasts of public outlays on health may not fully take into consideration the effects of economic growth on privately purchased substitutes as well as on the health levels themselves.

Government department and agencies, and even more so semipublic enterprises, may also be unwilling to provide the planners with the required information if they suspect that such disclosures may result in administrative, parliamentary, or public criticism of their affairs. Unless the planners are to duplicate the work of both the administrative and semipublic sectors, this lack or incompleteness of data will seriously hamper the preparation of plans.

The main administration constraint on planning stems, however, from disbelief in the fulfillment of the plan. At some stage of the planning process, departments will be asked to submit outline plans for their fields of activity under certain economic assumptions. These plans are then put together, checked for inconsistencies, and, if necessary, adjusted. They now form the framework within which the operational plans of the various departments have to be worked out and implemented. But suppose that a department doubts the ultimate ability or willingness of the government to execute its plan. It is then faced with a dilemma: If it plans its own projects according to the assumption of the master-plan, it may fail to provide correctly for the fields for which it is directly responsible; but if it disregards these assumptions and follows its own forecasts, it foils the plan. Consider the hypothetical reaction of the heads of a department in charge of the production of domestic consumer goods to a plan aiming to increase investment by halving the present rate of growth of private consumption. They will probably tell themselves that if the plan turns out to have been too ambitious their adherence to it will result in a dearth of consumer goods, while if the productive capacity in these industries is expanded more rapidly than planned the fulfillment of the main targets of the plan will cause some underemployment of plan and machinery. They may be expected to opt for the latter possibility.

This type of behavior arises because the responsibility for the overall fulfillment of the plan is usually more vaguely defined than that for specific fields of activity. It will be especially apparent when government agencies or enterprises, such as national airlines or ministries entrusted with road-building programs and so forth, have to carry out bits of the plan by themselves.

WHEN PREDICTION AFFECTS THE PREDICTED EVENT

The success of social and economic planning depends ultimately on its ability to affect the behavior of human beings. This is largely determined by factors over which the planner has no control; the resultant constraint on planning is obvious. But there is another paradoxical one due to the effect of the plan on the "planee."

Plans tend to be well publicized, thus becoming one of the instruments of their own fulfillment. To the public the plan is a statement of the government's intentions. If it expects that the government will stick to its plan, the latter, by its mere existence, will affect behavior. Will the government policy aim at high rates of growth and high levels of employment? Can it be expected to discriminate in favor of exports? The answer to these questions will be reflected in the behavior of business firms and households. After all, in a mixed economy, with much governmental intervention, certainty with respect to government behavior is of great importance.

However, as a result of the publication of a plan, behavior may depart from that assumed by it. Currency devaluation provides a well-known example. Foreknowledge of it increases the demand for foreign currency and decreases its supply. By thus aggravating the deficiency that the devaluation was planned to correct, it renders the planned policy ineffective. To ensure that the expected rate of inflation does not exceed some given limit, the published plan must quote a lower figure. A "true" forecast that reflects the expected future will probably never materialize if published; only forecasts that are "false" in this sense—that is, would never materialize if not publicized—will. Thus an internally consistent plan ceases to be such once published, while an originally inconsistent plan may become consistent through its publication.

POSTSCRIPT

Is there any sense in planning under such constraints? The answer depends on what we expect of planning. Perhaps the most important function of indicative planning is the systematic scanning of the feasible alternatives available to society. In broad outlines, this is possible even under the existing constraints. Furthermore, the planning process itself, through the repeated search for inconsistencies in the plan, serves ultimately to loosen some of the above enumerated constraints. Indicative planning is not very costly in resources. As long as we do not expect it to be fulfilled down to the last iota but rather view it as a framework for reaching rational decisions, a cost-benefit analysis would probably reveal the planning process to be more than just worthwhile.

DISCUSSION

YAACOV ARNON (Israel): I would call the main constraint on planning and its execution the Inverse Oedipus Effect, because Oedipus did not know, and therefore did, but the plan's effect is that you know, and therefore you do not do.

Now if publication makes plans go wrong, how do you solve this problem? Most planners think that their main weapon in executing a plan is to explain how it is done and why. After all, we are talking about indicative, not compulsory, planning. If you say prices will rise by 8 percent next year, people may go and buy more and prices will rise more. But if you say wages will rise 8 percent next year, this is the minimum and various pressures will see to it that they will certainly rise more.

There is a constraint on the execution of a plan caused by the difference between political leaders and the population. We had this problem in Israel during recent years. The government parties say they want to decrease income differentials, but when the low income groups get a wage increase the higher income groups set the same increase percentage. The constraint here is political.

EPHRAIM KLEIMAN (Israel): What does one do about publication? If publication of a plan changes the plan, behavior, and so on, then in theory this is a feedback, which can perhaps be worked into the system. But the public may not react to publication as expected. In practice, planners often deal with the situation by falsifying facts and not publishing the true plan. Indeed, though morally unpleasant, this may be the only solution but even so may not always work.

A social policy may indeed sometimes have the opposite effect of that intended because its sponsors did not see all the ramifications. This may be the experts' or the politicians' fault.

Let us say a high protective tariff is imposed for income distribution reasons, in the hope that capital will profit and workers will get higher wages because the goods they produce are protected. Yet the secondary effects may upset this picture. Policy makers often look only at the immediate effects, not at the secondary effects, with this sort of result.

POLITICAL, SOCIAL, AND ADMINISTRATIVE CONSTRAINTS ON PLANNING
Leopoldo Solis M.

THE PERSPECTIVE OF THE STATE

The purpose of planning in LDCs is not only to maximize the increase in the GNP but also to enforce structural changes in society, without which development cannot effectively reach the masses.

While pursuing its objectives, planning confronts political and social constraints that, if left alone, progressively deform the existing social structure. Administrative constraints may reflect the social and political constraints at the operative level, or they can curb the planning objectives by their own weight.

With regard to the planning objectives of LDCs, the state is not a predetermined unit of actions and decisions, since such a unit by promoting structural changes in society will change its nature in the process. The state is the apex where politics and economic converge. The agent best reflecting the different governmental organizations and their conflicts is the head of the state.

From the perspective of the national state, the capacity for qualitative changes becomes the only measure for judging political efficiency. Political inefficiency—the lack of capacity for qualitative changes in the social structure—will manifest itself by increased rigidities and by authoritarian actions and decisions.

An underdeveloped state unable to adapt itself to social change will increasingly make use of its police functions, in detriment to its political stability. A state cannot increase its political strength without a minimum of social consensus if it does not create adequate political organizations.

POLITICAL OBJECTIVES

Planning is not a neutral activity, free from the influence of political forces. When the state makes a decision such as to increase economic growth at a maximum rate, it is defining a political objective. If it considers that planning should be an instrument for the structural transformation of the economy, it is also defining a political objective.

Political objectives are fundamental to planning. The technical characteristics of planning are fundamental only inasmuch as they influence the political objectives. Social consensus is related to the basis of planning, which is the fixing and negotiation of its objectives. The required covenant of political objectives must be the outcome of political interaction between the rulers and the ruled if it is to have the necessary political strength.

Political interaction influences the final objectives. The initial purpose is to redistribute the economic values of the society; simultaneously, the social values in formation should be consolidated. Planning creates conflicts, but also it increases the cohesion and the negotiating power of the state. An initial decision to change is transformed into an objective of qualitative evolution.

POLITICAL CONSTRAINTS

The constraints on the implementation of a state's planning policies are exerted by groups or persons who have obtained a privileged situation enforced by their role within the market economy or the political apparatus.

There are explicit or implicit pressures that affect the decisions in the area of planning. These pressures are exerted by foreign investors and their representatives, the national entrepreneurial class, labor aristocracies, and political or bureaucratic elites.

Foreign Investors

Foreign investors and their representatives hinder economic and social planning whenever the objectives of the state do not correspond to those of the multinational corporations concerned.

The objectives and consequent actions of the multinational corporations may conflict with those of the state as regards sovereignty over the natural resources of the nation (especially in investments in mining) or the allocation of investments in the productive structure (foreign investments in superfluous consumption goods, when social priorities indicate investing in certain branches of intermediate and heavy industry, or in the production of popular goods for consumption).

There are concrete differences between the state and the corporations over export and external financial policies. Experts may be convenient for the host country but inconvenient for the multinational corporation, given the latter's costs, or because they would displace production from its own headquarters. In financial policy actual practices frequently conflict with the national objective that foreign investors should basically finance themselves externally so that they will not absorb the internal savings needed by the national corporations, by small- and middle-sized national firms, or by other sectors such as agriculture and housing.

National Entrepreneurial Classes

National Entrepreneurial Classes may constitute a serious obstacle to the planning objectives of society, since they exercise a very powerful influence (economical and political) over the state. At times this influence is even implemented by political bribery or by the actions of their representatives in the high echelons of government.

The influence of the entrepreneurial classes is also ideological. They normally defend the traditional values of European liberalism. But some of their members are more subtle, defending positions associated with nationalism (to increase commercial protection) and advance progressivism (to weaken their adversaries).

The influence of the national entrepreneurial classes acts against the objectives of planning from two angles: by their pressure for maintaining too high rates of commercial protection for longer periods than necessary; and by demanding high levels of sumptuary consumption, both from internal and external supply. They transmit imitation effects to the rest of the society, especially to the middle classes, and bring about unnecessary expenditure of scarce foreign exchange. Importers who mainly use imported inputs and entrepreneurs subsidized when they import industrial machinery exercise their influence to maintain fixed rates of exchange, which generate additional profits for them.

Labor Aristocracies

Labor aristocracies have become a substantial constraint on the objectives of planning. Their wage demands have been increasingly divorced from rises in productivity. They not only add inflationary stimulus but also induce investors to use capital-intensive technologies.

The pressures and actions of labor aristocracies are opposed to a policy of maximum employment. Directly the actions of their unions discriminate against the majority of the working class; indirectly they encourage technological substitution. Labor aristocracies are not eager to allow the majority of the workers access to the benefits of development.

Political and Bureaucratic Elites

The political and bureaucratic elites are the actual decision makers. Their legal powers and their capacity to convince give them considerable influence on the objectives and operations of planning. Their possibilities for modifying or rectifying the policies of the state are abundant—they encourage as well as punish. These elites follow a simple tactic: at first they utilize their best technicians for justifying the position convenient for them; if this is not sufficient, they exercise all the weight of their authority or the power that backs them.

The power of the political and bureaucratic elite can be internal (budgetary, legal, and organizational), or their strength may come from outside the state. The direct influence of the high level bureaucrats and the disruptive capacity of some politicians are generally sufficient for modifying objectives and operative decisions.

Frequently the actions and decisions of the political and bureaucratic elites are a fundamental and direct political constraint on planning. They have interests of their own that are related to their roles in the ministries, public enterprises, or political organizations. And links may be established between a sector of the political elite and groups of associated interests. As the result of a tacit or explicit agreement, the elite gives patronage to the interests of the lobbying group.

If the members of the political and bureaucratic elite are not linked to outside interests, their own requirements or ambitions encourage them to decide according to a conservative pattern. Decisions turn out to be those that cause a minimum conflict in the social structure and do not create enemies with present power. This mode of bureaucratic decision making is almost indispensable for continuing with a promising career or for not risking the power of their political or bureaucratic organization in conflicts of which it is not always possible to predict the outcome.

SOCIAL CONSTRAINTS

The historical evolution of most underdeveloped countries has created a social structure that constitutes a constraint on planning. The emergence of the middle class is one of its major characteristics.

Middle classes have emerged in a development pattern different from that of already developed countries. In nineteenth century Europe, industrialization brought urbanization. In the LDCs urbanization came before industrialization. Today the cities of the LDCs sell to a protected market, while the farms sell at international prices and buy the more expensive goods that are sold by the cities. The interdependence is not one that guarantees higher future consumption for all but may extract possibilities of improvement for the rural and urban poor.

The emergent middle class changed the traditional power structure, and their influence over the state has increased considerably. Their demands for increased urban services are generally satisfied at the expense of other investments of greater economic productivity and social benefit.

The middle classes are the strongest supporters of cosmopolitan patterns of consumption. They absorb the scarce resources of a nation in nonsocial patterns, not only by the immediate enjoyment of the benefits of production but also by greater consumption today, at the expense of investments most required to meet social needs. These consumption patterns have negative effects for the majority of the population and for future generations of the underdeveloped countries.

ADMINISTRATIVE CONSTRAINTS

Some of the most frequent administrative constraints are lack of adequate information, division between the planning and the fiscal functions of a government, and obstacles to a qualitative reorientation of public expenditure.

These may simply be a lack of information. Alternatively, services of statistical information in the different governmental organizations and in the private sector may use incompatible methodological approaches that do not permit intersectoral, interorganizational, and general analysis.

Information services should provide adequate information, ordered in such a way that the options for attaining short- and long-run objectives are known in advance. All feasible alternatives must be included and ranked accordingly. When these requirements are not fulfilled, planning faces a substantial constraint.

A frequent administrative constraint is conflicts that arise between planning and fiscal authorities. At the operative level, when planning is not closely tied to fiscal policy it turns out to be a mere cabinet exercise. Planners should participate in the evaluation of specific projects, in the analysis of current expenditures, and in the elaboration of the annual investment programs. If they do not participate in the budgetary process, one of the most powerful instruments of a government—the way it finances and allocates its resources— is out of their reach. In some cases fiscal authorities act against the planning objectives of the state. Hence it is important to work for cooperation between the two authorities.

Through links with fiscal policy, operative relations with other governmental institutions are established and it is possible to participate in the analysis of budgetary requests, in the discussions where the upper limits of overall expenditure and the final adjustments are decided. This participation strengthens the process of planning.

Coordination between fiscal policy and planning influences monetary policy by reconciling the availability of resources with the financial needs of the plan, and both with the objectives of monetary stability. The necessary link between price and exchange policy is also established.

Planning should be related to fiscal decisions and be able to affect the amount of resources and the return on investments. But planners must also be entitled to give opinions on laws that affect the planning process. Although laws do not create a social reality, they have restrictive or enforcing characteristics that can constrain or strengthen the planning process.

At the level of decisions, there are constraints that make a qualitative re-orientation of public expenditure extremely difficult.

The first constraint is the rigidity in the structure of public expenditure. It is associated with the fact that the largest part of public expenditure in any given year is allocated according to decisions taken one or several years before.

The second constraint results from organizations that managed large amounts of resources in the past having in the present teams of highly trained technicians for generating and promoting ideas and projects. Organizations that act in areas that were neglected in the past are not capable of generating investment projects of acceptable quality. The institution (ministry, public enterprise) that spent most in the past usually has a greater capacity for spending in the present, being consequently the one that absorbs more funds, though in many cases it does not direct its expenditures according to the planners' priorities.

A third constraint concerns the participants in the process of planning. Each individual participant has a perspective associated with his profession and work. Therefore, he tends to emphasize the importance of his particular points of view and to neglect the opinion of other individuals or bodies.

The operational obstacles to planning can be located when one recognizes the financial stringencies of the short run. One starts to confront the obstacles by efficiently linking current expenditure with capital investments to further the political objectives.

THE STRATEGY OF THE STATE

Political analysis is useful only when it is selective and concrete. For strategic purposes it is not sufficient to recognize constraints as general categories. Groups, factions, and even individuals have to be identified if one is to have a better idea of who is defending the goals of planning and who is making obstacles for the social objectives of the state. An adequate strategy can only result from a detailed analysis of the concrete reality.

The constraints to planning mentioned are related to each other. Their interdependence is such that they cannot be overcome one by one. Only a plan that takes into consideration all the fundamental constraints can offer a solution.

Social constraints cannot be overcome in the short run. Any significant change in consumption styles and any reorientation of investments in the private sector can be, at best, a very slow process. The actions in the area of social constraints are certainly fundamental, but from a strategic point of view they have to be postponed until serious educational efforts can be undertaken.

To overcome administrative constraints one needs men and power. The information needed to make decisions and evaluate policies in a very interdependent society cannot be obtained without the direction of capable technicians. Good engineers, economists, and mathematicians are indispenable for generating and promoting the required projects. But the best experts cannot do much if they do not have the backing political power.

The area of political constraints is the area in which immediate action is required. Unless the strategy helps to overcome these constraints, not much can be done about the social and administrative constraints on planning.

The pressure groups that constrain planning are not homogeneous. The strategy should try to unify the most active and dynamic groups and individuals, while at the same time making increased efforts to divide the more traditional and inefficient groups.

The sequence of the strategy has to be timed so that the active and dynamic groups see that the power of the new alliance is increasing fast and thus are encouraged to join it. Although many nonrational elements can give an impetus to the creation of a progressive and modernizing alliance, the rational of Realpolitik is usually stronger than subjective judgements.

Necessarily, the nuclei of the alliance must have power of their own, besides the power of the aggregate. They must be politically linked to sectors of society that would be benefited by a qualitative reorientation of development. And they require responsible leaders, who know the secrets of fast movement, restraint, and final consolidation.

The first step towards a progressive and modernizing alliance can only be taken when there is self-confidence and conviction about a feasible better future.

DISCUSSION

YAACOV ARNON (Israel): There is an inertia in every society, which makes it impossible to achieve structural changes over four or five years without a revolution. The constraints in a society that make it impossible to move too fast are not constraints on planning. They are one of the things planning has to take into account.

I agree that planning is a political exercise and its goals are based on political thinking. A democratic government, once elected to power, knows what it has promised but may have difficulties because it has to take into account not only those who elected it but the whole population.

The main constraint on planning is uncertainty. Goals, and even policies, may be set for a four or five year period. But there are extraneous factors the planners know nothing about when they are making their plan. This uncertainty increases over the period of the plan. It is much more difficult to plan the fifth year of the plan than the first.

In a mixed economy the government should intervene only to the extent that the private sector is not responding to the targets of the planning authority. Strong vested interests can be a serious constraint on planning, which often cannot be overcome.

A 5-year plan is a constraint on government departments, which they dislike. Ministers like to have a freer hand. Let us say that planners reach the conclusion that if there is a 3 percent rise in private consumption, agricultural output in a certain field should not be increased—and then private consumption rises by 5 percent. The minister of agriculture may then be attacked because there are not enough vegetables or something else on the market.

The planned 3 percent rise in private consumption may involve supplying 20,000 refrigerators. But the minister of trade and industry may think there is a need for 40,000. There you have a real administrative conflict, which is very difficult to resolve. This kind of division of responsibility is one of the constraints on planning.

DAVID WEINSCHAL (Israel): There are conflicts among participants in the budgetary process and among planners: first, about the order or priorities for social, economic, and political aims, because of differences in value judgements and interest; second, about interpretation of facts and data. Politicians and experts have to collaborate in the planning process to reach conclusions and often do not find a common language. This is a serious constraint on planning. Improvement of information systems and of empirical analyses may limit the area of disagreements.

Disagreements also exist about subjective expectations. Thus in Israel there is no agreement on the volume of immigration in the coming years. There are optimists and pessimists, but there is no scientific way of forecasting such trends. Disagreements about expectations create conflicts and constraints on planning.

However, the main constraint on planning is the power structure, since decisions taken in the planning process tend to lead to changes in it.

GERT ROSENTHAL (Head, National Planning Office, Guatemala): One can plan for certain pressure groups, in which case they would support this. One can plan formally or informally. Planning can also be an advisory service. The type of constraints Dr. Solis describes are the natural constraints on the development process per se, rather than on planning.

There is a real ideological constraint on planning as regards the degree of state intervention in economic development. In many Latin American states pressure groups with economic or political power object to such intervention on ideological grounds. From this to opposing planning as a process is a small step.

AARON WIENER (Israel): The free professions may constitute an important constraint. If we have a phlegmatic political structure, we have a phlegmatic type of planning. And the political structure may be set up according to disciplines taught at universities.

Projects produced by professionals are greatly similar to projects in developed countries and may be repeated even if experience over 10 or 20 years proves them unsuccessful. The most attractive projects for LDCs are usually not submitted for evaluation. These are examples of constraints produced by professionals.

ALEJANDRO SUELS (Venezuela): There is a basic contradiction between the desire for maximum support for the government's planning process and its freedom to execute its plans. The more sections of the population the government wants on its side the more vested interests are going to be brought to bear on its plans. This can be a serious constraint.

Sometimes this kind of conflict can be avoided but more often not.

M. EMILIO CASTANON (OAS): In many states the evaluation of results is sacrificed in order to maintain conformity to certain doctrines.

NUSRET FISEK (Turkey): Mr. Solis' constraints affect more the implementation than the design of the plan. Implementation is the weakest point in the planning process. Most planners have no experience of implementation. If they underestimate the experience of the administrators, the plans become very difficult to execute.

LEOPOLDO SOLIS M. (Mexico): I have no quarrel with the view that constraints on planning are in fact general constraints on development.
When a planning office is run by an economist, it has a structure that could be improved. Planning has become participating to an extent justifying planning agencies run by agronomists and engineers.
If there is a strong government department and a weak one, the planners should try to work through the strong one.

THE USE AND ABUSE OF MODELS IN DEVELOPMENT PLANNING
Paul Streeten

All thought presupposes implicit or explicit model building and model using. But models must be realistic, relevant, and useful. The trouble with many current models is that they are shapely and elegant but lack the vital organs.

SYSTEMATIC BIASES

Model thinking shows four systematic biases, which are related to each other and overlap. These can be called adapted ceteris paribus or automatic mutatis muntandis; one-factor analysis; misplaced aggregation; and illegitimate isolation.

Adapted Ceteris Paribus or Automatic Mutatis Mutandis

The conclusions of orthodox liberal and Marxian economics, though derived from very different premises, converge in this respect. The separation of parameters from variables in Western orthodox models is partly determined by what is appropriate for advanced industrial nations, partly by ideology and vested interests, and partly by convenience of analysis. Thus psychological attitudes and valuations and social institutions are normally assumed to be given and adapted. We assume, for example, that there is a legal framework; that contracts are enforced; that an efficient civil service carries out government orders and an honest judiciary adjudicates; that people are able and willing to work if opportunities arise; that they are literate, skilled, and able to cooperate with discipline, appearing on time and carrying out orders; that money spent is efficiently spent and not diverted into the pockets of corrupt officials; and that alternatives are considered largely on their pecuniary merits. It follows that none of these matters is considered a suitable area for planning.

In the Marxian scheme (though not always in Marx's own writings) what are parameters become dependent variables. Cultural, political, and social institutions are a superstructure determined by the methods of production. It reflects these conditions and creates tensions between the degree of development of the forces of production and the prevailing relations of production (the institutions and attitudes). These tensions give rise to revolution. After the revolution, the attitudes and institutions reflect the new conditions of production. Hence social, cultural, and political attitudes and institutions, the so-called "relations of production," though dependent variables, are, after a time-lag, adjusted to the extent required by the dynamic productive forces. Once again, though for fundamentally different reasons planning the superstructure is not in question. It would be futile before the revolution and unnecessary after it.

Thus the conservative judgment that a reform of attitudes and institutions is undesirable and the Marxian judgment that it is either impossible or inevitable lead to the same conclusion, distracting attention from conscious policy directed at a radical reform of the so-called "noneconomic" factors in economic development. Textbooks, articles, and plans pay lip service to the need to reform the social framework before economic planning can begin. But these declarations are usually forgotten later when the discussion turns to such conventional concepts as income, employment savings, and investment. At that stage either the assumption of <u>ceteris paribus</u> (other things being equal) is tacitly reintroduced, so that the conventional economic variables can be considered in isolation; or the assumption of automatic <u>mutatis mutandis</u> (due alteration of details) is made, implying that where other things cannot be assumed constant they will without special policies be adapted to the required extent as a result of economic transformation.

The intellectual framework that reflects this bias is supported by value judgements and by vested interests. As we shall see, reforms of institutions and human attitudes violate entrenched interests and are therefore more painful to implement than financial expenditure programs.

In a bias-free model the distinction between parameters and variables would be determined not by ideological preconceptions but by the situation to which the model is intended to apply and by the questions asked about this situation. To be useful models will have to be, at least initially, much more specific to individual cases and much less general and theoretical. In particular, the distinction between parameters and variables should not run along the line drawn between "economic" and "noneconomic" factors operating in a situation. Thus social and political reform should neither "precede" nor "follow" economic development; social reform must accompany development, reinforce it, create the conditions necessary for it, but is itself promoted and determined by development. The process is one of continual mutual causation. There is no "primacy" of either economics or politics.

One-factor Analysis

Economists frequently select one factor as the strategic variable in development, although the choice of this factor is subject to fashion and ideology. If the physiocrats stressed land as the source of all wealth and the classical economists labor, capital has until recently played the strategic role. Keynes's emphasis on the income-creating aspect of capital was combined with Marx's emphasis on its output-creating aspect in the Harrod-Domar model, which has strongly influenced planners. The relationship of the equation of the rate of growth of income to the savings ratio divided by the capital-output ratio has been one of the chief vehicles by which Western economic thought has been carried into the discussions of the plans of underdeveloped countries.

Capital is sometimes regarded as a necessary and sufficient condition of growth, sometimes as the strategic variable. Yet numerous other conditions both account for past growth in advanced countries and are required for development in underdeveloped countries. A new one-factor analysis has tended to replace the old one. Education or Technology has become the fashion. There is often little thought as to education of whom, for what, how long, in conjunction with what other factors, which will be singled out as discussion progresses. Perhaps we shall soon study the returns from appropriate child training, which produces experimental innovating personalities, as we are already studying the returns from expenditure on child prevention.

Misplaced Aggregation

Almost all concepts formed by aggregation suitable for analyzing Western economies must be carefully reconsidered before they can be applied to underdeveloped economies. "Capital," "income," "employment," "unemployment," "price level," "savings," and "investment", presuppose conditions that are absent in many underdeveloped countries. "employment" presupposes a fairly homogeneous, mobile labor force, willing and able to work and responsive to incentives. In a society of isolated communities, some of them apathetic or with religious prejudices against certain kinds of work, illiterate and unused to cooperation, the notion "labor force" does not make sense. Similarly "underemployment" or "disguised unemployment" presupposes that if only demand and machines were available men and women would be able and willing to work. In fact, much more would be required: for instance, a breakdown of caste prejudices, of apathy, of lack of interest in money rewards, or of resistance to cooperation, discipline, and punctuality. Any attempt to calculate disguised unemployment also presupposes a value judgment as to the length of the appropriate working day and working week.

If economies are divided into sectors between which there is little or no substitution, either in consumption in response to changes in relative prices, or in production in response to changes in relative factor rewards, aggregation of incomes or prices is inappropriate. Even though the indigenous sector may sell its surplus in the market and even though some of its members may occasionally participate in the transactions of the money sector, if the indigenous sector neither depends upon nor interacts with the capitalist sector aggregation can be meaningless. The income of an industrial enclave may grow, while real income per head of the indigenous population stagnates or declines. In what sense is average income rising? The problem is not merely how to get at the facts in the indigenous sector and how to appraise them properly. More fundamental is the problem what weights to attach to a small decline of essentials and to a large increase of nonessentials. Paasche and Laspeyres indices may give contradictory results. Habits of thought induce us to use concepts that are applicable to one set of conditions, because substitution is possible, responses exist, and value judgments are appropriate, in an entirely different context, where these presuppositions, of legitimate aggregation are absent. The statistical manifestation of this would be contradictory results according to which of several equally plausible sets of weights were applied to the same change. Using base period weights we should register a rise in income per head and therefore conclude that development is proceeding, while we have begged the political question, "development for whom?"

The distinction between consumption and investment can have various justifications. In the context of development it is based upon the assumption that investment enables us to produce more later than we would otherwise have done, while consumption is current enjoyment. But if more food and better health now reduce apathy and raise ability to work, they share in the characteristics of investment: consumption, too, is productive of more output.* If different

---

*It has been estimated that the combined effect of malnutrition and ill health in Ecuador reduces the average worker's production

investment projects require different sums to bribe corrupt officials, what guide is their cost to the resources used up? To abstract from the differences in such cases is to pour out the baby with the bath water.

It is correct to say that a man is male, a woman female, but it does not make sense to ask: "Is your family male or female?" Similarly, it is what philosophers call a category mistake to ask what is the capital, income, employment, price level, and so on of a society sharply divided into noncommunicating sectors. Just as words can be spelled but letters of the alphabet cannot be spelt, so asking questions about certain aggregates commonly used in advanced industrial countries as if they applied to underdeveloped countries is improper. The solution of a jigsaw puzzle consists in putting each piece where it belongs, not in lumping them together arbitrarily.

Two separate problems arise here. First, category mistakes are made where a category is applied to a field of experience to which it is inappropriate. It is quite possible for this category to be appropriate for advanced countries, but not for underdeveloped ones, just as it is legitimate to ask "Where is the University?" in some cities but not in Oxford.

Second, there are instances in which the category might be appropriate if we knew what it meant when applied to a situation of underdevelopment. Thus the distinction between consumption and investment can be misplaced aggregation in either sense, depending upon the definition. If investment is defined as abstaining for the sake of higher consumption later the first problem may arise. But if investment is defined as any input that yields higher output later, irrespective of whether it involves abstaining or not, the second problem arises and the error is not a conceptual one but one of failing to group certain activities under investment that, in advanced countries, are classified exclusively as consumption.

Illegitimate Isolation

The converse of misplaced aggregation, but related to one-factor analysis, which is a manifestation of it, is the bias of illegitimate isolation. It consists in assigning the role of sufficient condition to what may or may not be one of several necessary conditions of development. If a component is illegitimately isolated from its necessary complements and then aggregated with others similarly

---

to 48 percent of his potential capacity, as opposed to 93 percent in the United States.

isolated, we get a combination of misplaced aggregation and illegitimate isolation. This bias can be illustrated by successive missions going to a country. The first says entrepreneurial incentives are inadequate and if we nurse these by low taxes, resources will soon become available. The next says resources are the bottleneck and decisions will soon come forth if resources are set free by high taxation to generate a high budget surplus. But the correct policy would be high taxation of certain incomes and property, perhaps land, combined with generous investment allowances or employment subsidies and other incentives, where these yield results. The division should not be resources versus incentives but certain incentives combined with certain resources.

Education, now often advocated as a panacea, may simply result in a group of educated unemployed and unemployables. Equipment may lie unmaintained and rusting. Irrigation water flows unused and reservoirs are silting because investment has not been coordinated with the right kind of education, land reform, and civil service reform. The price we pay for misplaced aggregation and illegitimate isolation is wasted resources and possibly hardened resistance to and growing cynicism about the process of development.

Perhaps the most serious criticism of certain planning models is that their very success becomes an obstacle to adaptation and innovation. Planning models introduce an additional rigidity into societies already stiff with rigidities. For this reason, in spite of declared intentions to the contrary, they are elements strengthening conservatism.

The alternative is not, however, to rely on laissez-faire and the free play of market forces. It is rather to combine contingency planning with rolling planning, so that there can be always adequate responses to new and unforeseen events, both favorable (such as an improvement in the terms of trade) and unfavorable (such as a cut in aid). While this involves sacrificing some of the political appeal of rigid five- or seven-year planning models, the contingencies can and should be presented to the electorate. A clear distinction should be drawn between forecasts and hypothetical prognoses. Hypothetical projections of current trends can be used to indicate required action to prevent or to accelerate these hypothetical trends. The true prophets are those who move the people to take protective or supporting action, not those who turn out to be right. It may therefore be a virtue of certain prognoses, or scenarios as they have come to be called, to turn out to be self-falsifying. Subtle planning models will allow for the possibility of over reaction to the prognosis of the plan.

SUMMARY AND CONCLUSIONS

In what respects should we particularly beware of possible traps in established doctrines and in what ways can these be improved or replaced? In addition to the already discussed problems of misplaced aggregation and illegitimate isolation, one might consider the following points:

- Be on guard against assuming continuous and smooth functions. Discontinuities and kinks may occur in relationships such as capital coefficients, supply of effort, production functions, foreign trade, and so on. Consider indivisibilities and complementarities.
- Be not content with less than at least two sectors where intersectoral relations are crucial to a problem. Clearly the marginal returns from disaggregation decline and may become negative, but Keynesian aggregation, too, is often misleading.
- Consider the implications of unstable equilibria, whether static or dynamic. Increasing returns, cumulative processes, and polarization are not as exceptional as the concentration on stable equilibrium suggests. Indeed, in development processes they are the rule.
- Include, where necessary, variables that are exogenous in advanced countries as dependent variables. Examples are administration, political power structure, motivations and incentives, population growth, and technical knowledge.
- Keep in mind the specific limitations of the free market system as a guide to certain important decisions. Distinguish clearly between free market forces and price policies. The latter are an instrument of planning.
- Beware of abstracting from time: the phasing of projects, the time-flow of consumption, and the effects on learning are crucial.
- Be content to provide (at least initially) sufficient conditions for certain sequences rather than full explanations. Discard these sufficient conditions only if they are contradicted by observations.
- Remember that an important function of a model is to show up the limitations of another model. Models may serve as limbering up exercises, demonstrating various possibilites. The great danger is that they rigidify into blinkers, forcing us to perceive reality in only one way.
- Never mistake validity for truth. Consistent logical or mathematical models, rigorously derived from stated premises, are valid but need have no connection with reality. The conclusions or the assumptions of empirical models must be verifiable in the light of observations. The identification of mathematical symbols with such concepts as "products," "income," "production functions," "capital," "employment," which are never operationally defined,

introduces a systematic confusion into the analysis. The confusion is concealed by the rigor of the deductions from the ill-defined assumptions. It is a frequent fault of economic model builders and model users that they fail to distinguish between consistency and realism, between validity and truth.

POSTSCRIPT

This conference should be concerned with distribution of status, prestige, participation, and satisfaction from work. But economists tend to deal with what can be measured, and income inequality can be measured.

There need to be no conflict between equality and economic growth, given proper planning.

There are broadly three schools of thought on redistribution of income: One view is that a sound price structure, involving the reduction of the relative price of labor as against capital, a better capital market, realistic exchange rates, and so forth. would allow LDCs to exploit their comparative advantage of unskilled labor, improve efficiency, and gradually improve income distribution while encouraging growth. The second view is that a revolutionary attitude to redistribution of assets and power is necessary. The third view claims that technological improvements are the key to better income distribution and growth.

My view is that all three are wrong, since no approach is adequate by itself. The revolutionists tend to forget that it is not enough to distribute assets to the poor. They must also be made to use them as constructively as the rich did. Otherwise you get equality but lower the standard of living. In the Soviet Union agriculture is not efficient and has not produced great equality either.

Getting a correct price level is also not enough in itself. If the distribution of land, property, educational opportunities, and so on is very unequal, it may enable more workers to be employed but will not distribute incomes more fairly between wage earners, the poor rural population, and the big land owners.

Nor will the technological approach alone work. The Green Revolution may increase food supplies but may well aggravate inequalities. Rich farmers become richer; the poor ones are often worse off than before, and some are actually dispossessed.

So the only correct approach is to combine all three facets: correct pricing and incentives, some redistribution of wealth and power (and power like income should be more evenly spread, not concentrated in a single group—whichever group this may be), and some technological progress. The use of only one instrument to the exclusion of the others may make matters worse than they were.

DISCUSSION

PINHAS ZUSSMAN (Israel): Too much emphasis is placed on the efficiency of resource allocation through the price mechanism. In Israel price distortions in agriculture amount to about 5 percent of the annual added value of the sector. Technological progress in agriculture here proceeds at an average of 3 percent per annum; that is, every year there is 3 percent more output without additional input. So two or three years of technological progress can offset all losses due to price inefficiency.

Making prices right is a tough political problem because income distribution and political pressure groups are involved. So in Israel, I think, we selected the right policy by not making prices right and by putting more emphasis on technological and institutional progress.

The argument that formal economic planning models tend to disregard changes in social and institutional attitudes may be true, but social change is usually slow. For plans of up to five years the assumptions that social institutions will not change much tends to be correct. However, formal planning models reduce contacts between factors concerned in development, letting computers make political decisions, which often don't fit the general scheme. In Israel, formal planning models have been unsuccessful.

A Participant: There is a fourth category, besides the three Professor Streeten mentioned. It is based on psychology, and lays stress on changing people and reforming institutions, generally increasing competence and improving decisions.

A different type of development model is a policy simulator, portraying the workings of systems and enabling the checking of different contingencies by policy makers. This type of model is not predictive or plan making.

THOMAS CARROLL (Inter-American Development Bank): The three prongs of Professor Streeten's fork may not be of equal length. In many developing states institutional reform must take precedence, because without it the price mechanism will not function properly. The kind of technology developed is dependent on the new institutional framework, whether the latter is created rapidly or by stages. Most agricultural inventions in eighteenth and nineteenth century United States came as a result of the family farming system. Technology is usually related to the kind of institutional organization preferred.

EPHRAIM KLEIMAN (Israel): The price mechanism has been a failure in improving income distribution. Partly because price mechanists disregarded the problem of income distribution, assuming that growth was the first priority and that if the general income level rises this is an improvement even if distribution is worsened, as long as nobody is worse off than before. How does a man react when his income is doubled but the gap between him and someone above him is trebled? We should try to find out how people feel about income distribution before making recommendations about it.

WILFRED BECKERMAN (Great Britain): Almost any tinkering with the price mechanism, at least in Britain, is on income distribution grounds. Agricultural support, subsidies to particular industries, rent controls, and tariffs are the result of this.

But the price mechanism has a nasty habit of coming in through the back door. The amount of funds for redistributive purposes flowing in and out of the government budget in Britain and the United States is much greater than their actual effect on redistribution.

In France family allowances and social benefits are very high. If they were eliminated the unions would demand and get big wage rises. In the United States social benefits tend to be passed back to the wage earner, while company taxes are passed on in prices. So attempts to redistribute income tend to feed back through the price mechanism.

Hence I have gradually reached the conclusion that if one wants to frame a policy looking after allocation of resources, income distribution, and a technical approach, one must work out a very elaborate model of the economy to ensure that what one is giving with one hand is not going to be taken away by the other.

LEOPOLDO SOLIS M. (Mexico): Professor Streeten is too pessimistic about models. In less developed states the problem is to avoid the shortcomings of orthodox economic thought. Models should suit the institutional framework and behavior relations common in such states.

As regards linear models in agricultural planning, a straightforward program easy to apply is needed if one wants to maximize incomes and water and land are available. You may get a result with higher value of output and possibilities of varied income distribution within the areas. Such models are useful.

IASSU ANDEMICAEL (Economic Affairs Officer, ECA): In some cases, price rectification, better income distribution and the choice of an appropriate technology may be of little help, especially if the country concerned is too small. In Africa there are 41 independent states, but only 4 have a population of over 20 million (Nigeria, Ethiopia, Egypt, and Zaire). Half of the African states have populations of 2 to 5 million only, and there it will be extremely difficult to establish industries requiring a certain minimum size. I would therefore suggest the importance of regional cooperation and the establishment of multinational industries.

PAUL STREETEN (Great Britain): My theme was the need to attack other than purely economic values, especially psychology and attitudes. I do not reject model making, but models must be realistic and not leave out variables not taught at the universities. Once it is accepted that there are, say, three prerequisites for success, it is not reasonable to argue that one of them is more necessary than the other.

We should avoid the fallacy of Marxians and some liberals that if one is given the thing dear to one's heart the rest will automatically follow too. The utopian socialists were basically more realistic, because they thought of how to change human beings and institutions to create the society we want.

I do not believe that redistribution of land or power automatically produces the right technology. In some states earning capacity could be redistributed gradually out of annual savings, increasing the earning capacity of the lower income groups.

Radical redistributionism can take the form of death duties or a capital levy, not only of revolution. But unless it is accompanied by technological steps it will lower total output and reduce the earning power of the redistributed assets.

Incentives are important, but need not consist solely of profits or money. In China, where they redistributed assets and improved technology, they seem to be using collective instead of individual incentives. But some incentives must be used, otherwise one only gets equality at a low level of living.

What happens to average incomes is a technical problem. I could set out the conditions under which the average income of the lowest 20, 30, or 40 percent would rise. This depends on the elasticity of substitution between wages and capital in response to such factors as relative price changes, technology, fiscal policy, education, and links between jobs and educational qualifications.

Taiwan has something to teach. It has got its prices right, has promoted exports after a period of import substitution, and has the right exchange rate and a quite effective land reform.

However, the most liberal trade regimes are rarely the most liberal politically. There is a certain negative correlation there, and, if we are concerned with equality not only in the economic sphere, attention must be paid to freedom of expression, participation, and so on.

A final remark on planning models: If we mean by development not only growth but also a certain quality of life, income distribution, and general participation, we must ask: "What are the causes of development?" This we do not know. First land was emphasized, then labor, then capital, then education, then technology. Yet these are not the strategic factors in development.

**USEFULNESS OF
PLANNING MODELS**
Bernard Ullmo

An economic model is a set of quantitative mathematical relations capable of orderly solution, which allows us to describe and understand the working mechanism of a section of an economy.
In principle, the orderly solution is not a requirement but an aid. It becomes common practice when computations are complicated or when the model is to be utilized more than once (as is normal when a plan is being prepared). The set of mathematical relations eliminates qualitative representations of the economic reality, giving preference to quantitative representations. "Quantitative," as against literal, indicates that the planned model describes a concrete economy characterized by the value of its representative or structural parameters. The original purpose of the national accounting system is to describe things. A genuine economic model must include, besides relationships that constitute only definitions, technical or behavioral relationships connecting an economic aggregate with other economic aggregates.
The planners of the Sixth French Plan had accumulated some experience with models: The physico-financial model (FIFI) played an important role in the planning process, and we will be continually referring to it. We will also examine necessary modifications when speaking about developing countries, making a comparative analysis where possible.
Two types of factors allow a model to be useful: the factors that assure its technical quality and the factors surrounding it (factors of the environment).

FACTORS THAT ASSURE THE TECHNICAL
QUALITY OF THE MODELS

Models are Designed to Clarify Problems,
not to put General Theories Into Practice

Let us assume that governments need planned economic development. We will not argue about the chosen type of planning, imperative or indicative, that is integrated into a socialist or a liberal scheme.

Is it beneficial to develop formal models when planning? What is the connection they ought to have with economic theory?

Every model requires theoretical elements, but these elements may be implicit or explicit, conscious or subconscious. It has the purpose of solving a well defined problem, such as giving quantitative values, resource constraints, and coherence. The French example illustrates this proposition.

A fundamental problem of the French economy is the structural tendency to disequilibrium in its balance of payments, which may reduce potentially rapid growth if it persists. A basic choice is posed: to close the economy or to expose it to foreign trade. Apparently the task is simplified if the first option is taken. If the second alternative is chosen one may ask why the planner introduces additional difficulties

Theoretical considerations explain his choice: they link economic dynamism and the scale of foreign trade; benefits accrue from specialization, from economies of scale, and from the increased dynamism of French industry under the pressure of foreign competition.

The benefits derived from specialization include cost and comparison advantages. The importance of economies of scale is due to the inadequacy of the decreasing returns hypothesis in every activity connected with the use of a natural resource. This is true of industry, especially of activities associated with a high level of value added to raw materials processed.

Accepting that the opening of the French economy to the world constitutes an essential economic choice, the Planning Authority assigns to the model a double objective: to examine the consequences of a decision about medium term growth and macroeconomic equilibrium; and to propose a corrective economic policy in case of disequilibrium.

To reach these objectives, the authors of the model FIFI want to base it on specific theoretical elements applying to the French economy in the period around 1965. Under this theory France has a competitive economy. This working definition derives from the hypothesis under which foreign industries are dominant, thus constituting a constraint for French industries.

The structure of the model, its main mechanism, and the results it presents are a consequence of the above problem:

It is a simulation model, making medium-term forecasts. This because the objective is to discover eventual disequilibrium. The main equilibriums in the medium term relate to growth, employment, prices, public finance, and foreign finance. To consider corrective policies constitutes a simulation problem. The model includes many instrument variables of economic policy. Full employment is not assumed to be assured, nor are public or foreign finance assumed to be in equilibrium; these elements may prove to be problems.

It is a semiglobal model distinguishing sectors that are exposed to international competition (80 percent of total foreign trade is carried out by industry), protected from this competition (building and public works, services, internal trade), and regulated (agriculture, energy, transport, and communications).

A competitive economy being assumed, foreign trade receives an original treatment: Prices play an essential role but not as relative prices, since, by hypothesis, foreign and French industries work with the same set of prices in the French market. Prices and costs, both of them endogenous in model, allow a margin of self-financing, taken as a base, to set the level of investments and the expansion of productive capacity. If this expansion is insufficient in relation to demand, part of which is induced by income from production, a second part being autonomous, the foreign balance will tend to worsen.

The economic policy tested by the model has the following effects on the equilibrium position of economic aggregates: A policy designed to develop or reduce autonomous demand has almost no influence on the foreign trade balance; a policy intended to support supply by reducing business costs may improve the equilibrium of growth, employment, prices and public finance, if concentrated on industrial activity.

The Sixth Plan particularly involves precise planning of public finance. The model, therefore, is well developed in this aspect and at present analyzes six different categories of authorities.

A Good Statistical Base is Necessary, but it
Must be Adapted to the Problem to be Dealt with

Quantification, Structural Changes, Model and Statistical Base

The need to quantify is not always evident to planners in developing countries. They maintain that good statistics are necessary for the forecasting models of developed countries that describe the future by extrapolation from the past. Underdeveloped countries must alter their economic structures and thus have to make a radical break with the past. This point of view may set goals (quantifiable or not) so ambitious as to be inconsistent with any firm economic reality; it is based on the illogical tendency, often encountered, to identify ambitious goals with planning quality.

The frequent utilization of a statistical base provides a sense of reality that seems to improve the standard of work. A formal statistical base is necessary to set realistic goals consistent with previous development or to introduce realistic changes in the different means employed. The quality of the model and its usefulness cannot go beyond the quality of the statistics used as a base. This should lead to the operation of the simplest models when the statistical base is fragile and to the rejection of the more sophisticated ones.

The Statistical Base Must Be Adapted to the Problem to Be Dealt With

The planner often ignores statistical facts. Statisticians tend to solve only problems that concern them and not those posed to them. Attaching the statistical service to the planning agency may attenuate some of the differences but cannot eliminate them.

In the planning models the essential elements are extracted from the time series of the national accounts; employment statistics are also used in developed countries. Time series adapt themselves better to economic models than do instantaneous nonrenewable samples, since they show the evolution of a certain phenomenon. To build a model one needs a relatively long and homogeneous series: two years (if possible separated by an interval) of national accounts information constitute a good start. Those sections with which the planner aims to deal should especially be developed.

After the Second World War, France's basic industries were practically destroyed; the main problem was reconstruction and administration in times of rationing and scarcity. Input-output tables, Leontieff matrices (in terms of volume), or the balance of raw materials (in physical quantities) for major basic products were the instruments best adapted for solving the problems of that period. Consequently problems of regulations dealing with divisions between consumption and investment and between public investment and private investment came to the top, and the French system of national accounts developed the economic matrix for aggregates that enabled one to trace original and redistributed income flows.

More recently problems associated with the competitiveness of industry have drawn attention to the price formation mechanism and to the methods used to finance investments. This leads to a discussion of the aggregated balance of nonfinancial enterprises, in which the set of nonfinancial operations concluded by each sector is described (price formation in one sector depends in fact on the costs of those operations); it also leads to an improvement in the matrix of financial operations.

SURROUNDING FACTORS OF MODELS

Additional Planning Instruments that Enable a Deeper Analysis of the Models

Structural Studies

Structure in economics has two complementary definitions. Perroux defines it as a set of stable fundamental relationships changing only slowly with time; this creates a need to quantify the fundamental ratios and the gradual evolution (the saving rate may be 5 percent or 20 percent). This definition contradicts the targets of planners of developing countries who search for a radical transformation of structures.

The second definition allows for greater precision in concepts. Different levels of causality exist in the economy. Econometrics deals with relatively superficial levels; the structural study seeks a deeper causality, demanding more detailed statistical information. For example, econometrics links the savings rate with the income of households. Initially it appears to be a simple causal relation: income (cause) is an explanatory factor of savings (result). But when Japan and Italy have a similar income per capita, the Japanese households' savings rate is much higher than the Italian. The reasons are differences in wage payments, habits, development of social security, and so on. The structural study allows a separation of significant explanatory factors. It shows why, contrary to expectations, the savings rate may rise when price increases accelerate.

Logically, structural studies ought to be solved before formal models. In practice, the French experience shows that formalization may come first and that, when it does, the study may have a natural outlet to one or more parameters of the model that prevents it from getting lost in the woods.

Cost-benefit Analysis

In France, these analyses are particularly related to public investment where costs are distinguishable but where benefits, when no sale in the market can be associated with them, are difficult to estimate; and large scale investments affecting surrounding factors.

Sometimes these analyses allow simulation with the central model FIFI sufficiently detailed to test certain aspects of big projects. FIFI has examined the macroeconomic impact of a large reduction in active farm population or of a larger immigration or of different systems in energy price policy. It was shown that the development of immigration has little influence on the level of employment in France but that it improves the balance of payments even though immigrants working in France transfer part of their income to foreign countries. In developing states these analyses are used to study productive or infrastructure projects but in a rather different form: Costs and benefits derived from the project are valued at a different price from that determined in the market. This "fictitious" price is provided by the planner either at his discretion or for a dual optimization model.

Despite conceptual advantages, such sophisticated techniques run some risks. They are useful in countries with developed statistics and technology. There, optimization causes marginal improvements in criteria to be used to choose between various well-defined projects. But such improvements may be too formal if projects are not well defined, as is frequently observed in developing countries. Therefore, to integrate the results derived from the analysis of a project, a detailed simulation model is preferable to an optimization model.

Systems of Models

French planners prefer a combination of a central model (semiglobal or disaggregated) and peripheral models, concentrating on a particular area. One can distinguish three main categories:
- Certain models analyze operations, such as household consumption or income tax, and have mainly an econometric meaning. Their task is to assure that the global results are consistent with those shown by the statistical analysis of the operation.
- Other models isolate and describe institutional sectors, that is, homogeneous categories of those taking decisions such as public enterprises or subagents of administrations.
- The others are transition models: Their main role is to translate the performed operations from one accountancy language to another.

The link between the central and peripheral models is made in two different ways. The peripheral models require certain framework data (such as growth of production and prices; and wage level) that arise out of the central model. The central model must consider certain results deriving from the peripheral models as exogenous data or as a general relationship summarizing the various relationships contained in the peripheral models. For instance, the household consumption model of FIFI for seven products is controlled by an extremely detailed model, and one tries to find in the central model the same income and price elasticities as obtained there.

Sometimes the central model absorbs the peripheral model: In the Sixth Plan, FIFI absorbed a detailed model that divided government authorities into six subagents; in the Seventh Plan it absorbed a detailed model of social security. This procedure cannot be followed without limit; it may turn the central model into a monster impossible to translate into matrix form.

Peripheral models, like structural studies, deepen the understanding of an area analyzed schematically by the central model.

Developing countries need ad hoc models for expanding existing knowledge of a certain area; models built for educational programs or professional training are the best examples in this field. In most cases models, central and peripheral, are developed by teams unaware of each other. Contact between models has to be assured. General information required by the ad hoc model should be computed by the central model; and general results from the peripheral model should be transferred to the central model.

Social indicators

Economists are concerned about accountable (national accounts) or quantifiable (demography, employment) data, seldom about social studies, since this field belongs to politics and is difficult to quantify. Yet there are good statistics for health, education, housing conditions, and so on. These statistics are not very comparable and, at present, are not used in formal or informal models. French planners refuse to develop a wider concept of national accounts under which they will not only describe tangible goods (and services) but also take into account external effects, thus creating a more satisfactory indicator than gross national product. Searching for a gross national welfare indicator seems to them a useless and arbitrary operation. Instead, they want to enlighten social and political debate by some synthetic indicators of the state of society and its functioning. There are five groups of indicators: material standard of living (health, infant mortality rate, life expectation at forty years); quality of working life (employment, daily hours of work, time spent in traveling from home to work and back); social cost of changes in the productive system (work intensiveness, work accidents, working conditions, temperature, lighting, division of work, degree of initiative); the environment (noise, pollution, proximity to nature); social integration (suicides, drugs, alcoholism, delinquency); and social inequality (income and wealth disparities, differences in the level of education and level of power). This widening of the fields of planning instruments may not be useful in developing countries. Nevertheless, these social indicators should be developed at least in health, nutrition, and education.

A Good Political and Administrative Element Is Necessary for the Appraisal of Models

The decision to develop the physico-financial model at the beginning of 1967 is attributed to the director of the planning authority. He was given no political instructions.

The first central projection made by employing FIFI was presented to the administration in the autumn of 1968. The financial planning groups included representatives of the director of the Planning Authority and of the Ministry of Finance. One has to remember that the Ministry of Finance plays a dominant role in the French government. Its tasks and traditional problems are short-term. As far as it is concerned, planning involves risks because of its medium-term budget orientations. On the other hand, the Economic Authority is small, with only advisory power, and relying on the technical quality of its work. A new organization should deal with international trade, balance of trade services, prices and competition, financing of the economy, public finance, fiscal policy, and social security.

This projection was modified and a new projection called "starting account" was developed and presented to the team in 1969. A technical team is formed, composed of young representatives of the administration, employers and trade unions, with the task of breaking down the model and forming an explanatory relay close to its respective organizations. The Planning Authority provides a set of variants to explain the mechanism and characteristics of the model without commenting on each of its equations. These are called sensibility variants because a central account serves as a point of reference. One studies the effect of changes in the value of a parameter or of a variable on the main economic aggregate. The analysis becomes progressively more complex. From sensibility variants we move on to stochastic variants (based on inaccuracies in the value of the parameters of the model), variants of analytical economic policy—for example, an increase in the collective equipment or an increase in income tax paid by individuals—and finally to "artificial" variants, simulating forms of economic development not used in the "starting account." For example, the Director of the Economic Authority presented in February 1970 three artificial variants to the Commission of General Economy and Financing: one leading to rapid growth and accelerated structural transformations, a second leading to moderation in demand (the policy advocated by the Ministry of Finance), and an intermediate variant.

French planning permits two phases: one relating to major future problems, the second called "phase of detailed work." The first phase was completed in August 1970, in the form of an "account of options." The second phase was summarized in June 1971. New specific variants were introduced; the employment commission studied the impact of an accelerated reduction in the length of the working day; the international trade committee analyzed the impact of a growth in exports; and so on. If the model is used this is due to the precautions taken by its builders and the Planning Authority. Without these precautions, it would be useless.

CONCLUSION

The physico-financial model suggests the necessity of accelerating the industrialization of the French economy and also the economic policy to be used.

The utilization of models is a necessary but insufficient condition for their usefulness. Exaggerated use of FIFI for the preparation of the Sixth Plan has created certain problems.

Under which conditions can a model be useful? It is better not to look for a comprehensive view of social and economic reality but to deal with specific problems. Underdevelopment is a fundamental problem but has no operative meaning for political action; thus it cannot be explained in terms of a model. A central model and a semiglobal model based on the System of National Accounts are not two opposite concepts; the existence of specific problems determines the structure of a semiglobal model, which will be developed in certain areas and not others. Specific models deal with precise problems and must be linked with the central model. The use of models risks fulfilling only a formal role if no in-depth studies are carried out that, in addition to their own development, enable development of certain parts of the model. The central model should be placed in the context of the planning process. It presents a coherent vision of the economic future, even if this vision is limited. This coherence serves as a federative frame to other planning instruments.

Models have a well-defined role to play in the planning process.

DISCUSSION

RUTH SILBERBERG (Israel): I fear that elaborate models, such as the French one, are suitable for developed states, where changes in the economy are marginal and planning is trying to direct development to increase efficiency and accelerate the growth rate. Such models are useful in very complex economies.

I am not sure that the French model is suitable for handling a situation in which changes are structural. Besides, in developing states detailed statistical information necessary for such models is not available, and there is a competition for the scarce manpower needed for planning. These states need some model so as not to get lost. But before deciding on the scope of the model, we have to decide about the strategy of the planning process.

J. ENNINFUL (Ghana): How do Mr. Ullmo's proposals apply to the problems facing developing states? How can systems be developed to suit these states' purposes?

IASSU ANDEMICAEL (ECA): Models are designed to clarify problems. What prevents them from helping to predict and explain economic phenomena? How far have the French models been successful in explaining and predicting? Another question is whether models can be devised to include social factors? What is the prospect of devising a single socioeconomic indicator of progress?

BERNARD ULLMO (France): I presented a case study of how French economists tackled some concrete economic problems in France. Structural studies permit the creation of a slightly formal, relatively simple model. In a developing state it is often possible to have a certain stabilization of consumption, which helps to isolate saving.

A global model does not have to be sophisticated to deal with a problem. A small Tunisian model aims to shed light on employment problems in Tunisia, under a constraint which is not absolute. The constraint is the simulation of Tunisian dependence on foreign capital. The model is simple. It does not pose general development problems or problems of neocolonialism but a very specific problem of foreign funds. This kind of model can be useful in developing states.

I should add that there is a risk of making abstract models that are unusable. Pardoxically, the complex French model deals effectively with very concrete problems. But we cannot export it, because it deals with our problems, not with those of others.

**A MICROECONOMIC
PLANNING MODEL
OF KOREA**
Irma Adelman
Sherman Robinson

INTRODUCTION

This planning model concentrates on economic policies that in the short run can be used to ameliorate income distribution but the application of which does not involve large stresses on the fabric of society. The model centers on such policy instruments as credit rationing, industrial and agricultural technology, various foreign trade instruments (such as tariffs, subsidies, export quotas), the government budget, tax policy, price policy, and inflation. It is neither an optimization model nor a projection model but has been developed as a framework in which one can examine the effects on income distribution of the policy measures mentioned and of variations in behavioral parameters.

Income distribution is regarded here as part of an interacting mechanism that involves the production and consumption activities of the economy and its institutional constraints. It is not possible, therefore, to investigate the distribution of income properly with a partial equilibrium approach. The present model attempts to describe how the behavioral patterns of the producers, of the government, and of the consumers all interact to determine the distribution of incomes among households. The distribution of income is also affected by persistent rigidities and imperfect adjustments to market equilibria. Therefore a general equilibrium model will not adequately describe the real world. Thus the model is neither a full neoclassical general-equilibrium model nor is it a pure disequilibrium or partial equilibrium model. It includes elements of both schools of thought.

The model is based on data from South Korea, and a number of behavioral relations in it reflect institutional characteristics specific to that country. The inclusion of particular institutional characteristics is very important for an income distribution model, since they modify the distribution of income and the allocation of products. The inclusion of institutional characteristics also permits

---

Sherman Robinson is a Professor in the Department of Economics, University of Maryland.

one to explore parametrically just how significant such special institutional factors are in determining income distribution.

Korea was chosen for a number of reasons. First, it has shown spectacular growth performance. Second, the Korean industrialization strategy is export oriented, avoiding some of the negative consequence affecting income distribution to which an import-substitution-led growth is susceptible. Third, there has been a labor-intensive production pattern, and this in a country with a highly educated, literate population. Fourth, as a result of the Korean War the accelerated growth process started from a relatively egalitarian distribution of wealth. Fifth, by international standards the current distribution of income in Korea is rather good. Finally, the data are fairly accurate. South Korea therefore provides a sound test case for the proposition that rapid growth can have favorable income distribution consequences

A GENERAL OUTLINE OF THE MODEL

The general description of the model and the more detailed presentation of each of its phases that follow do not include the mathematical formulation or a discussion of its technical aspects.

The model is dynamic; each period of time is decomposed into three phases. The economy is visualized so that at the beginning of each period producers form their demands for loanable funds on the basis of expected sales and expected input prices. Credit is then rationed either by setting an interest rate and allowing the market to clear at that rate or by setting a target rate of credit expansion and allowing the rate of interest to adjust in order to clear the credit market.

Thus, the output of the first phase (Stage I) is the allocation of credit among firms and sectors. The second phase of the model (Stage II) is a general equilibrium phase in which production, consumption, employment, income, and other economic decisions are made. Prices and wage rates are assumed to adjust so as to clear all markets. The results of this phase are the realized values of production, income, employment, wages, exports, imports, and so on. The third phase of the model (Stage III) consists of functions that update the relevant variables and formulate expectations that are then fed back into Stage I of the model for the next period.

In each period the three phases are solved serially. Variables assumed to be fixed at Stage I are allowed to vary as Stage II. Thus, the overall model distinguishes between expectations and realizations. At the third phase the differences between expectations and realizations are incorporated into the forecasting functions for the expected variables that are used in the next period.

Stage I

In this phase it is assumed that firms have expectations concerning the overall demand for the output of their sector, wages by skill category and firm size, and the structure of capital costs. These expectations guide the entrepreneurs in the formulation of their demand for the stock of capital with which they desire to produce the output they expect to sell. Firms are assumed to seek minimization of costs; they start with given output targets, a given wage structure, and the structure of expected capital costs; and they then seek to hire capital so as to minimize the costs of producing the specified sectoral outputs. The firms will bid for capital until the ratio of wages to marginal products is equated across all factors for each firm. This process determines the firms' demand for capital goods and so for the available credit.

In any given period, there are five sources of credit: (1) accumulated retained earnings from the previous period, (2) household savings, (3) foreign capital inflow, (4) government savings, and (5) the financial sector. The first two sources can be funnelled either through the banking system or the unorganized money market, while the other three sources always constitute the organized market. The structure and degree of financial intermediation and the possible changes in the relative importance of the unorganized money market influence both the cost and ultimate total volume of credit.

Two forms of credit rationing are considered. In one form of the model the absolute cost of capital according to firm size and sector is specified, and firms are allowed to 'buy' as much as they wish at the set prices subject to 'credit worthiness' constraints. The unorganized money market is sought by the demands which were not satisfied through the banking system and offers to lend at a specified higher rate of interest. Unloaned funds in the unorganized market are assumed to flow back to the organized sector. In the second form of the model the total volume of credit available through the banking sector is determined (by the third phase of the previous period) and the cost of new investment capital adjusts so that the aggregate demand for credit from the organized market and the given supply are equated. The price of capital in the unorganized market is determined in the same way, but is subject to a lower bound on the differential of interest rates in the two markets. If the price in the unorganized market reaches the lower bound, it is assumed that any excess supply of credit flows to the organized market.

Another possible version of the model is one in which both the rate of interest and the volume of credit supplied are determined. In this case credit is rationed and directly allocated to firms by the government. In this situation, the unorganized market is much more important since it is the only equilibrating mechanism available. All three of these possibilities have some empirical application in Korea.

The credit worthiness of firms represents constraints on their ability to borrow both domestic and foreign funds. The constraints are expressed as minimum self-financing ratios (that is, ratios of retained earnings from previous periods to the amount of investment desired). In general, an important role of the unorganized money market is to permit a firm to relax its credit worthiness constraint and so borrow additional funds at a higher cost. A diagramatic representation of Stage I is shown in Figure 5.

Stage II

This phase is a microeconomic market model in which prices and quantities (except for the quantity of capital employed by each firm, which is calculated at the outset) are variable. Stage II represents the core of the overall model; and its solution determines all wages, prices, production, employment, profits, and income, as well as consumption and the distribution of income.

This phase is itself divided into several stages. In the first stage the quantity of real capital goods that each firm actually receives is calculated: the amount of desired investment determined at Stage I is divided by the weighted price of the capital required by that firm in order to expand its capacity. The weights are the capital coefficients of the sector to which the firm belongs. Having calculated the actual investment undertaken by each firm and thus updated its capital stock, production and profit functions are formed in order to obtain the quantity of products supplied by the firms and the quantities of inputs demanded by them. The demand for investment goods according to branches of origin is calculated by applying the capital coefficient matrix to the sector of investments (according to destination) derived at the outset. The demand for intermediate goods is calculated by assuming fixed input-output coefficients and using Leontieff-type material balance equations. Levels of employment are determined by firms so as to maximize their profits, given that prices and capital are fixed at each iteration.

The markets for the different categories of labor are of two types: those for which the supply is fixed, and those for which the supply is a function of the wage rate. In general, the supply of higher skill categories of labor is assumed to be constant, while the supply of low-skill labor to the industrial sector is partly determined by migration from the rural sector and is clearly a function of both rural and urban wages. Equilibrium wage rates are determined by equating the aggregate demand for labor with aggregate supply for each of the skill categories.

FIGURE 5

Stage I: Allocation of Investment by Firm Size and Sector

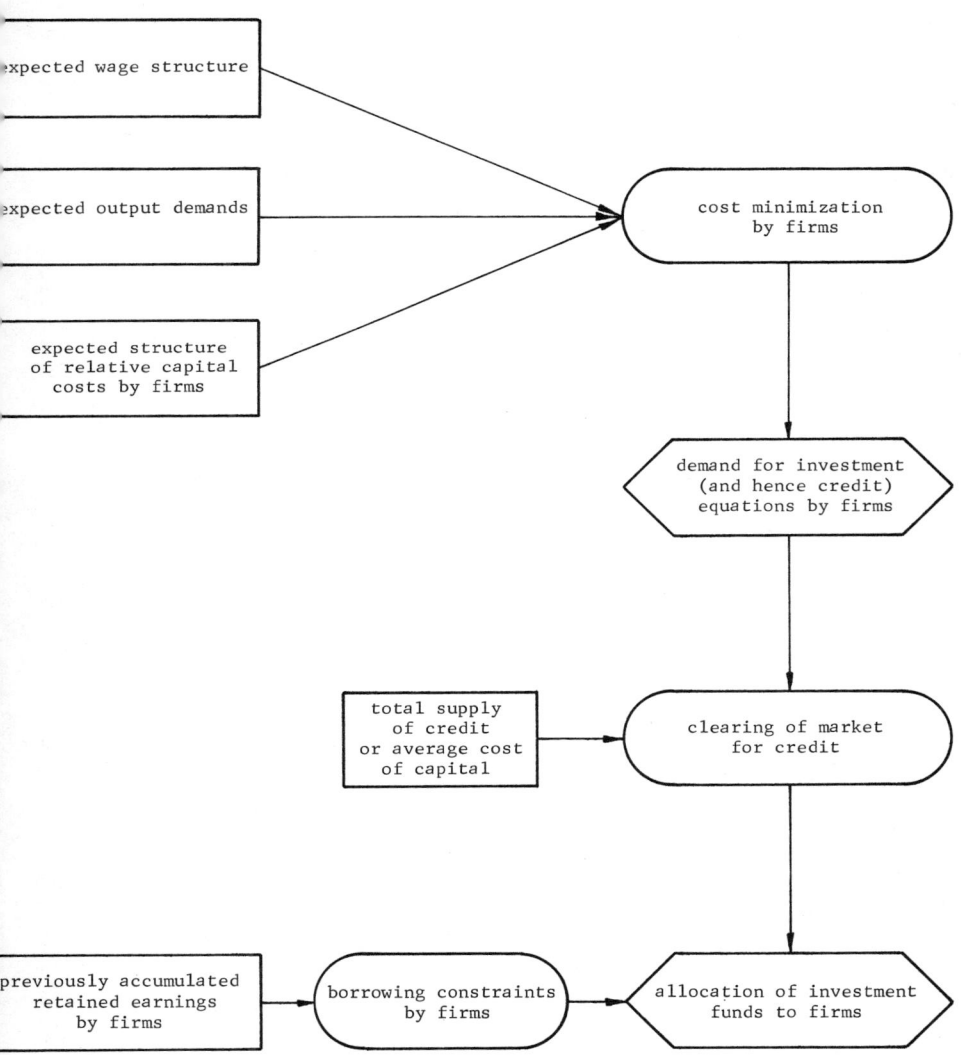

FIGURE 6

Stage II: Determination of Wages, Employment, Prices and Profits

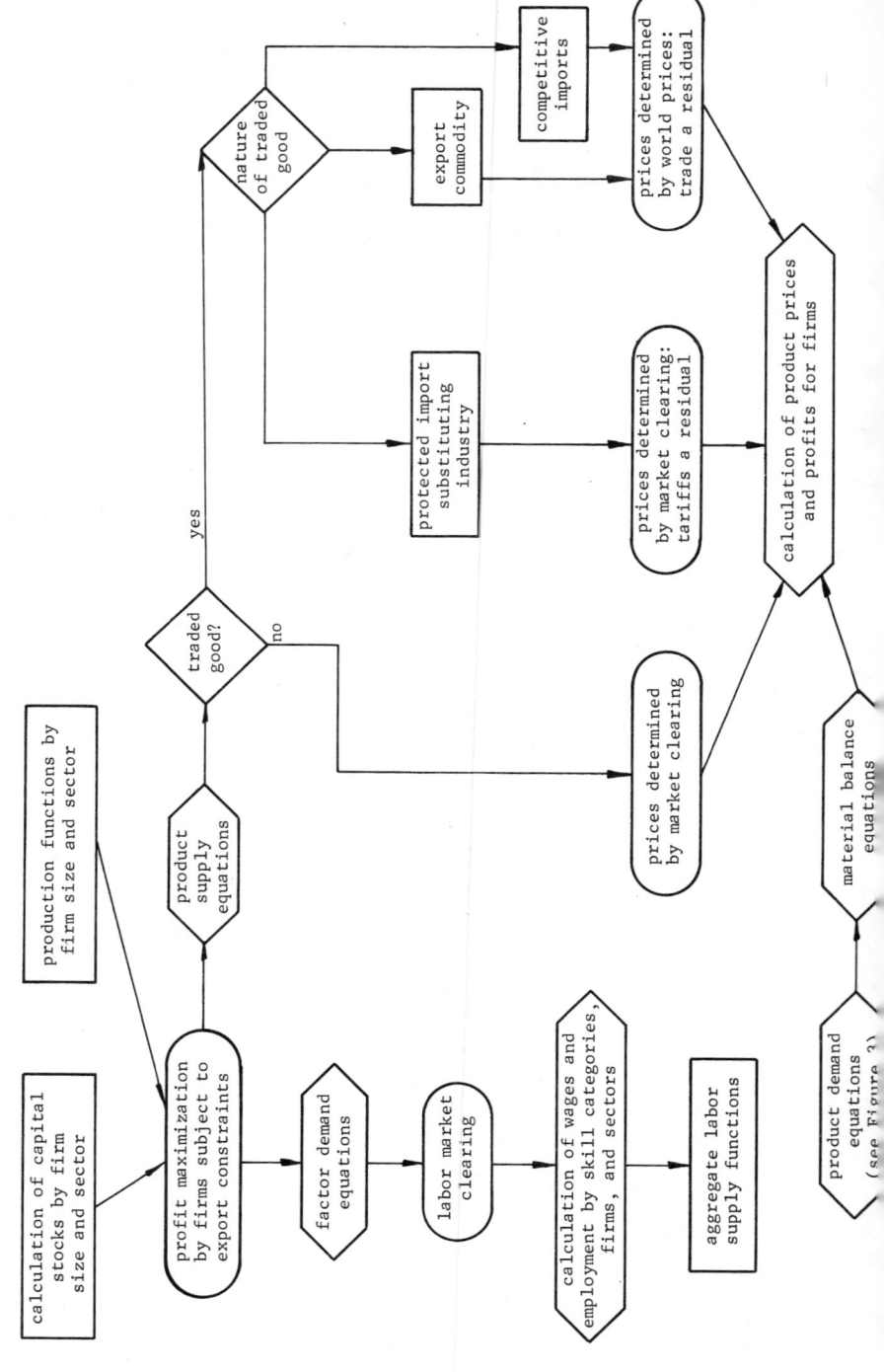

FIGURE 7

Stage II: Demand for Products

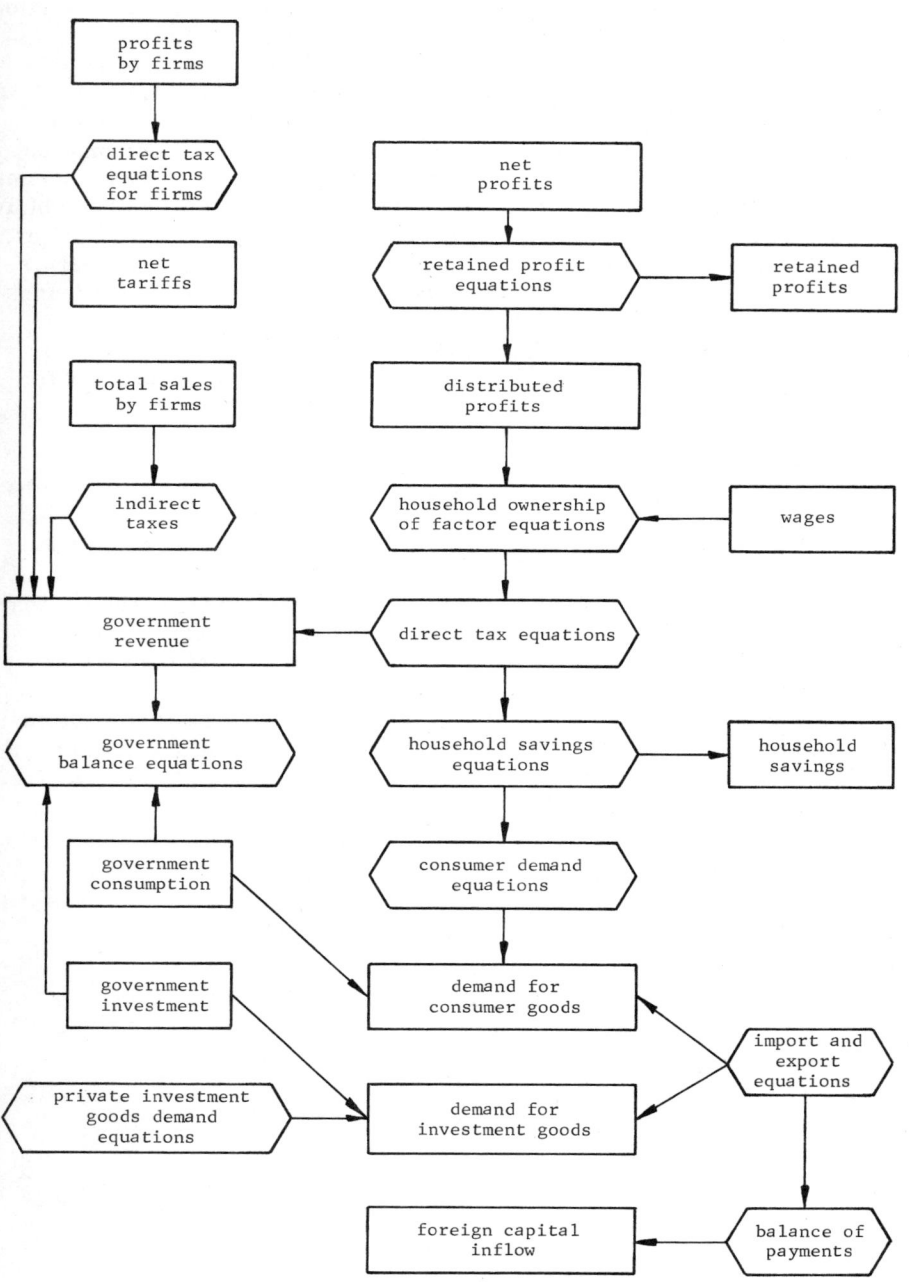

Apart from wages, the income of households also comprises distributed profits, interest, and transfer payments. It is assumed that households supply the different types of labor in fixed proportions. The total household expenditure on consumption is a function of disposable household income. Households are grouped according to their consumption patterns and a different expenditure function is formulated for each of these groups. Consumer demand for goods (according to their branch of origin) is determined by consumption functions with price and income elasticities for each type of consumer good and class of household. The supply of consumer goods is obtained as the residual of the material balance equations mentioned earlier. Prices are determined by an iterative procedure, where at every iteration quantities supplied and demanded are compared and prices are adjusted according to the degree of excess demand.

A general diagramatic representation of Stage II is shown in Figure 6. The flow diagram in Figure 7 shows how the demand for products is determined.

Stage III

The objective of this phase of the model is to update all the variables that were fixed or exogenous in the two previous phases. There are three different types of such variables: (1) variables that are simply data; which are updated by setting them equal to their value in the solution of Stage II; (2) variables that are data unique to Stage II; and (3) variables that reflect expectations for the next period and for which there are distributed-lag expectation functions in Stage III. The underlying model for revising this last category of variables is one of adaptive expectations. Current expectations are based on past performance and the difference between past performance and past expectation.

**TRANSLATING PLANNING
INTO RESULTS—
THE CASE OF
THE IVORY COAST**
Mohamed Diawara

In the Republic of Ivory Coast, given the existing situation, the goal of planning has been to achieve the maximum possible growth.

The president of the republic, Mr. Houphouet-Boigny, believes that the ultimate goal of the planning is the individual and collective promotion of the people of the Ivory Coast through economic and social development. A better standard of life can be achieved only if structural and social changes are based on a high ratio of economic growth. However, growth is not the ultimate aim of the policy of the Ivory Coast. It is only a way of promoting a new society freed from the evils of underdevelopment.

The methodology that has been gradually implemented is the following:

First stage: Direct analysis of the possibilities of growth in different fields. Such a direct approach makes it possible to determine the production, investment, and employment goals in various sectors on the regional and national levels.

Second stage: Checking the coherence of the global scheme to be implemented by comparing it to the tables of resources and uses and to financial transactions accounts. This checking may lead to a revision in certain sectors, mainly in those, such as building, public works, transport, and various services, in which production has to correspond to the demand. Thus this second stage permits the establishment of a coherent scheme that can be presented as a draft or a plan.

Third stage: At this point, with the ability to calculate the primary and secondary effects of various projects, it becomes possible to ameliorate the model obtained during the second stage. The aim is to achieve an optimal utilization of national resources.

In 1960 Ivory Coast economists could not base themselves on retrospective analyses in order to foresee future evolution. Even the study of existing economic and social structures did not permit the dynamics of the growth to be evolved. Moreover, existing data on current activities, revenues, expenses, and so on were scarce and often not trustworthy. Thus at the beginning planning had to be empirical: a number of surveys were launched, a number of sectors and projects studied. Procedures of implementation and incentives to promote the possibilities of growth had to be established.

The quality of the work improved as more and more surveys and studies became available.

The third stage, concerning the optimal utilization of resources, could be implemented only after January 1964, when technical data permitting the comparison of the interest and value of various projects became available. The constant improvement of national accountancy made it possible to trace the changes in the economic structure of the country, draw some lessons from the gaps between the forecasts and the factual results, and secure some precious indications concerning the goals for the 1971-75 period.

PROBLEMS IN CARRYING OUT THE PLAN

The main difficulties in the "translation of planning into facts" gravitate around a few big themes common to most developing countries: the difficulty of stimulating the will of the people to achieve the goals of the plan; the conformity of public investments to the plan; the incentives and coordination to be given to departments and public bodies responsible for the investments; the dynamics of the private sector and the international context; the numerous subventions or foreign loans among the capital investments necessary for development projects.

These major themes are accompanied by technical difficulties involved in the practical implementation of projects. I mean the all-too-frequent underestimation of delays or costs in certain fields, such as the infrastructure or agroindustrial projects based on new crops. Such underestimations naturally lead to an important gap between reality and the original calculations concerning rentability.

The Difficulty of Stimulating the Will of the People to Achieve the Goals of the Plan

The problem of stimulating the people to work toward the goals of the plan arises because outside the small circle closely associated with planning few understand the aims or ways of economists. It is difficult to translate the aims of the plan into a language accessible to those who will have to implement it at various levels. In the

Ivory Coast this fundamental problem has been reinforced by various specific factors: To begin with, the stress put at first on economic growth, and on production, may have masked the goals of quality that did exist but may not have been sufficiently emphasized. Mobilizing people to produce for the sake of production is a difficult task in the rural sector. Second, a model of growth calling for foreign investments (and foreign labor and know-how) has been chosen; it implied the export of agricultural and forest products. Such an approach may have been misunderstood, except by a small group of high executives, as not corresponding to the image of a national development. It must also be noted that in the beginning, in order to facilitate the success of certain projects negotiated with foreign investors, it was not desirable to publicize certain intentions. Thus in 1962, during the formulation of the "Perspectives Decennales 1962-70," only a few persons had a global perspective of the planning in the Ivory Coast.

Finally, the Ivory Coast lacked persons with the qualifications needed to play an important role within the administration and the rural sector, persons able to direct the diffuse desire for change and progress into the channels of planified goals. Hence what prevailed was projects directed by competent executives, a concept that did not help much in the sphere of training and mobilization of peasant leaders. However, the explanation campaigns launched by president Houphouet-Boigny contributed to the establishment of a dialogue: the persons who had evolved the plan explained its goals; the general public voiced its opinions and complaints.

A phenomenon specific to the Ivory Coast has been the growth all over the country of associations for the economic and social development of groups of villages, small towns, regional centers, and so on, usually founded and directed by intellectuals born in the region. Their success and dynamism depends essentially on the personal qualities and the availability of the directors. A certain number of these associations are very successful and can be relied upon for development campaigns such as those conducted within the frame of the Funds for Regional Amelioration, (F.R.A.R.).

Conformity of Public Investments to the Plan

The conformity of public investments to the planning data has always worried those responsible for planning. Under public investment one should include all investments made through the administration or various paragovernmental bodies, regardless of the origin of the funds.

The main problems concern the amount, origin, and allocation of resources. The problem of the amount of resources allocated to public investment was not crucial in the Ivory Coast: almost 121 billions of francs C.F.A. (in "constant francs" 1965) were allocated to public investment for the implementation of the "Loi-Plan 1967-70" and covered all the projects provided for by this law.

The inevitable distortions appeared at the two other levels: origin and allocation of resources.

Among the governmental investments planned, priority was given to activities crucial for the economic, social, and cultural development of the country. The emphasis put on this "essential core" guaranteed the allocation of resources whatever the situation. The "optional slice" deals with priorities for which resources will be made as soon as possible.

The "essential core" represents a very important part of the total public investment—about 87 percent in the Loi-Plan 1967-70 and in the five-year plan of 1971-75.

The Loi de Finances of 1962 (Finance Law) initiated a new structure for the budget, dividing it into an operational and an equipment budget, each of which had independent resources. The excess revenues of the operational budget revert to the equipment budget (B.S.I.E.), which includes public investment based on domestic revenues or loans, as well as on foreign loans, but not subventioned projects.

When the B.S.I.E. was created the General Administration of the Plan was part of a big Department of Economy, Finances and Plans. The secretary concerned had in mind to provide the government with a functional executive tool able to implement planning. The B.S.I.E. remains equal to its task due to its close coordination with the Lois-Programmes proposed by the secretary of the Planning Department.

In 1968 a new tool was provided for the "translation of planning into facts": three-year laws—detailed and precise three-year programs for all public investments whatever the nature of the financing (including bilateral aid or multilateral aid).

The first Loi-Programme covered the period 1968-69-70, the following one that of 1969-70-71, and so forth. The continuous planning initiated was as precise and as exhaustive as possible. Due to the close coordination with the Ministry of Finance and with foreign aid bodies, the Lois-Programmes proved helpful in the adjusting of public investments to planning aims. The method also leads, when need arises, to continual revisions and corrections, and permits the foreseeing and defining of the goals of future programs. Thus the data for the first year of the plan beginning in 1976 should be available already in 1973 because the Loi-Programme currently prepared covers the years 1974, 1975, and 1976.

The Loi-Programme for the years 1973, 1974, and 1975, the last one voted, is the first formulated according to the technique of "programing according to goals."

However, the Lois-Programmes triennales (three-year programs) and the Special Investment and Equipment Budget represent only a formal financial translation of the Plan and do not guarantee its implementation, which requires operational structures in the field.

Administrations of young independent states, such as the Ivory Coast, are not geared to implement complex development programs. Management and coordination with governmental or paragovernmental bodies responsible for the execution of public investments were among some of the important problems that arose. The solution adopted was to found governmental corporations active in specialized fields, among them SODEPALM, or Corporation for the Development and Exploitation of Palm Oil; SODEFOR, Corporation for the Development of Forest Plantations; SOGEFIHA, Corporation for the Management and Financing of Housing; O.N.F.P., National Office for Professional Training.

Two Government corporations deal globally with a definite area: A.R.S.O. is in charge of operation San Pedro and responsible for the development of the southwestern interior area; the Regional Authority for the valley of the Bandama deals with the problems created by the dam and lake of Kossou.

There are also numerous corporations in which the government owns more than a third of the capital, such as the Societe d'Energie Electrique de la Cote d'Ivoire, E.E.C.I. (Electricity); or S.I.E.T.H.O. (Corporation for the Development of Tourism and Hotels).

The contacts between such bodies and the Department of Planning are numerous and close. Almost all of them are under the obligation to provide a program of their activities covering several years and reflecting the aims of the Lois-Programmes and to submit it to the secretary of the Department of Planning. An official appointed by the government controls the activities of most of these bodies. His nomination depends upon the secretary of the Department of Planning.

Thus the Department is able to control the abovementioned bodies and to orient them towards the implementation of its goals. However, the establishment of these executive bodies did not create the administrators and technicians capable of managing them. Often it was necessary to ask for foreign technical assistance. The satisfactory results of the activities of many governmental companies comprise the training of administrators and technicians so sorely lacking at the time the Ivory Coast became independent.

The liberal planning policy adopted by the government of the Ivory Coast has led to a rapid ratio of growth. The translation of this liberal planning into facts was outward oriented and had to bear the brunt of changes in the flow of foreign investments depending on the fluctuations of foreign markets.

The considerations of private investors in a world-wide setting are paramount in the implementation of import industrial projects that do not fit paragovernmental bodies because these lack the necessary funds or technicians and because of the danger of creating monsters without outlets for their products. The promotion of projects for the production of paper pulp or for the mining of iron ore is based on the conviction of the investors that there are markets for these goods and that conditions prevailing in the Ivory Coast warrant the investment.

The policy of cooperation with the private sector has proved successful in many important fields and has given a concrete form to various attractive projects promoted within the liberal framework of exchanges of capital and competent executives.

As soon as the Ivory Coast became independent, a series of investment laws gave priority to enterprises furthering the economic and social development of the country. The enterprises were granted a priority status but not a monopoly of certain exemptions. In exceptional cases, they enjoy, over a long period, special fiscal concessions complemented by a statutory agreement formulating reciprocal obligations between the state and the enterprise.

The enterprises enjoying a priority status are closely linked with the Department of Planning, which has to approve their operating accounts, balance sheets, and production program. This system is the main but not the only device to orient private investments into channels furthering the goals of the Plan. It includes contributions private enterprises must pay into the National Investment Fund; tax reductions on industrial and commercial profits granted to investments compatible with the goals of the Plan; and "certificates of conformity to the Plan" granted by the Department of Planning, which confer benefits from an additional discount on certain credits by the Banque Centrale.

Finally, two governmental bodies have been created to promote private investment projects oriented towards the goals of the Plan: O.P.E.I. (Office for the Promotion of Ivory Coast Enterprises), the name of which tallies with its aims; and the Bureau for Industrial Development, dealing with the research for more important projects requiring foreign investments, which provides studies and surveys on financing. The young economy of the Ivory Coast, based on agriculture and in particular coffee and cocoa, is very sensitive to the fluctuations of the foreign market. In order to be more independent in this area it has to diversify its exports. This is one of the main goals of the Plan.

The role played domestically by the Fund for the Stabilization and Support of Prices of Agricultural Produce is only a palliative measure. However, it is very encouraging that in 1971, a very average year for the production of coffee and cocoa, the economy of the Ivory Coast held its own.

Dependence on Foreign Capital

The necessity for foreign capital in order to finance governmental investments sometimes makes it difficult to translate planning into facts. Indeed, the effective availability of such resources conditions the realization of 42 percent of the projects foreseen by the Loi-Plan 1967-70. The difficulties caused by this dependence of developing countries are well known; they include prolonged discussions of the projects, doubts about the respective proportion of subsidies and loans to be granted; and recourse in extremis to financing sources dearer than those that have not approved projects the government does not wish to be delayed or modified to fit the investors' suggestions. The good administration of the Ivory Coast, its reputation of being a "good payer," and the evidence of its economic expansion have enabled it to obtain within the necessary time limits the foreign aid required for government investments. Though discrepancies appeared between the foreseen costs and the real costs of this aid, the relations with the various bilateral and multilateral bodies are excellent. The projects are so successful that certain bodies are eager to present them as show cases that could facilitate similar activities in other African countries.

The three-year Program Laws include all types of foreign aid. Thus they enable economists to pinpoint the assistance that has been pledged and the aid that has not been forthcoming.

Implementation of the 1967-70 Plan

The most detailed data available on implementation pertain to the Plan covering the years 1967-70. The general evolution of the economy of the Ivory Coast during the decade 1960-70 showed a yearly average growth rate of 8 percent, calculated at constant prices—one of the highest in the world. The growth of the initially unimportant, badly structured industrial sector at an average yearly rate of 18 percent has also been spectacular.

The growth of agriculture, which started at a higher level of production, has progressed at 5 percent per year. Efforts have been made, mainly since 1964, to diversify agricultural production. Agricultural produce intended for industry or export has almost doubled in the last ten years. Forestry has almost tripled.

The development of industry was based on import substitution and has caused a profound change in the production structure of the country: The weight of raw materials within total output grew from 16 percent in 1960 to 24 percent in 1970.

The development of agriculture and forestry has helped the growth of industry. The distribution of imported goods has been improved but that of local products intended for the domestic market is still unsatisfactory. The transport and communications system has been developed. The road system was greatly extended during the early sixties; during the late sixties the port of San Pedro and a new network of roads in the southwest area were started. The rapid growth of the port of Abidjan, the continual modernization of the railway infrastructure, the rapid development of air transport, and a marked advance in telecommunications also occurred during this period.

Considerable efforts were made to develop the infrastructures necessary for sanitary and educational facilities. The costs involved represent respectively 12 percent and 27 percent of the general budget.

Private consumption has grown approximately by 7 percent per year (at constant prices) during the early sixties and by nearly 7.5 percent during the late sixties. The decade 1960-70 was thus a period when a carefully thought-out and determined policy initiated a process of continual progress and expansion.

The detailed study of the implementation of the Plan 1967-70 allows for a precise comparison between the provisions of the Plan and actual results. The most impressive is the average annual growth rate of domestic raw materials production: 7.8 percent at constant prices for a plan foreseeing 7.9 percent.

The analysis of growth according to sectors reveals certain deviations from the forecasts that should cause no concern. Although the primary sector played a more active role than foreseen (its average growth rate was 4.3 percent, exceeding the 3.8 percent foreseen), the general evolution proceeded according to plan: smaller relative importance of domestic raw material production (30 percent in 1970 as compared to 39.4 percent in 1965) and of exports (71.30 percent as compared to 80.5 percent); first results of the diversification of agricultural produce (the share of coffee and cocoa in exports was 77.7 percent as compared to 81.7 percent ten years previously). However, the forecasts concerning the exploitation of forests greatly exceeded expectations.

The goals of the Loi-Plan 1967-70 concerning the secondary sector were ambitious, calling for an annual real growth of 25.4 percent. In fact, this sector developed at a rate of 12.5 percent during the period under consideration. It was necessary to conduct more thorough agronomic tests in the sugar complex in the North. Despite many delays, the secondary sector grew rapidly, though manganese mining has stopped entirely. The salaried labor force has grown annually at a rate of 11.4 percent. Salaries have grown, in real terms, at an annual rate of 19.8 percent. The domestic production of raw materials almost reached the goals of the plan (23.8 percent as compared to the forecast of 24.4 percent). I stressed above the incentive given to investment by the priority status granted to certain enterprises. These companies played an important role in the development of the secondary sector. In 1970 their number was 64 out of 357 existing enterprises; however, they accounted for 65 percent of the investments, 60 percent of the manpower, and 55 percent of the turnover.

The tertiary sector grew at the rate of 8.6 percent per year as compared to the 8 percent forecast. An important part of the production of this sector is the distribution and transport of agricultural produce.

Though the implementation of the Loi-Plan 1967-70 was very satisfactory, there were points where the forecast didn't tally with the results.

The global amount of resources has been satisfactory. However, as compared to the plans there was less recourse to budgetary savings and foreign subsidies, while a bigger role was played by the Fund for the Stabilization and Support of Agricultural Prices and by foreign loans. The total resources available to the Ivory Coast are insufficient to maintain a high rate of economic growth and to assemble, without exerting an excessive tax pressure, the funds required for government investments and for debt redemption. The difficulty of containing within reasonable limits the growth of the operating expenses of existing bodies should be stressed in this context. Good results were achieved by the Ivory Coast in this field; forecasts for the period under consideration were exceeded by only 5 percent.

Future Difficulties and Prospects

The greatest difficulty in the implementation of the Plan, as far as the future is concerned, is the slow growth of educational structures and lack of proper qualifications. Since the number of pupils tends to increase faster than the Plan anticipated, the qualitative lack may become a major hurdle preventing the integration of a sufficient number of Ivory Coast citizens into the production framework.

This may create a situation in which more and more youngsters totally cut off from the rural world and badly prepared for the modern industrial sector will be seeking employment. In this sphere the translation of planning is most difficult. Educational reform cannot be decreed; it requires imagination and competence. It calls for continual planning at every level in fields that cannot be quantified.

Finally, despite planning and a constructive government policy, regional development has been more uneven than foreseen: The efforts to promote a greater variety of crops have been particularly successful in the forest area—where their results will be fully felt only around 1975. Progress in the savannah area, although impressive, was slower than was hoped. In the industrial field the importance of the Abidjan area has grown. The rural exodus continues at a high rate. However, the western and northern areas have progressed more than the other regions in agricultural production and rate of pupils in elementary schools. This may indicate that with time the gaps will narrow.

The balance sheet for 1971, a year when conditions were unfavorable (decrease in the production of cotton and coffee, lower prices for cocoa) shows that the economy of the Ivory Coast has held its own under stress. The primary sector has progressed at a satisfactory rate (+ 4.7 percent as compared to 1970); the secondary sector (+ 17 percent as compared to 1970) has caught up with the forecasts made at the end of the 1967-70 plan. Thus the global results may be considered very encouraging.

The greatest difficulties encountered were carefully studied.

Educational reform has been given priority; it is the essential goal of the strategy for the period 1970-80 aiming at the promotion of the people of the Ivory Coast.

The emphasis on regional development is reflected by the efficiency of translating it into facts: The integration of regional representatives of the Plan is being speeded up. A National Office for Rural Promotion is being set up to encourage activities promoting the least developed areas. Certain favorable indications can be noted in the decentralization of industry, for example, in textiles, a field where the Ivory Coast is particularly successful. The results of the efforts concerning Kossou and San Pedro will be felt soon. The big agricultural projects in the north are being successfully implemented.

STRICT IMPLEMENTATION OF THE PLAN

A very important campaign involving modern dynamic managerial techniques has been launched to increase the efficiency of government companies. This campaign may stimulate greater productivity and better understanding of the goals. The officials appointed by the secretary of planning may thus become more efficient and stricter in furthering the goals of the plan.

The system of the three-year Program-Laws, according to which government investments are made, was considerably sharpened by the adoption of programing according to goals by the Program Law for 1973, 1974, and 1975. This method regroups according to goals the ways and means of translating planning into facts. Thus, even at the operational level, the emphasis is put on the essential goals to be reached rather than on individual projects. This method should lead to continual interaction between planning and implementation, and the Loi-Programme should now be able to explain its main goals anew every year, attracting a bigger proportion of managerial and executive personnel.

The next Plan may be concerned mainly with the goals to be reached; the ways and means will be defined only globally. This new method of planning corresponds to the new concepts regarding development of the Ivory Coast economy. Wider choices emphasize the main guidelines and allow a better understanding of goals. The stress is put on qualitative regional goals and on coordination needs. The ultimate goal is the quality of the society to emerge before the end of this century, with the emphasis on the type of society and the environment; the ways and means will have to be provided by the successive Loi-Programmes.

The coming decades should be very exhilarating, representing a new step in the translation of planning into results, insofar as these results will not be indications of growth but of a participation in a better kind of life.

A well-drafted plan should represent an optimal utilization of resources. Under these conditions, the achievements of an ambitious plan are more significant than the total implementation of a plan presenting only projects easily realized.

The challenge of maintaining a long-term annual growth rate of 8 percent is being met over a period of 15-20 years. This success has practically no precedent and makes it imperative to persevere the methods that have made it possible.

Ivory Coast has planned for development in a liberal frame, and the activities of the state become more and more redistributive as expansion gives it more financial possibilities.

DISCUSSION

LE VAN PHUC (Vietnam): Have the recent rises in the prices of primary products in the world market influenced the goals of planning in the Ivory Coast—for instance, by reinforcing the tendency to invest in agriculture and raw material utilization rather than in industry, which has little chance to be internationally competitive?

Another question is whether the concentration of urbanization around Abidjan and on the coast, when one has to aim at the optimum utilization of resources that are scattered, is reasonable? Would it not be better to create urban centres in the interior?

JULIO CESAR ESTRELLA (Dominican Republic): How do you propose to harmonize the difficulties that arise between various administrative staffs in order to execute your plan?

ELIEZER BRUTZKUS (Israel): I question the close connection between planning programs, their implementation, and the development of the Ivory Coast. It seems that the Ministry of Planning is involved in routine economic procedures that have little to do with planning, especially as regards investment.

The progress made by the Ivory Coast was probably due to its economic structure and system of government rather than to long-range planning.

Economic planning in developing states should fix certain price levels, which are to correct the location of productive forces (for example, the exchange rate and interest and the price of land and water). The influence of these price levels and of fiscal or monetary policies will control economic development better than the intervention of planners. The government's direct involvement should be restricted to ecology, social problems, and the infrastructures. Planners should concentrate on determining the most suitable policies for investments, the balance of payments, and education.

MOHAMED DIAWARA (Minister of Planning, Ivory Coast) being absent, the discussion was answered by Ouattara M'Lan (Director of Studies, Ministry of Planning, Ivory Coast): We have maintained private enterprise—for instance, in the exploitation of iron in the Western region. Often distribution of output is done better by the private sector, which has acquired experience in this sphere, rather than by state companies. Where private enterprise is lacking we have established state companies or mixed companies.

Our planning policies have helped growth. The Ivory Coast became independent in 1960, and we worked out development projections for the decade 1960-70 quite precisely. Only planners could have done this. This allowed investors and public bodies to see what the development possibilities were and act accordingly.

We are devoting 27 percent of our budget to education and another 17 percent to health. But the question: How productive exactly is the education system? must be faced.

The Ivory Coast still depends on exports of coffee, cocoa, and wood. We are trying to diversify agriculture by plans to develop palm oil, pineapple, and coconuts, and have already reaped a few benefits from this. We do not believe industrial development should be pushed beyond what our resources warrant. We base it on the processing of agricultural products. We have not excluded the possibility of assembling motor vehicles.

Until now, our progress has been based on agricultural development. We are aware that, for political reasons of national unity, not only Abidjan and the urban areas should be the beneficiaries of development. Not only towns but most of the villages in the interior of the country have modernization programs, and the government is subsidizing the building of new houses. We are trying to create employment in these areas, so that the young people will have an incentive to remain in agriculture instead of moving to Abidjan. This involves an agricultural prices policy, an education and health policy, and a housing policy.

It is possible to have a planning office attached to the president's Office. But if the people working in planning have no political weight, their best plans will not help. Planning should not be detached from political responsibility.

If you talk to a finance minister in 1973 about plans for 1980, he will tell you that he has to find funds for his urgent current expenditures and will deal with you later. But when he has a politically influential minister of planning to contend with, he will take him into consideration and cooperate.

We started by dealing with the easiest problems. A government is not forgiven serious errors, so it is important to recognize weaknesses. One such weakness is our education, which has not been effective and has to be reformed. This is now being planned.

PLANASA: A DYNAMIC PLAN FOR A DYNAMIC PROBLEM—PARTIAL INDICATIVE PLANNING IN THE BRAZILIAN EXPERIENCE

Rubens Vas da Costa

Rapid population growth is one of the key characteristics of the LDC. Rural-urban migration has led to rates of urban population growth twice as large as the average national rates. Urban population growth of 5-6 percent per annum, common in many countries, leads to doubling every 12 to 15 years.

Thus the problems of economic development in these countries are extremely dynamic. National plans often fail to take into consideration the rapid increases in the demand for goods and urban services. When finally published, they are often obsolete or fall short of actual needs.

The LDCs require a mechanism capable of periodically revising plans so that they can be easily adjusted to new circumstances and needs. But this is not enough. We need to bring into the plans elements of self-correction as well as the means to assure that, when the backlog of needs is overcome, the attainment of goals will be assured on a self-sustained basis.

NATIONAL PLAN OF POPULAR HOUSING

The very ambitious PLANHAP, National Plan of Popular Housing, aims at financing until 1982 two million dwellings for owner occupation by low-income families earning between one and three minimum wages.* Total investments in PLANHAP will amount to Cr 30 billion (U.S. $5 billion equivalent) to eliminate the housing deficit in that income range and, after 1982, to provide an adequate supply for new families.

---

*In 1973, the minimum monthly wage in Rio de Janeiro was Cr 312.00 (U.S. $50.00 equivalent).

NATIONAL PLAN FOR SANITATION

The goals of PLANASA are ambitious. By 1980, 80 percent of the urban population of Brazil, that is, 65 million people, will be supplied with water of good quality, and 50 percent of the urban dwellings will be connected to sewage mains. The goal must be the control of water pollution. Total investments under PLANASA will amount to Cr 10 billion (U.S. $1.5 billion), 60 percent of which will be financed with loans from the Banco Nacional de Habitacao, or BNH (The National Housing Bank).

Because the growth rate of the urban population of Brazil has been 5 percent per annum and in certain large metropolitan areas has exceeded 6 percent per annum, severe deficiencies in the supply of potable water and in the treatment and disposal of water wastes accumulated. These services are generally a municipal responsibility, and financing was inadequate because the municipalities were weak. Local revenues failed to cover current costs, necessitating continued transfers from state and federal budgets for capital investments. Many municipalities lack managerial talent to plan, build, and operate the services.

In 1967 the Federal Government requested the BNH to establish a financing program for water and sewerage. By then only 50 percent of the urban population had access to water. Water treatment was in some cases inadequate and pressure was low in many cities, resulting in poor service to the consumer.

The BNH started by financing the expansion and modernization of existing water services. This required the adoption of realistic water rates, inflation-hedged and covering all current costs, including loan service. This was a considerable improvement but not enough. The piecemeal financing of municipal water companies was a static solution to a dynamic problem. The needs for city water supply sources are ever expanding. They grow faster than the urban population but are generally subject to economics of scale if adequate financing is available. However, financing almost 4000 municipalities, many of which competed for the same water resources, was wasteful. A new plan was needed.

Characteristics and Components

Because the need for good quality water is very dynamic in a country where the urban population is fast growing, the answer is a dynamic plan. The success of the PLANASA is conditioned by water rates covering costs and yielding a surplus to finance expansion. It also requires a thorough reform of the administration, the establishment of realistic goals, the elimination of the governmental capital subsidy after the backlog of demand has been met, a flexible water rate schedule assuring rates that low-income families can afford, as well as rates that induce conservation where water is scarce and stimulate consumption where resources are ample. Charge to middle- and higher-income families will yield a surplus that will cover the subsidized rates for low-income families.

Three main components assure the dynamic characteristic of the PLANASA: permanent reprograming, a dynamic feasibility model (that is, feasibility is assured at any point in time), and the growth of the State Water and Sewage Fund (SWSF) with the growth of demand. The SWSFs are revolving funds, owned by the States and agent managed, and are the key financial institution in PLANASA. They are capitalized by the state budgets and returns from prior loans Loans made with the SWSFs' resources bear an interest rate at least equal to the growth rate of the state urban population. These loans are fully indexed against inflation. After the goal has been met, the contribution from the state budget to the SWSFs will cease. Afterwards, the needs for renewal and expansion will be financed with resources from the SWSFs and loans from the BNH, without resources to state funds. The resources of the SWSFs grow as projects financed by the BNH are executed and will be available only to projects under PLANASA. Total assets of the SWSF are estimated to reach the equivalent to U.S. $600 million by 1989.

A PLANASA model showed that the backlog of water supply may be overcome in five to ten years, depending on the amount of resources available, and will meet the increase in demand during that period with the investment of approximately Cr 10 billion. A feasibility report was prepared for each state establishing that this problem could be solved given adequate institutional reforms and a rational water rate policy.

Enactment and Establishment

PLANASA was enacted under the authority of the BNH and later was included in the National Plan for Economic and Social Development. Each state was to sign an agreement with the BNH adhering to PLANASA and obtaining legislation to borrow from the BNH the amounts necessary to carry out the programs to provide the counterpart funds needed to establish a State Water and Sewage Fund and to comply with the rate policy recommended by the BNH, as well as with other administrative requirements of PLANASA, such as the creation of a state controlled W&S Company to build, maintain, and exploit W&S systems throughout the State.

The Municipalities were required to turn over to the State W&S Company assets and liabilities in exchange for its stock and a concession to the Company to exploit those services.

The BNH finances 50 percent of the investments required, provided the state and municipalities finance the other half. The terms of the BNH loans are interest of up to 8 percent, indexation of the loans, repayment in 18 years plus a maximum grace period of 3 years. The BNH makes additional loans to the state, which, in turn, turns over the loan proceeds to the SWSF, so that no state is required at any time to use more than five percent of its tax revenues for investment in W&S systems. In practice, this has meant that in the poorer states of northeast Brazil BNH loans have reached 80 percent of the required investments. To compensate for the large disparities in income amongst states, interest charges under PLANASA vary from 4 percent to 8 percent per annum, in accordance with the per capita state tax revenues.

Financial and Administrative Institutions

To carry out such a thorough reform in the financing of water services, a system of institutions had to be created or strengthened. BNH loans, for instance, are made to the state water companies via a state bank. The state banks thus render services for a fee under PLANASA. The state development banks* are generally the guarantors of BNH loans, also for a fee. The participation of banks in the financing of PLANASA assures a businesslike attitude. W&S Companies contract out with private construction firms, generally through tenders.

A list of the financial and administrative institutions that play a role in this plan will facilitate the understanding of PLANASA.

Financing Entity (FE)

The FE is responsible for furnishing to the SWSF the necessary financial resources to meet the commitments agreed upon with the BNH. The FE normally is the state government. Its principal source of funds for the SWSF is the state budget. However, the FE may obtain funding from other sources (nonstate funds) if it wishes to accelerate the execution of the investment program.

---

*In Brazil most states operate state banks, which compete with privately owned commercial banks; and development banks, which compete with privately owned investment banks.

Managing Organism of the SWSF (MO)

Charged by the state to manage, program, and loan the resources of the SWSF and the repayment made into the SWSF by the Water Company, the MO is also responsible for assisting the state government in mobilizing resources from the state budget and loans from other sources to fulfill the SWSF commitments.

Financial Agent (FA)

This is a bank owned by the state and accepted by the BNH as borrower. The FA borrows from the MO resources of the SWSF and is the depository of its funds. The FA relends both the proceeds from the BNH loans and the resources of SWSF to the W&S Companies. To maintain the values of its resources, all loans made by the FA are hedged against inflation. The FA is responsible for collecting repayments from the W&S Companies and returning them to the BNH and to the SWSF.

The Guarantor

BNH requires an acceptable guarantor of its loans to the state W&S Companies—generally, a state-owned development bank.

Promoting Agent (PA)

The Promoting Agent formulates the state sanitation policy. Its activities include:
- the collection and organization of information for state sanitation programs.
- the promotion of financial participation by municipalities in PLANASA, as well as the obtaining of concessions for the companies for the exploitation of the municipal water and sewage services. The municipality may be asked to contribute up to 15 percent of its revenues during the period of construction to the SWSF. Responsibility for the services will be transferred to the SWS Company. This will release resources for other municipal uses.
- the promotion of studies and the preparation of projects according to requirements established in PLANASA.

Final Borrower (Concessionary)

The Concessionary is charged by the state to execute works, perform services, and operate the systems financed by loans through the FA. It is also responsible for repayments of loans received from the FA. The Concessionary is normally the State W&S Company.

Technical Entity (TE)

The TE is employed by the BNH to assist in the analysis of projects and in supervising the execution of the works financed under PLANASA.

The large number of bodies operating under PLANASA are needed to assure an adequate division of responsibilities and specialization required for such an ambitious program in a short time span. On the other hand, transfer of responsibility to the state companies releases thousands of administrative and managerial personnel and generates considerable savings.

The consolidation of W&S responsibility in a single company in each state (23 companies, altogether), makes possible the centralization of research work, computerized billing, more efficient procurement, training of personnel,* technical assistance, and overall maintenance services.

Rate Schedule

PLANASA's most important features assure that all human settlements in Brazil will have access to water of good quality at rates their populations can afford. The rate increases initially needed to assure this policy objective are very small in relation to the water charges to the inhabitants of the larger cities of each state and will be fully compensated for by the increased efficiency of the centralized water administration as coverage reaches and exceeds the minimum goal, when rates in real terms will begin to decline.

The single rate schedule for each state also keeps municipalities from competing for industry location using artificially low water rates as an incentive. Lack of enforcement of waste disposal standards constituted another element leading to unsound social decisions. Low-income consumers (up to 15 m^2 per month) are assured that the monthly bill will not exceed 5 percent of the regional minimum wage and that this percentage will decline toward 3 percent with increased efficiency. To establish the rate structure a feasibility study was made considering the situation and the necessary changes in water rates. Results showed that with small rate adjustments one can reach

---

*The BNH is promoting jointly with the water companies, the ministries of education and labor, and other institutions, the training of 60 thousand personnel of the water companies, from the top management down to water treatment station operators. This goal will be met before 1980.

the goal in less than ten years, without the need to commit more than 5 percent of tax revenues. Only in the state of Piaui* the federal government had to donate Cr 13 million to assure the feasibility of the PLANASA, and in the state of Acre, in the Amazon region, approximately Cr 10 million were required from the Federal Government.

The rate schedule is optimized through a simulation computer model sensitive to changes of investment required. Recently a state government suggested a change in priorities for political reasons, resulting in an increase of 7 percent in the average rate throughout the state. The priority schedule maximizes the return on the investments by serving at first the most profitable settlements.

Adherence of the States to PLANASA

All states have agreed to adhere to PLANASA. In the state of Sao Paulo the constitution of the state company should be concluded shortly. This may be the second largest corporation in the state and one of the largest in Brazil. After completion of the agreement, BNH will lend approximately Cr 2 billion to the newly created State W&S Company through the Banco do Estado de Sao Paulo.

In the state of Rio Grande do Sul PLANASA is feasible only if the municipality, Porto Alegre, turns over its W&S department (DEMAE) to the existing State W&S Company, CORSAN. DEMAE's large cash surplus is used by the municipality for other purposes. The local legislative is controlled by the opposition party, and the transfer of DEMAE's assets to CORSAN is doubtful. Rio Grande do Sul may be the only state to stay out of PLANASA. In the smaller states of Mato Grosso and Acre only administrative problems have to be solved.

A number of municipalities have refused so far to turn over their concession for water and sewerage exploitation and to transfer assets and control of their water supply companies. They will have to agree because neither financing from the BNH nor transfers from state or federal budgets will be available. Considerable pressure by tax payers and waters users may be exerted to adhere to PLANASA, since improvements or expansion require tax or water rate increases.

The BNH loaned Cr 2.5 billion for W&S projects up to July 1973. These loans, together with the resources contributed by the states and municipalities, will generate Cr 7.2 billion in investments in 556

---

*Piaui, located in the Brazilian Northeast, has the lowest per capita income in Brazil.

settlements throughout the country. Initially, 25 million people will benefit from improved water works supplying good quality water.

The sewerage program has been initiated only in seven states, because the water supply system has to reach a certain point before sewage loans are entertained. Only the state of Paraiba has complied with this requirement. In Sao Paulo the financing for water and sewage projects was given on conditions harder than those slated under the PLANASA agreement. The capital cities of the states of Para, Pernambuco, Bahia, Sao Paulo, and the city of Rio de Janeiro (Guanabara State) have received loans to expand and improve their inadequate sewage services. Additional loans will be made available to the state companies as water supply projects advance.

The planning mechanism of PLANASA and the administrative, technical, managerial, and financial machinery established under it assure that it will reach its goal within 10 years. The resources flowing back to SWSFs from repayments of loans made to the State W&S Companies will suffice to finance improvements and to expand capacity. SWSF interest rates are at least equal to the growth rate of the urban population of the state. After goals are met, no further state resources will be needed. The State W&S Companies will reinvest their profits in expansion projects and improve services.

Other problems of a dynamic nature, involving the production of goods and services bought in the market place, may be solved by creating self-sustained financing mechanisms with an internal rate of capitalization equal to the growth rate of the demand. Personnel training, sound pricing policies, well-established priorities, and simulation computer models are other important requirements. The PLANASA pioneer experiment in Brazil with partial indicative planning has met with considerable success and is inspiring similar solutions to other problems.

DETERMINANTS AND CONSEQUENCES OF GROWTH OF ISRAEL AGRICULTURE
Yair Mundlak

Israel agriculture, in the twenty years 1952-71, achieved a high average annual growth rate of 8.8 percent by expansion of resources and by technical change. At the beginning of the period new land was brought into cultivation and new water projects provided agriculture with increasing quantities of water. Agriculture was also favored in the allocation of investment funds, and its capital stock increased relatively fast. But in recent years the growth of resources except for capital, has for all practical purposes come to an end. Consequently, technical change has accounted for an increasing part of the total growth in output. Of the average annual growth rate of 12.1 percent achieved in 1952-62, 58 percent is attributed to technical change. The average annual growth in 1962-71 was 5.4 percent, of which 96 percent was due to technical change.

The growth of agricultural output decelerated partly because of the constancy of land and water and partly due to demand limitations. The expansion of production of high value products such as vegetables, fruits, and livestock is determined by the growth of markets for them. The potential of Israel agriculture allows a higher rate of growth than that dictated by expansion of local demand. To utilize this potential, agricultural exports and import substitutes were developed. The rate of export development largely dictated the overall growth rate of agricultural output.

The decline in the growth rate of agricultural output has reduced the share of agriculture in total output, employment, and capital stocks. This shift in resource utilization (particularly of labor) took place without major disturbances, since employment opportunities were provided throughout the country, not least by establishing industries on farms. Consequently, only 31 percent of the agricultural labor force is now fully occupied in agricultural production.

PRODUCTION

Israel agriculture has expanded rapidly. Its output in 1971 was more than nine times larger than in 1949. The developments during the twenty years 1952-71 are summarized in Table 23. The period 1949-51, one of intensive settlement, is not dealt with here.

Apart from annual variations due to weather, output has grown constantly, but at a declining rate. The average annual rate of growth for the period 1952-62 was 12.1 percent as compared with 5.4 percent for the period 1962-71.

What are the causes of the big increase in output and of the decline in the rate of growth? To answer this question let us review the trends in the utilization of inputs. Table 23 presents quantity indexes of the various inputs, with 1954 as the base year. The labor force index rose from 99 in 1952 to 126 in 1959, then remaining stable until 1965. From 1966 it fell, returning to 97 in 1971. Thus the output index rose from 78 to 425 with no change in labor. Since all other factors increased during the period, it seems that technical change had an important labor saving component, or that the elasticity of capital-labor substitution in agriculture was rather high.

The index of the cultivated land rose from 97 in 1952 to 115 in 1959 and has remained more or less at the level since; thus

TABLE 23

Output and Inputs—Quantity Indexes, 1952-71 (1954 = 100)

	Output	Labor	Capital	Land	Water
1952	78	99	86	97	71
1953	79	96	93	99	85
1954	100	100	100	100	100
1955	101	106	109	101	115
1956	125	107	122	103	126
1957	139	110	138	107	126
1958	159	121	151	110	152
1959	201	126	167	115	150
1960	214	126	183	114	161
1961	237	128	197	116	155
1962	262	126	211	114	170
1963	265	124	224	112	173
1964	297	127	234	116	155
1965	274	124	246	116	166
1966	279	116	257	114	192
1967	327	112	272	117	169
1968	324	99	276	116	192
1969	331	96	279	116	187
1970	379	99	285	115	201
1971	425	97	289	116	202

land cannot account for the growth in output since 1959. And although there has been a continuous increase in the amount of water used for irrigation, much of it took place in the early years of the period reviewed.

The capital stock of agriculture grew faster and more consistently. Its index rose from 86 in 1952 to 197 in 1962, and 289 in 1971. Clearly, the growth of agricultural output cannot be fully accounted for by increases in conventional resources. The conclusion is that there has been a change in the productivity of resources, that is, a technical change.

If we attribute to technical change the part of output growth not accounted for by conventional inputs, we obtain an average annual rate of 5.8 percent for such growth in the period as a whole. By aggregating inputs, using as weights their shares in total output, we obtain an increase in total factor of 3 percent per year. The difference between the annual growth rate of output of 8.8 percent and that of total factor gives the rate of technical change. (See Table 24.)

During the 1952-62 period the annual growth of 12.1 percent in agricultural output resulted from a 5.1 percent increase in aggregate input and a 7.0 percent increase in productivity. The corresponding figures for 1962-71 are a 5.4 percent increase in output, a 0.2 percent increase in total factor, and a 5.2 percent increase due to technical change. Both output and technical change decelerated as compared with the first subperiod, but the weight of technical change within the total growth of agricultural output increased enormously. In fact, 96 percent of the growth of output in the second period resulted from technical change as compared with 66 percent in the first period.

Labor and capital may continue to grow should demand for such growth exist. Their development during the second subperiod can be viewed as reflecting market conditions. This is not the case with land and water, the quantities of which are determined exogenously. If these inputs will remain constant, they cannot contribute to growth in the future and technical change will continue to do most of the work, as in recent years.

Technical change took various forms: Increase in yield per "natural unit" such as land and cows; (2) change of output composition in favor of products with higher returns; (3) introduction of new products yielding higher returns; (4) decline in labor as compared with other inputs.

The first component represents the improvement of the efficiency of the biological process of agricultural production. The third component implies changing the production function by introducing new products. Both of these activities depend on progress made in local research and on knowledge imported from abroad. Good research and organization, as well as trained farmers, make the process of adaptation of new technologies function smoothly.

TABLE 24

Output and Inputs—Average Rates of Growth*
(percentage per annum)

Period	Output	Labor	Capital	Land	Water	Total Factor	Technical change
1952-71	8.8	0.0(0.51)	7.0(0.34)	1.0(0.05)	4.6(0.10)	3.0	5.8
1952-62	12.1	2.4(0.53)	9.0(0.32)	1.7(0.05)	8.7(0.10)	5.1	7.0
1962-71	5.4	-2.9(0.47)	3.5(0.38)	0.2(0.05)	1.9(0.10)	0.2	5.2

* The weights for computing total factors are in parentheses.

The new technologies introduced gave good results and spread rapidly. For instance, cotton was introduced to Israel in 1954. In 1960 it was grown on 24,500 acres, accounting for 29 percent of the irrigated field crops. In 1971 irrigated cotton was grown on 73,000 acres, constituting 57 percent of the irrigated field crops. Another example is the technology of growing vegetables and flowers in greenhouses or under plastic. The area of covered vegetables doubled between 1968 and 1971, reaching 9.2 percent of the total vegetable area in 1971. The area of flowers grown in this manner also doubled in the last three years. Flowers became an important commercial crop only in recent years but by 1971 were already grown in 275 villages.

The gain in efficiency resulting from changing the composition of output in favor of high value products largely depends on the demand for such products.

DEMAND

While agricultural output expanded in the 1952-71 period at an average annual rate of 8.8 percent, population increased at an average annual rate of 3.3 percent. If growth is to be sustained, outlets for the product have to be found. The expansion of local per capita demand is largely determined by the rise in real incomes and relative prices. Food is the major component of agricultural output. The main developments in per capita consumption of food are given in Table 25. The years 1952-54 were still a period of food rationing. The elimination of controls led to expansion of per capita food consumption at an average annual rate of 4.5 percent in 1954. However, this rate declined to 3.0 percent for 1960-66 and to 2.3 percent in 1966-71.

The change in food consumption was largely due to changes in real disposable income (measured here by per captia private consumption) and to changes in the relative prices of food.

During all subperiods per capita consumption of food grew less rapidly than its production. The difference was exported. Exports of unprocessed agricultural products rose from $17 million in 1952 to $63 million in 1962 and $155 million in 1971. The average annual per capita increase in agricultural exports was 3.2 percent in 1960-66 and 6.6 percent in 1966-71. There has also been a considerable rise in exports of processed food.

The most successful import-substituting product was cotton, first introduced in 1954. Israel has become a net exporter of cotton.

The growth of agricultural output could not have occurred without the development of the export market, which made it possible to divert resources to high-value export crops. This shift is recorded as a technical change. Consequently, the rate at which the export markets develop will increasingly determine the rate of technical change in agriculture.

TABLE 25

Rates of Change of Per Capita Consumption
and Relative Prices
(percentages)

	Per Capital Consumption of Food at Constant Prices	P*	Total Private Consumption per Capita at Constant Prices
1952-54	3.7	+0.4	5.3
1954-60	4.5	-1.2	4.8
1960-66	3.0	-1.7	5.1
1966-71	2.3	+0.3	3.6

*The average annual change of food prices relative to the aggregate price of private consumption.

THE DECLINE IN THE RELATIVE IMPORTANCE OF AGRICULTURE

Agricultural output constituted 10.6 percent of total output in 1952, reached a peak of 13.1 percent in 1958, and then declined to 6.9 percent in 1971. (See Table 26.) Without technical change the share of agriculture in the utilization of resources would have declined at the same rate. Technical change makes it possible to produce a given output with fewer resources, but this is also true for the rest of the economy.

If the share of agriculture in total resources declines faster than its share in output, this indicates a faster rate of technical change in agriculture than in other sectors. In Israel the share of agricultural labor declined somewhat faster than the share of agricultural output, but this was not the case as regards the share of capital. Thus technical change seems to be more labor saving in agriculture than in other sectors, while the substitution of capital for labor may be easier in agriculture.

Agriculture accounted in 1971 for about 9 percent of the labor force and the capital stock. The equality of the two indicates that the capital-labor ratio in agriculture is the same as in the rest of the economy. This result is true only for recent years. Throughout most of the period reviewed the share of agricultural labor was larger than the share of agricultural capital, which means that agriculture was labor intensive.

The share of agriculture in total investment is less than half its share in total output. If this trend continues, the share of agriculture in the capital stock will decline sharply in the near future.

TABLE 26

The Relative Importance of Agriculture in the Economy
(percent of total)

	1952	1956	1960
Output	10.6	11.3	11.3
Labor	17.4	16.9	17.1
Capital	15.0	14.5	14.2
Investment	8.5	15.8	11.4
Export	38.0	41.0	30.0
	1964	1968	1971
Output	9.6	7.8	6.9
Labor	13.9	10.4	8.9
Capital	11.7	10.9	9.0
Investment	5.8	5.9	4.1
Export	19.0	19.0	17.0

TABLE 27

Distribution of Farm Labor Force—
The 1971 Census (preliminary results)

	Total[a]		Kibbutzim and Collective Moshavim		Moshavim	
	Thousands	Percentage	Thousands	Percentage	Thousands	Percentage
Farm population aged 14 and above	204.6	100.0	77.3	100.0	64.9	100.0
Thereof: not participating in the labor force[b]	65.6	32.1	19.3	25.0	15.7	24.2
Participating	139.0	67.9	58.0	75.0	49.2	75.8
Thereof: working only on farm	42.8	30.8	18.3	31.6	15.1	30.7
working on and outside farm	26.2	18.8	—	—	18.8	38.2
working only outside farm	70.0	50.4	39.7	68.4	15.3	31.1

[a] The total includes Kibbutzim, Moshavim, private farms, and the Arab sector.
[b] Students, aged, and sick.

Finally, the export component of agriculture is relatively high. Throughout the period the weight of agricultural exports was twice as high as the weight of agricultural output.

The trend observed above in the agricultural labor force is common to all developing economies regardless of their stage of development. Rates of change might differ, depending on the specific conditions of the country and the ability of the urban sector to absorb agricultural labor. Unemployment in the cities discourages mobility of labor out of agriculture. Here the Israeli experience is interesting: The movement of labor out of agriculture did not involve population moves from farms to cities. Israel is a small country, and industry is fairly well spread; so one can live on the farm and work elsewhere. But the kibbutzim developed industries to provide employment for their unoccupied agricultural labor. These industries are succeeding well, and in some kibbutzim the industrial output exceeds the agricultural output.

This development is reflected by the occupational distribution of the agricultural labor force, summarized in Table 27. Of those participating in the labor force, 50 percent work in nonagricultural activities. This figure is higher for the kibbutzim, (68.4 percent) and lower for the moshavim (31.1 percent).

We thus differentiate between occupational mobility and geographical mobility, the former being most important in the context of economic growth. However, occupational mobility is not usually achieved without geographical mobility, which has social and economic repercussions putting a very high social cost on the process.

DISCUSSION

RUBENS VAZ DA COSTA (Brazil): Dr. Mundlak does not do justice to Israeli agriculture because he lumps together periods of 10 years. From 1969 to 1970 the increase in output was 15 percent. In 1971 output grew by another 12 percent. Thus after a period of rapid output growth ending in 1962 there was a period of slow growth, but now Israeli agriculture has against started to expand rapidly. Is this because you specialize in sophisticated commodities like flowers and avocados or because you are using your land and water resources better?

In 1971 Israel agriculture was expanding a little faster than the economy as a whole.

My first question is how much growth can be attributed to fertilizers, insecticides, pesticides, better farming methods, and improved animal husbandry. My second question is how you define labor. Is it the number of people engaged in farming, or does it also take into account the number of hours worked?

LEOPOLDO SOLIS M. (Mexico): What is the effective rate of protection for Israeli agriculture, and how did the terms of trade between agriculture and other sectors move during the two periods Professor Mundlak referred to?

MEIR MERHAV (Israel): Planning and pooling of resources played a major role in the rapid growth of Israel agriculture. The introduction of industry into kibbutzim was enabled by planning and pooling of resources. And introducing cotton was not due to market forces but was fostered from above. Nor is there any coercion involved in this type of planning but rather voluntary cooperation. In fact, this is a good example of successful planning.

JOSEPH SHATIL (Israel): Between 1948 and 1952 the Jewish population of Israel doubled, there was much insufficiently used land, and the country was short of food. So rapid growth of food output was essential, the demand for it being great. The government deliberately fostered it. In the late 1950s the first agricultural surpluses appeared, prices dropped by about one-third, and there were two years of crisis.

The needed reorientation took different forms: Kibbutzim started to industrialize; in moshavim, individuals sought outside work.

Cotton, introduced in the early fifties to employ surplus labor, became profitable only when mechanized—and then was grown almost exclusively by kibbutzim (which had no labor surplus).

Now there is a trend in both moshavim and kibbutzim towards highly mechanized, labor-extensive agriculture and towards exports.

The deceleration in the growth of agricultural output is connected with the limitations on land and water in Israel. Therefore strict planning was introduced after the 1959-60 crisis—not only of water quantities but also of production, marketing, and planting in many different agricultural branches. This planning is done by cooperation between farmers' organizations and the government. The said organizations being efficient, it is possible to execute the plans made fairly accurately.

LE VAN PHUC (Vietnam): Israel's agriculture switched from labor intensive to capital intensive. It must have borrowed to make the change possible. When there was excess labor, due to the shift, industry was brought in to alleviate the situation. But, since the shift came first, the farmers must already have borrowed up to their maximum capacity. So how did they borrow to set up industrial plants? Did the government deliberately foster industrial development in kibbutzim by very easy credit or credit without collateral?

IASSU ANDEMICAEL (ECA): What were the major problems encountered by kibbutzim, moshavim, and private farms during the last 20-years?

RICHARD ABLIN (Israel): A study of Israel agriculture can bring out the right and the wrong types of planning. One must distinguish between the rate of growth of productivity and the level of productivity.

Much of Israel's agriculture was misplaced, mainly owing to protective price distortions. The distorted prices were created to encourage import substitution, and resulted in a sector parts of which are basically uneconomic. Yet within this distorted structure there could be rapid growth of productivity.

This is the wrong type of planning. Eggs, poultry, and meat in Israel, for example, have a very high cost per dollar of added value or per dollar saved. Yet the activities contributing the added value to these products may be quite efficient.

So one is being efficient doing the wrong thing. The reason for the high cost per dollar saved in these cases is that some of the major components of added value have to be imported at high cost (for instance, feed). This offsets the relatively high efficiency of the Israeli contribution to the final output. The real national income is reduced by this kind of efficient agriculture.

On the other hand, the improvement of the technical level in Israeli agriculture, spreading knowledge of new opportunities, and so on are a real area of government responsibility. Such extension services improving skills and the technical level cannot be left entirely to private enterprise. Much of the productivity improvement resulted from this type of government activity.

There were also cases of unhappy directive intervention by planners, such as to produce only one particular type of tomato. These failed and only caused trouble.

YAIR MUNDLAK (Israel): Any government action requires a plan; so it is not a question of either you plan or you don't. The real questions are what we mean by planning and what is the relationship between plans, policy, and policy instruments. One can object to the policy or the instruments used, but hardly to planning as such.

The industrialization of the kibbutz, Dr. Merhav, is a pure example of private market forces, not of policy. Each kibbutz acted as an entrepreneur in the market place. No one told them to do what they did.

Industrialization in kibbutzim started a long time ago, with the motive of finding solutions for older members. It did not seek encouragement from the government, which only later became an address for help.

But this does not mean we do not need planning.

It was not a plan but policy, since the beginning of Jewish settlement in Israel, that land belongs to the nation not to the farm—that it must be nationalized. Water is by and large nationalized too; and, even if it belongs to the private individual, there is a water law that dictates its use. This is not a question of limiting the water we use (it is limited by nature) but of distributing available water to farmers.

There is a policy concerning the size of the farm unit given to individual farmers. This policy has not been updated and causes problems related to the question how the three types of farms adjust to the situation. The size of the land area given to moshavim was decided in the 1920s according to two criteria: first, self-labor (no more land than the farmer can cultivate himself, with his horse); and, second sufficient land to allow him to earn an income comparable to urban wage earners. But today you replace the horse with a tractor, and urban wage rates have risen; so one needs a very different size of farm. Nevertheless, the plan, the laws and the practice have not changed. This is exactly the danger of plans and dogmas. The instruments of the past have become an ideology.

Even in Israel, we sometime refuse to recognize this fact in public debates. So I showed in my Table 27 what actually happens: In moshavim 30.7 percent work only on the farm, but 31 percent work only outside the farm. Working only outside the farm means that the wife takes care of the poultry and on a citrus orchard not requiring much work except during the season. The husband works elsewhere.

We have a 5-year plan for agriculture, drawn up every two or three years. This is mainly a framework for evaluating different policies and for allocating public funds invested in agriculture. Branches considered important for agricultural development get heavily subsidized public credits.

The interest rate for farmers is subsidized and well below the market rate. There are also planned production quotas, based on the total output demanded by the plan, which is drawn up in cooperation with production and marketing boards. Some of these boards, such as the vegetable one, learned from experience that they were interfering too much, restricted their operations and ceased controlling various products during various seasons. The experience of the poultry board is also discouraging. In recent years it failed to stabilize prices and quantities.

We thus have a framework for taking action, but it is not always used correctly. The policy and the instruments may not always have been the right ones.

In agriculture there are random variations. Two of the three years 1969-71 were very good in terms of rainfall, and one in terms of citrus prices in Europe. That is why I preferred to deal with the rate of growth for 1962-71. Results in 1972-73 will be less good than in 1969-71.

Fertilizers and insecticides are very important. We use them heavily. Positive results are partly due to good management, which also means not overusing them. We had an interesting experience in cotton. In the second or third year after it was introduced it suffered from bollweevil, and there were heavy losses. The year after we sprayed heavily to kill it, but the crop was not profitable because of the high cost of spraying. So good management calls for balancing the insect population against the costs of spraying and selecting the right level of spraying.

There is certainly a great deal of protection and subsidizing in our agriculture. Since wages here are linked to the cost-of-living index, the government takes care not to cause big jumps in the index. Hence the Israeli consumer has hardly felt the change in the prices of primary commodities. Relatively to other countries, Israeli food prices are cheap, due to government subsidies. This is not really protection for agriculture; in fact it deprives agriculture of some handsome opportunities. It is aimed at producing stability. The question is what trade-off there should be between stability and efficiency. The present policy may not be very wise.

Farm organizations have usually demanded protection and planning. But when world prices started to rise in the last few years, they started to have second thoughts and turn to the free market ideology. For, owing to planning, they don't get the free market price of cotton. They get the historical price with some adjustments.

By and large Israel is competivite in most of its agricultural products, despite having to irrigate many products not irrigated by our competitors. We don't produce enough meat since we do not have the land for pasture. Until recent years, the price of beef was determined by conditions in land-intensive countries. This has now changed, and marginal output in the world market may now come more from fattened, fed beef. In this we may have a comparative advantage, as in poultry and turkeys.

We have protection in two major groups of products, milk and fruit. The question is not so much one of subsidies as of strict controls on imports of dairy products and fruit. I am not trying to justify this situation.

**REALISM IN EDUCATIONAL
PLANNING IN LDCs**
Eli Ginzberg

THE IMMODEST ECONOMISTS

Economists are imperialists. For several decades they have concerned themselves increasingly with education, and in the process they have sought to dominate the arena in terms of their policy preconceptions. But economists like other imperialists are often on the move: in the 1950s and into the late 1960s they were strong advocates of increasing national investments in education in both developed and developing countries, convinced that significant social gains would be realized from raising the skill and competence of the population. In the last few years they have begun to carp at increasing expenditures, claiming that they were compounding rather than resolving problems by misdirecting too much investment into education or by misallocating resources among the different levels of education.

Specifically, the critics point to many previously unrecognized injurious effects from such overinvestment. Educational investments at best have a long-deferred pay-out period—a generation or so, similar to reforestation. The inevitable tendency for the better educated to drift to the cities and to remain there, adding to the pool of unemployed educated persons, further distorts the distribution of talent. A major challenge that most developing countries face is to keep more able people on the farms, where they can, it is hoped, contribute to the vitalization of agriculture. Since holders of diplomas and degrees will not accept jobs they consider beneath them without a long search for suitable work, the larger number of graduates, the higher the unemployment rate. Since most people who complete secondary or tertiary education have acquired little technical knowledge or skill, it is wrong to see the educational system as a producer of the new manpower that the advanced sector requires. The government bureaucracy not only provides the major source of employment for a high proportion of college and university graduates but also maintains a salary scale heavily tipped in favor of the educated, thereby adding to labor market distortions and income inequalities.

Excessive investments in education have additional untoward results. When the ablest university graduates find it difficult to continue their studies or secure a satisfactory position with career prospects, they may go abroad; and many never return. Even though it costs much less to educate a child during the first years of school than in secondary school or in college, sizable sums are wasted because many youngsters who start school drop out after one or two years without having achieved basic literacy.

While some of these criticisms have surfaced in developed nations, they are most frequently directed at developments in the LDCs.

THE RESPONSIVE POLITICIANS

The economists probably encouraged the political leaders in most LDCs to do what they would have done in any case, namely to increase rapidly public spending for education.

The end of World War II saw many newly independent developing countries. For most, opposition to the colonial power that had ruled them was stronger than commitment to a national identity. Hence the leadership faced the urgent task of buttressing the idea of nationhood, an effort in which a substantially expanded public school system could assist. Curriculum, books, and language could all be put into the service of the new state. Although the financing of education by the new national government did not assure the eclipse of strong regional and local values and traditions, the underwriting of all or most of the educational budget provided the central government with leverage to further the ideas and ideals of nationhood. The leadership had little else to work with.

Politicians are engaged in a ceaseless struggle to win and hold adherents, a process in which they are more likely to succeed if they can respond positively to the expressed and latent aspirations of their constituents. The people in most LDCs, especially in countries that had recently ejected their colonial overlords, saw education as the open sesame to a new and better life. Nor was this an unwarranted assumption. The average man knew from long and painful experience that all power and privilege belonged to the educated few who alone had access to the good jobs and honorific positions. The only way up the occupational and income ladder was through education. Small wonder that the political leadership in every developing country was under steady siege to enlarge appropriations for education. The most benighted farmers hundreds of miles from the seat of government pressed for a local school with only slightly less intensity than the urban masses who were directly exposed to the forces of modernization.

The intensity of the demand for education exerted strong pressures on the politicians, individually and collectively. Limited in potential leverage, managerial competence, and financial resources, the central government, through expanding educational budgets, could show positive action for every section of the country, for every class, for both sexes. The fact that educational opportunities for large numbers could be provided for relatively little money—in warm climates classes are often held out of doors and operate with little equipment—added to the attractiveness of a public educational program. No national budget could stand the costs of a nation-wide effort at road building, a substantial regional investment in new plants, the rapid spread of electricity, or the provision of even modest health services in both cities and the rural hinterland. The only national program with the potential for delivering a new and constructive service to large numbers of the population, and eventually for all, was the development of local schools. Accordingly, the politicians were favorably inclined.

Many in leadership positions anticipated that, in addition to the contribution that it can make to nation building and to social welfare, education would help dissolve some of the rigidities that stand in the path of modernization. Clearly a developing country cannot grow and prosper until most of its population become literate.

Political cohesion, military security, economic specialization, and social cohesion depend on easy and rapid communications, and this can be achieved only if the mass of the population are able to read and write. The tragic disaster of Pakistan may have been embodied in its creation, but it was made certain and the date of its collapse advanced by the conscious decision of the military-business oligarchy to starve education in the belief that an illiterate population would be more tractable.

The political leadership in most developing countries moved to funnel more money into public education on the grounds that education is essential for the strengthening of nationhood, for improving the conditions of the common man, and for speeding modernization. For the most part, those with decision-making power saw little danger and many advantages to increasing governmental expenditures for education. And they acted accordingly.

SOME INCONTROVERTIBLE REALITIES

The educational push was made easier by the fact that, except for scientific and technical training, increasing school enrollments do not constitute a drain on scarce foreign exchange. Nor do they represent a diversion of scarce manpower resources, for once the expansion gets under way many graduates flow back into the system as teachers.

Moreover, since most teachers come through the humanities track, the schools do not compete for scarce scientific and technical personnel with the modern sector. In fact, the ability of the educational system to absorb a high proportion of the liberal arts graduates is a source of satisfaction and relief to the political leadership since it substantially reduces the numbers who would otherwise be found in the pool of educated unemployed.

Another favorable aspect of the education explosion derives from the low social cost of keeping large numbers of young people in the educational pipeline. Some political leaders believe that there is less potential for social unrest if more opportunities are provided in secondary and higher education than if the urban labor market is further flooded with unemployed adolescents and young adults.

In developing countries where market demand is weak the operation of a large secondary school, or, even better, a large college, may provide a significant stimulus to the local economy through the combined expenditures of students and staff. Thus, every competent politician will lobby aggressively for a new school in his district.

Although we now have a clearer view of the reasons that have led most developing nations to expand rapidly their educational systems, important financial, organizational, and social constraints have begun to emerge.

The first problem is financial. In the developing world, education has become the single largest component of the national budget, larger than defense or public health. The share of education in gross national product advanced rapidly in the 1960s, much faster than the growth in total output. Still another sign of financial pressure is the fact that annual expenditures on education have been increasing at a rate of over 10 percent, which cannot be indefinitely sustained.

In addition, the high-cost sectors of the educational system are expanding at a differentially faster rate. In Africa and Latin America in the 1960s the secondary and tertiary levels had an average annual rate of increase that was double that of the primary level; in Asia the tertiary level had an annual rate of increase that was double that of the primary level. The steady spread of primary education throughout the world, even if the goal of 100 percent enrollment by 1980 will not be met, assures ever mounting pressure for the expansion of secondary education, which in turn inevitably implies pressure to enlarge the tertiary structure.

This internal dynamic for rapid expansion, particularly of the secondary and tertiary levels, carries an ominous financial implication, since the ratio of cost per student-year among the three levels in some developing countries is of the order of 1:10:100.

The financial difficulties that loom ahead have led politicians, planners, and, belatedly, educators, to take a closer look at the educational system. In many developing countries only half of those who enroll in first grade remain to complete the primary cycle of five or six years. In fact, between one-fifth and two-fifths of the entire budget for education is spent on youngsters who do not remain in the system long enough to acquire basic literacy.

A recent report on Ceylon—a leader among LDCs in providing broad access to education—states that because of dropouts and repeaters it took 107 learning-years to produce one "O" level graduate, all but 10 of which represent slippage if we postulate that all who enter the system at grade one aspire at least to "O" certificate.

To take another example, Colombia: In the middle 1960s, "less than one quarter of new entrants to primary schools completed five years, barely a quarter of entrants to secondary education completed six years, and under half of students in higher education completed their courses." One need not adopt the extreme position that all who drop out along the way have failed to benefit from the years they spent at school, but these high attrition rates suggest that there are wide margins for improved articulation among student, school, and society.

There are additional grounds for concern with the relevance of most educational systems in developing countries. They are geared in the first instance to serve as a selection device aimed to control the flow from the broad base to a narrow apex. The educational explosion also led to major societal disequilibria, three of which warrant attention: the rural-urban balance, the educated unemployed, and the brain drain.

Since the principal objective of most entering students is to move up the educational ladder, the curricula of primary and secondary schools have not been structured to assist dropouts to adjust to their local environment. The rural school does not see its role as that of helping the sons and daughters of local farmers to improve their occupational and life skills. And even less attention has been paid to the possibilities of providing learning opportunities for parents—opportunities to acquire literacy, technical assistance in farming, health instruction, and other critical work and life skills. The internal orientation of the curriculum rural school has helped to speed the migration of the better educated to the cities.

The expansion of secondary and tertiary education far in advance of the capacity of most developing economies to expand employment in the modern sector is largely responsible for the steadily growing pool of educated, unemployed young persons. The overexpanded higher educational system has been aided and abetted by distorted wage structures, poorly managed civil service systems, and the slow erosion of outmoded expectations prevalent among the student body and their families.

A third negative result of the increased output of higher education, particularly in advanced scientific, technical, and medical occupations, which is now substantially in excess of acceptable career opportunities, has been the brain drain. A recent report states that one-third of the scientists in the United States and one-sixth of those in Canada came from developing countries.

Even if the financial underpinnings for a fast expanding educational system in the developing world were assured, there would be little point in perpetuating an educational system that has such a high order of built-in frustration, in which so many start and so few succeed; in which the curriculum has little or no relevance to the lives of the rural population; and that causes many college and university students and graduates to spend years in unemployment or underemployment looking for suitable job openings—if they do not relocate abroad. The financial stringency, however, makes such a reappraisal mandatory.

DIRECTIONS FOR REFORM

Since one-half to two-thirds of the population in most LDCs are rural based, the educational system in a developing country must seek to be more responsive to the needs of the rural population. Since the modernized urban sector will not generate new jobs fast enough to provide employment for those who are already in the cities, the rural hinterland must be looked to as the source of employment for many young people now entering the labor force.

As a beginning, the political leadership in developing countries must increase the tax sources for the support of the local school. Exclusive reliance on the central government assures inadequate financial support. One approach tried with some success in a few countries is to use the educational support provided by the central government to encourage greater local efforts to raise part of the total capital and operating budget. Sometimes the local citizenry will volunteer their labor in slack seasons to build or expand the school. Or they will take it upon themselves to raise part of the teachers' annual salaries.

Schools cannot run on money alone; they require competent teachers and supervisors. But professionals are loath to return to the hinterland once they have experienced urban life. Moreover, professionals will not perform effectively on the orders of higher authority. The challenge, therefore, is to redesign the civil service system in such manner that a period of service in a rural school system is a prerequisite for a more desirable position in the system and for career advancement.

Curriculum reform is essential. In the acquisition of basic literacy skills, and particularly in the fifth, sixth, and seventh grades, the subjects studied and the knowledge acquired should be related to the rural environment. It is not the task of the primary schools to teach boys how to become better farmers and girls how to be better housekeepers and mothers, but it should be their task to help these young people apply what they learn in school to solving the problems they will encounter after they leave school.

Teachers should work in close association with others who bring services to the rural population, particularly the agricultural extension worker, the public health worker, the community aide. If these government workers do in fact provide useful services, which are directly visible in increased agricultural output, reduced illness, and expanded recreational opportunities, it should be possible to encourage the local population to pay at least some part of the cost of these services.

One final comment on the rural educational center. A system of community radios linked to regional programing may offer significant opportunities for a combined instructional-recreational effort at low cost.

The counterpoint suggestions for the urban sector of the educational system follow. Here, too, curriculum reform is the priority: the secondary school must not continue to operate primarily as a sieve to identify students suitable for higher education. There is urgent need for terminal programs with strong career orientations. This does not mean that secondary education should become overtly vocational. It does mean that emphasis should be placed on helping students obtain basic knowledge and mastery of techniques that will facilitate their employment in the local economy.

It would be a costly error if the educational authorities were to opt for a substantial expansion of vocational schools. Good vocational schools are expensive to operate; the recruitment and retention of qualified instructors present special difficulties; maintaining up-to-date equipment is almost impossible. There may be a place for a limited number of good vocational schools in a developing economy, but only for a few.

Because of the dominant role that the civil service plays in most LDCs, a willingness on its part to select for training and promotion a reasonable proportion of persons at each level on the basis of their performance rather than on educational criteria might help to reduce the pressure of young people to acquire credentials. Second, a wage and salary structure less biased in favor of degree holders might help to reduce the flood of students battering at the gates of the university.

Finally, if Professor Blaug's approach of shifting more of the costs of higher education to the individual were energetically pursued and if information about the faulty expectations of the value of degrees per se was more widely disseminated, the mad scramble for higher education might be somewhat abated.

IN PERSPECTIVE

The political leadership's decision to expand expenditures for education is not determined primarily by economic considerations but reflects its assessment of value considerations, social pressures, and the search for broadened career opportunities that propel developing countries. At most, powerful constraints may set limits on what politicians and planners can do in the educational arena, as well as in others. But that still leaves them with wide scope for the design and implementation of alternative educational strategies and tactics. The principal directions for change are to improve the productivity of basic education, reform the curriculum of the rural school, and narrow wage differentials based on educational achievements.

What criteria should political decision makers use to determine the level and specificity of educational expenditures? With respect to level, they should recognize that, the economists notwithstanding, education is more than an investment, the productivity of which is to be measured in terms of prospective earnings. Education has importance to the individual and society through its potential impact on value formation, the transformation of the political structure, and the improved development of human potential. Admittedly, education by itself cannot assure economic growth and social development. But a failure to broaden and deepen the access of the population to the pool of knowledge will result in its continuing backwardness.

But this positive view about the constructive potential of education must not hide the incontestable fact that many educational expenditures can be wasteful and some can be injurious. The political decision makers who appropriate monies and the educational bureaucrats who guide their use must try to raise the productivity of educational expenditures and avoid the pathological consequences of expanding the system. Neither task is easy but the acknowledgment that more expenditures are not necessarily in the public interest is the first stage to improved understanding; the search for improved patterns of expenditure is the second.

Some LDCs have invested too much in education and most of them have made serious errors in their suballocations. But it remains to be demonstrated that individual and social betterment is possible without mobilizing more effectively the latent potentials of people or that this can be accomplished without large-scale educational investments. If politicians have the wisdom to stop short of generating more social turmoil than they can contain, they have little to fear from a liberal stance towards the financing of education. It is the tragedy of most LDCs that their populations are mired in poverty from which they cannot quickly extricate themselves. Hence the words of the Preacher are particularly appropriate: "Wisdom is a defense and money is a defense, but the excellence of knowledge is that wisdom giveth life to them that have it."

THE OVEREXPANSION OF HIGHER EDUCATION IN LESS DEVELOPED COUNTRIES AND ITS REMEDY
Mark Blaug

Since about 1950 higher education has been the fastest growing part of the educational system the world over, whether measured in terms of enrollments or of financial outlays. The main reasons for this higher education explosion are the rapid growth of incomes per head in both developed and less developed countries after the relatively stagnant years of the 1930s and 1940s; and the policy of subsidizing higher education in order to produce the qualified manpower which was thought to be required (in an absolute physical sense) to secure economic growth. Yet almost all less developed countries are now suffering from overinvestment in higher education, hand-in-hand with underinvestment in primary education, and this pattern of misallocation is harmful to the prospects of future growth in these countries.

EVIDENCE OF COST-BENEFIT ANALYSES

Higher education has been growing faster than either primary or secondary education in almost all countries over the last fifteen or twenty years. As the facts are not likely to be disputed, let us immediately ask: What is wrong with all this? Why not let higher education expand faster than the lower levels of the educational system?

It is not generally realized just how expensive higher education really is. Table 28 shows that one university student in a less developed country in effect displaces 90 primary school students. Furthermore, while higher education is expensive everywhere, its relative cost is much higher in LDCs than in developed countries.

Even this proves nothing. What we want to know is whether the benefits of higher education warrant the extra cost. We cannot measure all the benefits. But let us at least look at the direct benefits and then speculate whether the indirect spillover benefits would affect the conclusion.

Table 29 shows that (1) the direct benefits for all levels of education are higher in the less developed than in the more developed countries; and (2) for the LDCs the direct benefits are more or less

TABLE 28

Ratio of Total Costs* by Educational Level
Per Student Year (Primary = 1)

Country Group	Secondary/Primary	Higher/Primary
Some rich	6.6	17.6
Some intermediate	6.6	20.9
Some poor (LDCs)	11.9	87.9

*Total costs are defined as direct costs plus forgone earnings.

Source: G. Psacharopoulos, Returns to Education. An International Comparison.

TABLE 29

Ratio of Average Annual Earnings Before
Tax of Labor by Educational Level

Country Group	Primary Education Over None	Secondary Education Over Primary	Higher Education Over Secondary
Some rich	—	1.4	1.7
Some intermediate	2.4	1.9	1.8
Some poor (LDCs)	2.4	2.4	2.7

Source: See Table 28.

the same at all levels of education. If the direct benefits are much the same at all levels while the costs of higher education vastly exceed those of primary and secondary education, it follows that higher education produces less value for money than primary or secondary education.

Rates of return on investment in education conveniently summarize the relationship between costs and benefits. Table 30 presents the findings for 18 countries around the world, 10 of which are LDCs. In all cases, primary education yields higher social rates of return than any other level. Moreover, the return on secondary education exceeds that on higher education in both rich and poor countries.

TABLE 30

Social Rates of Return on Investment in
Levels of Education (percentages)

Country Group	Primary	Secondary	Higher
Some rich*	—	10	9
Some poor	25	15	12

*Compulsory primary education in rich countries makes it impossible to calculate rates of return on investment in primary education: the reference group of people without any schooling is missing.

Source: See Table 28.

Efficient allocation of investment in education implies equality between the social rates of return at all levels of education. The results, therefore, show apparent underinvestment in primary education in almost all LDCs. Given the existing quality of education, too much is being spent on the higher levels and too little on the lower levels of the system. I must emphasize that this is a conclusion about quantities: rate-of-return data cannot tell us what would happen if the content of primary schooling were radically altered; they cannot even tell us how far to carry the reallocation of resources, because rates of return only provide signals of direction, not statements of actual amounts to aim at.

However, the discrepancies between rates of return on the different education levels are, in most cases, so large that even huge shifts of resources over a period of five to ten years would not close the gap. Insofar as the dropouts in primary education are mainly due to poverty and deprived home background there is little the educational authorities can do to increase attendance rates in primary schools. But free meals, free uniforms, and free busing, not to mention smaller classes and better trained teachers, can do much to increase enrollment rates; and all these measures would compete for budgetary funds with the rising outlays on higher education.

The argument in favor of shifting expenditures towards primary education is probably strengthened by introducing the vexed question of "spillover"* and by noting that the public sector in LDCs typically

---

*Many commentators have drawn attention to the so-called spillovers of education, which are not reflected in personal income flows.

overpays the graduates it employs, raising the rate of return on higher education above what it otherwise would be. Of course, we can make a good case for putting more emphasis on primary education by considering noneconomic objectives, such as equality of educational opportunity, national cohesion, and political stability. The point is, however, that even if we take a much narrower view of the instrumental ends of education—to maximize the rate of growth of national income—there is now a consensus between the views of most economist and of most educators: primary education must be given top priority.

WHAT TO DO ABOUT IT?

What can we do about it?
The simplest way of attacking the problem is to impose enrollment ceilings in higher education. It makes no difference whether a government first imposes quantitative controls on enrollments and then selects among the potential entrants by an examination or whether it purports to offer a place to all who are "qualified" and then raises the standards of the entrance examination to the point that only a fraction of the potential students succeed in obtaining a place. The latter method, however, strikes gullible voters as "fair" because it promotes the meritorious. It is even possible to admit everyone to higher education who has graduated from a high school and then to select among these by a first-year examination. This postpones the decision by a year, but after that is equivalent to selection at entry. Which of these particular techniques is adopted in any country depends entirely on historical traditions.

The policy of rationing places in higher education, either directly, or indirectly via admission standards, is practiced in a number of LDCs. But it is everywhere under attack as "undemocratic" and historical experience shows that the decision to abandon it quickly becomes irreversible. However, there is more than one way to kill a goose: it may be possible gradually to raise tuition fees to cover the full costs of higher education, thus reducing the private rate of return to higher education, with predictable effects on the private demand for places. If these were accompanied by more scholarship programs for poor students or, better still, by loans for everybody

---

We know very little about them, and there is not even agreement among economists as to what form they take. It would be a bold planner, therefore, who could claim that certain levels of the educational system generate greater spillovers than others.

repaid out of a "graduate tax" on future incomes combined with scholarships for the very poor, it might be made politically palatable to LDC electorates.

Shifting more of the costs of higher or secondary education to parents and students would not affect the benefits and costs of education to society, since these do not depend on how education is financed. If it is financed out of taxes, part of the costs are borne by single people and childless couples; if it is financed out of fees, the costs are borne exclusively by those who consume education. In either case the resource costs are exactly the same and so are the social benefits. The argument for raising fees, therefore, is entirely dependent on the notion that demand is responsive to private costs and that higher fees will lead to a reduced demand for places. Although the empirical evidence for this proposition is thin—few countries have performed the experiments that would have generated the evidence—it is certainly eminently plausible.

But can a government that lacks the political will to place a ceiling on enrollments be expected to have the political will to raise tuition fees? The answer may well be yes, because a move to raise fees can be hitched to the politically popular demand for equality of educational opportunity. A survey of the social composition of students in higher education would soon demonstrate in every country that the average university student is, to put it mildly, much better off than the average taxpayer. These figures could be publicized and with it the true resource costs of university education as against the private costs to students and parents.

Of course, not all university students are rich, but an increase in fees is perfectly compatible with an increase in scholarships. This is a case in which we can have our cake and eat it: we can choose any social composition of students we like, provided we are willing to subsidize in relation to parental income. To be sure, if we increase fees and then use all the extra revenue to finance poor students, we defeat the original purpose of bringing about a decline in enrollments. We thus face a typical problem of trading off the objective of shifting more of the costs to parents against that of equalizing access to higher education, subject to the constraint that total numbers must decline.

What we must not do is to give scholarships solely on grounds of past educational performance; the effect of that is necessarily to give more to the children of the well-to-do. We must tie the scholarship principally to parental income, although thereafter past educational achievement may be given some weight. It is easy to assess educational performance, but it is very difficult to assess parental income, particularly where the bulk of parents are self-employed professionals who evade income tax as a way of life. To give up because of these difficulties is to give up the goal of equal educational opportunity, a goal to which almost all LDCs subscribe as an article of faith. Unfortunately, the article of faith is usually satisfied by abolishing fees at the lower levels of education, leaving access to the upper levels to be determined by merit. What could be fairer? The recognition that this sort of argument is utterly fraudulent is precisely the object of the propaganda campaign that ought to precede the drive to raise university fees.

Parental income could be assessed on the basis of the father's occupation and a scale of average incomes per occupation could then be established on the basis of the best evidence available. Parents would be presumed to earn the incomes corresponding to the scale but an appeal board could be set up to adjudicate any claims of incomes below the scale. The entire system could be administered on a regional, provincial, or state level; and the scholarships would be given to students, not to institutions, for resaons that are perhaps obvious. This rough-and-ready method would be unfair in some individual cases. But social policy is made for groups, not for individuals; and at least such a crude method of assessing the income of parents would establish the principle that financial assistance should go to the poor and not to the clever.

Better still would be cost-covering fees, a modest scholarship program for the poorest from the most backward areas and student loans for everyone, to be financed by a special "graduate tax" on future income (if there were any income, not otherwise). If the loan were so generous as to cover all fees and maintenance expenses, this might well increase demand for higher education, which is the last thing we want. Raising fees and loans proportionately, however, would discourage the demand for places, because the graduate tax would constitute a net increase in the private costs of higher education over the situation prevailing hitherto. The magnitude of the loan and the corresponding graduate tax could be varied to produce whatever scale of higher education might be thought desirable. Such a scheme would give students a greater incentive to study and might encourage poorer students and more women to seek higher education. It could be defended politically on grounds of the benefit-principle of taxation—graduates earn more and there is no reason why the average taxpayer who earns less should be asked to subsidize higher education for the privileged few—and on grounds of equity—it is the only system that gives everyone equal access to funds and then taxes them alike. It would be even more acceptable on egalitarian grounds if the graduate tax were made progressive; and why not? It is an incidental advantage that this tax would be much easier to collect than income tax: it is much more difficult to hide the facts about one's education than it is to hide the facts about one's income.

The loans proposal works as a full-fledged system in the Scandinavian countries. Most poor states operate a loan system, albeit for a very small proportion of students.

A final word. The case for restricting the growth of higher education is not based on the fact that many LDCs must now face the problem of graduate unemployment. Rather it is based on evidence about the social yield of investment in education after adjusting earnings for the average probability of unemployment associated with successive levels of educational achievement. This is no mere technical distinction. Educated unemployment as such can be used as easily to defend educational expansion as educational contraction. After all, the educational authorities might say that since the fault lies with the functioning of the labor market, one may as well expand educational facilities, thereby keeping people off the labor market as long as possible. The fallacy in this argument is simply neglect of the resources used in producing more educated people, which are automatically taken into account when calculating rates of return on educational investment. Besides, the trouble with educational expansion as a method of mopping up labor, as distinct from the expansion of some other equally labor-intensive industry, is that the output of education is necessarily more educated people. Thus, educational expansion does not simply postpone the problem; it postpones it only to magnify it in the future.

CONCLUDING COMMENTS

This by no means exhausts all that the educational authorities can do to shift resources out of higher education and into primary education. The problem can be tackled qualitatively: by vocationalization of the secondary school curriculum, by ruralization of the primary school curriculum, and perhaps by the abolition of examinations of the standard type. But, although much may be said in favor of these proposals, their effect on enrollments in higher education is likely to be extremely gradual, whereas the idea of shifting more of the costs to students and parents would make an impact in two or three years. Besides, economists are hardly the best sort of people to talk about curriculum and examination reform. The same is not true of intervention in the labor market, and particularly the reform of public salary scales.

I agree with Professor Ginzberg that vocational secondary schools are no solution to the problems of LDCs. But I disagree with him about the "ruralization" of the curriculum. I do not believe that if one introduces an agricultural bias into primary and secondary schools in largely agricultural states this will make the children into farmers, put a stop to the flight from the countryside, and thus relieve urban unemployment.

The British tried to promote this idea in all their African colonies still in the nineteenth century. African parents would not stand for it, because an agricultural bias confined to schools in rural areas creates a feeling among rural parents that their children are getting a second-class education. And if you apply the bias to urban schools too, urban parents will complain that it has nothing to do with city life. But, most important of all, a bias in the curriculum does not affect people's occupational choices or their ultimate decision to live in a village or in town. It is fine to emphasize books with references to the countryside, teach biology, or refer to the animals and plants around, but not to teach people about farming at primary schools.

Curriculum reform should aim at teaching children to think and reason instead of to memorize. Examinations should test the ability to reason. This may not promote economic growth but will maximize the children's knowledge and might even make education fun.

No economist has proved a simple relationship between the kind of curriculum schools have and the kind of performance people produce on jobs in later life. It may well be that the most important thing about schools is attitude training. Punctuality and respect for authority may well be the most important values fostered by primary schools, while the capacity to take initiative and act on familiar information may be among the most important values conferred by secondary and higher education.

DISCUSSION

JOSEPH GILLIS (Israel): To solve educational problems by financial manipulation seems to me just a little too pat and simple. I also see a weakness in Professor Blaug's statistics. What I want to know is what proportion of children of primary school age were not getting education before and what proportion of older children were not getting education before. The increases are not meaningful.

My other question is: "How much education?" This surely depends on the society. In a very developed country, such as the United States, one would require a higher level than in a technologically less advanced society. But the amount of education reacts back on the society and influences it.

In Israel all have free primary education. Some 60,000 children enter grade I each year. Around 40,000 continue to secondary education. Only about 20,000 to 25,000 finish secondary education, of which about half pass matriculation. Between 11,000 and 12,000 matriculation certificates are issued every year. All these are very round figures.

In Israeli universities, technological institutes, and so on there are places for 40,000 to 50,000 students per annum. Thus the number of matriculants is insufficient to fill existing places at universities here. So one might think that efforts would be made to broaden secondary education, those on whom universities are to draw. Instead, big efforts are being made to expand universities, perhaps because the people at the universities are closer to the seats of power and have more influence.

As regards professional education: forecasts of how many doctors or engineers will be needed in future were normally not worth the paper they were written on. This applies especially in small countries like Israel. Two or three years ago, a highly competent committee estimated our needs for technologists in the next decade. They said we would be short of 4,000 electronic engineers by 1975. This year another committee reported that in 1974 we will have 2,000 unemployed electronic engineers. There is no reason to believe the second estimate any more than the first.

In practice, few enterprises anywhere have closed down or slowed down because of shortage of engineers, while limiting engineering studies because there may be unemployment among engineers can be self-defeating.

I was horrified by Professor Ginzberg's attitude to education as "a lottery." I was familiar with the British lottery system. The brightest working class boys got scholarships to universities; so the working class was successfully skimmed off. The results are visible. In most scholarship examinations the boys from expensive public schools do better.

We have to find a system that does not limit higher education but uses it as an integrating factor in the social structure.

Professor Blaug spoke about teaching children how to think. But how? We tried a small experiment here, and I am unhappy about the results. We tried to teach the concept of how to break down a problem and translate it into equations. We gave this a modern dress, calling it Computer Science. When we examined the children at the end of the year they were all very interested in computers but their ability to think was not better than that of other children.

How much education should we give? It is already impossible to function reasonably without being able to read or write. The time is coming when it will be impossible to function reasonably without higher mathematics.

Finally, what one can do for society in exchange for education cannot be measured by one's salary or by one's contribution to the gross national income.

URI LITVIN (Israel): I am not sure that rates of return can give us a sound answer to whether there is overinvestment in higher education. They cannot show the quantitative shift required to transfer resources from higher to primary education. The solution depends on the elasticity of demand for labor of different kinds, on the supply of primary education, and so forth. Besides, we are interested in marginal rather than average costs of education. Rates of return are average. And they can alter drastically if teachers' salaries are raised, since this would lower the return on primary education while raising that on higher education.

I do not believe there should be free education. But there was an attempt in Israel to raise higher education fees, and the Ministry of Education soon found out that it was a hard thing to do, that many people believe free education is a goal in itself. To change this thinking, one would have to reeducate the politicians, if not the population.

NUSRET FISEK (Turkey): There are social and educational constraints on planning education as Professor Ginzberg suggested. First, peasants object if you teach their children to change their way of life, though not if you teach them mathematics, history, or reading. Second, adapting the rural curriculum to the betterment of rural life means reducing the chance of children to go on to secondary education. One cannot both provide a good classical primary education and educate to be better farmers without extending the duration of schooling.

The first objection to changing the system will come from the wealthier farmers, who object to limiting classical primary education because they want their children to go on to higher education. They will also oppose cooperatives, which could make them lose their place in the community. So they will press the politicians not to change the educational system, and they will be heard because they have influence.

Thus there is a political obstacle to educational planners. And anyone doing such planning must keep in mind the social and political factors and allow for the need to overcome pressures from community leaders and politicians.

The percentage of persons with higher education is much lower in LDCs than in developed states. In Turkey there is a very low unemployment rate among those with higher education. Hence the emphasis on having more higher education in mnay LDCs. Some social and economic factors, such as the desire for social mobility, reinforce it. There are 600,000 Turkish workers in Europe. A survey asked them how much education their children should get. Some 60 percent said they should have higher education; And these parents have no education at all, or at best primary education, themselves.

Why is this social demand for higher education so high? Because in LDCs there is a big difference between people with higher education and people without one. So everyone wants higher education.

We must therefore try to minimize the differences between the incomes and social status of people with higher education and people without it. It is necessary to create employment possibilities for people with different levels of education. (In Turkey, the main reason for higher education after secondary education is the desire to find a suitable job.) Without reducing income differentials and creating employment for the less educated, we shall not achieve a proper educational balance in LDCs.

OUATTARA M'LAN (Ivory Coast): It is true that ruralization of the curriculum in LDCs is subject to political constraints, because in the internal regions it is often thought that schooling is the solution promising progress.

For the school population the school seems at first a path of liberation from a traditional society. But after only a few years it becomes clear that it is nothing of the kind.

Education costs heavily. Notably, recurrent maintenance charges are heavy as compared with the investment needed to build a school, college, or university. For every franc invested in a school or university five or six francs must be spent to make it function.

In the Ivory Coast all are agreed the curriculum should be ruralized, that the requirements of the economy should be listed. But this masks some dangers. The first danger is to plan education for the children concerned only. The aims of education are progress, modernization, and productivization of the economy as a whole. So we must not forget the majority of the population, who are not children. Within the limits set by our financial resources, we have to adjust education to the number of types of work and jobs that will be created. So we have to expand the meaning of "education."

We have to examine the development projects contained by our plans, see what they mean in terms of investment, and estimate their exact impact on future employment.

This poses a grave question: it is easy to talk about planning education, but very difficult to decide who should be admitted to each stage of education and who should not. Planners tend to dismiss this second question by saying it is not their responsibility, that it is a specific problem facing each state. Yet this is a problem that must be faced.

In most African states the methods of the past colonizing power have been maintained. Yet when one says that one should limit entries to the different grades of education, make it necessary to pass competitive examinations to pass from one type of education to another, and that some selection is necessary, it quickly becomes clear that without a very centralized, almost dictatorial political system one cannot prevent various elements from disturbing the educational plan. And the wealthy can always send their children to Britain, France, or the United States if local examinations show that they should not move up to the higher educational level.

Just because this problem is so complex planners must deal with it. Everyone wants to push his children as far forward as possible. But we must forecast the employment quotas as well as the quotas of those educationally able to fill the jobs concerned.

It may seem paradoxical that education can be dangerous, but in my country this may well be true. When I said education must take into account not only children but the whole population, I had at the back of my mind that in the Ivory Coast we have been considering a complementary nonschool system. We call it the National Office for the Promotion of Rural Affairs, and it concerns itself not only with the young who could not attend primary school but also with the adult and the aged participating in the productive process. In this manner we hope to fill in—perhaps not effectively enough but adequately—the holes left by the classical education system.

ISAAC KERSTENETSKY (Brazil): As regards overexpansion of higher education, Brazil is an exception. During the last 12 years primary education in Brazil expanded by some 60 percent, secondary education by over 200 percent, and higher education by 500 percent. But to look at quantitative indicators or the rate of return is insufficient to evaluate what happened in Brazil.

More than half the students and professors in our higher education are in law, economics and so on, while we lack sciences.

We have a fairly sophisticated system of primary education in the south, but in many areas in the northeast primary education teachers did not finish primary education themselves. So we are probably expanding too fast, looking only at the quantitative indicators or our higher education but paying insufficient attention to the quality of primary and secondary education.

Though for the past four years our growth rate has been very fast (over 10 percent), we should be able to take care of the expansion of the supply of labor, even with a growth rate of 7 percent. But the relationship between the profile of the demand for labor, the profile of the economic structure, and the type of training we are giving to our population may produce serious bottlenecks.

My point is that the evaluation of education systems and their relationship with economic development must be made not only in terms of the rate of return but also by simple surveys evaluating in detail the quality and conditions of education in different areas.

URI AVNER (Israel): I should like Professor Blaug to comment on the possibility of increasing benefits by reducing rates of dropout from higher education and by increasing the output of higher education.

Research is a very expensive activity. Could one reduce costs by inventing new methods of training or of producing highly trained staff?

For instance, open universities may help people to get higher education without the need for high investment and costs.

I should also like to hear Professor Blaug's comments on the new prospects of international mobility of academicians, hitherto handicapped by problems of licensing. What will be the implications for cost-benefit analysis if this mobility will also extend to people trained in developing countries?

ELI GINZBERG (Ford Foundation): The concept that there is too much money for higher education, displacing people from primary education, is too much for me. Unless one analyzes in each state the supply of young persons able to go to school and can prove that teachers go out to the less populated areas, the fact that you have an overinvestment in higher education in Sao Paulo will not mean that without it more children in the Amazon basin would go to school.

In terms of my knowledge of India, Afghanistan, and Ethiopia, productivity of primary schools is very low, and improving school lunches, busing, and so on may not improve it much.

Hence I do not know if we are dealing with comparable items, with taking money from one pot and putting it into another.

Earnings are a tricky concept in LDCs. One might squeeze some more productivity if people did not hang around the university, but at the cost of much social friction in the family. There is the problem of income foregone.

As for fee-loans, why ask LDCs to introduce something so unsuccessful in the developed world? I am for it, but in the United States we have done little for greater equity via the fee-loan approach; and some other devices, such as the open universities suggested, may be a better way of cutting costs.

Professor Gillis misunderstood my use of the word lottery. It simply suggests that there are a very few opportunities for social mobility through the educational system. This may not be desirable, but in the developing world one had better use existing structures until better ones are available. I just gave a small amount of credit to the expansion of higher education as a method of social mobility.

In manpower planning, programming, and forecasting I would advise great caution, especially in gearing an educational system to this. The economy has a way of growing in directions nobody thought about. It is dangerous to let the government assume too much responsibility for forecasting. The alternative is to put more responsibility on the individual to take the risk. Pay him as much as you can, and assume that most educated persons will finally fit into the economy in one way or another

I was much interested in the evidence from Turkey on social constraints to rural change. I do not want static ruralization. But all educational systems should consider career relevance. There should be some relationship between the system and the local econom where many people are going to remain.

I would agree with M. M'lan that thinking about an educational system only in terms of school-age youngsters is a gross error. Primary education can also be addressed to adults. I also suggested to do something on public health and extension training with parents.

If parents do not understand the significance of primary education, this means trouble and may cause dropouts at school. The bad experience of the Israelis with improvement of the Orientals going through the school system is a function of the fact that ability to make use of schooling effectively has much to do with interaction within the family. The results may remain discouraging for the Israelis for some decades yet.

But it is not easy to get the parents to move along together with the youngsters. Unless one has enough control over the educational system to have qualitative measures paralleling the quantitative ones, one simply does not know what is happening. In New York City we now push children through secondary schools just for not making trouble at school. You get a diploma for not making trouble. I agree with Professor Blaug that learning to sit still or follow orders may be an important part of education, but it would be nice to know that the man can also read and write or something. Yet we put on the back of the diploma what he is supposed to know, without knowing that he knows.

I do not think higher education has to be as expensive as it is. We may do better by not trying to hold the line and being inundated by pressure from aroused democrats, but instead reducing the number of courses. We should move from elite education to mass education.

MARK BLAUG (Great Britain): To answer Professor Gillis: I have figures on the proportion of the age groups enrolled in the three-levels of education for 45 countries. They cover 20 years. The age groups are, for primary education usually 7 to 12; for secondary education, from 12 (sometimes 14) to 18; and, for higher education, from 19 to 22. As regards the 45 countries concerned, the figures show that the rate of increase in enrolling proportions of the respective age groups has been fastest in higher education. So my argument stands.

The question how much education people need calls almost for a lecture in itself. The concept of need for some sort of physical requirement for educated people has no meaning since there is no absolute technical need for people with given educations. Manpower forecasting is a modern science fiction. And if you produce a product requiring a special input of skill, one can get round the lack of such skill by substituting a lower skill supplemented by training, or by substituting machines.

One cannot judge people's productivity by looking at their work, as it cannot be divorced from the organization and the tools with which they work.

To an economist a scarce skill is one that is productive. So what we mean by saying that higher education is productive is that it imparts some values, attitudes, or knowledge that are scarce in society and therefore commands high earnings. But then sometimes the labor market works badly and scarce people earn less, not more.

There is much literature on the question of reforming the curriculum to maximize children's reasoning ability. When I learned trigonometry, I memorized all the formulas for sines and cosines but did not know why they worked. I want a reform that would show students that, once they understand that the formula for a cosine is the opposite of that for a sine and why both formulas work, they need not memorize them, because they will be able to derive them from elementary principles in five seconds. I want to maximize the understanding of concepts.

In the United States, typical elementary school examinations will contain about 50 percent of questions on memorization and about 50 percent on understanding. But in a typical LDC 90 percent of the questions will involve memorized facts, and fewer than 10 percent actual understanding of concepts. My kind of curriculum would reduce the number of questions the answer to which depends on remembering a fact and increase the number of questions calling for understanding of concepts and their formation.

It is possible to argue that too much or too little is being spent on education by governments relative to other things, but this is tricky. You have to compare with investments in infrastructure, transportation, health, and what not. So it is best to stick to the more modest problem of how to allocate best a given education budget. Anyway, such data as exist show that you cannot make an argument from cost-benefit analysis in favor of spending more on all kinds of education.

Rates of return would, of course, differ if teachers' salaries were different. These constitute some 30 percent of the total cost of education. But output forgone constitutes at least 50 percent.

Many states, including India, have loans to students, but they cover only a small proportion of students. Only Ghana tried out a comprehensive student loan scheme for two years. They did not give the system a chance before closing it down. In the United States the experience is mixed. In Scandinavia the loans work, but perhaps only because Scandinavia is the way it is. So there is room for doubt, but I am optimistic and feel the experiment should be tried by some LDCs.

Professor Fisek spoke of the stigma to poor students of being selected for scholarship or interest-free loans as against other students. There is a certain danger that a policy favoring the poor may be resented by the poor, but I am very struck by the fact that these arguments are always used by middle-class people to defend the universal provision of free higher education or some other social service. Our choice is between special selection for the poor, putting up with their resentment, if any, and providing the service free, when the poor will not be resentful but also will not avail themselves of it—so that we end up with free higher education largely consumed by middle-class children. You can't have your cake and eat it. Either you are selective to promote equality, or you are nonselective and leave inequality. Universal free education would promote equality only if there were no examinations. The moment there are, middle-class children will get most of the cake. The only way out is to discriminate in favor of disadvantaged students.

M. M'lan hinted at nonformal education. This exists in the form of adult literacy classes, in-service training programs, youth centers, youth clubs with some educational activities, mothers' classes, and educational components in agricultural extension. In Tanzania more people seem to be involved in such nonformal education than in formal education. But no one has ever applied cost-benefit analysis to nonformal education. I have a hunch that it might prove to yield greater benefits per unit of cost than formal education.

To answer Mr. Avner's questions: The rate of return on higher education is lower than on primary or secondary education. It can be raised by increasing benefits or by cutting costs, so why not by cutting costs?

By reducing dropouts the cost per graduate would be cut. But the rate of return does not tell you what direction to move in and how large the move should be. So whether one should reduce higher education or raise its return by reducing dropouts remains a question. One should remember, however, that by reducing dropouts you increase the number of graduates, which affects the earnings of graduates. So what you do to the rate of return will depend on the country and the circumstances.

As regards Mr. Avner's question about diversifying higher education instead of reducing it, or separating research from teaching, one would have to calculate the rates of return before expressing an opinion about which of the alternative courses is the soundest. For this, the experiments would have to be made first.

On occupational licensing: One of the reasons there is so often excess demand or supply of educated people is because educational cycles are so long. Hence these cycles lose touch with the labor markets. They should be shortened. Why have four-year university courses. Better to have two-year junior colleges leading on to a third and fourth year if one wants them. This is desirable not only because it gives students more choice but because it makes higher education more sensitive to the labor market. It allows it to react in two years instead of four.

Occupational licensing should be attacked. There is a brain drain of doctors from LDCs to developed countries partly because there is effective international occupational licensing in medicine, with the result that all LDCs prepare people who can step into New York hospitals. No wonder they do. If there were no occupational licensing, LDCs could train more public health experts and fewer surgeons. One needs a different mix of doctors in LDCs, but you don't get it since medicine is taught the same way everywhere and there is occupational licencing. Lawyers and teachers are now aspiring to the same thing.

Thus occupational licensing is conducive to the malfunctioning of the educational systems and labor markets in LDCs.

**RAPPORTEUR'S REPORT—
GROUP C**
David Kochav

There is a paradoxical situation in the field of planning. Planning of some kind is practised by 74 out of 83 developing states; yet there is widespread scepticism regarding its usefulness, not only among politicians but even among the planners themselves.

This scepticism was clearly expressed here, and some fundamental issues of planning were discussed. The first was whether planning is really necessary and useful. Most participants felt that LDCs needed planning. Experience shows that the development process is so complex that some analytical framework to guide policy makers and their advisers is required.

As the late Prime Minister of Israel, Mr. Levi Eshkol, once said: Planning is like an old Turkish road built in Palestine before the First World War. One does not ride on it, because it is too busy. One rides to the side of it. But if it did not exist, one could easily get lost in the desert.

However, the answer to the question whether in fact planning has been useful is unclear. The evidence seems conflicting. Most participants felt that planning can be useful, but only if certain conditions are fulfilled.

What does planning really mean? It is a process that should improve policy making by the government and the private sector. Most LDCs have indicative planning to help their governments to frame appropriate development policies. The planning process itself is often more important than the final plan that emerges. This process should be designed to achieve a reasonable combination of objectives, not disregarding the inherent trade-offs between them.

Planning must formulate policy measures that the government is willing and able to execute. Though planning often concentrates on the public sector, effective incentives and disincentives are needed to guide the private sector to actions furthering the desired development effort. Planning leading to excessive government controls or government intervention in individual firms (as in some LDCs) can even be harmful. A detailed five-year plan that the government tries to execute in an inflexible way may also do more harm than good.

David Kochav is from Israel.

The final purpose and test of a plan is its implementation. However it is an oversimplification to expect a plan to be literally implemented, and it is wrong to measure the success of a plan by its accuracy in predicting future performance. Planning and prophecy are in essence contradictory. The object of planning is to change the course of future events. Unpredictable developments and other uncertainties must affect actual performance. The dynamism of the development process makes precise forecasting almost impossible. To quote from Professor Streeten's paper: "The true prophet, like Jonah, is he who moves people to take protective or supporting action, not he who turns out to be right. The success of planning depends on its effect on economic and social policies and its ability to deal actively with unexpected changes. This basic point is often misunderstood."

A precondition for useful planning and implementation is some degree of mutual understanding between planners and policy makers. Planning is a political process. It must be based on a sound professional input but can only be properly framed or executed through politics. The relationship between political leaders and planners is usually troubled, and those more frustrated are the planners. Politicians are mostly interested in the final product—the plan, which they often want to be ambitious and optimistic. They have little patience for deliberations on trade-offs or models and would prefer to de-emphasize the need to sacrifice certain objectives in order to achieve others. They want all the good things at once, and quickly. (Yet sound economic and social development is a lengthy process.) They often regard the plan mainly as a means of gaining domestic support or foreign aid rather than as a program of action for themselves. They do not want to limit their freedom to frame budgetary and other current policies.

On the other hand, planners rightly concentrate on the difficult choices among conflicting objectives. But they often show little understanding or sympathy for the political realities.

Some understanding between politicians and planners is essential for useful planning. Decision makers should not abuse the professional integrity of planners, and planners should not be blind to political constraints. It was strongly emphasized at this conference that medium-term planning cannot be divorced from current policy advice. Effective implementation demands that planners work closely with current policy advisors on budgetary, fiscal, monetary, and income policies. Unless planners are intimately involved in current policy advice and formulation, their planning is unlikely to be effective.

Most of the participants share the view that development planning should have multiple objectives, including both rapid growth and fairly equitable income distribution. I would tend to share the view that development strategies designed to encourage labor-intensive and in some cases small-scale farms and industries may help to achieve better income distribution with growth. The multiplicity of objectives should affect policy measures. As Professor Streeten suggested, a three-pronged approach is needed: first, a system of incentives and disincentives leading to desired action through the price mechanism; second, institutional reforms; and third, technological changes to adapt technology designed in developed states to the needs of LDCs. Most participants agree that working through the price mechanism alone will not achieve the desired objectives. Reconstitution of the institutional and social framework is also needed, though there are wide differences of opinion as to how far the reforms should go.

Ideologies have been built on the basis of each of the three prongs. Yet many participants agree that the three lines of action are complementary rather than conflicting.

Nevertheless, we do not yet have an integrated area of development in which the economic, social, and technological elements could be coordinated. Nor do we know clearly which specific measures should be applied.

Much additional work is needed by economic planners to frame an integrated theory of development. This conference has at least contributed to a restatement of some of the questions. But we really have a good deal of homework to do.

PART V
CLOSING ADDRESSES

CLOSING ADDRESS
Simon Kuznets

We should look at this conference in terms of the basic objective of Rehovot Conferences in general—to provide a useful dialogue between the scholars and the practitioners of policy on an international scale, with special attention to the problems of developing states.

This Rehovot Conference, as well as that of 1965, had some valuable features. One is the freedom of the dialogue between the thinkers and the doers here, as compared with the constraints besetting such dialogues between a statesman and an adviser in any given country.

The freedom with which the social scientists and economists have revealed their doubts and qualified their statements here was very impressive. It is the kind of freedom not often practiced by scholars when asked for advice by statesmen on a recurring problem. Then, the answer is usually given without qualifications.

The second valuable feature of this Rehovot Conference was the diversity of experience in practical matters reflected by the dialogue. The third, crucial feature is that Rehovot Conferences take place in Israel—a state that has dealt with very difficult development problems for years and has succeeded in providing satisfactory answers to many of them. This is a most valuable background.

Yet despite favorable conditions, the ideal could not be fully realized. I refer to some difficulties in the hope that future conferences might be able to deal with them: First, there was a tendency on the part of some academic scholars to talk to each other, so that in a sense two dialogues were going on rather than one. There was a limit to the possibility of discussion, due to the tempo of organization of the meeting. And with many papers covering a wide variety of topics, perhaps the coverage was a bit too wide.

All these are minor blemishes as compared with the accomplishments. With the large number of papers presented and discussed and the large number of people involved, tremendous efforts must have been invested to enable this conference to take place without any major hitches. I have considerable experience of conferences and must confess that my admiration for the organizers here, in purely technical terms, is unbounded. To have this sort of continuous auspices in Israel for this type of dialogue is a remarkable achievement and privilege.

CLOSING ADDRESS
Abba Eban

Your Excellencies, ladies and gentlemen:

Development on a world-wide scale has been a central feature of the international landscape for some 30 years. So it is natural for world opinion to ask: "Cannot the lessons by now be classified and experimentally analyzed, with the end of eliciting laws of general application?" Though some eminent universities have already made the economics of development a specific discipline, the time is not yet ripe for generalized theories. For one thing, the knowledge that no plan can be immune to its social and political background, and that political leaders have preferences and caprices, imposes subjective restrictions on any attempt to deduce firm scientific doctrines. We have also learned here about the fallacy of making rapid economic growth the sole criterion of planning.

Economists confessed the weight of volatile, psychological factors they must face. Physicists and biologists do not have this problem. Yet this does not mean that everything is arbitrary and uncalculable, that we must throw planning away, shut our eyes, and lunge forward hopefully into an uncharted horizon. The presence of economic theory and planning yields better results than their absence. But each case is particular, and in fact development science is a vast and growing aggregate of case histories.

There must be separate discussion of development between and by governments. But when education ministers meet education theorists, when ministers of health meet authoritative physicians in the field of public health and endemic disease, when ministers of agriculture meet agronomists, irrigation experts, and planners—they are doing something not done very often. Ministers, officials, and academicians have unlimited conference opportunities, yet meetings where a frank dialogue takes place between those responsible for action and those who investigate, analyze, and classify are comparatively rare.

The relationships between statesmen and experts vary widely, ranging from obdurate scepticism to almost superstitious reverence. Our experience here has led us to an intermediate attitude. The general feeling at the end of every Rehovot Conference is that there is a reciprocal value in compelling political leaders to understand some of the classified, empirical knowledge of the experts, while compelling the academicians to face some of the practical limitations on their theories. Something fruitful emerges to the benefit of both.

Israel will maintain and expand its development role, in cooperation with all states that find advantage and utility in such cooperation. Rancor degrades too many sectors of international life. Sometimes I feel that the only thing all governments have in common is a precise knowledge of each others' imperfections. But in the long run, the fortunes of developing states will be determined not by the polemics that divide them but by the solidarity that should unite them in common action. We shall not be intimidated by the rhetorical violence of others to lose sight of these larger long-term visions.

I wish to express satisfaction, gratitude, and respect to the scientists and scholars at this conference. We shall continue to make Israel a meeting ground between leaders of the scientific movement and those charged with the burdens of policy and administration in states where many millions are still cut off from a reasonable prospect of health, welfare, and creative self-expression.

The Eighth Rehovot Conference will convene in the summer of 1975, I hope that you and many others will be here with us then.

APPENDIX A

ORGANIZATION OF THE SEVENTH REHOVOT CONFERENCE

The Seventh Rehovot Conference was organized by the Continuation Committee of the International Conference on Science in the Advancement of New States. It was sponsored jointly by the Hebrew University of Jerusalem and the Weizman Institute of Science.

HONORARY PRESIDENTS

Abba EBAN
Minister for Foreign Affairs,
 Israel

Pinchas SAPIR
Minister of Finance,
 Israel

Moshe SANBAR
Governor of Bank
 of Israel

Prof. Israel DOSTROVSKY
President of the Weizman
Institute of Science

Abraham HARMAN
President of the Hebrew
University of Jerusalem

CHAIRMAN OF THE REHOVOT CONFERENCES
Abba EBAN
Minister for Foreign Affairs, Israel

SECRETARY-GENERAL
Dr. Amos MANOR

SCIENTIFIC PREPARATORY COMMITTEE

Chairman:
David HOROWITZ
 Chairman, Advisory Council and
 Committee, Bank of Israel

Deputy Chairman:
David KOCHAV
 Chief Economic Adviser,
 Ministry of Defense, Israel

Members:

A. AGMON
 Ministry of Finance, Israel
S. AMIR
 Minister for Foreign Affairs,
 Israel

Prof. S. ECKSTEIN
 Bar Ilan University
D. GENICHOVSKY
 Bank of Israel

Prof. H. BARKAI
Hebrew University of Jerusalem
Prof. H. BEN SHACHAR
University of Tel Aviv
Prof. N. BURES
Technion, Haifa
A. CHELOUCHE
Exchange Bank of Chicago

Dr. F. GINOR
University of Tel Aviv
D. GOLAN
First International
Bank of Israel, Ltd.
Dr. S. MAITAL
University of Tel Aviv
Miss. R. RAELI
Ministry for Foreign
Affairs, Israel

SCIENTIFIC SECRETARIES

D. GENICHOVSKY, Coordinator
Bank of Israel
Dr. R. ABLIN
Bank of Israel
J. FISHER
Bank of Israel

Dr. S. HANONO
Ministry of Finance,
Israel
Dr. R. MEERON
Bank of Israel
N. MENUCHEN
University of Tel Aviv

E. SAVIR
University of Tel Aviv

CONFERENCE SECRETARIES
Mrs. Rahel HAIK
Mrs. Faye RIMON

PRESS OFFICERS
Mr. Nechemia MEYERS
Mr. Ian EFRATI

ACKNOWLEDGMENTS

The assistance rendered by government and public institutions and private individuals abroad as well as in Israel is gratefully acknowledged.

ABROAD: Agency for International Development, Washington, D.C.
The Asia Foundation, San Francisco
Joseph Handleman, Miami Beach, Florida
United Nations Educational, Social and Cultural Organization, Paris
IN ISRAEL: The Bank of Israel
The Ministry of Finance
The Ministry for Foreign Affairs
The Rothschild Trust

APPENDIX B

LIST OF PARTICIPANTS*

AFRICA

BOTSWANA
Mr. M. MADISA
   Coordinator, Rural Development, Ministry of Finance

CENTRAL AFRICAN REPUBLIC
Mr. Emanuel BIZOT
   Head, Department of Human Resources, Ministry of Planning International Cooperation and Statistics

ETHIOPIA
Mr. Terrefe ASSRAT
   Regional Coordinator, Ministry of Agriculture
Dr. Assefa MEHRETU
   Director, Institute of Development Research, University of Haile Sellassie
Mr. Ahmed TAIB
   Agricultural Extension Coordinator, CADU, Chilalo Agricultural Development Unit

GABON
Mr. Robert RENOMBO
   Ministry of Finance and Economy

GHANA
The Hon. Lt. Col. J. ENNINFUL
   Special Assistant of Head of State and Commissioner for Finance and Economic Planning
Mr. Charles ADU-BAAH
   Rural Planning Officer, Ministry of Labor and Social Welfare
Mr. Thomas ANSAH-DAWSON
   Project Officer, Agricultural Development Bank
Mr. Andrew Anderson ARTHUR
   Acting Principal Regional Planning Officer, Ministry of Finance and Economic Planning
Mr. Perry Sarpong MENSAH
   Regional Planning Officer, Ministry of Finance and Economic Planning

IVORY COAST
H. E. Mohamed DIAWARA
   Minister of Planning
Mr. Ouattara M'LAN
   Director of Studies, Ministry of Planning
Mr. Joseph NITTE
   Director of the Office of the Minister of Planning
Mr. Nicholas TOPPE
   Ministry of Planning

---

*Designations given are those held as of conference date.

KENYA
Mr. Elega Herman AKIDUHA
District Planning Officer, Ministry of Finance and Planning

LIBERIA
Mr. Emmanuel O. GARDINER
Assistant Minister for Sector Programming, Ministry of Planning and Economic Affairs
Dr. Abeoudu Bowen JONES
Director of Research Institute of Public Administration

MALAWI
Mr. C. F. KANJO
Senior Economist, Ministry of Finance

NIGERIA
Mr. Samuel Oliyemi FALAE
Senior Planning Officer, Federal Ministry of Economic Development
Mr. Johnathan Olufunmi OGUNDEYI
Senior Agricultural Officer, Public Service Committee
Mr. Nwamfem Bertrand OJIMBA
Higher Community Development Officer, Cabinet Office

RWANDA
Mr. Jean BIRARA
Governor, Bank of Rwanda

SIERRA LEONE
Mr. I. S. BANGURA
Deputy Financial Secretary, Ministry of Finance
Mr. E. TUBOKU-METZGER
Assistant Economist, Economic Adviser's Office, Ministry of Finance

KINGDOM OF SWAZILAND
The Hon. Robert P. STEPHENS
Minister of Finance
Mr. Peter DAVIES
Economist, Ministry of Finance

UPPER VOLTA
Mr. Kassoum CONGO
Director of the Upper Volta Branch of la Banque Central des Etats de l'Afrique de l'Ouest

ASIA AND THE MEDITERRANEAN

CYPRUS
Mr. Georgios V. HADJIANAS-TASSIOU
Senior Planning Officer, Planning Bureau

GREECE
Prof. Elias T. BALOPOULOS
Under-Secretary of State for Planning and Government Policy, Ministry of Planning

ISRAEL
Mr. David HOROWITZ
Chairman, Advisory Council and Committee, Bank of Israel
Dr. Ephraim KLEIMAN
Senior lecturer in Economics, Hebrew University of Jerusalem
Prof. Yair MUNDLAK
Dean, Faculty of Agriculture, Hebrew University Rehovot

JAPAN
Dr. Koichi MERA
  Senior Economist, International Development Center

KHMERE (CAMBODIA)
Mr. CHEN SUN
  Secretary-General, Ministry of Planning
Mr. Phien KIM
  Chief of Production Office, Ministry of Community Development

KOREA
Mr. Mahn Sup KWAK
  Chief, Municipal Development Section, Pusan City Government
Prof. Chung Pum SONG
  Chairman, Board of Directors, Teachers' Mutual Fund

LAOS
Mr. Arya LYFOUNG
  Chief, Planning and Implementation, Agricultural Activities Province of Sayabourg
Miss Singkham PHONVISAY
  Assistant Director of Nam Tane Irrigation Project, Department of Agriculture, Ministry of National Economy
Dr. Pane RASSAVONG
  Commissioner of Planning, Ministry of Planning and Development
Mr. Phouanghphanh SANANIKONE
  Director, Economic and Social Analysis, Ministry of Planning and Development

NEPAL
The Hon. Govind Prasad LOHANI
  Member (Research), National Planning Commission

PHILIPPINES
Mr. Nelson DAVILA
  Research Assistant, Department of Public Works, Transportation, Communication, Planning and Development
Mr. Filologo PANTE Jr.
  Director, Economic Planning and Research staff, Planning and Policy Office, National Economic Development Authority
Mr. Jose P. PATALINJUG Jr.
  Chief Agrarian Reform Program Officer, Department of Agrarian Reform
Mr. Guillermo Carubio TRINIDAD
  Regional Development Director, Presidential Economic Staff

SINGAPORE
The Hon. JEK YEUN THONG
  Minister of Culture

THAILAND
H. E. Dr. Boonrod BINSON
  Minister of State Universities
Mr. Kitti ITWITYA
  Economist, Financial and Monetary Planning, National Economic Development Board
Mr. Vacharee SANGIEMCHANYA
  Senior Economist (Regional Employment Planning), National Economic Development Board
Miss Netnarumon SIRIMONTHON
  Junior Economist, National Economic Development Board

TURKEY
Prof. Nusret FISEK
  Director, Institute of Community Medicine, Hacettepe University
Prof. Necmi SONMEZ
  University of Ankara

REPUBLIC OF VIETNAM
H. E. Ing. Le THUAN ANH
  Minister of Planning and Development
Mr. Le BA NHON
  Director for Coordination of Foreign Assistance, Ministry of Planning
Mr. Le VAN PHUC
  Expert, Economic Development Fund

CENTRAL AND SOUTH AMERICA

ARGENTINA
Dr. Jose Maria DAGNINO PASTORE
  Department of Economics, Catholic University of Argentina

BARBADOS
Mr. Lewis CAMPBELL
  Head, Agricultural Division, Caribbean Development Bank

BOLIVIA
The Hon. Julio PRADO Salmon
  Minister in Charge of National Council for Economy and Planning
Mr. Javier CAMPERO PAZ
  Director, Planning and Economic Policy, National Council for Economy and Planning, Office of the Presidency

BRAZIL
Dr. Rubens Vaz da COSTA
  President, National Housing Bank
Mr. Novaes Pontes JUAREZ
  Head, Department of Rural Development, Banco Nordeste do Brasil

Dr. Isaac KERSTENETZKY
  President of the Brazilian Institute of Geography and Statistics

COLOMBIA
Prof. Jorge MENDEZ
  University of Bogota

DOMINICAN REPUBLIC
H. E. Dr. Julio Cesar ESTRELLA
  Minister of Development

EL SALVADOR
Mr. Alfredo Benjamin NOYOLA
  Executive Secretary, National Council of Planning and Coordination

GRENADA
Mr. Neville Dominic NEDD
  Acting Chief Technical Officer, Ministry of Agriculture

GUATEMALA
The Hon. J. LAMPORT Rodil
  Minister of Finance
Mr. Gert ROSENTHAL
  Head, National Council for Economic Planning

HAITI
Mr. Andre JEAN-LOUIS
  Specialist, Development Project, Department of Agriculture, Damien

JAMAICA
Dr. Gladstone G. BONNICK
  Chief Technical Director, National Planning Agency
Mr. Lincoln Alberto MCINTOSH
  Regional Planner, National Planning Agency

MEXICO
Mr. Leopoldo SOLIS M.
  Director, Economic Studies, Office of the Presidency
Prof. Victor URQUIDI
  President, El Colegio de Mexico

NICARAGUA
Mr. Rudolfo MEJIA
  Director, Agrarian Institute of Nicaragua

PANAMA
Lic. Manuel A. RUIZ G.
  Director-General, Institute for the Development and Promotion of Human Resources
Mr. Manuel VELARDE CARDOZA
  Assistant of Mr. Ruiz

PARAGUAY
Dr. Jose Enrique PAEZ
  Deputy to Executive Secretary, Department of Planning

PERU
Prof. Daniel SCHYDLOWSKY
  Senior Research Associate, Center for Latin American Development, Boston University, Massachusetts
Dr. Valentin VASQUEZ MENDOZA
  Director, Economic Planning Department, Institute for Public Administration (ESAP)

VENEZUELA
Dr. Alejandro SUELS
  Deputy Director-General of CORDIPLAN

NORTH AMERICA

UNITED STATES OF AMERICA
Prof. Irma ADELMAN
  College of Business and Public Administration, Department of Economics, University of Maryland
Dr. Elihu BERGMAN
  Assistant Director, Center for Population Studies, Harvard University
Prof. Carlos DIAZ-ALEJANDRO
  Department of Economics, Economic Growth Center, Yale University
Prof. Stephen ENKE
  Consulting Economist, Defense Programs, General Electric Company
Prof. Bruce F. JOHNSTON
  Food Research Institute, Stanford University
Prof. Simon KUZNETS
  Professor of Economics, Emeritus, Harvard University

Prof. Harvey LEIBENSTEIN
Department of Economics,
Harvard University

Prof. Gustav PAPANEK
Chairman,
Department of Economics,
Boston University

Prof. Gustav RANIS
Director, Economic Growth Center, Yale University

EUROPE

FRANCE

Mr. Bernard ULLMO
Head, Economic Projections Section, National Institute of Statistics and Economic Studies,

FEDERAL REPUBLIC OF GERMANY

Dr. Juergen DONGES
Institute of World Economics, University of Kiel

GREAT BRITAIN

Prof. Wilfred BECKERMAN
Head, Department of Political Economics, University College, London

Prof. Mark BLAUG
Head, Research Unit in Economics of Education, University of London Institute of Education and London School of Economics

Prof. Ian. M. D. LITTLE
Professor of the Economics of Developing Countries, Nuffield College, Oxford University

Prof. William Brian REDDAWAY
Editor, The Economic Journal, University of Cambridge

Prof. Paul P. STREETEN
Warden, Queen Elizabeth House, Oxford University

SPAIN

Mr. Javier IRASTORZA Revuelta
Secretary-General, Economic and Social Development Planning Commission, Office of the Government

INTERNATIONAL ORGANIZATIONS

AGENCY FOR INTERNATIONAL DEVELOPMENT, Washington, D.C.
Mr. Robert MUSCAT
  Associate Assistant Administrator, Office of Policy Development and Analysis, Bureau for Program and Policy Coordination

EUROPEAN ECONOMIC COMMUNITY, Brussels
Dr. Hans Broder KROHN
  Director-General, Development and Cooperation
Dr. Eberhard RHEIN
  Assistant to the Director-General of Development & Cooperation

FOOD AND AGRICULTURE ORGANIZATION, Santiago
Prof. Solon BARRACLOUGH
  Project Manager, Agrarian Reform and Rural Development Project, Santiago, Chile

FORD FOUNDATION
Prof. Eli GINZBERG
  Consultant and Director, Conservation of Human Resources, Columbia University, New York

INTERNATIONAL BANK FOR RECONSTRUCTION AND DEVELOPMENT (World Bank) Washington, D.C.
Dr. John ADLER
  Director, Programming and Budgeting Department
Prof. Hollis B. CHENERY
  Vice-President, Development Policy

Mrs. Helen HUGHES
  Chief, Industrialization Division, Economic Department

INTER-AMERICAN DEVELOPMENT BANK, Washington, D.C.
Dr. Thomas CARROLL
  Head, Agricultural Economics Division

ORGANIZATION OF AMERICAN STATES, Washington, D.C.
Dr. Armando CASSORLA
  Special Assistant for CIES/CIAP Affairs, Office of Executive Secretary for Economic and Social Affairs
Prof. Emilio CASTANON PASQUEL
  Director, Social Affairs Department

ORGANIZATION FOR ECONOMIC COOPERATION AND DEVELOPMENT, Paris
Mr. Paul Marc HENRY
  President, OECD Development Centre

UNITED NATIONS ECONOMIC COMMISSION FOR AFRICA, Addis Ababa
Dr. Iassu ANDEMICAEL
  Economic Affairs Officer, Economic Research Unit

UNITED NATIONS ECONOMIC COMMISSION FOR ASIA AND THE FAR-EAST
H. E. Dr. Boonrod BINSON
  as member of the Mekong Committee for Thailand
  (See Thailand)

UNITED NATIONS EDUCATIONAL, SCIENTIFIC AND CULTURAL ORGANIZATION, Paris
Prof. Richard HOGGART
Assistant Director-General for Social Sciences, Humanities and Culture

UNITED NATIONS CHILDREN'S FUND, New York
Mr. Tarlok SINGH
Deputy Executive Director in charge of planning

ABOUT THE EDITOR

YOHANAN RAMATI is director of Yohanan Ramati, Investment Consultants and Real Estate. He is Managing Editor of the Jerusalem monthly, the <u>Israel Economist</u> and contributes regularly to the paper <u>Ma'ariv</u>.

From 1959 through 1969, he was councillor and member of the City Executive in Jerusalem, serving as Chairman of the Assessments Committee, the Public Works and Water Committee, Deputy-Chairman of the Town Planning and Building Permits Committee, and as a member of the Finance Committee.

Mr. Ramati received his M.A. in Economics, Politics, and Philosophy from Oxford University.

RELATED TITLES
Published by
Praeger Special Studies

AGRICULTURAL DEVELOPMENT PLANNING:
Economic Concepts, Administrative Procedures,
and Political Process
                  Willard W. Cochrane

EDUCATION, MANPOWER, AND DEVELOPMENT IN SOUTH AND SOUTHEAST ASIA
                  Muhammad Shamsul Huq

MICRO ASPECTS OF DEVELOPMENT
                  edited by Eliezer B. Ayal

PATTERNS OF POVERTY
                  Charles Elliott

THE UNITED STATES AND THE DEVELOPING WORLD: AGENDA FOR ACTION, 1974
                  edited by James W. Howe and
                  the Staff of the Overseas
                  Development Council

URBANIZATION AND THE DEVELOPING COUNTRIES: Report on the Sixth Rehovot Conference
                  edited by Raanan Weitz